Kobe University Monograph Series in Social Science Research

Series Editor

The Kobe University Monograph Series in Social Science Research is an exciting interdisciplinary collection of monographs, both authored and edited, that encompass scholarly research not only in the economics but also in law, political science, business and management, accounting, international relations, and other sub-disciplines within the social sciences. As a national university with a special strength in the social sciences, Kobe University actively promotes interdisciplinary research. This series is not limited only to research emerging from Kobe University's faculties of social sciences but also welcomes cross-disciplinary research that integrates studies in the arts and sciences. Kobe University, founded in 1902, is the second oldest national higher education institution for commerce in Japan and is now a preeminent institution for social science research and education in the country. Currently, the social sciences section includes four faculties—Law, Economics, Business Administration, and International Cooperation Studies—and the Research Institute for Economics and Business Administration (RIEB). There are some 230-plus researchers who belong to these faculties and conduct joint research through the Center for Social Systems Innovation and the Organization for Advanced and Integrated Research, Kobe University.

This book series comprises academic works by researchers in the social sciences at Kobe University as well as their collaborators at affiliated institutions, Kobe University alumni and their colleagues, and renowned scholars from around the world who have worked with academic staff at Kobe University. Although traditionally the research of Japanese scholars has been publicized mainly in the Japanese language, Kobe University strives to promote publication and dissemination of works in English in order to further contribute to the global academic community.

More information about this series at http://www.springer.com/series/16115

Piotr Szwedo · Richard Peltz-Steele ·
Dai Tamada
Editors

Law and Development

Balancing Principles and Values

KOBE UNIVERSITY

Springer

Editors
Piotr Szwedo
Law and Administration
Jagiellonian University
Kraków, Poland

Richard Peltz-Steele
School of Law
University of Massachusetts Dartmouth
Dartmouth, MA, USA

Dai Tamada
Graduate School of Law
Kobe University
Kobe, Hyogo, Japan

ISSN 2524-504X ISSN 2524-5058 (electronic)
Kobe University Monograph Series in Social Science Research
ISBN 978-981-13-9422-5 ISBN 978-981-13-9423-2 (eBook)
https://doi.org/10.1007/978-981-13-9423-2

This Springer imprint is published by the registered company Springer Nature Singapore Pte Ltd.
The registered company address is: 152 Beach Road, #21-01/04 Gateway East, Singapore 189721, Singapore

Introduction

Development is a heavily loaded term. With the fast pace of scientific discovery and the deepening tendrils of globalisation that have become characteristic of contemporary social life across the globe, *development* has become a recurring and convenient shorthand term across a myriad of contexts. For instance, the term *development* is invoked to describe the maturation of the body and mind, the multiplication of social opportunity, the expansion of an economy, and innovation in art and science. The term is a particularly appealing semantic choice as it connotes progress. *Development* may be taken to insinuate that humanity is—or ought to be—fundamentally concerned with purposeful growth, realisation, and the incremental march towards Utopia. It is not uncommon for people to conceptualise the pursuit of their ambitions as *development*. In fact, who could, or would want to appear to, be *against* development?

Yet experience has shown that the meaning of *development* is very much a subjective matter; it is a question of perspective. When one seeks to define *development*—a necessary task if policies must be devised to achieve it—suddenly the term proves curiously evasive. For, as it turns out, the *development* that tracks innocent infancy to weathered maturity may also describe the consuming proliferation of some malignancy. The *development* that fosters an economy from simple localised barter to sophisticated global trade is also a process that may enrich the elites yet crush the impoverished. The development that cultivates one's social and cultural identity also may incite nationalism and tribalism.

Etymologically, *development* has its roots in the Old French verb *desveloper*. The prefix *des-* within this context has the meaning of 'apart', and the root *velop* (or *velup*) signifies *to wrap up*.[1] In Latin and Italian, *viluppare* means *to enwrap/to bundle*.[2] However, the terms *progress* and *growth,* which in everyday use, may serve as synonyms of *development*, have different etymological origins: *progress*,

[1]Walter W. Skeat, *A Concise Etymological Dictionary of the English Language* (Cosimo Classics, 2005) New York, p. 139.

[2]*The Compact Edition of the Oxford English Dictionary*, vol. I, (Oxford University Press, 1971), pp. 279–280.

from Latin *pro-* meaning *forward* and *gradi* for *to walk. Progress* is thus to *move forward.*[3] *Growth* is based on the verb *to grow*, having its roots in various Germanic languages, including Old English and various Scandinavian languages, and is related to the process of the production of shoots in plants.[4] Interestingly, the above etymological analysis paints *progress* and *growth* as a one-way operation of increase—a rather linear process—whereas *development* seems to be a process of multidirectional character. It is therefore legitimate to expect that the term *development* as a normative and discursive concept may well be distinct and more complex and multifaceted than its synonyms in everyday use.

What is more, development is a phenomenon that is often qualified by some descriptor. Invariably, there is a development *of*—e.g., *human development, economic development, community development*, or *state development*, and so on. The nature of the subject determines the character of the process. This statement leads to a distinction between personal development understood as self-realisation within the context of individual freedom, and the development of communities based on the idea of the common good or interest. The scope of what is defined to be *common* in particular cases determines the need to put aside or relegate *particular* interests and privileges. This statement is true for relations between both individuals and collectives/states.

At the level of international law and international relations, *development* is also conceptualised as a *meta*-value that encompasses other legally entrenched values. More than sixty years ago the United Nations General Assembly observed that: 'a balanced and integrated social and economic development would contribute towards the promotion and maintenance of peace and security, social progress and better standards of living, and observance of, and respect for, human rights and fundamental freedoms for all'.[5] The underpinnings of a *human right to development* were conceptualised even earlier, in the Universal Declaration of Human Rights of 1948. Article 22 provides that: '[e]veryone, as a member of society, has the right to social security and is entitled to realisation, through national effort and international co-operation and in accordance with the organisation and resources of each State, of the economic, social and cultural rights indispensable for his dignity and the free development of his personality'.[6]

The above-cited provision provides two relationships that are key in understanding the complexity of *development*: namely the connection of development with *human dignity* and with *international cooperation.* Development is instrumental to other values and has an important goal: namely the championing of human dignity. Our inherent dignity is at the same time the 'foundation of freedom, justice and peace in the world', as the 1948 Declaration's Preamble stipulates in its

[3]Walter W. Skeat, *A Concise Etymological Dictionary,* fn. 1, p. 413.

[4]Icel. *grōa*, Dan. groe, Swed. *gro*; *ibidem,* p. 224.

[5]United Nations General Assembly Resolution 1161 (XII), *Balanced and Integrated Economic and Social Progress,* UN Doc. A/3716 (1957).

[6]United Nations General Assembly Resolution 217 (III), *A Universal Declaration of Human Rights,* UN Doc. A/811 (1948).

first sentence. The way of understanding *human dignity* influences the perception of other human rights and of development. As dignity is a multidimensional notion, the legal and normative conceptualisation of *development* still requires a comprehensive approach, which the present publication aspires to apply. Arguably, legal analyses that take place within rigid positivistic frameworks lead to inevitable reductions and circularities in thinking. Imprecise legal terms are defined by other, often blurry, legal concepts. In order to avoid *ignotum per ignotuis* approaches to such matters, legal methodology ought to be expanded by reference to other social and human sciences: history, economics, anthropology, and ethics.[7] Most often *dignity* is only understood it its modern, Kantian, sense. However, its predominant understanding in international legal scholarship[8] may be isolated from alternative achievements in the study of ethics. Dignity's role in the approach to sustainable development gives it a strong anthropocentric character. Together with its inclinations towards human rights, it serves the re-theorisation of international law, which has traditionally been based on the paradigm of sovereign states. The idea of a global community of individuals that coexists in parallel with an international community of states gives rise to important arguments for the construction of a New Global Law.[9]

Article 22 of the 1948 Universal Declaration also states that *development* may necessitate *cooperation.* This statement also has both legal and ethical implications. The term 'cooperation' has its roots in the Latin prefix *co-* 'together' + *operari* 'to work'.[10] Development is therefore based on common action and may not be achieved differently but through work. On an ethical level, and according to the Book of Genesis, man was put in the Garden of Eden 'to work' (Lat. *ut operaretur, Genesis* 2, 15). Therefore, the obligation to work was not a punishment but an integral part of human convocation. Within such reasoning, the duty of states to cooperate with one another is merely a consequence of this very early and fundamental ethical imperative. Cooperation is not only an obligation but also a means of achieving other objectives such as addressing international problems of an economic, social, cultural, and humanitarian character (*cf.* arts. 1, 55 and 56 of the United Nations Charter). What is more, cooperation is also essential for the achievement of sustainable development.[11]

The Preamble to the United Nations General Assembly 1986 Declaration on the Right to Development states that: '[d]evelopment is a comprehensive economic,

[7]Catholic Social Teaching refers to both concepts in key circulars such as *Dignitatis humanae* of the Second Vatican Council and *Populorum progressio* by Pope Paul VI.

[8]*Cf., Max Planck Encyclopedia of Public International Law*, available at: http://opil.ouplaw.com/home/EPIL, paras. 5 and 6.

[9] Rafael Domingo, *The New Global Law* (Cambridge University Press, 2010).

[10]*Oxford Dictionary of English,* ed. by Angus Stevenson (Oxford University Press, 2010), p. 384.

[11]The latter term has gradually displaced the 'permanent sovereignty over natural resources' in international legal documents, *cf.* 2005 World Summit Outcome, UN General Assembly Resolution A/RES/60/1, especially paras 48–56; cf., Nico Schrijver, *Natural Resources, Permanent Sovereignty over,* in *Max Planck Encyclopedia of Public International Law,* fn. 10, para. 16.

social, cultural and political process, which aims at the constant improvement of the well-being of the entire population and of all individuals on the basis of their active, free and meaningful participation in development and the fair distribution of benefits resulting therefrom'.[12] Development is vital for international economic relations where the need for the harmonisation of economic progress and of other non-mercantile considerations is becoming essential. There has been an important shift in this field of international law following the entry into force of the 1994 Marrakech Agreement establishing the World Trade Organization. In its Preamble, the 'expansion of production and trade in goods and services' is balanced with 'optimal use of the world's resources in accordance with the objective of sustainable development'.[13] A similar conceptualisation of *sustainable development* is also present in the 1987 Brudtland Report where is based on two elements: the concept of 'needs', in particular the essential needs of the world's poor, to which overriding priority should be given; and the idea of the limitations imposed by the state of technology and social organisation on the environment's ability to meet current and future needs.[14] This definition assumes that development ought not to take place in isolation between different communities. It requires economic cooperation and aid, but, moreover, the creation of equitable opportunities for all.[15] Development is therefore based on an ethical dilemma: either it takes place with due regard to the needs of others—namely the poor in other parts of the world and of future generations or no development takes place whatsoever. *Sustainable development* is not a fixed state of harmony; rather, it is a process of change striving to be consistent with the present and future needs.[16] It is a process in which, although, law plays an important role; other normative orders are also implicated; therefore, *development* should not be analysed only in relation to one of them.

Here, Ermanno Calzolaio counsels caution, invoking Javolenus's maxim, *omnis definitio in iure periculosa est* (i.e. any definition in law is dangerous). Development has many faces. We err when we idolise development per se, placing it upon a pedestal as an axiomatic end in and of itself. Rather, our task should be the mastery of development as a pliant tool, a means to the ends that we choose—whether they be economic growth, environmental protection, human rights, or comprehensive human happiness. Mastery begins with understanding. If development is not reducible to some common meaning, then it can never be more than a vacuous rhetorical device of convenience. At the core of development, as a prerequisite to the realisation of its true potential, there must lie some universality of scope.

[12]Adopted by General Assembly resolution 41/128 of 4 December 1986 (A/RES/41/128).

[13]Agreement establishing the World Trade Organization, adopted in Marrakesh on 15 April 1994 (UNTS, vol. 1867, at 154).

[14]Report of the World Commission on Environment and Development (the Brudtland Report), Our Common Future (1987), p. 41.

[15]*Ibidem*, p. 42.

[16]*Ibidem*, p. 17.

The present publication represents neither the initial nor the final efforts of imbuing the term *development* with meaning, though we hope that it represents steps in the right direction. A proper study of the notion of *development* is, as Calzolaio argues, 'multifarious and multidisciplinary'. Ours is the search for the universality that is required to turn the development construct into reality—even if the reality manifests differently in different cultural contexts. It cannot suffice to examine development from one perspective alone, whether a perspective of nationality, cultural identity, ideology, or discipline per se. Myopic approaches to development are often organised in silos, expanding a self-referential vernacular that is increasingly impenetrable and meaningless to others involved in the pursuit of development, albeit preoccupied with silos of their own. Rather, a *universal* language of development, and a path towards mastery of development as means to worthy ends, must be explored through a vibrant trade in ideas and intellectual engagement.

In that vein, the scholarly interrogation of the notion of development in the present publication reveals a concept much older and much better known to the human experience than do modern treatments. The contemporary sustainability movement hardly invented the notion of public regulation to preserve the 'common heritage of mankind'. Franck Duhautoy finds that state control of water resources in Plato's Ancient Greece was justified by the public interest. Tomáš Gábriš credits—or, perhaps, blames—the Ancient Greeks for our very conception of development as an invariably linear process. At the same time, Duhautoy finds that the commodification of vital resources is equally ancient. He traces the tension between *res communes* and privatisation, with an intriguing balance struck at *res nullius*, from Antiquity (namely Ancient Rome) to the Middle Ages, to, in turn, the present, concerning the exploration of the solar system. The same *public–private* tension plays out across socio-legal and cultural traditions, as witnessed in the Talmud, the Quran, and the modern customary law of Libya.

Concerning current discussions on development, these parallel conceptual streams—one grounded in human heritage and collective social rights, the other in commodification and private economic rights—whilst they have on occasion been complementary, they are often competitive. Christine Mengès-Le Pape and George Garvey point to Pope Leo XIII's 1891 Encyclical on the Rights and Duties of Capital and Labour (cf., *Rerum Novarum*), as a landmark effort to overcome this contradiction. The Vatican sought to temper the explosive economic growth of the Industrial Revolution with accountability for the social welfare of the workers who constituted the human engine of productive process. This demand—namely that development not forego humanity—became central to Catholic social teaching. Flavio Felice and Luca Sandonà examine the influence of this approach on the thought of Luigi Sturzo during his exile from fascist Italy, informing Sturzo's conception of 'constitutional economics'.

More often than not, though, the social and economic emphases in development law and policy diverged in the twentieth century. Even when Sturzo was no longer *persona non grata* in post-war Italy, Christian Democratic economic planning embraced the European *ordoliberalism* of the day, enthroning *competition*, Felice and Sandonà argue, as 'the hermeneutical key of economic policy'. The exigency of post-war reconstruction threw the development needle full tilt in the direction of economics, drowning out the idealistic paeans of breakthrough human rights instruments such as the Universal Declaration—which, as Garvey observes, recently turned seventy.

The 'cultural decade' of the 1960s brought to the fore the dichotomy of social and economic thinking concerning development. This tension can be detected in the World Bank's investment dispute resolution treaty, a product of 1960s' globalisation. In this vein, Tamada highlights the burgeoning controversy over whether social impact is relevant today to the legal interpretation of the term 'investment', as conceived half a century ago. Tracing a similar dynamic, Mengès-Le Pape and Garvey explain how the Vatican, with Pope Paul VI's historic encyclical of 1967, *Populorum Progressio*, had championed the introduction of humanism into the global economic development agenda. This once bohemian notion of 'integral humanism' is now revived as perhaps humanity's best chance for peace.

For all the world's efforts since the advent of the post-World War II world order, 'the end of history' seems to have never arrived. As Gábriš describes Fukuyama's ultimate abandonment of the end-of-history thesis, neither the establishment of world government nor the neoliberal, post-Soviet 'renaissance of constitutionalism' has delivered the basic necessities of the world's population, much less world peace. To generalise Gábriš's analysis of Brian Tamanaha's work, the simple equation *development=modernisation* has failed. The enterprise of development has turned out to be impossibly more complicated than any constituency had anticipated. Economic investment seems only to deepen economic dependence. Socialist planning seems unable to ignite ingenuity. Constitutional democracy seems only to aggravate inequality.

Thus, Gábriš challenges us to consider that development is neither inevitably linear nor amenable to universal definition. To be sure, we may agree on universal *ends*, such as food security, shelter, clean air, and drinkable water. But development concerns *means*, not ends, and when speaking of means, one size does not fit all. In this vein, Zuzana Selementová discusses the concept of *common but differentiated responsibilities* (CBDR) as a necessary strategy in responding to climate change. Whilst the concept of CBDR still allows room for disagreement over the meaning of development, Selementová demonstrates that it is the traditional economic measures of development that fall short as they fail to account for human factors including access to education and health care.

In fact, the failure of twentieth-century development policy, predicated principally on foreign aid, might have cleared the field for the conceptualisation and reconstruction of *development* in the very vein of *integral humanism*, as Mengès-Le Pape proposes, or, in Garvey's terms, for an 'integral development'. Today, there is much talk about *sustainable development*. Calzolaio explains the seemingly contradictory, if not arguably oxymoronic, nature of that term, as it seems intent on reconciling current economic growth and long-term environmental welfare. What is more, the term *sustainable development* sounds prospective, as it invokes the interests of future generations. But the term might as well be an effort to remedy our past failure to reconcile capitalism with humanism. *Sustainable development* has come to represent the far-ranging investigation of context that must inform our mastery of development from an integral perspective.

If the meaning of development in the traditional economic context of investment disputes might be sufficiently elastic to accommodate factors including social welfare and cultural impact, as Tamada suggests, then the notion of *sustainable development* might be an apt vessel for a *common but differentiated* approach to development across the board. In fact, Daniel Zatorski proposes that *sustainable development* could do just that in relation to the world of commerce, as he links international sales law with corporate sustainability across the common ground of ethical values. Similarly, Adam Szafrański, Piotr Szwedo, and Małgorzata Klein reveal the tension that arises between free trade, on the one hand, and values in the area of Internet regulation, on the other. Unbridled capitalism, under the guise of free-market fundamentalism, threatens the deontological particularities and social fibre of disparate societies. For instance, the choice of a society to protect its minors from harm through exposure to adult content could be undermined by neoliberal demands to pare down regulation. They propose that the law of development can remedy such tensions by ensuring that economic prosperity does not demand as its price the debasement of social values.

Perhaps unsurprisingly, this leveraging of economic advantage with integral humanism is strikingly reminiscent of Pope Leo XIII's efforts to impart economic actors with the responsibility for human welfare. It was that very 'logic of Christianity', in Garvey's words, through which Pope Francis has enfolded 'human ecology', namely by the inclusion of environmental sustainability into Catholic doctrine through the 2015 encyclical, *Laudato Si'*—124 years after the *Rerum Novarum* and by way of the *Populorum Progressio*. Is integral development within reach at last?

There are rare examples, such as the case of South Africa, where the law has sought *to command* that development strives for worthy social goals while maintaining constitutional democracy. Arguably, South African efforts are reminiscent of Sturzo's thought about the role of constitutional economics in real-world practice. Richard Peltz-Steele and Gaspar Kot explain that the post-apartheid constitutional process has been designed to radically shift power from governing institutions to human constituents, in part by transcending the classical divide between public and private sectors. As a result, the private sector is subject to public scrutiny. For instance, large-scale projects purported to be developmental are scrutinised to ensure that they are genuinely beneficial to communities and are not only likely to make the rich richer at the expense of the poorer layers of society. Peltz-Steele and Kot argue that the same mechanism might be equally useful in Europe, where states are wrestling with public investments aimed at stimulating private development.

In the South African experience, the potential of *sustainability* to promote integral development is well demonstrated by the emergent complexity of problems in natural resource management. Jan Glazewski and Wojciech Bańczyk both demonstrate how South African legislators and jurists are thinking broadly about competing policies that purport to effect development. Similar to those who advocate a progressive approach to the interpretation of investment treaty obligations, South African authorities, in considering whether to approve commercial activity such as mineral extraction, often reject purely economic considerations. According to Bańczyk, these analyses properly consider the collateral impact on discrimination, poverty, labour, and civic participation, as well as the conservation of the environment. At the same time, Glazewski demonstrates that customary subsistence fishing can pit environmental conservation against social values such as cultural identity and reparation for past injustices. Unsurprisingly, deriving sound policy and replicable principles from such mélange of concurrent and competing priorities is easier said than done.

So we find ourselves feeling our way forward in new territory, searching for a definition of *development* that will work hard enough to accomplish all we ask of it. When modern international institutions were born after World War II, we were content with *development* as an idealised path that emanated from the experience of the world's most industrialised and prosperous nations. Foreign aid for aggressive modernisation was the requisite catalyst. Later, in a fit of neoliberalism, we reimagined development as a natural progression—an inevitable consequence of social and economic systems when left to their own devices. We redirected resources to facilitate free markets and personal responsibility. Neither of those strategies delivered us the better world we had imagined. And all the while, humanists from the sidelines had decried the fever pitch of economic drivers that seemed to churn social ruin in their wake.

By the end of the twentieth century, a more nuanced approach to development began to emerge—one that rejects panoramic and panacean policymaking in favour of qualitative legal intervention in human, economic, and social activity. International institutions have assumed the ambitious agenda of mapping the highly interdependent economic, social, and cultural conditions that must be navigated to integrate a wide range of competing for policy priorities. Is there a new, pliant understanding of development, imbued with humanism, capable of placing us back on course towards the 'end of history', or placing our diverse humanity on many courses towards the 'end of history'?

As discussed earlier in this introduction, the term *development* comes to modern usage by way of Old French. Referring to the undoing of containment, or envelopment, *developing* is a 'cousin' to such terms as *unfurling* and *unwrapping*. As recently as the eighteenth century, the notion of a slow and steady progression was central to conceptualising *development.* Thus, the term suggests the gradual revelation of something within: something as yet unknown; something that, once revealed, is capable of changing our circumstances and our very nature. Therein lies the universality of *development*: not in its meaning as an ultimate end or destination, but our journey in its pursuit. We differ over methodology—over course. But we labour together to unfurl the revelation of our deliverance.

Contents

About the Editors

Piotr Szwedo is Associate Professor (Dr. Habil) in the Department of Public International Law at Jagiellonian University (JU) in Krakow. He has authored and co-authored books in Polish ('Środki odwetowe w prawie Światowej Organizacji Handlu', Wolters Kluwer Poland 2008), English ('Cross-Border Water Trade: Legal and Interdisciplinary Perspectives', Brill 2018) and French ('Injusticiabilité', Mare et Martin 2014, 'Les sources de droit dans les pays européens et francophones', Mare et Martin 2017). He also published in the Journal of World Trade, I.CON International Journal of Constitutional Law, Max Planck Encyclopedia of Public International Law, Denver Sports and Entertainment Law Journal, Catholic University Law Review and others. He also has been Visiting Lecturer at the universities of Kobe (2010, 2019), Nantes (2012), Marburg (2012), Kaunas (2013), Orléans (2013, 2014, 2016, 2017, 2018), Macerata (2017, 2018), Paris-Sorbonne University Abu Dhabi (2016, 2017) and China University of Political Science and Law (2019). His main areas of research are international economic law, water law and legal aspects of sustainable development.

Richard Peltz-Steele is Chancellor Professor at the University of Massachusetts Law School in the USA. He teaches torts and comparative law and researches in information law and policy, and development and human rights. He has authored or co-authored a treatise on access to information and legal education casebooks on access to information and tort law. He has published on information law, data rights, and torts in US law reviews, most recently Villanova, Oklahoma, and Indiana International and Comparative; in the Punjab Research Journal Social Science (India); and in books in the USA and Europe. He serves on the editorial board of the Journal of Media Law and Ethics (USA) and has done peer review for journals in India, Netherlands and South Africa. He blogs at TheSavoryTort.com and tweets @RJPeltzSteele. Before moving to New England in 2011, he taught and advised on access to information law and policy in the state of Arkansas, holding appointments by the governor, the chief justice, and the legislature.

Dai Tamada is Professor of International Law at the Graduate School of Law, Kobe University. He holds LL.M. (Kyoto University 2000) and Ph.D. (Kyoto University 2014). His research areas cover international dispute settlement, international investment law, law of treaties, and law of the sea. He has been Research Committee Member in several Government organs, including MOFA, METI and MOJ. His recent publications include Malgosia Fitzmaurice and Dai Tamada (eds.), *Whaling in the Antarctic: Significance and Implications of the ICJ Judgment* (Brill/Nijhoff, 2016), Dai Tamada and Philippe Achilleas (eds.), *Theory and Practice of Export Control: Balancing International Security and International Economic Relations* (Springer, 2017), and Dai Tamada, "The Japan-South Korea Comfort Women Agreement: Unfortunate Fate of a Non-Legally Binding Agreement", *International Community Law Review*, vol. 20, no. 2 (2018), pp. 220–251.

Chapter 1
"Law & Development" in the Light of Philosophy of (Legal) History

Tomáš Gábriš

Abstract This chapter is to provide a number of insights into the interface of philosophy of (legal) history and Law & Development movement, challenging the idea of linear historical "progress" in constitutional law and human rights, seemingly approaching some ephemeral final goal of history. Taking general philosophy of history as a starting point, in fact, the idea of Francis Fukuyama on having reached the end of history in the form of a worldwide victory of liberal democracy was in the meanwhile abandoned even by the author himself. Still, looking at constitutions of many states, Fukuyama's thesis seems to be largely accepted by the legislators of today in their view of liberal democracy and human rights standards as the final and superior stage of evolution, the "end of history". Current discussions on the so-called material core of constitutions, meaning unchangeable constitutional principles and values (of liberal democracy, human rights, etc.), precluding any future changes, go along the same path. The same view used to be accepted by proponents of the Law & Development movement as well, internalizing the modernist view of linear historical evolution leading towards yet greater progress attainable through legal tools. However, this view has been challenged in recent decades by numerous postmodern thinkers in general and by philosophers of history in particular. They are doubting the idea of progress and of linear development in history, as well as of the acceptability of imposing Western standards onto other cultures throughout the rest of the world. Based on these and some other arguments, in this chapter we shall try to reconsider the relevance of the Law & Development movement in the light of currently prevailing philosophical views.

Keywords Law · Development · Legal history · Philosophy of history · Historiography

T. Gábriš (✉)
Faculty of Law, Comenius University in Bratislava, Safarikovo nam. 6, P. O. Box 313, 810 00 Bratislava 1, Slovak Republic
e-mail: tomas.gabris@flaw.uniba.sk

P. Szwedo et al. (eds.), *Law and Development*, Kobe University Monograph Series in Social Science Research, https://doi.org/10.1007/978-981-13-9423-2_1

1.1 Law & Development, Legal Development and Legal History

1.1.1 Law & Development Versus Legal Development

Law & Development, often understood as "modernization through law" was paid attention to recently by the well renowned scholar, Brian Tamanaha.[1] This movement was traditionally building on the assumption that market reforms and governmental reforms in numerous countries of Eastern Europe, Asia, Africa or Latin America require legal backbones. Their legal regimes were therefore to be modelled on Western legal systems, requiring uniformity and comprehensiveness, a monopoly of power, equal application of the law, rationality, rule-bound decision making, bureaucratic organization, an emphasis on rights and duties of individuals, and an instrumental view of law (to serve identified social needs), with the system run by legal professionals. It was namely generally held that "a more highly developed legal system leads to a more highly developed economy or polity"[2] and therefore, Law & Development initiatives mainly took the form of transplanting Western legal institutions into developing or otherwise underdeveloped countries.[3] The majority of the work done in this respect was funded by prominent international entities such as the World Bank, the Ford Foundation, the Carnegie Endowment for International Peace, the American Bar Association, the UN Development Program (UNDP), the U.S. Agency for International Development (USAID), the Inter-American Development Bank, the European Bank for Reconstruction and Development, the United Kingdom's Department for International Development, the Asian Development Bank, the Japan International Cooperation Agency, and others.[4]

Thereby, Tamanaha points out that "Law & Development" is to be strictly separated from the so-called "Legal Development", which simply means development of the law itself, taking a form of continuous or discontinuous evolution, influenced by numerous social factors, being studied by the discipline of Legal History.

However, we shall claim in this chapter that even the traditional approach to "Law & Development" proper has to do with legal (constitutional) history—namely, with a philosophy of legal history, and more specifically, with the idea of linear development and progressive evolution towards the ideals perceived as historically superior, similar to Hegelian and Fukuyamian concepts of the end of (constitutional or legal) history.

[1] Tamanaha [1].

[2] Id.

[3] Id. at 210–211.

[4] Id. at 217.

1.1.2 Development and Legal History

Many of the "modern" disciplines of legal scholarship and legal education trace their origins to a research on the relationship between law and other disciplines—literature, psychology, economics, and so on. In contrast, legal history has always been perceived only as a history of law, not as a relationship between law and history. However, it is precisely from this neglected point of view, close to the philosophy of law or to the philosophy of legal history, that one may better understand the importance of the "legal development" as well as of the "Law & Development"—based on a deeper understanding of the interconnections between law and history. Law is namely a historical phenomenon on its own—immanently—foremost terminologically, as well as through its traditional institutes, but also through the historical traditions of legal scholarship and of legal professions. From a different point of view, in addition, history (not just the history of law) is a topic that appears in law also explicitly—when invoking the past in laws and constitutions.

The "Law & Development" movement itself implicitly implies an underlying historical (and philosophical) approach to law as well. Namely, the idea of the historical evolution of law and society, with the possibility of its influencing through the introduction of legal backbones of the desired social, economic and political development (progress). This makes the proponents of this movement seem like they truly believe (in Hegelian terms) in ideas ("spirit") changing the material world, in contrast to the Marxist perception of law as being only a reflection of the material conditions of society, unable to surpass the historical period of its origin. Specifically, in terms of the "Law & Development" movement, its representatives apparently believed that the liberal democracy, human rights standards as well as all the respective conditions of life would take the forms of the Western models, simply through a transplantation of the "superior" Western legal standards (perceived as a sort of the "end of evolution" both in legal as well as in social and economic terms; especially after the fall of the rival idea of evolution towards the utopian communism in 1989).

At present, however, the continuous and linear interpretation of history in the sense of ever higher progress is being questioned and often faces an outright rejection by current philosophers of history, together with the belief in the transformative force of law on its own. This also lies at the heart of Tamanaha's article on Law & Development. Still, a thorough analysis of the idea of continuous evolution and progress (development) in law towards a liberal democracy and basic human rights guarantees is yet to be undertaken, in order to be able to reassess and revisit also the ideas of the "Law & Development" movement, finding a place for this movement in the postmodern world. In order to at least attempt to undertake such an introductory analysis here, we shall explain first the postmodern approaches to the ideas of progress and evolution in the philosophy of history, and then apply these ideas onto the perception of history by legislators (lawyers), finally coming to a reformulation of the status and role of the "Law & Development" phenomenon.

1.2 The Philosophy of History and the Philosophy of Historiography—Towards the Philosophy of Law & Development

1.2.1 The Philosophy of History—A Return to Multiple Traditions?

The birth of the concept of the "philosophy of history", similarly as with the "philosophy of law", is associated with the person of G. W. F. Hegel, albeit the idea of development of human society with the passage of time was not alien even to the ancient civilizations. Both Greek and Jewish cultures, for example, distinguished between the cyclical and linear understanding of the passage of time—the sacred time, along with the alternation of seasons of the year, were cyclical, while the historical development was linear. Thereby, in the case of the Greeks, linear evolution was descending, human race falling down on its route from the golden age to the ever-worsening periods of history. In contrast, in the case of Jewish culture, there was an unspecified end of history expected in the linear future.[5] Linear understanding in the sense of approaching the definitive (and glorious) end has been introduced specifically in Christian thought, with its chiliastic and messianistic understanding of history (awaiting the second arrival of Christ).[6]

Not surprisingly, building on Christian traditions, even the secular society formulated its own versions of the narrative on the end of history. Thus, while Giambattista Vico[7] still talked about the rotation of *corso* and *ricorso* (rise and fall of cultures and empires), the French enlightened thinkers such as Voltaire, Turgot and Condorcet, believed in the idea of linear evolution and ever-greater progress.[8]

Turgot, for example, understood progress as determining the meaning of history, while specifically emphasizing the importance of economic growth in social development. Still, Condorcet's understanding of the historical progress was even more ambitious. Based on historical material, he tried to connect the past with the future through the presence. By his methodological approach, he hoped to offer an objective interpretation of human progress, with the possibility of anticipating future tendencies. His historicism, fuelled by Hegel and other philosophers of history of the 19th century, kept on influencing the philosophy of history up until the 20th century, when K. R Popper voiced his attacks on historicism.[9] Condorcet namely divided human history into stages of development, great historical epochs, separated by epochal changes such as invention of letters, the contributions brought about by Greek science, the invention of the printing press, and the birth of modern science.

5Cf. Umlauf [2, p. 117].

6Id. at 119.

7In his work The New Science (1725, Scienza Nuova).

8Valent and Chovancová [3].

9Popper [4].

Subsequently, while Kant made a turn from nature to man, emphasizing the human perception of organizing the surrounding world rather than humans being conditional upon external experience and senses, Hegel then overestimated this idea to the extent that he considered thinking and being as identical. That is, he claimed that there was no difference between idea and reality—everything that we think of, exists, and everything that exists is the subject of an intangible idea, thinking. An idea was understood by Hegel as an impersonal principle, reason, spirit. This spirit evolves in the world and in a man, upon the principle of so-called dialectics, that is, by overcoming contradictions. Every idea, which is a subject matter of a thesis, is negated by its antithesis, and from this denial, which is not absolute, there is a synthesis arising. Such a synthesis, in his view, is also a new proposition (thesis) that awaits its antithesis and following synthesis, to further replicate the process of dialectical evolution. However, this development is not infinite—the spirit goes through three historical developmental stages until the end of history is reached. Specifically, in the first phase, the idea or spirit develops in itself. In the phase of antithesis, the idea is separated from itself in the form of nature. In the third phase, the idea and nature merge into the "absolute spirit". That is the end of history and of the development of the spirit (the idea). It was this Hegel's idea of the end of history and of the purpose of history that inspired Karl Marx and his followers to believe that the end of history was in fact not the regime of the Prussian state, as Hegel believed it to be in his works,[10] but rather that it would be the phase of Communism.

The evolution of thought after Hegel went in the German-speaking countries both towards idealistic thought, focusing on intangible ideas and will,[11] as well as towards materialistic thought, culminating in the thinking of Karl Marx and Friedrich Engels. Marx namely emphasized the development on a material basis instead of the development of ideas and spirit. In his view, the material basis influenced and conditioned the development of the spiritual superstructure and not vice versa, meaning that the method of production influences the division of society into classes, always creating the dominance of one class, which must be overthrown at the end of the respective historical epoch. In addition, in Marx's view, the material basis determines not only social stratification, but also morals, art, religion, and law. Therefore, he could also claim that the law is the will of the ruling class promoted to law.[12] Marx thus understood the state as a power tool for organized violence and for the suppression of one social layer by another. He believed that after the victorious Communist revolution all mechanisms of regulating society such as the state and law would cease to exist, and the individual, on the basis of voluntariness and one's own awareness, as a new

[10]In 1990s, the American political scientist Francis Fukuyama, under the influence of Hegel, reported that the end of history has come through the victorious liberal democracy after 1989. However, this was opposed by Samuel Huntington's prediction of the "clash of civilizations" as the next phase of the development, denying "the end of history".

[11]See the works of Arthur Schopenhauer (1788–1860), who draws everything in the world from human will, and he considers the world only in terms of will and imagination.

[12]*Manifesto of the Communist Party by Karl Marx and Frederick Engels, February 1848*, Marxists (Aug. 29, 2018, 10:04 AM) https://www.marxists.org/archive/marx/works/download/pdf/Manifesto.pdf.

person, would endorse the principles of the new community where any social conflicts would cease to exist—in a world where everyone rationally understands their duties towards the community.[13]

Marx and Engels thereby believed that by revealing the primacy of the material basis to the ideological superstructure and by revealing the patterns of their historical development, the laws of the development of human society were uncovered. Namely, based on the method of production, Marx and Engels believed the human development was linearly evolving towards progress, through the alternating socio-economic formations—from the primitive society through slavery, feudal society, bourgeois society, up to, finally, a communist society. This development, similarly as it was put by Hegel, was seen as a transition from the "state of necessity" into the "state of freedom", where no one works under the pressure of urgency and external effectiveness.[14]

This utopian idea of the end of history was in fact tested in the 20th century when the communist parties in Eastern Europe and also in some non-European states attempted to implement it. Most of these attempts, however, failed—at first, it became clear that the need to preserve state and law persists even after the revolution. To explain this, a new developmental stage was introduced between the bourgeois society and the communist society, being called Popular Democracy and its later form being labelled as Socialism. However, society itself rejected this concept, and, at its latest in 1989, the "historical return" to the bourgeois stage of development, law and society, with the ideology of a liberal democracy, took place in Eastern Europe. That is why the American neo-conservative political scientist Francis Fukuyama wrote in 1989 an article called "The End of History", and later edited the book The End of History and the Last Man (1992), where he argued that the liberal democracy is the actual end of history, after overcoming the competing theory of the Marxist interpretation of history. In the spirit of Hegel's concept of evolution towards freedom, Fukuyama believed that after 1989 history was in fact culminating in a period of the highest possible degree of freedom.[15] It was this freedom that the West wished to import also to the rest of the world, making the victory of liberal democracy absolute and beyond doubt.

However, even this idea recently got into a crisis. Witness to this is the fact that in the meantime, Fukuyama himself abandoned his theories after Samuel Huntington had published his Clash of Civilizations.[16] Instead of the end of history, Fukuyama now constructs a new concept of the philosophy of history—he claims we are entering now the stage of the struggle for identity, understood as a national and cultural identity that can be individual and independent of Huntington's "civilizations".[17] The concept of identity is thereby similarly invoked also by the current Ghanaian-British-American philosopher Appiah, who believes we are in wars of identity because we

[13] Valent and Chovancová [5].

[14] Hegel inspired Marx also as far as labour and production is concerned. Cf. Singer [6].

[15] Umlauf [2, pp. 333–334].

[16] Fukuyama [7].

[17] Fukuyama [8].

keep making the same mistake: exaggerating our differences with others and our similarities with our own kind…[18]

Albeit this might sound new, in fact, this approach only follows what Hannah Arendt had already diagnosed about our times fifty years ago… Hannah Arendt's historical thinking, duly expressed in her book The Past and Future, is namely based on an (not very well argued) idea that up until the 19th century, history represented a chain of historical traditions, regardless of whether this tradition was explicitly expressed, and whether the alternating generations were aware of it. Arendt herself sincerely admits that it was only the case of the Romans' receptivity of the Greek culture that proves they were expressly aware of the tradition. The second historical moment of an openly proclaimed awareness of the tradition then followed only in the period of romanticism at the beginning of the 19th century. However, romanticism with its emphasis on local and national traditions, has also, in Arendt's view, outlined the approaching departure with tradition perceived until then as an intergenerational chain.[19] According to Arendt, this departure from tradition was brought about at the philosophical level by three major philosophical figures—Kierkegaard, Marx and Nietzsche. All three were undoubtedly following Hegel, who was one of the major thinkers to perceive the whole of historical development not as a chain of tradition, but rather as a continuous thread, in the spirit of a secular linear understanding of history leading to one ultimate end of history, irrespective of local and national traditions emphasized by romantics.

It was thus in the end of the 19th century that the importance of the "chain" of traditions was lost, claims Arendt, since Kierkegaard, Marx, and Nietzsche have abandoned in their thinking all the "traditional" past authorities and values, thus opening the door to a complete erasure of the concept of tradition, role of which was newly assumed by the idea of a linear evolution of history with its own rules and with the ultimate goal of history (be it liberal democracy or communism).

In the 20th century, respectively already by the end of the 19th century, men have additionally abandoned not only "tradition", but according to Arendt also the whole "triad" of tradition, religion and authority, being three closely interconnected elements, previously connecting the generations. Under Arendt, the "traditional" concept of philosophy of history was thus replaced by a newly-conceived philosophy of history, perceiving the evolution of humanity as being globally uniform, heading towards the future set out specifically in the 20th century by totalitarian regimes convinced of their truth as to the ultimate goal of development of human society, regardless of any local (temporary) specificities.[20]

According to Arendt, the aforementioned changes of the 19th and 20th century were primarily the consequences of an influence of scientific thinking in the field of natural sciences, believing that modern science can reveal all the patterns and laws of natural relations and forces. Modern thinkers under this impression accepted that the same patterns and causality must exist and can be discovered even in the

[18] Appiah [9].

[19] Arendt [10].

[20] Antaki [11].

case of the evolution of human society. This discovery was proclaimed by no less important figures than Hegel (in the spirit of idealism), Marx and then Lenin and Stalin (in the materialist sense). Similarly, according to Arendt, along with belief in the possibility of influencing the development of nature, the idea of influencing the evolution of mankind has emerged—being probably also the idea behind the Law & Development movement.

Of course, since the work of Arendt is often more of a general and speculative nature, it may be questionable (and a challenge for further research) for professional historians, whether the turn of the 19th and 20th century has indeed definitely rejected past values and traditions as well as their overall concept. Similarly, one can but contemplate whether the reported abandonment of traditions in the 19th and 20th centuries is irreversible, or whether, under the impression of postmodernism, multiculturalism and globalization, this development steps back—towards re-inventing the traditions, as could be suggested by the current hunger for their "revival" under the heading of "identity".

Thus, to conclude this section, we have apparently still not reached the end of history, albeit this is not fully acknowledged yet neither by legislators, nor by the representatives of the Law & Development movement, who still seem to stick to the traditional "historiography" believing in having uncovered the laws of history, evolving towards the "end of history".

1.2.2 Philosophy of Historiography

Having mentioned historiography, it is important to explain that the philosophy of history (with its origins and peaks in Vico, Voltaire, Hegel, and Marx) must be distinguished from the philosophy of historiography.[21] The fundamental difference between these two philosophical areas lies in the fact that while in the "philosophy of history" (in English, also referred to as "the substantive, material philosophy of history") the historical development itself is being explained (mostly in a "speculative" way), while in contrast, within the "philosophy of historiography" (in English, it is also referred to as "analytical philosophy of history") the subject of inquiry is the scholarly discipline and methodology of the discipline that examines the past.

Interestingly, in the same way as Arendt linked the emergence of the modern philosophy of history with the model of natural sciences, she also explains the breaks in the way history is being written about, that is, in the philosophy of historiography. Namely, instead of Homer's, Herodotus's and Thucydides' "impartiality", under the impression of the natural sciences belief in "objectivity" and in the possibility of the objective knowledge of laws of social development was introduced, influencing the form and methodology of historical scholarship and writings.[22] Similarly, Arendt explains the opposite developmental trend in historiography—in the 20th century,

[21]Cf. Tucker [12].

[22]Arendt [10].

doubts about "certainty" and "truth" in historical scholarship emerged, in the sense of epistemological doubts as to the possibility of an objective evaluation of history by historians. However, Arendt does not go so far as to dispute the ontological foundations of history (i.e., objective history, objective existence of the past), in the sense of existence and truthfulness of historical facts on their own. As a matter of example, she offers a historical fact of an attack on Belgium by Germany committed on 4th August 1914, which is an example of a historical fact that is difficult to dispute. Still, Arendt specifically and openly speaks about nationalistic (*Nazi*) and Socialist (Communist) practices of rewriting history (and creating false, new traditions).

Arendt's preoccupation with and criticism of relativistic approaches to historical facts and their various interpretations (including misinterpretations and falsifications), was an early reaction to decades of intensely expanding constructivist and narrativist approaches to historiography and history, which were present among the philosophers of history and historiography especially between the 1960s and 1990s. The essence of these approaches was to discuss the possibility of objectivity in historiography, the possibility of objective reconstruction of historical events and of the ability to discover any "laws" in historical development. In particular, postmodern authors—Arthur Danto, Louis Otto Mink, Hayden White, Paul A. Roth, and also the Dutch author Frank Ankersmit, considered every piece of historical writing to be only a "construction" of a historian, attributing to the past certain characteristics from an *ex-post* perspective.

In this regard, however, it should be remembered that although Arendt accepted that historians should not believe in the existence of any historical laws or of the linearity of historical evolution, and that the explanation of historical events and facts should instead always take the form of an *ex post* search for roots and causes (*Ursachen*) of historical events, without the possibility of absolute certainty and without the right to completeness of the explanation, at the same time, Arendt herself cannot be considered an outright postmodernist constructivist of narrativist.

Similarly, returning now back to the problem of relationship between law and development, in both of its forms—of Law & Development as well as Legal Development—, it seems that our modern legislators stand in opposition to both constructivist and narrativist postmodern approaches to historiography. However, they also stand in opposition to Hannah Arendt's perception of historiography. Namely, judging from the wording of national constitutions, laws and from the traditional approaches to Law & Development, modern legislators still believe they have discovered the universal laws of history and are writing their own one and only correct (hi)stories—an idea that both Arendt and postmodernists refuted!

1.3 The Legislator as a Legally Binding Historiographer?

The philosophy of history and the philosophy of historiography are not objects reserved solely to historians—they are strongly influenced by philosophical discourses and narratives of the period, historically e.g. by the works of the French phenomenologist Paul Ricoeur, or even by the older authors such as Henri Bergson and Marcel Proust. In addition, it is also appropriate to distinguish between history and historiography on the one hand, and so-called collective memory, respectively, memory of a nation on the other. In the latter case, the past is used foremost as a tool of national remembrance, in fact, of national "mythology". According to critics, the issues of "memory" are therefore much closer to politics than to actual history and historiography, although in practice their combination may also occur, which, according to sceptical opinions, is particularly a problem for small nations, constructing their past (history) politically. Critics thereby argue that while history as a science should be characterized by the objectivity achieved through the use of fundamental methodology, objectivity is being distorted by political interests in the field of collective or national memory, which ultimately leads to the fact that the national memory itself often takes instead of the form of uncontested national myths rather the form of disputes among several alternatives, which are often mutually exclusive, and compete with each other.

Indeed, legislative evaluation of the past and its canonical interpretation in constitutions and laws seem to represent an unhappy mixture of non-scientific mythology mixed with the political fight. To offer here some examples, let us have a look at a number of legislators acting as historiographers and codifiers of national memory (or rather mythology): to continue with the Eastern European historical examples in this chapter, let us work here with constitutions and laws from this part of the world, having its specific experience with distortions of historiography under the totalitarian regimes of the 20th century, but also having rich experience in the current constructions of national memory.

Proud references to the famous past are a usual part of constitutions in this part of the world.[23] Interestingly, it is mostly the Eastern European countries that use this way of symbolically remembering their linear historical evolution towards independence and liberal democracy reached often only at the end of the 20th century. In contrast, there is only a few Western European examples of this kind—one can find explicit references to the past e.g. in the constitution of Andorra, where the constitution calls for respecting the seven-centuries-old motto "virtus, unita, fortior", which is to be retained in Andorra as its basic principle. Another, minor reference to the past is to be found in France—the French constitution proclaims the ideas of the declaration of the rights of a man and of citizen (dating back to the French Revolution) and the preamble to the Constitution of 1946 to contain the leading values and principles of France. Finally, Portugal is the third of the rare Western European countries that

[23]References to the shameful past of totalitarianism are mostly contained in laws on memory of the nation. As an example, in the Slovak Republic, the role of preservation of national memory is being fulfilled by the Nation's Memory Institute, established by Act no. 553/2002 Coll., on making available the documents on the activities of the state security units from the period 1939–1989 and on the establishment of the Nation's Memory Institute (Act on the Memory of the Nation). The period of 1939–1989 is labelled in the Act as a period of unfreedom, "when citizens did not have the opportunity to live in a democratic country, to decide freely on their own state and on themselves, and when the activity of democratic institutions was limited or suppressed, and when there were permanently and systematically violated human rights."

recall their past in the constitution—namely the victory of democracy over the fascist dictatorship in Portugal. All the other Western European states lack any canonical "historiography" in their constitutions.

In contrast, in the case of the Eastern European countries, the situation is remarkably different—just one look at the constitution of Hungary makes it clear that Hungary emphasizes explicitly its discontinuity with the communist period and instead underlines its continuity with the historical Hungarian Kingdom and its Holy Crown. Similarly, Belarus refers to its centuries old development; Bosnia and Herzegovina point to the continuity of their state; the Czech Republic invokes both the traditions of the Bohemian Kingdom as well as of the Czechoslovak Republic; Poles commemorate their Christian traditions, as well as their struggle for independence and the traditions of the first and second Poland; the Constitution of Lithuania similarly mentions its centuries long existence and the fight for freedom and independence. In contrast, Estonia begins a story of its glorious past only in 1918, when it was established as an independent state. The Constitution of the Republic of Macedonia narrates its story of a struggle for independence, just like the Moldovan Constitution, remembering the "state continuity of the Moldovan people in the historical context". Russia commemorates the historical unity of its state and emphasizes the love for the country inherited from ancestors. Serbia briefly mentions the traditions of the Serbian people. Slovakia remembers "the political and cultural heritage of their ancestors and the centuries-old experience of the struggle for national existence and own statehood, along with the spiritual heritage of Cyril and Methodius and the historical legacy of Great Moravia". A specific case is the Constitution of Croatia, which speaks of a thousand years long identity of the Croatian nation and of the continuity of its statehood in various forms—from the 7th century principalities, medieval state created in the 9th century, the establishment of the Kingdom in the 10th century and the preservation of Croatian identity in the times of the Hungaro-Croatian union, free election of a Habsburg ruler in 1527, approval of the indivisibility of the Habsburg Empire, up to the events of the 19th and 20th centuries leading to the independence of Croatia in 1995.

Thus, one can conclude that particularly in Eastern Europe constitutional documents often contain a sort of canonical historiography, usually serving as a symbolic clarification of the reason and legitimacy of the respective states, their independence and unity, offering thereby a blend of official historiography and collective memory (national mythology).

Most of these constitutions were enacted in the 1990s, in the period after the breakup of the Eastern Bloc and after the disintegration of the multinational states of Eastern Europe such as Yugoslavia or Czechoslovakia, in a period which was perceived as "the end of history"—accepting the seeming victory of liberal democracy (at least in Europe). At that time, even in Eastern Europe, the ideals of constitutionalism were revived, combined with an emphasis on natural law, with the restoration of constitutional justice (constitutional courts), the judicial control of administrative authorities and the emphasis on the material concept of the rule of law. This was a situation shared alike by some South-European and Latin American states as well, where the renaissance of constitutionalism also resurfaced after the abandonment of totalitarian and authoritarian non-democratic regimes in the 1970s.

In most of these states (of Europe and Latin America), the renaissance of liberal democracy is connected to the notion of so-called neo-constitutionalism, as the next step in the evolution of constitutionalism. In sum, there are three basic manifestations or signs of neo-constitutionalism being discerned[24]:

(a) The birth of material cores of constitutions that make some principles and institutes more rigid, while the supervision of them is entrusted to strict constitutional control by constitutional courts or other similar mechanisms.
(b) The combination of morality with the law in the form of a number of constitutional norms and principles, which have explicit moral content and meaning (especially at the level of fundamental rights and freedoms).
(c) Changing the roles of lawyers, especially legal scholars, leading them not only to describe the law, but to interpret, implement and apply it or even change it, always in the spirit of the values and principles expressed in the constitution.[25]

The constitution is thus to guarantee that the "end of history" in the form of liberal democracy will never be abandoned and it will be preserved as the guiding principle of these states. The liberal and democratic principles, representing a so-called material core of constitutions (never to be changed or abandoned), should thereby serve as an interpretive tool for the application and implementation of law at a sub-constitutional level, thus applying constitutional values and principles (of liberal democracy) in daily legal practice. Therefore, it may be said that instead of the "rule of law" rather the "rule of the constitution" is the main motto of today, the unchangeable material cores of the constitutions representing and encompassing the highest standards of liberal democracy and basic human rights, being the end of history codified by legislators, authors of the constitutions, acting as legislative historiographers drafting legally binding historiographies.

However, this approach is closer to the concept of collective memory and national mythology, rather than to the current trends in the philosophy of history and philosophy of historiography. Namely, postmodern approaches are hesitant to recognize any pattern or final stage of evolution that mankind would be approaching in a linear way, which makes even the liberal democracy as the end of history questionable.

This can best be illustrated by a brief overview of the thought of some radical postmodern, but also some moderate current philosophers of historiography. In Western Europe and on the American continent, the wave of interest in the postmodern philosophy of history and historiography, operating with the argument of the narrativity and constructive nature of historiography, took place mostly in the 1970s-1990s. The essence of these debates was to discuss the possibility of objectivity in historiography or the possibility of objective reconstruction of historical events and discovery of historical laws. This was thereby not a completely new discussion. These topics have been discussed in European historiography already by the end of the 19th century, at

[24]Cf. Lloredo Alix [13].

[25]Cf. Atienza and Chiassoni [14].

least since Ranke's thesis "*so wie es eigentlich gewesen ist*", and since subsequent efforts of positivism in historiography—i.e. efforts to use "truly scientific" methods in historiography.[26] Since the mid-20th century, the discussion on the essence and possibilities or limitations of historiography has come to life again, for example in the works by E. H. Carr and W. H. Walsh.[27] From the 1960s onwards, critical voices from both Anglophone and French historiography,[28] opened the door to perceive history as a construct of the mind. Thereby, generally, constructivists agreed on one essential thing—they all advocated the possibility of presenting different historical works on the same past, and questioned the ability to write history in Ranke's sense ("*so wie es eigentlich gewesen ist*"), as well as the possibility of revealing any laws in history or even the end of history…

Let us start with A. Danto, a narrativist historiographer, who claimed that historians often use phrases that alone create a story from any historical event—for example, marking an event as the beginning of a "thirty-years' war" suggests in advance a story lasting for 30 years, ex-post transmitting future knowledge back to the past. According to Danto, moreover, historians deliberately choose later events that they link up with the previous events, creating thus a narrative again, albeit necessarily incomplete and distortive. A complete description of any historical event would namely require us to discuss all the relevant stories—but that would require knowing the future, so as to know whether something relevant will happen in the future that will change our view of the past event, creating thus a new narrative. Due to all of this, it is virtually impossible to tell all relevant stories about the past, claims Danto.[29]

Another narrativist historiographer, L. O. Mink, continues in a similar vein, and claims that historiography is characterized by a particular kind of historical understanding. According to Mink, we come to such an understanding through a specific holistic grip, which is sometimes called a synoptic judgment. Historical understanding, according to him, will only be gained when we look at the past in total, when we place the past events in context or place them in a narrative sequence (into a story). It is precisely this holistic view that, according to him, distinguishes the historical approach from a purely scientific one and provides for a certain autonomy of historiography.[30] Mink thus questions the "scientific" character of historiography.

Additionally, the great importance of the personality of the historian for the final form of the historiographical work was emphasized at the turn of the 1960s and 1970s by another narrativist historiographer, Hayden White. He formulated a theory of four so-called tropes (metaphor, metonymy, synecdoche, and irony), as lenses or structures through which historians perceive the object of their interest. The dominant view, according to White, will give the historian concrete optics, which will affect the resulting version of the past. In fact, Hayden White thus confirms that historiography

---

[26]Little [15].

[27]See e.g. Walsh [16].

[28]Braudel [17].

[29]Danto [18].

[30]Cf. Mink [19].

is not strictly confined to the sources used. At the same time, however, H. White did not deny that the historian is working with real facts.[31]

A rather different view of the reality of historical facts was proposed by Paul A. Roth. His approach is being referred to as irrealism, basically meaning that according to Roth, in fact, we do not have one fixed past, but multiple pasts. Roth thus argues in favour of the uncertainty of the past and of the pluralism of historical depictions from the pen of individual historians. Roth hence gave up the idea of one true (objective) past and of any fixed (objective) historical facts.[32]

However, Roth's approach was perceived as too extreme, and did not become dominant even among narrativists or constructivists; even Roth himself gradually gave way to a milder standpoint. In general, however, constructivists agree on one essential thing—they all advocate for the possibility of presenting different depictions of the same historical past, and question the ability to write history in Ranke's sense of "*so wie es eigentlich gewesen ist*". Basically, all of these pluralistic postmodernist approaches (see a book by Frank Ankersmit: Historiography and postmodernism (1989)[33]) are casting doubt on an objective historical truth.

This radical view would, nevertheless, mean, that each legislator-historiographer can indeed construct any depiction of the legal past, which then subsequently becomes the sole acceptable version of the past. Such approaches were, however, harshly criticized by "classical" historians and philosophers of historiography (Perez Zagorin, Chris Lorenz and John Zamito[34]) who complained that postmodern narrativist do not know how historians actually work and therefore cannot objectively judge their methods.

In the light of this criticism, the postmodern narrativist Ankersmit has taken (in the book Historical Representation, Stanford, 2001) a more moderate position, similarly as the French theorist and philosopher of historiography living in the USA—Roger Chartier. He is of the opinion that, despite the strong influence of the historian's personality on the choice of methods and sources, when using recognized methodology of historical science, the results of historiography have a certain truthful claim.[35] Thus, should the imperatives of historical science (similar to the so-called historiographic operations in the works of Michel de Certeau[36]) be observed, history can claim its own mode of truth, and a scientific nature. This attitude is thereby, according to several authors, approaching the theory of "possible history" developed by German historian Reinhart Koselleck.[37] He namely claimed that albeit individual works of historians differ, all of them can be acknowledged the status of reconstructions of "possible history". The postmodernist relativization of history was thus in the later works softened to the extent that historiography can be accepted as a science with

---

[31] White [20, 21].

[32] Roth [22].

[33] Cf. Ankersmit [23–25].

[34] Cf. Zammito [26].

[35] Chartier [27].

[36] de Certeau [28].

[37] Koselleck [29].

its own research specificities and its own mode of truth, but with specific standards and respected methods of scientific research that have to be followed.

What does that mean for a legislator acting as a historiographer? Our interim conclusion can be the following: Albeit the philosophy of (legal) history does not acknowledge the linear evolution and existence of any final stage in evolution, rather, in contrast, the enlightened ideas of progress are being doubted and challenged, no guarantees for the perception of liberal democracy as the final end of history can be offered, albeit this is being done in legal documents, especially constitutions. There, linear evolution towards the "end of history" is being "codified" often in a legally binding manner, being an approach which might be challenged from the postmodernist position. However, it is acknowledged nowadays that at least a certain degree of acceptance and trust can be credited to these historiographies, should they be based on recognized scholarly operations, leading to at least a "potential history".

1.4 Towards the Philosophy of (Law &) Development?

In the previous sections we expressed some doubts as to whether it is correct to recognize an end of history seen in the liberal democracies and human rights standards enshrined in the material cores of neo-constitutionalist doctrines. Naturally, a related question arises—if one refutes the idea of progress and linear development towards the end of history, is it acceptable to support the establishment of liberal democracies through legal means in other parts of the world, e.g. within the Law & Development movement? That would namely mean to perceive the values of liberalism, democracy and human rights as a kind of Hegelian-Fukuyamian end of history that is to be promoted by legal means. Is this approach still tenable in the postmodern world, or do we need a new philosophy of Law & Development, taking into account the findings of the general philosophy of history and of historiography?

On this basis, while the historiographical accounts in the constitutions and other laws can be accepted on condition of having had respected the basic historiographical operations and standards, the idea of the end of history as pronounced in many constitutions and as presented nowadays in the material cores of constitutions, should be considered problematic. Even the whole concept of the traditional Law & Development movement could be challenged on the pretext of being a neo-colonialist or post-colonial approach to non-Western or non-European countries and cultures (identities).[38] Any new version of the Law & Development should thus take into account the current doubts as to the one and only correct answer to the questions of good and morals and as to the linear route towards the end of history.

Two possible solutions are being offered here currently—one of postmodernists, refusing any reduction to universal values and goals, and the other, represented by philosophers such as J. Habermas, K. O. Apel, or Ch. Taylor.[39] All of the latter group

---

[38]Cf. Loomba [30].

[39]Cf. Habermas [31].

suggest there is an objectively accessible and rationally acceptable solution, which can be seen in a dialogue, communication, discourse. The discursive approach is often being considered a compromise between two—pluralistic and monistic—versions of metaphysics. Namely, for pluralists, communication allows for the competition of ideas, while for monist, it gives a hope to reach the one and only correct, reasonable solution. The communicative and discursive approach could thus be a reasonable basis also for the philosophy of development in law, and specifically for the "Law & Development" field—perceiving development as an ongoing communication and discourse.

1.5 Conclusions

Despite the fundamental scepticism about the use of postmodern philosophy in legal disciplines, one can still see the positive aspects of such a move, specifically in theoretical legal disciplines, which often overlap with philosophy, history or other humanities. Postmodern philosophy can be of added value in these areas by questioning traditional interpretations and by posing new (types of) questions. Thereby, the traditional methodology of legal scholarship is still not to be abandoned, to prevent untenable over-interpretations or misinterpretations. Conservativism of classical methods in combination with bold postmodern assumptions can together provide acceptable results of new original scientific research while being in line with current philosophical trends.

In this chapter, situated at an intersection of philosophy, law, and history, we have tried to reassess the underlying concepts and search for a potential new basis of the "Law & Development" field. Both philosophy of history as a rather speculative area of thought, as well as the philosophy of historiography (studying how history is being written down by historians), were challenged recently by postmodern approaches. Numerous conclusions and inspirations can thereby be drawn for the research area of "Law & Development", mostly challenging the "traditional" superiority of Western models and standards, as well as challenging the idea of the liberal democracy and guarantees of basic human rights as being the end of history to be accepted by the rest of the world. Instead of these traditional viewpoints, we advocate for a more communicative and discursive form of the "Law & Development" movement, perceiving the development in law as a process—i.e. in procedural terms.

References

1. Tamanaha, B. Z. (2011). The primacy of society and the failures of law and development. *Cornell INT'L L.J.*, *44*, 209.
2. Umlauf, V. (2010). Synopse dějinnosti a koncept historie: Hermeneutické eseje o filosofii dějin.
3. Valent, T., & Chovancová, J. (1996). Kapitoly z filozofie dejín, pp. 16–17.
4. Popper, K. (1957). The poverty of historicism.

5. Valent, T., & Chovancová, J. (2012). Filozofia pre právnikov (filozoficko-právne aspekty), pp. 135–136.
6. Singer, P. (1983). Hegel: A very short introduction.
7. Fukuyama, F. (2018, August 29). *Huntington's Legacy*, The American Interest. https://www.the-american-interest.com/2018/08/27/huntingtons-legacy/.
8. Fukuyama, F. (2018). Identity: The demand for dignity and the politics of resentment.
9. Appiah, K. A. (2018). The lies that bind. Rethinking identity: Creed, country, color, class, culture.
10. Arendt, H. (2002). Between past and future.
11. Antaki, M. (2006). The Critical Modernism of Hannah Arendt. *Theoretical Inquiries in Law, 8*, 251, 258.
12. Tucker, A. (Ed.). (2009). A companion to the philosophy of history and historiography.
13. Lloredo Alix, L. M. (2014). *¿Estamos ante un cambio de paradigma en la filosofía del derecho? El neoconstitucionalismo y la crisis del estado social. Are we Facing a Change of Paradigm in Today's Legal Philosophy? Neo-constitutionalism and the Crisis of Social State*, Universitas. Revista de Filosofía, Derecho y Política, nº 19, pp. 157, 170.
14. Atienza, M., & Chiassoni, P. (2010). *Debate sobre el positivismo jurídico. Un intercambio epistolar. Con un comentario de Álvaro Núñez Vaquero*. Analisi e Diritto, pp. 289–318.
15. Little, D. (2010). *New contributions to the philosophy of history* (p. 97).
16. Walsh, W. H. (1951). An introduction to philosophy of history.
17. Braudel, F. (1997). Les ambitions de l'histoire.
18. Danto, A. (1965). Analytical philosophy of history.
19. Mink, L. (1987). Historical understanding.
20. White, H. (1973). Metahistory.
21. White, H. (1978). Tropics of discourse.
22. Roth, P. A. (2002). Ways of pastmaking. *History of the Human Sciences, 15*, 125–143.
23. Ankersmit, F. (1994). History and tropology: The rise and fall of metaphor.
24. Ankersmit, F. (2001). Historical representation.
25. Ankersmit, F. (2012). Meaning, truth, and reference in historical representation.
26. Zammito, J. H. (1998). Ankersmit's postmodernist historiography: The hyperbole of "opacity". *History and Theory, 3*, 330–346.
27. Chartier, R. (1997). On the edge of the cliff.
28. de Certeau, M. (1975). The writing of history.
29. Koselleck, R. (2000). Vergangene Zukunft. Zur Semantik geschichtlicher Zeite, p. 206.
30. Loomba, A. (2005). Colonialism/Postcolonialism.
31. Habermas, J. (1994). Justification and application: Remarks on discourse ethics (studies in contemporary german social thought).

Chapter 2
Populorum Progressio: Development and Law?

Christine Mengès-Le Pape

Abstract In his *Populorum Progressio* Encyclical of 26 March 1967, Pope Paul VI raised the link between development and law as one of the most pressing matters for his and for future generations. This encyclical letter was preceded by the era of social teachings of the Church that had begun at the end of the 19th century with the *Rerum novarum* Encyclical. Pope John Paul II explained in *Annus centisimus* that Pope Leo XIII had already offered an initial conception of development to be applied to the juridical relations between masters and workmen. That doctrinal work was further extended by Pope John XXIII, in his 1961 *Mater et magistra* Encyclical, from social rights to the support of less developed areas, which was to be determined on the basis of justice and equity, and not by a mechanical application of the laws of the marketplace. Less than two years after the close of the Second Vatican Council, the advent of the *Populorum Progressio* Encyclical occurred within a global context marked by burgeoning prosperity in the West and by the often violent decolonisation process. Nations that had just gained independence were hopeful as to the prospects of improving their legal systems, of contributing to their own development, and of assuming their rightful place in the international community. Despite aid programmes, the disparities between developed and developing nations had increased dramatically. The study of the Encyclical *Populorum Progressio* may enable a better definition of the notion of development which, according to Pope Paul VI ought not be restricted to purely economic growth, but as 'man's complete development which should be understood and pursued in conformity with the dictates of moral law. The Encyclical may provide answers to questions as to the purpose of development, founded on social and legal equality, with the formula, 'development: the new name for peace'.

Keywords Catholic Church · Global poverty · Global development · Social justice · Law and morality

---

C. M.-L. Pape (✉)
University Toulouse, 1 Capitole, 2 rue du Doyen-Gabriel-Marty, 30142 Toulouse Cedex 9, France
e-mail: Christine.Menges-le-pape@ut-capitole.fr

P. Szwedo et al. (eds.), *Law and Development*, Kobe University Monograph Series in Social Science Research, https://doi.org/10.1007/978-981-13-9423-2_2

2.1 Introduction

Just over 50 years ago, on 26 March 1967, during the celebration of the Resurrection, Pope Paul VI published the Encyclical *Populorum Progressio, on the Development of Peoples*, first written in French and translated—after the *sta tutto bene* (i.e., the endorsement) of the Pope[1]—into Latin and other languages.[2] The announcement of this encyclical letter, which had aroused considerable interest, took place within the context of increasing disparity between the world's nations with the gap widening between, on the one hand, the affluent and developed countries, and, the poor and less developed countries on the other, albeit in a world that had increasingly become closely interdependent. The opening words of the Encyclical are: '[t]oday it is most important for people to understand and appreciate that the social question ties all men together, in every part of the world'.[3] Prior to the *Populorum Progressio* encyclical, Pope Paul VI had developed strong ideas concerning the globalisation of the social question that he had expressed through speeches he had made during his apostolic journey to India and his visit to the United Nations headquarters,[4] the letter to the

---

[1]Presentation of the Encyclical *Populorum Progressio*, by Paul Poupard, *La documentation catholique*, 1967, col. 1018; Cardinal Paul Poupard, «Capire la Populorum Progressio», *Quaderni di fede e mondo in Sviluppo*, Assise, edizioni Pro Civitate Christiana, 1968; «L'idea dello sviluppo integrale: la ricerca dei veri valori nelle encicliche», *Nuntium*, n° 31–32, Pontificia Università Lateranense, 2007; *Le développement des peoples, entre souvenir et espérance*, Paris, éditions Parole et Silence, 2008. François Perroux, *Dialogue des monopoles et des nations*, Grenoble, Presses Universitaires de Grenoble, 1982; *L'économie du XXe siècle*, Paris, PUF, 1961; Pour une philosophie du nouveau développement, Paris, Fleurus, 1967. Paolo-G. Carozza, «The structures of developpement and the structure of the human person», *Questione sociale, questione mondiale. La permanente attualità del magistero di Paolo VI*, Rome, Vita et Pensiero, 2017; Marc Feix, «Développement des peuples et développement durable, de *Populorum Progressio* au Forum social mondial», *Revue des sciences religieuses*, n° 82/1, 2010; Michel Schooyans, «*Populorum Progressio*, vingt ans après», Vatican, 1987; Ignace Berten, «*Populorum Progressio*, quelle actualité?», *Développement et civilisations Lebret-Irdef*, février 2008; Vincent Cosmao, «*Populorum Progressio*, trente ans après», *Bulletin du Centre Lebret «Foi et Développement»*, n° 250/251, février et mars 1997.

[2]The French and the English versions present certain differences—for instance, the term 'humanisme intégral', is rendered in the English version as 'true humanism', and the term 'devoir communautaire' is rendered as 'ties with all men'.

[3]Encyclical *Populorum Progressio*, n° 3 'Today it is most important for people to understand and appreciate that the social question ties all men together, in every part of the world. John XXIII stated this clearly, and Vatican II confirmed it in its Pastoral Constitution on The Church in the World of Today. The seriousness and urgency of these teachings must be recognized without delay. The hungry nations of the world cry out to the peoples blessed with abundance. And the Church, cut to the quick by this cry, asks each and every man to hear his brother's plea and answer it lovingly'.

[4]'We come to you as a messenger of Jesus and his teaching. Many of you know His life and doctrine and, like Mahatma Gandhi, express reverence for Jesus and admiration for His teaching. 'I am the light of the world', Jesus said; and today the world stands in great need of this Light, to overcome the strife and division, and the menace of unprecedented violence, which threaten to engulf mankind. The people of India and of Asia can draw light and strength from the teaching and spirit of Jesus, from His love and compassion, in their efforts to help the less fortunate, to practise brotherly love, to attain peace among themselves and with their neighbours'. *Journey to India, homily of Paul VI, Bombay*, 4 December 1964.

Director of UNESCO in August 1965,[5] messages for the *Social Weeks of France* and for the celebration of Christmas 1966,[6] and, lastly, through the *Motu Proprio: Catholicam Christi Ecclesiam* with which he created the Pontifical Council *Justitia et Pace*.[7] Among the issues raised by the Encyclical of March 1967 is the question of the relationship between law and development in which the political and the spiritual are so obviously linked, with the express acknowledgement that both spheres are distinct, just as both powers—namely, the Church and the State—are sovereign, each with its own sphere of competence.[8]

In his speech of 20 April 1967, the Pope pointed out the links between the natural and the supernatural, the secular and the religious; he quoted the philosopher Nicolas Berdiaeff's paradoxical formula: '[b]read for myself is a material issue, bread for my

[5]'It is a question of the full development of man and humanity which opens to all the way of truth; the truth of science—a major factor of cultural, technical and economic progress—as well as moral and spiritual truth, which alone is capable of fulfilling man's highest aspirations'. *Message of His Holiness Paul VI to Mr. Rene Maheu, Director General of UNESCO for the World Congress of Ministers of Education*, 26 August 1965.

[6]Presentation of the Encyclical *Populorum Progressio*, by Monseigneur Paul Poupard, *La documentation catholique*, 1967, col. 1017.

[7]*Motu Proprio: Catholicam Christi Ecclesiam*, 6 January 1967: '*Deinde de Pontificia Commissione studiosorum, a Iustitia et Pace appellata.*

Haec Commissio sibi proponit populum Dei universum excitare ad plenam adipiscendam conscientiam muneris sibi hisse temporibus demandati; ita quidem, ut hinc pauperiorum populorum progressus promoveatur ac socialis iustitia inter nationes foveatur, illinc vero subsidia nationibus minus progressis praebeantur, quorum ope eaedem incrementis suis per se ipsae consulere possint. Quam ad rem huius Pontificiae Commissionis erit:

(1) *colligere ac summatim perscribere praestantiores scientiae investigationes ac doctrinae adiumenta, quae pertineant sive ad cuiusvis generis incrementa, in campo scilicet educationis et mentis culturae, rei oeconomicae et socialis, et in ceteris eiusdem generis; sive ad ipsam pacem, in iis omnibus rebus, quae progressus causam superent*;

(2) *operam conferre, ut altius pervestigentur, quod attinet ad doctrinam, ad pastorale munus et ad apostolatus actionem, generales quaestiones, quae progressus et pacis causa proponantur*;

(3) *curare, ut haec doctrina atque huiusmodi nuntiorum collectio in notitiam omnium Institutorum Ecclesiae, quorum intersit, perferantur*;

(4) *vincula nectere inter omnia Instituta, hoc quidem Consilio, ut apta virium coniunctio foveatur, validiores nisus fulciantur, itemque caveatur, ne ad idem propositum, cum virium impendio, varia incepta et opera contendant.*'

[8]This definition will be given in the Encyclical *Deus Caritas est*: 'The just ordering of society and the State is a central responsibility of politics. As Augustine once said, a State which is not governed according to justice would be just a bunch of thieves: '*Remota itaque iustitia quid sunt regna nisi magna latrocinia?*'. Fundamental to Christianity is the distinction between what belongs to Caesar and what belongs to God (cf. *Mt* 22:21), in other words, the distinction between Church and State, or, as the Second Vatican Council puts it, the autonomy of the temporal sphere. The State may not impose religion, yet it must guarantee religious freedom and harmony between the followers of different religions. For her part, the Church, as the social expression of Christian faith, has a

neighbour is a spiritual issue'.[9] He was thus emphasising a proximity that 'leaves intact—Paul VI notes in his speech to the Intergovernmental Committee of the World Food Programme—the clear distinction between a spiritual society, like the Church, and a temporal society constituted by the countries'.[10] This issue, which maintains the distinction but at the same time establishes reciprocity between the two powers, has been studied through various sources rooted in the *Lex Divina*, that is to say, in the will to build the 'Kingdom of Heaven' on earth. As an introduction to the publication of the text, in April 1967, the French bishop, Monsignor Paul Poupard, from the Secretariat of State, presented the sources he had used, including Holy Scripture and Holy Tradition, along with other sources indicating the novelty of the doctrine. References to Holy Scripture can be found in *Populorum Progressio*, in particular verse 16:26, Matthew, applied to those who promote the supremacy of wealth: '[w]hat does it profit a man, if he gain the whole world but suffer the loss of his own soul?',[11] then the verse 8:2, Mark: 'I have compassion on the crowd',[12] or the letter of James: '[i]f a brother or a sister be naked and in want of daily food, and one of you say to them, "Go in peace, be warm and filled" yet you do not give them what is necessary for the body, what does it profit?'.[13]

Pope Paul VI went on to maintain the social teachings of the preceding Popes including those contained in the *Rerum Novarum* and *Immortale Dei* by Pope Leon XIII, *Quadragesimo anno* by Pope Pius XI, *Fideidonum*, and several broadcasts, by Pope Pius XII, and in Pope John XXIII's apostolical letters *Mater et Magistra* and *Pacem in Terris*.[14] Lastly, the Second Vatican Council is cited multiple times—seventeen, according to Monsignor Paul Poupard—with *Lumen Gentium*, the Decree *Apostolicam actuositatem*, and especially the Pastoral Constitution *Gaudium et Spes*, 'because its teaching is serious and its application urgent'.[15] The Encyclical goes on to

proper independence and is structured on the basis of her faith as a community which the State must recognize. The two spheres are distinct, yet always interrelated.'

[9]Presentation of the Encyclical *Populorum Progressio*, by Monsignor Paul Poupard, *La documentation catholique*, 1967, col. 1017.

[10]'The action of Church is not entirely on the same level as your own, and the convergence of efforts and points of view leaves intact the distinction that exists between a spiritual society like the Church and the temporal society constituted by the countries you represent.' (Cf. *Populorum Progressio*, No. 13), *Address of His Holiness Paul VI to the Intergovernmental Committee of the World Food Programme,* 20 April 1967.

[11]Encyclical *Populorum Progressio*, No. 40.

[12]Ibid., No. 74.

[13]Ibid., No., 45.

[14]Presentation of the Encyclical *Populorum Progressio*, by Monsignor Paul Poupard, *La documentation catholique*, 1967, col. 1017.

[15]Encyclical *Populorum Progressio*, No. 3: 'Today it is most important for people to understand and appreciate that the social question ties all men together, in every part of the world. John XXIII stated this clearly, (6) and Vatican II confirmed it in its Pastoral Constitution on The Church in the World of Today. (7) The seriousness and urgency of these teachings must be recognized without delay.

The hungry nations of the world cry out to the peoples blessed with abundance. And the Church, cut to the quick by this cry, asks each and every man to hear his brother's plea and answer it lovingly'.

deal with the doctrinal novelty; references are made to modern authors, theologians, philosophers, and economists. In the text, the writings of Jacques Maritain are cited (*L'Humanisme intégral*[16] and *Les conditions spirituelles du progrès et de la paix*),[17] as well as the writings of British economist, Colin Clark (*The Conditions of Economic Progress*).[18] There are further references to the writings of the Jesuit, Henri de Lubac, (*Le drame de l'humanisme athée*), of the Dominican M-D Chenu, close to the worker-priests, with his publication, *Pour une théologie du travail.*[19] We also find expressions of Oswald von Breuning's *Economics and Society Today*,[20] of *The Pastoral Letter on Development and Peace* by Monsignor Larrain Errazuriz, the President of the Latin American Episcopal Council[21] who, it must be remembered, had in 1962 distributed 180 acres of land to 18 peasant families.[22] Among the experts consulted, it would be a grave omission not to mention the Dominican Louis-Joseph Lebret, founder of the 'Catholic Association Economy and Humanism'[23] about whom Pope Paul VI had written that: '[h]is memory must be kept, his work must be continued, his dream of Christian civilisation must be fulfilled'.[24]

Thus, the sources, cumulatively, make clear the intentions that underpin the Encyclical: they are reminders of 'the duty for the Church—which was founded to establish the Kingdom of Heaven on earth and not to conquer an earthly power—to be in the service of man'.[25] The message of the Encyclical thus ranges from the denunciation of injustice to the aim of achieving justice and peace via the means of development; from 'a cry in agony to an appeal for hope'.[26]

---

[16]Maritain [1, 2].

[17]Maritain [3].

[18]Clark [4].

[19]Chenu [5, 6].

[20]von Nell-Breuning [7].

[21]Emmanuel Larrain Errázuriz, Bishop of Talca, Chile, President of CELAM, *Lettre pastorale sur le développement et la paix*, Paris: Pax Christi (1965).

[22]Presentation of the Encyclical *Populorum Progressio*, by Paul Poupard, *La documentation catholique*, 1967, col. 1018.

[23]Lebret [8].

[24]Presentation of the Encyclical *Populorum Progressio*, by Paul Poupard, *La documentation catholique*, 1967, col. 1018.

[25]Encyclical *Populorum Progressio*, No. 3: «Founded to build the kingdom of heaven on earth rather than to acquire temporal power, the Church openly avows that the two powers—Church and State—are distinct from one another; that each is supreme in its own sphere of competency».

[26]Encyclical *Populorum Progressio*, No. 13: «The hungry nations of the world cry out to the peoples blessed with abundance. And the Church, cut to the quick by this cry, asks each and every man to hear his brother's plea and answer it lovingly».

2.2 The Denunciation of Injustices

The text of the Encyclical highlights the deep crises that, despite the general prosperity of *Les Trente Glorieuses* (i.e., 'The Glorious Thirty' [years of relative prosperity between 1945 and 1975]), have actually been greatly increasing and have become chronic and global. During his journeys to Latin America (1960), Africa (1962), the Holy Land, and to India, Pope Paul VI noted the blatant disparities at play: '[t]here We saw the perplexing problems that vex and besiege these continents, which are otherwise full of life and promise. We gained first-hand knowledge of the difficulties that these age-old civilizations must face in their struggle for further development'.[27] Those pathologies that mainly plague poor countries are analysed—in Aristotle's and Saint Thomas Aquinas's views—as consequences of a perversion of purpose that benefits only a few and serves particular or unfair interests, in total disregard of the collective good; they are the effects of degenerate political and economic laws, termed 'inhuman principles'[28] in the French translation of the Encyclical.

First, the authors point at the failure of political systems, and blame oppressive structures for their pursuit of power. The Encyclical refers to how 'a privileged minority enjoys the refinements of life, while the rest of the inhabitants, impoverished and disunited, are deprived of almost all possibility of acting on their own initiative and responsibility, and often subsist in living and working conditions unworthy of the human person'.[29] The Encyclical opposes all attempts to exercise hegemonic domination. The imperial dream throughout history of ruling over the world is being criticised. To illustrate its rejection of the *dominium mundi*, the authors of the Encyclical refer to the recent colonial past, along with the condemnation of its excesses by stating: '[i]t is true that colonising nations were sometimes concerned with nothing save their own interests, their own power and their own prestige'.[30] However, those abuses of power are far from over, and the Encyclical warns against the re-emergence of 'a new form of colonialism that would threaten civil liberty, exert economic pressure or create a new power group with controlling influence'.[31]

---

[27]Encyclical *Populorum Progressio*, No. 4.

[28]Encyclical *Populorum Progressio*, No. 70. Cf., 'Why is it, then, that they give in to baser motives of self-interest when they set out to do business in the developing countries?'. NB., French version of the Encyclical, is more forceful—cf., 'pourquoi reviendraient-ils aux principes inhumains de l'individualisme quand ils opèrent en pays moins développés?'.

[29]Encyclical *Populorum Progressio*, No. 9: 'Then there are the flagrant inequalities not merely in the enjoyment of possessions, but even more in the exercise of power'.

[30]Encyclical *Populorum Progressio*, No. 7: 'Though insufficient for the immensity and urgency of the task, the means inherited from the past are not totally useless. It is true that colonizing nations were sometimes concerned with nothing save their own interests, their own power and their own prestige; their departure left the economy of these countries in precarious imbalance—the one-crop economy, for example, which is at the mercy of sudden, wide-ranging fluctuations in market prices. Certain types of colonialism surely caused harm and paved the way for further troubles'.

[31]Encyclical *Populorum Progressio*, No. 52: 'It is certainly all right to maintain bilateral and multilateral agreements. Through such agreements, ties of dependence and feelings of jealousy—holdovers from the era of colonialism —give way to friendly relationships of true solidarity that are based

'Just as much as totalitarian ideologies are criticised by *Populorum Progressio*, so are political systems which aim to isolate. The text denounces such systems to which it refers as 'civilisations jealous of their own advantage alone'.[32] and it also highlights the dangers of nationalism and racism. The Encyclical thus defines nationalism as an institutional system that 'disunites nations and poses obstacles to their true welfare',[33] and racism as 'a cause of division and hatred within countries whenever individuals and families see the inviolable rights of the human person held in scorn, as they themselves are unjustly subjected to a regime of discrimination because of their race or their colour'.[34] Then comes the criticism of the economic norms considered unfair. Undoubtedly, due to the Cold War, *Populorum Progressio* barely mentions communism. That said, however, the Pope went so far as to state that 'total collectivization and the dangers of a planned economy which might threaten human liberty and obstruct the exercise of man's basic human rights'.[35] But the danger that the authors caution against at greater length is that of capitalism; *Populorum Progressio* condemns 'unbridled liberalism' which presents 'free competition as the

on juridical and political equality. But such agreements would be free of all suspicion if they were integrated into an overall policy of worldwide collaboration. The member nations, who benefit from these agreements, would have less reason for fear or mistrust. They would not have to worry that financial or technical assistance was being used as a cover for some new form of colonialism that would threaten their civil liberty, exert economic pressure on them, or create a new power group with controlling influence'.

[32]Encyclical *Populorum Progressio*, No. 49: 'If prosperous nations continue to be jealous of their own advantage alone, they will jeopardize their highest values, sacrificing the pursuit of excellence to the acquisition of possessions. We might well apply to them the parable of the rich man. His fields yielded an abundant harvest and he did not know where to store it: But God said to him, Fool, this very night your soul will be demanded from you'.

[33]Encyclical *Populorum Progressio*, No. 62: 'There are other obstacles to creation of a more just social order and to the development of world solidarity: nationalism and racism. It is quite natural that nations recently arrived at political independence should be quite jealous of their new-found but fragile unity and make every effort to preserve it. It is also quite natural for nations with a long-standing cultural tradition to be proud of their traditional heritage. But this commendable attitude should be further ennobled by love, a love for the whole family of man. Haughty pride in one's own nation disunites nations and poses obstacles to their true welfare. It is especially harmful where the weak state of the economy calls for a pooling of information, efforts and financial resources to implement programs of development and to increase commercial and cultural interchange'.

[34]Encyclical *Populorum Progressio*, No. 63: 'Racism is not the exclusive attribute of young nations, where sometimes it hides beneath the rivalries of clans and political parties, with heavy losses for justice and at the risk of civil war. During the colonial period it often flared up between the colonists and the indigenous population, and stood in the way of mutually profitable understanding, often giving rise to bitterness in the wake of genuine injustices. It is still an obstacle to collaboration among disadvantaged nations and a cause of division and hatred within countries whenever individuals and families see the inviolable rights of the human person held in scorn, as they themselves are unjustly subjected to a regime of discrimination because of their race or their color'.

[35]Encyclical *Populorum Progressio*, No. 33: 'It is for the public authorities to establish and lay down the desired goals, the plans to be followed, and the methods to be used in fulfilling them; and it is also their task to stimulate the efforts of those involved in this common activity. But they must also see to it that private initiative and intermediary organizations are involved in this work. In

guiding norm of economics' and 'paves the way for a particular type of tyranny'.[36] According to Pope Paul VI, the law/rule of free trade alone must be rejected because it alone can no longer rule international relations. Moreover, concerned with the needs of the social collective, the *Populorum Progressio* encyclical refuses to endorse the right of property—enshrined by the French Declaration of 1789 and by the Civil Code—as absolute and unconditional.[37] A quote from Ambroise de Milan expresses this such communitarian sentiments in stating that: '[t]he earth belongs to everyone, not to the rich',[38] which means, the encyclical goes on, to state that 'the right of private property is not absolute and unconditional'.[39] In sum, 'as the Fathers of the Church and other eminent theologians tell us, the right of private property may never be exercised to the detriment of the common good',[40] and, thus, the *Populorum Progressio* places the fundamental needs of the collective above private rights per se.

But governments may also commit injustices. To prevent the political and economic abuses denounced in *Populorum Progressio*, the Holy See warns against violent popular reactions and 'revolutionary uprisings that engender new injustices, introduce new inequities and bring new disasters'.[41] *Populorum Progressio* adds that: '[e]vil may not be dealt with in such a way that an even worse situation results'.[42] Nevertheless uprisings may be legitimate 'where there is manifest, longstanding tyranny which would do great damage to fundamental personal rights and dangerous harm to the common good of the country'.[43] Intellectuals may see this as encouragement of Liberation theology, support for Jacques Maritain's *Neo-Thomism* and Yves Congar,

this way they will avoid total collectivization and the dangers of a planned economy which might threaten human liberty and obstruct the exercise of man's basic human rights'.

[36] Encyclical *Populorum Progressio*, No. 26.

[37] Declaration of human and civic rights, of 26 August 1789, article 17, 'Since the right to Property is inviolable and sacred, no one may be deprived thereof, unless public necessity, legally ascertained, obviously requires it, and just and prior indemnity has been paid'; Civil Code of France, article 544: 'Ownership is the right to enjoy and dispose of things in the most absolute manner, provided they are not used in a way prohibited by statutes or regulations'.

[38] Encyclical *Populorum Progressio*, No. 23. *De Nabute*, c. 12, n. 53: PL 14. 747; cf. Palanque [9].

[39] Encyclical *Populorum Progressio*, No. 23: *The Use of Private Property*, 'He who has the goods of this world and sees his brother in need and closes his heart to him, how does the love of God abide in him? Everyone knows that the Fathers of the Church laid down the duty of the rich toward the poor in no uncertain terms. The earth belongs to everyone, not to the rich. These words indicate that the right to private property is not absolute and unconditional'.

[40] Encyclical *Populorum Progressio*, No. 23: 'No one may appropriate surplus goods solely for his own private use when others lack the bare necessities of life. In short, as the Fathers of the Church and other eminent theologians tell us, the right of private property may never be exercised to the detriment of the common good. When private gain and basic community needs conflict with one another, it is for the public authorities to seek a solution to these questions, with the active involvement of individual citizens and social groups'.

[41] Encyclical *Populorum Progressio*, No. 31: "Everyone knows that revolutionary uprisings engender new injustices, introduce new inequities and bring new disasters".

[42] Encyclical *Populorum Progressio*, No. 31.

[43] Ibid.

Marie-Dominique Chenu, and Louis-Joseph Lebret's justifications. Furthermore, the encyclical put forward the notion of social sin—i.e., the sin of omission in the face of such disparities that may be rectified only by the practice of justice and peace.

2.3 A Development for Justice and Peace

Pope Paul VI, in emphasising the urgency to act, had stated: '[w]e must make haste. Too many people are suffering'.[44] To relieve the suffering of the people, the solutions proposed by atheistic and materialistic philosophy and above all, by liberal overconsumption, appear to be inappropriate. *Populorum Progressio* proposes a *third way* leading first to man's integral development, and subsequently to mankind's common development. Such intervention on the part of spiritual authority may be justified by the long presence of the Church in human affairs, 'she [i.e., the Church] seeks but one solitary goal: to carry forward the work of Christ himself under the lead of the befriending Spirit. For Christ entered this world to bear witness to the truth, to save and not to sit in judgment, to serve and not to be served'.[45] First Pope Paul VI advocates the personal development of man Here the advice brings together tradition and modernity. The text is reminiscent of Aristotle and Thomas Aquinas's thinking with the principle of distributive justice expressed by Roman jurists, in the *suum cuique tribuere* maxim, so as to guarantee their citizens their full human development, and to give them their rightful place in the community of nations.[46] But, above all, the authors apply the integral humanism of Jacques Maritain who proposes to the citizens to ensure their human fulfilment. It is a call for growth in humanity: each person can grow in humanity, enhance his/her personal worth, and perfect him-/herself. Self-development, however, is not left up to man's option; the Encyclical refers to the duty of growth as: '[t]hus human self-fulfilment may be said to sum up our obligations'.[47] Man's self-development, carried through by personal efforts and responsible activity, is destined for a higher state of perfection. And the authors list the areas of personal growth: education, freedom from poverty, health, adequate means of subsistence, job security, involvement in responsibilities, freedom from all forms of oppression—that is to say: to do more, to know more, to have more, so as

[44]Encyclical *Populorum Progressio*, No. 29, 'We must make haste. Too many people are suffering. While some make progress, others stand still or move backwards; and the gap between them is widening. However, the work must proceed in measured steps if the proper equilibrium is to be maintained. Makeshift agrarian reforms may fall short of their goal. Hasty industrialization can undermine vital institutions and produce social evils, causing a setback to true human values'.

[45]Encyclical *Populorum Progressio*, No. 12.

[46]Encyclical *Populorum Progressio*, No. 6, 'Moreover, those nations which have recently gained independence find that political freedom is not enough. They must also acquire the social and economic structures and processes that accord with man's nature and activity, if their citizens are to achieve personal growth and if their country is to take its rightful place in the international community'.

[47]Encyclical *Populorum Progressio*, No. 16.

to be more. On the other hand, in this vision of growth, the criticism of materialism is more nuanced. The authors make a distinction between the liberal law of profit, considered as harmful, and industrialisation whose contribution to humanity overall has been considerable.[48]

Concerning colonisation, there is similar nuance at play. The Encyclical honours 'those colonizers whose skills and technical know-how brought benefits to many untamed hands, and whose work survives to this day'.[49] Here we get a glimpse of the work conducted by missionaries, such as the work of Charles de Foucault who compiled a dictionary of the Tuareg language.[50] This contribution of missionaries demonstrates how the final goal of *integral humanism* may be directed only towards God. The encyclical reads: 'it is a transcendent humanism which is the highest goal of human self-fulfilment'.[51] The term *integral humanism* contrasts with that of a *closed* or *horizontal humanism*—i.e., that which is deprived of a *vertical* dimension—that is better suited to communist and capitalist materialisms. Pope Paul VI does not seek for opposites to converge; he blames materialism for remaining an incomplete, ambiguous, purely formal and even distorted form of humanism. In *Populorum Progressio*, one can read: 'man can set about organizing terrestrial realities without God. But closed off from God, they will end up being directed against man. A humanism closed off from other realities becomes inhuman'.[52] Conversely, growth, regarded as a vocation for each, enters the theology of History proposed by the Social Doctrine of the Church: 'All men are called to this full development. Civilizations spring up,

[48]Encyclical *Populorum Progressio*, No. 26, 'But if it is true that a type of capitalism, as it is commonly called, has given rise to hardships, unjust practices, and fratricidal conflicts that persist to this day, it would be a mistake to attribute these evils to the rise of industrialization itself, for they really derive from the pernicious economic concepts that grew up along with it'.

[49]Encyclical *Populorum Progressio*, No. 26, 'The structural machinery [those colonizers] introduced was not fully developed or perfected, but it did help to reduce ignorance and disease, to promote communication, and to improve living conditions'.

[50]Encyclical *Populorum Progressio*, No. 12, 'We need only mention the efforts of Pere Charles de Foucauld: he compiled a valuable dictionary of the Tuareg language, and his charity won him the title, "everyone's brother". So We deem it fitting to praise those oft forgotten pioneers who were motivated by love for Christ, just as We honor their imitators and successors who today continue to put themselves at the generous and unselfish service of those to whom they preach the Gospel'.

[51]Encyclical *Populorum Progressio*, No. 12, *Man's Supernatural Destiny*, 'Self-development, however, is not left up to man's option. Just as the whole of creation is ordered toward its Creator, so too the rational creature should of his own accord direct his life to God, the first truth and the highest good. Thus human self-fulfilment may be said to sum up our obligations. Moreover, this harmonious integration of our human nature, carried through by personal effort and responsible activity, is destined for a higher state of perfection. United with the life-giving Christ, man's life is newly enhanced; it acquires a transcendent humanism which surpasses its nature and bestows new fullness of life. This is the highest goal of human self-fulfilment'.

[52]Encyclical *Populorum Progressio*, No. 42, 'The ultimate goal is a full-bodied humanism. And does this not mean the fulfillment of the whole man and of every man? A narrow humanism, closed in on itself and not open to the values of the spirit and to God who is their source, could achieve apparent success'.

flourish and die. As the waves of the sea gradually creep farther and farther, so the human race inches its way forward through History'.[53]

This vocation for growth leads to another aspect; that of the common development based on assistance to the needy. This *duty of solidarity* is accomplished through legal and technical measures that will prove difficult to apply. Faithful to Council Vatican II, *Populorum Progressio* resumes the tradition of the principle of the universal destination of goods as a limit to the right of property: '[a]ll other rights, whatever they may be, including the rights of property and free trade, are to be subordinated to that principle'. Pope Paul VI went on to list possible acts of solidarity, including the payment of higher taxes for development, paying more for imported goods, emigrating from one's homeland to help emerging nations, protecting the natural family such as it is in God's plan, and furthering 'the nobility of work', by personal and common efforts of every worker. For, 'when work is done in common, it unites the wills, minds and hearts of men'.[54]

The Encyclical also deals with the issue of the surplus of affluent nations that ought to be made available to poorer nations, and encourages the creation of a world fund requested by Pope Paul VI during his journey to Bombay. Then there is the part that collaborative programmes can play as they are necessary for 'directing, stimulating, coordinating, supplying and integrating'[55] the work of individuals and intermediary organisations. For this collaboration, Pope Paul VI insists, in accordance with the Encyclical *Ecclesiam Suam*, on the necessity for dialogue between affluent and poor countries in favour of cooperation and against debt servitudes. By these practices of solidarity, the Holy See promotes not only the integral development of man but that of the whole of humanity, towards the fraternal goal of the common good. According to *Populorum Progressio*, such development is the new name for Peace.[56] On Christmas Day 1975, in his homily for the closing of the Holy Year, Paul VI announces the forthcoming civilisation of love as 'the wisdom of fraternal love, which has characterized the historical journey of the Church'.[57] It is not hatred,

---

[53]Encyclical *Populorum Progressio*, No. 22, *Issues and Principles*.

[54]Encyclical *Populorum Progressio*, No. 27, *Nobility of Work*, 'Further, when work is done in common—when hope, hardship, ambition and joy are share—it brings together and firmly unites the wills, minds and hearts of men. In its accomplishment, men find themselves to be brothers'.

[55]Encyclical *Populorum Progressio*, No. 33, *Programs and Planning*.

[56]Encyclical *Populorum Progressio*, No. 76, *Development, the New Name for Peace*.

[57]Homily of Paul VI, Christmas—Closing of the Holy Year, 25 December 1964: '*La sapienza dell'amore fraterno, la quale ha caratterizzato in virtù ed in opere, che cristiane sono giustamente qualificate, il cammino storico della santa Chiesa, esploderà con novella fecondità, con vittoriosa felicità, con rigenerante socialità.*

Non l'odio, non la contesa, non l'avarizia sarà la sua dialettica, ma l'amore, l'amore generatore d'amore, l'amore dell'uomo per l'uomo, non per alcun provvisorio ed equivoco interesse, o per alcuna amara e mal tollerata condiscendenza, ma per l'amore a Te; a Te, o Cristo scoperto nella sofferenza e nel bisogno di ogni nostro simile. La civiltà dell'amore prevarrà nell'affanno delle implacabili lotte sociali, e darà al mondo la sognata trasfigurazione dell'umanità finalmente cristiana. Così, così si conclude, o Signore, questo Anno Santo; così o uomini fratelli riprenda coraggioso e gioioso il nostro cammino nel tempo verso l'incontro finale, che fin d'ora mette sulle nostre labbra l'estrema invocazione: Vieni, o Signore Gesù (Apoc. 22, 20)'.

struggle, or greed that will be its dialectic, but love, the love-generating love, and the love of man for fellow man.[58] And he declares that the civilisation of love may be 'defenceless but it is invincible'.[59]

2.4 Conclusions

Fifty years ago, the Encyclical *Populorum Progressio* on the development of peoples was issued to denounce the injustices of an increasingly interconnected world that was appearing increasingly more inhuman. The encyclical contains general instructions above all as to the proper path to development—i.e., that which aligns with the purposes of justice and peace—to fuller growth. This message was novel, mostly due to the fact that Pope Paul VI was addressing not only the Church, but also all of humanity. In June 2007, Cardinal Paul Poupard explained the consequence of this novelty, by recalling the visit of Pope Paul VI to the assembly of the International Labour Organisation (ILO) on 10 June 1969. The main aim is to prepare a common legislation 'to express in rules of law that solidarity which is becoming ever more definite in the consciences of men'. In his speech at Geneva, the Pope had called for the development of an international law aimed at realising the quest to build a civilisation of love—in his address to the ILO assembly, the Pope had stated that 'your legislative work must continue boldly and strike out resolutely along new paths, to guarantee the common right of peoples to their integral development and enable in each instance all peoples to become the artisans of their destiny'.

References

1. Maritain, J. (1936). *L'humanisme intégral*. Paris: Aubier.
2. Maritain, J. (1938). *True humanism*. New York: Charles Scribner's Sons.
3. Maritain, J. (1966). Les conditions spirituelles du progrès et de la paix. In *Rencontre des cultures à l'UNESCO sous le signe du Concile Œcuménique Vatican II* (p. 66). Paris: Mame.
4. Clark, C. (1960). *The conditions of economic progress* (3rd ed., pp. 3–6). New York: St. Martin's Press.
5. Chenu, M.-D., o.p. (1955). *Pour une théologie du travail*. Paris: Editions du Seuil.
6. Chenu, M.-D. (1963). *The theology of work*. Dublin: Gill.
7. von Nell-Breuning, O., s.j. (1956). *Wirtschaft und Gesellschaft* (Vol. 1, pp. 183–184). Grundfragen, Freiburg: Herder.
8. Lebret, L.-J., o.p. (1961). *Dynamique concrète du développement* (p. 28). Paris: Economie et Humanisme, Les editions ouvrières.
9. Palanque, J. R. (1933). *Saint Ambroise et l'empire romain* (336 ff). Paris: de Boccard.

[58] *Idem*.

[59] *Idem*; Patrick de Laubier, *La civilisation de l'amour selon Paul VI*, Paris, Frédéric Aimard, éditeur, 2013.

Chapter 3
Luigi Sturzo's Socio-economic Development Theory and the Case of Italy: No Prophet in His Homeland

Flavio Felice and Luca Sandonà

Abstract Luigi Sturzo's (1871–1959) popularism is an economic and political theory that has many commonalities with the German social market economy. Because of his anti-statism, the fascist regime forced Sturzo to remain in exile for twenty-two years. In this period, Sturzo mainly lived in the United Kingdom and in the United States of America additionally absorbing Anglo-Saxon approaches to capitalism and authentically fusing these with a Catholic perspective. In his views on development, Sturzo pointed out that the free market must not only exist within the rules of free competition, but must also possess an ethical perspective based on the centrality of the human person. In the light of Sturzo's political thought, we can assert that political and social institutions should support the inclusion of all people, especially of the most poor and marginalized, according to the principles of subsidiarity and solidarity. Consequently, Sturzo's 'constitutional economics' rejects welfarism, emphasizes the freedom and responsibility of civil society, while questioning potentially inflationary and deficit spending policies. Such conceptual framework based on the centrality of the intermediate bodies (family, associations, groups, enterprises, etc.) could today also be useful for the socio-economic development of the least developed countries given that Sturzo's approach balances the necessity for the competitiveness of a free market economy with the necessity from social justice drawn from Catholicism. However, from an historical point of view, although Christian Democrats had governed Italy uninterruptedly from 1946 to 1992, they had not develop Sturzo's approach to economic policy. Their economic planning had been in line with the Italian tradition of State capitalism, especially after the death of Alcide De Gasperi in 1954. At the beginning of the 1990s, the Christian Democrat economist Nino Andreatta rediscovered Sturzo's ideas.

Keywords Socio-economic development · Luigi Sturzo · Popularism · Constitutional economics · Christian democracy

---

F. Felice (✉)
University of Molise, Campobasso, Italy
e-mail: flavio.felice@unimol.it

L. Sandonà
University of Trieste, Trieste, Italy
e-mail: lsandona@units.it

P. Szwedo et al. (eds.), *Law and Development*, Kobe University Monograph Series in Social Science Research, https://doi.org/10.1007/978-981-13-9423-2_3

3.1 Introduction[1]

In a recent pamphlet on the history of industrial policy in Italy, Franco Debenedetti,[2] a top manager and entrepreneur that serves as president of the pro-market Bruno Leoni think-tank of Turin, dedicated a chapter to Luigi Sturzo. This chapter is titled *Luigi Sturzo, una voce contro* (i.e., 'a dissident/contrary voice'). The question thus is: against what? Debenedetti answered that Sturzo seemed to be the only social scientist that was contrary to state interventionism that defined the Italian model of economic development from the end of WWII to the end of the First Republic (viz., 1992). Other than Sturzo, Luigi Einaudi was also a promoter of a sort of humanist liberalism to encourage virtuous economic behaviours. Vilfredo Pareto and Maffeo Pantaleoni were neoclassical liberalists. The subsequent generation of thinkers had included Francesco Forte, who supported socialist liberalism, Sergio Ricossa, who supported the Austrian school of economics kind of liberalism, and Alberto Quadrio Curzio, who argued for social liberalism.

Antonio Masala[3] methodically reviewed the diverse range of European free market economic models, including classical liberalism, Ordoliberalism, neoliberalism, and so on. He pointed out that Alfred Sherman,[4] one of the ghost-writers for Margaret Thatcher, had confessed that many of his ideas were drawn from Sturzo's liberalism, which was the only example radically founded on Catholic ethics and natural law. For this reason, Dario Antiseri[5] distinguished between Sturzo's popularism/liberal Catholicism that continued the tradition of Antonio Rosmini Serbati and Einaudi's Catholic liberalism that, in turn, was founded on classical liberal economic principles and only adapted in reference to human and Catholic values.

The analysis of Sturzo's popularism seems particularly interesting in light of recent re-emergence of populism in politics and, according to some,[6] even in the Catholic Church. Sturzo's popularism is based on the inclusive character of political, economic, and social institutions. Furthermore, it supports a balanced polyarchy of powers at the international, national, and local levels; interprets as complementary the concepts of government and governance; and contrasts any form of concentration of power in the hands of the few. What is more, populism emphasizes the charisma of the leader, challenges democratic institutions, and conceives the people's will as being of divine nature.[7] In this contribution, Sect. 2 introduces the thought of Luigi Sturzo, with special reference to his connections with the German social market economic tradition; Sect. 3 reviews Italy's economic history underlying the lack of

[1] This section was written by Luca Sandonà.

[2] Debenedetti [16].

[3] Masala [23].

[4] Sherman [31].

[5] Antiseri [7].

[6] Zanatta [39]. For a more detailed analysis of the phenomenon of populism, see L. Zanatta, *Il populismo*, Carocci Editore, Roma, 2018.

[7] Serio [30].

impact of Sturzo's teaching; and Sect. 4 analyses the revival of Sturzo's thought, as propounded by Nino Andreatta, a Catholic economics professor at the University of Bologna who has moved away from Keynesism and towards popularism/liberal Catholicism. Lastly, the conclusion (Sect. 5) attempts to address the reasons that Sturzo had failed to become a prophet in his homeland.

3.2 Luigi Sturzo's Socio-economic Development Theory[8]

It is thus true that the application of 'ordoliberal' theories has only recently reached Italy, and only indirectly.[9] However, we cannot but acknowledge that the thought of authors such as Ludwig Erhard, Walter Eucken, and Wilhelm Röpke have profoundly influenced aspects of Italy's economic and political culture. With regard to popularism, we maintain that Fr. Luigi Sturzo—a priest, scientist, politician, and statesman—knew only too well how to express clearly the social philosophy of the authors mentioned earlier. A significant testimony reaches us from a letter sent by the West German Chancellor Konrad Adenauer to Giuseppe Palladino on 25 September 1959, a few days after the death of the Sicilian priest: 'I esteemed Fr. Sturzo as one of the great politicians who out of a profoundly felt sense of Christian responsibility, after the chaos of the last war, have worked in every sense to build a new Europe; I hope greatly that Fr. Sturzo's prayers may help me to cooperate, in turn, in the spirit that animated his intention, to resolve the problems that will present themselves for the Christian West'.[10] Having returned to Italy in 1946, after a long and sorrowful exile since 1924, which had led him first to France, then to England, and, eventually, to the United States, Sturzo wrote prolifically as a freelance journalist for newspapers and academic journals in which he was vehemently critical of the mounting statist climate of that era. A climate that translated into government and parliamentary support for state intervention in the economy.

In an article of 29 December 1957, entitled *Paura della libertà* ('*Fear of Freedom*'), Sturzo wrote: 'Unfortunately there exists among us, like it or not, a hybrid industrial business, [comprising] the staticised one and the private one; the former with monopolistic privileges, ample state guarantees, a facility of means, and no sense of risk; the latter with a longstanding tradition of state-given favours, facility of means and with a sense of risk; even industrial operators who seek particular favours lose sight of the value of economic freedom and the real interests of national productivity'.[11] These are not the words of an impenitent libertarian, an anarcho-capitalist who dreams of who-knows-what strategies to privatize lunar real estate. Quite the contrary. These are the words of the father of Italian and European politi-

[8]This section was written by Flavio Felice. An earlier version of this text was published in the international scholarly journal, *Global & Local Economic Review*.

[9]Forte and Felice [20], Forte et al. [19].

[10]Palladino [26].

[11]Sturzo [35].

cal and economic Catholicism—one of the greatest interpreters of modern Christian social thought and one of the most authoritative social scientists of the 20th century.

That article is of considerable importance. It is interesting to note how Sturzo affirms that no form of 'solidarity' appears practicable where the coexistence of 'statism' and 'market economy' emerges, while a policy oriented towards solidarity would be possible only where the 'free market' is accompanied by a state policy of 'cooperation' and of 'occasional' and 'agreed intervention'.[12] These would be the circumstances that would allow for a fair and healthy policy. Ultimately, Sturzo qualifies his political-economic position with the characteristics typical of a social market economy. Not by chance does he take the German and US economic-entrepreneurial reality as an example, nor is it by chance that Röpke cited Sturzo's work as one of his inexhaustible sources of inspiration. The social market economy that Sturzo advocated takes three conceptual elements into consideration: First, that freedom is unique and individual: 'one loses political and cultural freedom if one loses economic freedom, and vice versa',[13] in disagreement with the Crocian 'political liberalism/economic liberalism' distinction, and in agreement with the unitary perspective of Einaudi, Hayek, and Röpke himself. Second, that freedom is an expression of self-discipline as well as of legislative regulation: 'for the coexistence and respect of reciprocal rights and duties'.[14] And third, that the main functions of the State are to 'guarantee and safeguard collective and private rights',[15] keep public order, assure national defence, and to maintain and safeguard the monetary and credit system. And, furthermore, to exercise vigilance and care for public finance, and to guarantee its proper administration. Only secondarily and 'subordinately does the state intervene, in a supplementary manner, in those sectors of social and general interest where private initiative is deficient, until these are able to resume their role'.[16] As becomes evident, Sturzo, just like the ordoliberals and the fathers of social market economics, does not deny that in cases of necessity the State should intervene, but he circumscribes such cases to situations of 'emergency', for a 'temporary' period and 'in a secondary and alternative manner'.[17]

The economic freedom of which Sturzo speaks 'is an economic freedom that conditions and facilitates the existence and development of the political and moral freedoms'.[18] In this sense, for Sturzo, the collapse of all those 'corporativistic illusions of the philo-fascist Catholics of yesterday' would come as a result.[19] Corporatism, for our author, did not and could not have any realization except in the sad Mussolinian

---

[12] *Id.*

[13] *Id.*

[14] *Id.*

[15] *Id.*

[16] *Id.*

[17] *Id.*

[18] *Id.*

[19] *Id.*

attempt to identify 'State-party-corporation', in the very realization of the fascist motto: 'all in the State, of the State, for the State, nothing outside the State'.[20]

Similarly, the identification of economic freedom with the existence and development of political and moral freedoms—integral and indivisible freedom—arguably cause the collapse of the illusions in the 'socialist and classist State'.[21] The experience of the Soviet Union and of its satellite countries, as well as the 'forgeries of Belgrade and Beijing' all demonstrate that, in the absence of economic freedom, 'free capitalism' is soon substituted by a 'State capitalism, a thousand times worse than the private one' and that the *dictatorship of the proletariat* would be nothing but 'the military dictatorship with the apparatus of profiteering functionalism'.[22] It is on this level of reflection that Sturzo comes to affirm that 'Western countries, more or less individualistic and dynamic, with so many differences of climate, productivity, economic development, customs, needs, history, and culture, and whose political conditions are full of contrasts, will never undergo—except by force—the suppression of their fundamental liberties, of which the economy is the necessary condition'.[23] In this picture, although State intervention at the time was generally more extensive than in the past, its impact would be lesser, and the productive energies coming from the private sector would represent an antidote against State interference precisely in those countries where the political structure was more solid and the industry healthier. Sturzo did not see Italy as being amongst those countries, given that Italy was inconsistent and evidently immature on the political level, and possessed an economic-productive system that was extremely weak and constantly de-responsibilised by State interventionism that, assuring monopolistic privileges (state guarantees), had ended up miseducating economic operators to the 'risk that educates' in a Schumpeterian sense.

In underlining the fact that, ultimately, State interventionism does not lead to policies of solidarity and respect for personal freedoms, but rather to the authoritarian subversion of a free society, Sturzo presents a pragmatic and impactful view. It is worth noting that Sturzo's idea of economic and political development is consistent with the notion of 'integral human development'; a quintessential notion within the tradition of the Social Doctrine of the Church. Sturzo's 'personalism' argues that only the individual acts and the social aggregates are the multiple, simultaneous, cumulative, and continuative projection of human action. On this anthropocentric basis, Sturzo's popularism advocates democratic participation to political activity, openness to inclusive institutions working in a spirit of polyarchy, and opposition to any form of concentration that favours the rent over the competition. On the other hand, Sturzo's 'solidarity' pertains to the moral character of civil and political action,

---

[20]On the contrary, it is precisely by recovering the experience matured by and in 19th-century social Catholicism that Sturzo develops a sensitivity towards the underlying human factors of the production process, proposing representation for work, understood in its most varied forms, within the administrative organisation of the Italian state. See Secco Suardo [29].

[21]Sturzo [33, p. 158].

[22]*Id.*

[23]*Id.*

rejecting State interventionism conceived as a form of assistentialism. In this view, humankind is seen as free and responsible, ignorant and fallible, yet always perfectible. However, if it is inspired by 'superior ideals', it can concur to the reflection of the divine on the civil institution in order to build a type of development not only in quantitative terms (growth) but also qualitative. This perspective, which connects *personalism* and *solidarity* in Sturzo's popularism, is centered on the belief that the *common good* is not determined by the State as well as that the State is not endowed with the right of achieving the common good in the name of social pluralism. On the contrary, Sturzo thinks that the common good is inspired by the principle of subsidiarity, as it derives from the spontaneous order resulting from the active role of each individual and intermediate body (such as the family and cultural/social/associative groups) without any pretence of imposing something on other people. In this context, Sturzo introduces the transcendent call of each human person to create institutions directly answering to God's invitation (to Man) to be co-creator. Put differently, Sturzo's proposal could be a sort of *people's capitalism*[24] or even, according to Guy Sorman's definition, of *barefoot capitalism.*

His harsh critique of this reality was aimed at a part of the Catholic political and intellectual milieu accustomed to referring to concepts such as *personalism* and *solidarism* as possible picklocks that could have unhinged—by overcoming—the typical institutions of the market economy, to give life to some form of an economy 'of Italy's own'. This was an illusory alternative to the market economy that threatened political and cultural liberties; illusory, inasmuch as—according to Sturzo—freedom is 'individual' and consequently 'whole and indivisible'.[25]

State intervention, which Sturzo considered necessary for civil living (living in *conformity*, according to the terminology of the fathers of social market economics) may precariously slip into statist interventionism: *not in conformity,* 'a destroyer of every institutional order and every administrative order',[26] when it appears as the 'systematic degeneration of state intervention, in fields not its own or by provisions harmful to the rights of citizens'.[27] Intervention is 'illegitimate' or 'harmful to the rights of citizens'[28]—Röpke and the interpreters of the Freibourg School would claim 'not in conformity with the market economy'—when the State does not limit itself to attempting to neutralise hostile factors in the joint activity between entrepreneurs and workers. The degeneration of statism would result in the monopolization of national capital, consequently contracting productivity, devaluating currency, generalising functionalism, and effecting a totalitarian drift.[29] As may be witnessed, for Sturzo the State was in its very essence the political form of civil society; what the *Res publica*

[24]In relation to this perspective, it would be interesting to compare Sturzo's economic and political theory of development with Michael Novak's original view on democratic capitalism. See De Girolamo [13, 14], Felice [17].

[25]Sturzo [33, p. 159].

[26]Sturzo [36].

[27]*Id.*

[28]*Id.*

[29]Sturzo [32].

was for the ancient Romans and the *Administration* in the Anglo-saxon tradition. Ultimately, and to put it in Sturzo's words, it was 'power and the administration of the common good'.[30]

The reasons for the anti-statism in a certain tradition of Catholic social thought (that current heir to Sturzo's thought), are expressed by the priest of Caltagirone himself when he affirms that statism unhinges the intermediated articulation of society; ultimately, by centralising power in the hands of State entities and bureaucratising civil society, it contravenes one of the cardinal points of the modern Social Doctrine of the Church, namely, the principle of subsidiarity, both in its horizontal and vertical dimensions.[31] It weakens a certain capacity for individual resistance in the face of the threat of invasion by bureaucratic bodies in the spontaneous life of social organisations. It transforms parties and unions into bureaucratic bodies of the State—where the State is strong—and of the anti-state, where the State is weak. Sturzo's fear is that 'one day today's power-centralizing state will collapse even with its half-chained freedom, and there the anti-state, itself a power-centralizing entity, will rise to power with the cadaver of political freedom at its feet'.[32] According to Sturzo, by subverting the rights inherent in the human person, statism also ends up subverting the powers and functions of the administration, producing an economic imbalance in, both, the production and distribution of goods and services, due to its irrational initiatives, elevated costs, and management deficit.

Sturzo's message on economics can be summed up in the maxim, typically used in the Ordoliberal context: 'the state, a referee and not a player in the free economic game'. Giuseppe Palladino, the Italian economist who executed the 'will' of the founder of the Italian Popular Party[33] and was one of the men closest to Sturzo in his final years, is credited with highlighting the great lesson in economics we received from Sturzo. Palladino writes in a volume dedicated to the US recessions from 1927 to 1957: 'In rethinking the past and recent economic and financial experience, we shall make reference above all to the critical position assumed by father Luigi Sturzo in the face of more relevant government and parliamentary directions on the

[30] *Id.*

[31] 'A State-controlled organization on subsidiarity puts up for discussion not only the repartition of competence and power between the various institutional levels, from local to European levels, but also puts up for discussion the repartition of competences in the horizontal sense, between operators having diverse characteristics—public, private and State-private—having in common the capability to carry out activities of general interest. This problem has already been addressed in different and in convergent ways applying a variety of theories, with the most important identifiable as federalism, the theory of subsidiarity and the model of Social Market Economy. These different approaches allow one to understand the various elements of the historical process. Their capacity to develop a cross-fertilization process can be attributed to the very nature of the ongoing processes involving the change referred to by all the three mentioned' Velo [38, p. 15].

[32] Sturzo [34].

[33] The Italian Popular Party was founded by Luigi Sturzo on 18 January 1919, and, in the opinion of the Italian historian Federico Chabod, it was '[t]he most notable event in the history of the Italian twentieth century'. It contributed to the end of the so-called 'Roman question', exacerbated by the capture of Rome by the Italian army on 20 September 1870 [11, p. 43].

topic of the state intervention in the economy'.[34] We particularly owe to Palladino the reception of Sturzo's thought in a manner strongly committed to understanding the national and international economic processes, and again owe to Palladino the understanding of Sturzo as one committed to giving answers coherent with his sociological presuppositions, and oriented towards the current of research we have defined as Ordoliberalism. Sturzo was conscious that *stability*, understood as full commitment, and *development*, in the absence of inflation, represent two demands of modern democracies, since such democracies are more sensible to the needs of the market. Their greater market sensibility results from their diminished derivation from those nets of social protection typical of archaic societies; consequently, the women and men of the post-war period were much freer, but at the same time much more exposed to risks deriving from possible economic crises and catastrophes.

In conformity with the ordoliberal lesson, Palladino, assuming Sturzo's principle of 'the sociology of the concrete' regarding the evils of statism, writes that 'since the series of economic and social relationships in a free society is always posed as a question of fair and proper competition, it is well to observe that the following principle of free competition was suffocated yesterday (in the past) by the illusion of being able to consider the market the playing field and referee of the economic game, and is more seriously threatened today by the error of deeming the state a party and referee of the game itself. And thus, the game remains a confused one, and its stability enters into conflict with the ulterior development of the economy'.[35] Ultimately, the lesson of Sturzo, mediated by Palladino's contribution, regarding the Italian reception of the ordoliberal lesson, takes into account the awareness that in a game or match, the best results are obtained when the following three conditions exist: the presence of good players ('conscious and updated economic workers'), clear and certain rules ('principles with which to regulate the hierarchy of interests and ends, starting from those individuals and of groups, of the categories and—in the universal sphere—of the individual nations') and an impartial referee.

The first error was allegedly committed in considering the market the playing field, in which senseless automatons with homogeneous—and thus indifferent—expectations exercised themselves in the public manifestation of the principle of free and perfect competition. This dual function was motivated by the conviction that it was sufficient for the State to serve as the guarantor of economic freedom, and, consequently, to have the function of impeding anyone from disrupting competition—which on its own could not have been other than perfect—out of respect for an interpretation of the concept of Adam Smith's 'invisible hand', according to which the instances of individual selfishness would be directed towards the 'greatest common good'. This mistake, according to Palladino, generated the misleading idea that universal and free competition would regulate the natural and spontaneous circulation of work, capital, and goods, resolving in this way the problem of the allocation of scarce resources on a global scale. So that, Palladino points out, 'healthy force of the economy's sure development'—which has from time immemorial been called

[34] Palladino [25, p. 171].

[35] *Id.*, p. 178.

selfishness—when not moderated by reason, can serve as neither brake nor limit. In this way, selfishness, exploiting the increased revenues of the larger companies, has obtained the upper hand over the weakest: 'And as companies have grown *in proportion* they have also become less numerous in the main sectors of the economy: the iron and steel industry, metallurgy, sources of energy, mechanics, credit, etc. In this way *individual selfishness* has often become *group selfishness* (monopolies, trusts, cartels), *class selfishness* (trade union monopolies) and *national selfishness* (economic imperialism and isolationism)'.[36]

By the end of the 1950s it was evident that the great economic and social question, conscious as it was of the market's incapacity to regulate itself and of the inestimable harm the state would do if positioned simultaneously as referee and as player, was being directed towards the search for a referee able to guide the economic sphere. People began to understand how anti-monopoly and anti-trust laws would not suffice, since in those sectors that had been left in the hands of a few companies, no law would ever keep a certain number of directors from meeting and making decisions that would influence the global market for a single good. Here Palladino sees three possible remedies. Having set fairness and stability as objectives of the economic game led by free men, he deemed that these objectives could be pursued as long as society addressed the quality of the economic players, took on the full consciousness of its individual and collective goals and, lastly, became definitively aware that only the principle of free competition 'is compatible with the economic game of a free society founded on the incentive of private property and on men's free individual choices, on the democratic method as workers, consumers and savers'.[37] Instead, where economic power is confused with political power in the international field, through control by nations, or worse, through a mixed economic system in the domestic realm, it is highly unlikely that results would be any more comforting than those of an economy left to itself, since the asphyxiating control of the entrepreneurial State would lead to increasing confusion of the political system with the economic system.

3.3 The Divide Between Sturzo's Thought and Italian Economic Development Model[38]

The Ordoliberal topic of a competitive economy as a *public good*, above all, after Wilhelm Röpke's contribution to developing the theory of the social market economy, has undergone a fair diffusion in Italy thanks to its positive evaluation by Luigi Einaudi, Luigi Sturzo, Benedetto Croce, and Guglielmo Ferrero in the period immediately following the First World War, to then, lamentably, be set aside by the second

[36] *Id.*, p. 179.

[37] *Id.*, p. 181.

[38] This section was written by Flavio Felice. An earlier version of this text was published in the international scholarly journal *Global & Local Economic Review*.

half of the 1960s. Even less fortunate had been the reception of Ordoliberal thought at the time of the drafting of the Italian Constitution.[39] With particular reference to this second context, Tommaso Padoa-Schioppa wrote: 'The norms on the economic relations contained in Part I of the 1948 Constitution appear to be largely inspired by the idea that public institutions should have an active role in the economy. It is an idea that joined the two dominant political forces of the time, the Marxist and the Catholic, in a vision that was strongly critical of "capitalism". Government intervention in the market, limits on ownership rights, the orienting of economic activity to social ends are thus grafted strongly onto the fabric of liberal origin'.[40] The author of that passage perceives how strongly the thesis is affirmed that to pursue a *social* value, it would be necessary to reduce the *market space* to make room for *government intervention*. In such a thesis, Padoa-Schioppa comments, we glimpse a negative judgement of the market—considered intrinsically *antisocial*—and a positive one regarding public intervention, judged *intrinsically beneficial*. Padoa-Schioppa comments: 'for some time there has been a consensus in economic theory in deeming the market's "failures" an exception rather than the rule; that, just as we were saying, "except for exceptions", the market system has in itself the capacity to achieve the ends of "safety, freedom, human dignity, salaries proportional to the quality and quantity of the work done" that the Constitution enunciates'.[41]

This same position has been expounded by Alberto Quadrio Curzio, according to whom, '[i]t would instead be better to say that, a middle way (though some would see it as a compromise) has prevailed between the liberal configuration favorable to the market regulated by the Western democracies, and the Communist-socialist configuration, favorable to Eastern planning. This middle way was advocated for principally by Catholics, but others' intentions could have distorted it, had political events permitted, in the extreme case, towards the collectivist planning solution'; and, again, that '[a]lready in Art. 1 of the Constitution, which affirms that "Italy is a Democratic Republic, founded on work", the possibility was left open to extend this concept even towards conceptions of the supremacy of the "working class". In fact, it does prove difficult to understand why "work" should come before the "human person" (spoken of in later articles) that expresses values that are far superior and of greater breadth that include, among other things, also that of work [...] There occurs [in the Constitution] instead, often, the reference to the intervention in production and state and public ownership as an expression of that "third way" which in our country has generated a growing and grave distortion with a protectionist bureaucratic attitude and state-run entrepreneurship activities for which only recently attempts at a remedy have been made'.[42]

An equally radical judgement on the insensibility to the market of a significant part of the fathers of the republican constitution was expressed by Giuliano Amato. In an essay on the market in the Italian Constitution he writes: '[i]t is a classic mixed-

[39]Rotondi [28].

[40]Padoa-Schioppa [24].

[41]*Id.*, p. 454.

[42]Quadrio Curzio [27].

feeling that which the Constituting Assembly, in its great majority, feels and asserts in regard to the market. It mistrusts the market at the same time that it defends it; and it defends it […] while being in the main insensible to a large part of the reasons for which it is right and fitting to do so'.[43] The result is an economic Constitution that oscillates between a kind of neo-corporatism and veiled government control, where the role of the little autonomous producer predominates, who, rather than seeking out and demanding respect for the laws of the market, regulates himself within his own community (*corporation*) of associate producers. All this in a general climate where efficiency and social justice are considered antinomies, and where political rhetoric finds it more convenient to emphasise the latter rather than the former. No one, in the context of drafting the Constitution would discuss anti-trust laws, the rules of the market, the limits that the market itself—and not the State—imposes on individuals; no one discusses conflicts and interests that legitimately and inevitably dwell there, and that determine the choices of consumers and workers.[44]

Those were years when no one questioned the model of State Participation. And in such years of boundless optimism due to the hope people were placing in growth after WWII, the *Ordoliberal* prudence and fears of bureaucratisation, in these years of the monopolisation of social services and of anti-statist recipes, favouring the principle of free competition, appeared as a dead weight that would have inevitably slowed the positive economic cycle triggered by reconstruction. These were the years when Italy was experimenting with the great deflation willed by then President of Banca d'Italia and future President of the Republic, Luigi Einaudi, and was entering the exciting and mythologised phase of reconstruction, through the policy of assistance and subsidies directed towards companies. The Italian industrial fabric that was reborn after WWII was the child of an industrial policy centred not on the market with its rules, but on state aid, with the distorting burden of both its bureaucratic technical apparatus and its expectations to enact its political programming.

This statist culture, with its diffidence towards the market and ignorance of the opportunity that the mechanism of free competition offered, was shaken by the process of European unification. The 1957 Treaty of Rome bore a series of directions, prohibitions, and limits in opposite direction to those taken by the Italian Constituent Fathers.[45] It took the direction of the market, and of the principle of competition, as the hermeneutical key of economic policy; not merely an applicative instrument of some occasional policy. In the direction of public intervention not aimed at interfering with the market, but at dictating rules to safeguard and promote competition, seen no longer as an alternative to social justice but its ally, and the sole authentic promoter of economic efficiency.

The opinion is widespread among economic jurists that the *ordoliberal* conception will influence significantly the underlying philosophies of the constitutive Treaty establishing the European Economic Community (i.e., 1957 Treaty of Rome). Maria De Benedetto writes: '[a]ccording to such a doctrine [ordoliberalism] the State,

[43] Amato [1].

[44] *Id.*, p. 13.

[45] Felice and Sandonà [18].

"strong but neutral", is called to carry out the functions of rebalancing and institutionally guaranteeing the mechanisms of the market: "the new neutrality imposes a public administration of the economy"'.[46] There, thus, enters into Italy, by way of Europe, the market culture,[47] the principle of competition, the consciousness that the market process represents not so much a possible non-value to be contained, as a value to be grown and nurtured to maturity.[48] Reference should be made in particular to articles 85, 86, and 90 of the 1957 Treaty of Rome, nowadays articles 101, 102 and 106 of the Treaty on the Functioning of the European Union (2007), in the part pertaining to the 'Common norms regarding competition, taxation and drawing the respective legislative bodies closer'. Contained in these articles is an affirmation of the principle of competition as the hermeneutic principle expressing the economic character—the *ordoliberals* would say the *Economic Constitution*—of the geopolitical area we call Europe. Agreements between businesses and associations are prohibited, as are all those practices that prejudice the market and restrict or distort free competition, enunciating, moreover, the irreducible irreconcilability between the presence of any companies that abuse their dominant position and the principle of competition.

3.4 Nino Andreatta's Revival of Luigi Sturzo's Thought[49]

In the immediate post-war period, Italy experienced market-oriented policy-making quite close to Sturzo's ideas.[50] In fact, Einaudi led the economic policy of De Gasperi's centrist government, which was mainly characterised by the introduction of agricultural reform that divided the large estates of the wealthy landowners in favour to the small private farmers. In the name of the principle of subsidiarity, De Gasperi also favoured small- and medium-sized firms as exemplifying popular entrepreneurship, which he praised. He maintained a serious fiscal policy in an attempt to achieve balanced budgets, and his approach to monetary policy was characterised by an aversion to inflation. In 1954, however, De Gasperi died and Amintore Fanfani, the leader of the Christian Democracy's left-wing, became the secretary of the party.[51] Fanfani was a professor of Economic History at the Catholic University of Milan; a scholar of international stature specialising in the relationship between Catholic ethics and cap-

---

[46]De Benedetto [12].

[47]Velo [38].

[48]'The reforms of Ludwig Erhard oriented towards the free market in West Germany near the end of the 1940 s offered an alternative model of development, and the consequent economic growth represented a strong impulse to the vast European liberalization' [37, p. 163].

[49]This section was written by Luca Sandonà.

[50]Bini [10].

[51]Bini [9].

italism.[52] He was a strong supporter of State interventionism as a means of achieving social justice. Consequently, Sturzo's economic and political ideas were definitively abandoned by Catholic policymakers, who went on to uninterruptedly govern Italy from 1955 to 1992.

The economic philosophy behind the second and third generation of Christian Democrats was rooted in the Camaldoli Code. As Antonio Magliulo[53] has pointed out, Fanfani and Dossetti also inspired the Italian Constitution according to a social conception of economic rights. In this debate on the fundamentals of Italian law, Einaudi, a member of the Constitutional assembly, was defeated because he 'thought that the state may actually encourage the formation of cartels and monopolies with measures such as duties, patents and meddling in investment, which reduces competition amongst rival firms. He proposed an amendment stating that the government must not favor the formation of cartels and monopolies and, if anything, it must submit them to public control. The amendment was rejected, because most voters considered that the formation of cartels and monopolies should have been regulated on the basis of a difference between "positive" and "negative" agreements among firms, without preventing the government from playing an active role in the economy'.[54]

We could thus affirm that the left-wing of the Christian Democrats elaborated a sort of Catholic Keynesianism. This approach was initially elaborated by the academic review *Cronache sociali*, that was published from 1947 to 1951. This journal was founded by Giuseppe Dossetti and other professors of the Catholic University of Milan, and had the aim of propagating an economic culture implicitly oriented by Catholic values and based on the centrality of the State. In particular, Giorgio La Pira, a professor of Roman law that will later become mayor of Florence, argued that only the State could address the expectations of the poor people because it was only public intervention that could build an inclusive economy. This perspective of government-oriented economy, in 1963, reflects the transition from a centrist to a centre-left government coalition. While the Second Vatican Council was under way, several members of the Italian Socialist Party were included in a government that was presided over by the Christian democrat Aldo Moro. At the end of the 1960s the centre-left government coalition intensified its economic planning. In the 1970s, the centre-left government introduced social welfare measures, approving a series of long-term economically unsustainable reforms that were based on the principle of their being accessible and free to all, such as the review of pension entitlements, healthcare, and education. In these years, the Italian economics academic community was dominated by Marxists, Sraffians, and Post-Keynesians.[55] The more conservative Italian scholars, included the left-wing Christian democrat economists Nino Andreatta and Romano Prodi, defined themselves, at most, as Keynesians. On the

[52] At the 1956 Democratic convention, John F. Kennedy, the future President of the United States, cited Fanfani's work as one of the principal causes of his entry in politics.

[53] Magliulo [21].

[54] Magliulo [22].

[55] Bini [8].

other hand, the right-wing Christian democrat politicians, such as Giulio Andreotti, did not refer to alternative economic theories of policymaking. They paradoxically praised state-owned enterprises given that they could directly recruit people. In this way, politicians could directly satisfy the electorate's demand for jobs, which would thus reciprocate the favour at elections.

However, Christian democracy was culturally led by the left wing, particularly in respect of economic policy. In fact, the left wing of the Christian democrats collaborated with some economic think-tanks, and included several economists as their parliamentary deputes, whereas the right-wing of the Christian democrats had only sporadic external contact with individual economists. However, the revival of Sturzo's thought was paradoxically promoted by Nino Andreatta, an economic advisor to Aldo Moro from 1963 to 1978. In 1976, Andreatta became a member of Parliament and founded with other colleagues the think-tank *Agenzia di Ricerche e Legislazione* (Research and Legislation Agency). Initially, Andreatta had been a strong supporter of economic planning. In the 1980s, the international political and cultural climate influenced Andreatta towards a market-oriented direction. Ronald Reagan's deregulation and supply-side economics, Margaret Thatcher's privatisation policies, the pro-market character of the Single European Act that intensified the process of European integration, and the prominence of the Chicago School of Economics in the academic literature were all factors that contributed to Andreatta's 'conversion',[56] as he himself put it. In particular, the figure of Michael Novak, a distinguished scholar of the American Enterprise Institute, was influential on Andreatta. Novak developed an original take on democratic capitalism that also sought to demonstrate the compatibility between Catholic ethics and a free-market economy. At the 'Money and Christian Conscience' conference, held on 10 and 11 April 1987 in Bologna, Andreatta quoted Novak's volume *The Spirit of Democratic Capitalism*, whose translation was in press by the publishing house Studium. Andreatta emphasised Novak's values of competition, professionalism, success, and human liberty. Andreatta cited long passages from Novak's arguments, including that 'the incarnation doctrine teach us to reduce our noble expectations and love the world as it is, elaborating a political economy capable of supporting the best parts of it'[57]; '[t]here are abuses of the competitive spirit, obviously, but competing—*cum petere,* searching together—although one against the other, is not a vice. But it is somehow the style of every virtue, it is an indispensable fact of human and spiritual growth of a free person'[58]; and that 'money has a neutral value. It can be administrated in a wise way or in a foolish one'.[59] In other words, in the light of Novak's vision, Andreatta criticized the mainstream approach to economics based on abstract and formalized models.

Furthermore, Andreatta seriously worked for some time on the foundation of a new Italian Popular Party, which ideologically referred to the original Italian Popular

[56] Andreatta [6].

[57] Andreatta [5].

[58] *Id.*, p. 317.

[59] *Id.*

Party founded by Sturzo in 1919. This project would be realised in 1993, after the demise of the First Republic deriving from problems of corruption and malfeasance among the political milieu. Anticipating the evolution of the Italian political history, Andreatta thought that 'it occurred to come back to non-denominationalism (*aconfessionalità* in Italian) of Sturzo's party … in order to understand our time'.[60] In this regard, Andreatta rejected the idea of a 'chimeric third-way', but proposed to 'acknowledge the difficulties of the perfection of the market economy' and consequently the necessity of creating a system of rules (liberalism of rules) to constrain 'economic, political, and financial criminality'.[61] Therefore, Andreatta stated, 'the market is not the only mechanism and, nevertheless, it is the best possible. The market can be obviously corrected. The political community has to guarantee the rules of the game […] and these rules have to be internalized in the professional activities of the economic agents'.[62] He also offered examples of when the rules fail to work: 'In Argentina, a Catholic country, there is the idea that the political power can change the rules of the market […] the diverse social groups tried to modifying the working and the rationality of the system. The consequence has been that Argentina, which was the 7th country in the world in 1930, is now the 45th [N.B., at the level of economic development]. Argentina has grown less than 1% from 1930 to today; at that time, it exported a quantity of goods equal to that of Canada and Australia, now it exports a quantity of goods equal to 10% of that of Canada and Australia'.[63]

Therefore, evidently, Andreatta emphasised Sturzo's anti-statism, anti-perfectism, anti-protectionism, and the morality-based view of the economy. In addition, Andreatta valorised Sturzo's methodological personalism, which emphasises freedom and responsibility of every person in her/his actions. In this sense, Andreatta affirmed that 'Sturzo's intellectual experience is lack of historical archaeology; I refer to the corporative view that often influences social Catholic tradition with the risk of a utopianism unconnected with reality'.[64] In fact, Andreatta underlined Sturzo's 'deep interpretation of history',[65] his aversion to 'the abstract modelling'[66] and his affirmation in 'strong and intuitive terms of the relevance and meaning of economic laws'.[67] According to Andreatta, the Christian Democracy's 'diffidence'[68] toward Sturzo lies in the fact that the economic culture of the 1930s of Chamberlain, Robinson, Berlain, and Minz was introduced in Italy through the Catholic University of

[60] Andreatta [2].

[61] N. Andreatta, *I cattolici e l'economia*, in conference proceeding, 'La politica economica degli anni ottanta: riaggiustamenti o progetto ideale', Centro culturale San Carlo, Milano, republished in La Rivista dell'Arel, nos. 3/2015, 1/2016, p. 302.

[62] Andreatta [3].

[63] *Id.*, p. 314.

[64] N. Andreatta, *Potere pubblico e mercato: la natura economica dei partiti di ispirazione cristiana*, conference of Luigi Sturzo, parties of Christian inspiration, and European democracy, Bologna, 8–11 March 1989. A version of this intervention was published in De Rosa [15].

[65] *Id.*

[66] *Id.*, p. 325.

[67] *Id.*

[68] *Id.*, p. 328.

Milan. This point of rupture was due to the idea of having 'much more degrees of freedom than those of the wise and old ideas of Sturzo, who was endowed with an historical sense of the economic laws'.[69] On the other hand, in Andreatta's view, Sturzo rightly opposed the dialogue between socialism and Catholicism because he believed that it would have created an 'economic bureaucratism'.[70] Thus, he was opposed to the establishment of ENI, i.e., the state-owned electricity production enterprise. In Andreatta's view, Sturzo was not only a courageous 'master' capable of contrasting mainstream ideas; he was also an exponent of a new era of popularist policy-making, and his ideas often served as points of reference for others. In fact, 'the operation of distinguishing Sturzo's ideas on state and politics from those on economy, accepting the former and rejecting the latter, [...] it was not a negligible failing on the part of the second generation of Christian Democrats, which ended the experience *à la De Gasperi* in 1954'.[71] It is not common to hear such reflective self-critical words.

3.5 Conclusion[72]

Sturzo originally proposed a people-centred market economy where competition was conceived as a part of, and conducive to, the *common good*. He thus opposed discretionary political interventionism that could potentially disrupt inclusive democracy. For this reason, in line with German social market economic theory, Sturzo spent his entire intellectual life theorising on the importance of social institutions as a bulwark against such arbitrariness driven by contingent political interests capable of perverting political institutions, and precipitating the advent of a totalitarian State.

Just as the market has proved incapable of simultaneously functioning as, both, playing field and referee upholding the rules of the economic game, so should the State not be both referee and player. The State cannot but carry out the role of referee. The political system should have distinguished itself from the economic, both, in the national and international contexts. Hence the need to distinguish the State as referee, the market as the playing field, and the operators as the players. With each actor faithfully playing its part, one may more readily deduce the possible antidotes to the risk of grotesque private economic concentrations degenerating into a system of public collectivism. The first remedy, identified by Palladino, is of an internal nature, and concerns the uncontrolled form of self-financing and the separation between the managing and ownership of shares of large corporations. The second is an external remedy and regards the State's commitment to optimally expanding market processes in order to impede a few sellers and buyers from dominating the market. Palladino wrote: '[w]ith the first corrective, capitalism must become popular and the democratic

[69] *Id.*

[70] *Id.*, p. 329.

[71] *Id.*, p. 331.

[72] This section was written by Flavio Felice and Luca Sandonà respectively to their contributions.

method be adopted by large companies. With the second, the solution to the economic problem must assume a worldwide dimension'.[73]

Sturzo's views were rejected by Catholic policymakers that governed Italy during the First Republic. Their economic culture was based on the centrality of State interventionism. The Italian Constitution and the Camaldoli Code substituted the social for the individualist view of economic rights. As Andreatta pointed out, the history of Italian economic policy for that period was thus in line with the 'social-democratic tradition'.[74] This seems quite odd and paradoxical taking into account that the principal government party, the Christian Democracy, was among the co-founders of the European People's Party in 1976.

Conversely, Sturzo's thought was rediscovered and valorised by Nino Andreatta, a development economist that converted from Catholic Keynesism to popularism/liberal Catholicism. Andreatta praised Sturzo's popularism because he understood that it was capable of elaborating a free-market economic view within a juridical framework, and based on the centrality of the individual. Such an inclusive economy balances the principle of competition with that of social justice, as well as the principle of subsidiarity with that of solidarity. Sturzo's *constitutional economics* emphasise meritocracy and efficiency. At the same time, it also includes the marginalised and the less talented because it provides subsidies and aid in order to stimulate and realise their abilities. In fact, Sturzo's view of development focus on civil society's primacy over the economy's function. The intermediate bodies are capable of satisfying the needs of the people with pragmatism, concreteness, and the involvement of all participants. In the liberal Catholic view, welfarism and deficit spending policies were thus radically rejected as the State ought only play a minimal role in the economic system.

It is in our view that Sturzo's approach to development could be useful even for the least developed countries as it is neither founded on the external support of other national and international/supranational organisations—which ordinarily imposes conditionality, such as structural reforms, for financial aid—nor on the role of a presumed enlightened elite that governs the State. Whilst, Italy's history, culture, and experience following World War II undoubtedly differs greatly from that of most of the world's most impoverished and underdeveloped nations, there are, however, lessons that may apply to these nations, particularly those with a Catholic heritage. Sturzo's development theory is based on a bottom-up approach centred on the irreducible and inalienable dignity of each individual and of the people. For instance, many of the problems associated with international aid-based policies are associated with elitist assumptions as to the value of Statist solutions, and with indifference towards the value of bottom-up policymaking. Whilst, Sturzo may have been, to paraphrase Scripture, a prophet not espoused in his land and in his time, the wisdom of his insights, however, has much to impart to those seeking sound development policies for impoverished nations nowadays.

---

[73]Palladino [25, p. 182].

[74]Andreatta [4].

References

1. Amato, G. (1992). Il mercato nella costituzione. *Quaderni Costituzionali, XII* (1), 7.
2. Andreatta, N. (1982). *Una cristiana laicità*, in *Assemblea degli esterni*, published in *Una leadership vigorosa, una nuova moralità*, in *Discorsi di un inverno*, Roma. (republished in La Rivista dell'Arel, nos. 3/2015, 1/2016, p. 256).
3. Andreatta, N. (1984). *Il mercato è la migliore delle macchine possibili*, in seminar. 'I Martedì di S. Domenico', Bologna (republished in La Rivista dell'Arel, nos. 3/2015, 1/2016, p. 311).
4. Andreatta, N. (1986). *La sinistra democristiana e il governo del paese: riflessioni autobiografiche tra memoria e proposta*. Il Mulino (No. 2, 1986, pp. 263–278) (republished in La Rivista dell'Arel, nos. 3/2015, 1/2016, pp. 66–76).
5. Andreatta, N. (1987). *La scuola cattolico-sociale: riflessioni di un economista oggi*, in *Danaro e coscienza cristiana*. Bologna: Edizioni Dehoniane (republished in La Rivista dell'Arel, no. 3/2015, 1/2016, p. 316).
6. Andreatta, N. (2012). *La politica dei giusti e la convenzione del mercato*, radio interview by Andrea Scazzola, Radio Due, 14 June 1992, transcripted in *Arel. La rivista*, 2, 23.
7. Antiseri, D. (2010). *Il liberalismo cattolico italiano dal Risorgimento ai giorni nostri*. Soveria Mannelli: Rubbettino.
8. Bini, P. (2013). The Italian economists and the crisis of the nineteen-seventies: The rise and fall of the 'Conflict Paradigm'. *History of Economic Thought and Policy, 1,* 73–103.
9. Bini, P. (2005, gennaio/giugno). Teoria, cultura e politica economica negli anni del 'miracolo' italiano: 1953–1968. *Storia del Pensiero Economico* 2(1):5–34.
10. Bini, P. (2008). Formule di governo e modelli di cultura economica a confronto. L'Italia dal centrismo al centrosinistra. In F. Anania & M. Simone (Eds.), *Quale modernità per questo paese, Numero monografico di Trimestre* (No. 3–4, pp. 21–38.
11. Chabod, F. (1961). *L'Italia contemporanea (1918–1948)*. Torino: Einaudi.
12. De Benedetto, M. (2000). *L'autorità garante della concorrenza e del mercato* (pp. 18–19). Il Mulino.
13. De Girolamo, M. (1987). Note sul pensiero economico di Luigi Sturzo. *Rivista di Politica Economica* (aprile-maggio).
14. De Girolamo, M. (1998–2001). *Da Sturzo a Novak. Itinerari etici di capitalismo democratico*. Roma: Edizioni Dehoniane.
15. De Rosa, G. (1990). *Luigi Sturzo e la democrazia europea*. Roma-Bari: Laterza (republished in La Rivista dell'Arel, nos. 3/2015, 1/2016, p. 324).
16. Debenedetti, F. (2016). *Scegliere i vincitori, salvare i perdenti. L'insana idea della politica industriale*. Venezia: Marsilio.
17. Felice, F. (2002). *Capitalismo e cristianesimo. Il personalismo economico di Michael Novak*. Soveria Manelli: Rubbettino.
18. Felice, F., & Sandonà, L. (2017). Italian values-grounded liberalism and german social market economy: a transnational convergence behind the treaty of Rome. *The Journal of European Economic History, 3,* 93–118.
19. Forte, F., Felice, F., & Forte, C. (Eds.). (2014). *L'economia sociale di mercato e i suoi nemici*. Soveria Mannelli: Rubbettino.
20. Forte, F., & Felice, F. (Eds.). (2016). *Il liberalismo delle regole. Genesi ed eredità dell'economia sociale di mercato* (2nd ed.). Soveria Mannelli: Rubbettino.
21. Magliulo, A. (2009). Il contributo di Dossetti e Fanfani alla costituzione economica italiana. *Il Pensiero Economico Italiano, 17*(2), 161–189.
22. Magliulo, A. (2018). The reception of Austrian economics in Italy. *Russian Journal of Economics, 4*(1), 65–86.
23. Masala, A. (2017). *Stato, società e libertà. Dal liberalismo al neoliberalismo*. Soveria Mannelli: Rubbettino.
24. Padoa-Schioppa, T. (1999). La costituzione economica dell'Italia. In F. Gentile & P. G. Grasso (Eds.), *La costituzione criticata* (pp. 452–453). Napoli: Edizioni Scientifiche Italiane.

25. Palladino, G. (1958). *La recessione economica americana* (p. 171). Angelo Signorelli Editore: Roma.
26. Palladino, G. (1995). *Don Sturzo oggi* (p. 53). Napoli: La Nuova Cultura Editrice.
27. Quadrio Curzio, A. (1999). *Il 'peccato originale' della Costituzione*. In F. Gentile & P. G. Grasso (Eds.), *La costituzione criticata* (p. 450). Napoli: Edizioni Scientifiche Italiane.
28. Rotondi, C. (2012). Economia sociale di mercato: la 'via italiana' tra liberalismo, liberismo e stato sociale. In G. Antonelli, M. Maggioni, G. Pegoretti, F. Pellizzari, R. Scazzieri, & R. Zoboli (Eds.), *Economia come scienza sociale. Teoria, istituzioni, storia* (pp. 113–133), Bologna: Il Mulino.
29. Secco Suardo, D. (1962). *I cattolici intransigent. Studio di una psicologia e di una mentalità*. Brescia: Morcelliana.
30. Serio, M. (2015). Populismo e culture politiche. In R. Chiarelli (Ed.), *Il populismo tra storia, politica e diritto*. Soveria Mannelli: Rubbettino Editore.
31. Sherman, A. (2005). *Paradoxes of power. Reflections on the Thatcher Interlude*. Imprint Academic.
32. Sturzo, L. (1956). *La società, sua natura e leggi. Sociologia storicista (1935)* (p. 109). Bologna: Zanichelli.
33. Sturzo, L. (1957). Paura della libertà, Il Giornale d'Italia, 29 dicembre. Republished in Sturzo L. (1998), Politica di questi anni. Consensi e critiche (gennaio 1957—agosto 1959), edited by C. Argiolas, (Vol. XIV, p. 158). Roma: Gangemi Editore.
34. Sturzo, L. (1998a). *Ceti piccoli e statalismo*, Il Giornale d'Italia, 29 luglio 1958. In C. Argiolas (Ed.), *Politica di questi anni. Consensi e critiche (gennaio 1957–Agosto 1959)* (Vol. XIV, p. 278). Roma: Gangemi Editore.
35. Sturzo, L. (1998b). *Paura della libertà*, Il Giornale d'Italia, 29 dicembre 1957. In C. Argiolas (Ed.), *Politica di questi anni. Consensi e critiche (gennaio 1957—agosto 1959)* (Vol. XIV, p. 158). Roma: Gangemi Editore.
36. Sturzo, L. (1998c). *Stato e statalismo*, Il Giornale d'Italia, 23 gennaio 1958. In C. Argiolas (Ed.), *Politica di questi anni, Consensi e critiche (gennaio 1957–agosto 1959)* (Vol. XIV, p. 371). Roma: Gangemi Editore.
37. Tupy, M. L. (2008). European Union, in Henderson D.R., German Economic Miracle, in Henderson D. R., The Concise Encyclopedia of Economics. Indianapolis: Liberty Found, Inc.
38. Velo, D. (2014). Social market economy and the future of European unification. In M. Gil Robles, F. De Quadro, & D. Velo, (Eds.), *The European Union and the social market economy* (p. 15). Bari: Cacucci.
39. Zanatta, L. (2016). *Un papa peronista?* in *il Mulino. La rivista*, 2, 240–249.

Chapter 4
International Financial Aid, Catholic Social Doctrine and Sustainable Integral Human Development

George Garvey

Abstract Following World War II, the secular international agenda emphasized processes of developing the economically challenged and post-colonial nations of the world. The project was led by the Bretton Woods institutions and the United Nations. Bretton Woods focused primarily on economic issues: The IMF would establish order and liquidity in the international financial markets, and the International Bank for Reconstruction and Development (World Bank) would rebuild from the war's devastation and ultimately aim for "the eradication of poverty." In contrast, the United Nations focused on the international recognition of human rights. Similarly, the Catholic Church expanded its teachings of social doctrine to address the same issues. Pope St. John XXIII addressed human rights and the roles of international organizations. Pope St. Paul VI emphasized economic and social development, particularly in relation to less developed nations. Catholic teachings regarding development have always gone beyond mere economic advances and have sought "integral human development." In the words of Pope St. Paul, "[w]hat must be aimed at is complete humanism. And what is that if not the fully rounded development of the whole man and of all men" (*Populorum Progressio* 42). This chapter summarizes the secular and "Catholic" approaches to international development with an emphasis on the parallel tracks of economic development and human rights. The chapter then analyzes the impact of policies related to the critical role of financial aid. The analysis considers, first, the extent to which financial aid has been effective in promoting the development of poor nations; and second, whether economic progress alone achieves a desirable level of "integral human development," as defined by St. Paul VI.

Keywords Human rights · Integral development · International financial aid · International Monetary Fund · *Populorum progressio* · St. Paul VI · Sustainable development · United Nations · World Bank

---

G. Garvey (✉)
The Catholic University of America, Washington, D.C., USA
e-mail: garvey@cua.edu

P. Szwedo et al. (eds.), *Law and Development*, Kobe University Monograph Series in Social Science Research, https://doi.org/10.1007/978-981-13-9423-2_4

4.1 Introduction

In the euphoria following the defeat of National Socialism and Fascism in the Second World War, the victorious powers sought to develop a new world order, one that would never again allow the forces that led to the War prevail. At least among the Western democracies the goal was pursued on essentially two tracks. One was a "human rights" track and the other an economic development track. Those powers that were defeated had demonstrated a brutal lack of regard for the rights of human beings. At its worst this was evidenced by death camps and death marches in Europe and the Pacific. Tyrannical rulers had no sense of inherent human dignity. Humans were instruments—things—to be subjected to forced labor or death.

The second track, i.e. economic development, recognized the role of a dysfunctional international economic order in the creation of the conditions leading to war. Developed industrial nations had adopted policies that would "beggar other nations." Imperial ambitions flourished as industrial nations sought economic hegemony, which of course would lead to political hegemony in Europe and Asia.

The western powers led by the United States and United Kingdom came together at the Bretton Woods Conference in New Hampshire to establish international institutions that would check any efforts to recreate the pre-war situation. The major Bretton Woods institutions, the International Monetary Fund and International Reconstruction and Development Bank (the World Bank), sought to establish a stable world monetary system, bring trade flows into relative balance, and provide funds for the development of underdeveloped nations.

Much of the International Monetary Fund's functions related to financial relationships between the world's developed nations. Financial stability was essential for the reconstruction of sound international relationships. The World Bank by contrast focused on aiding the underdeveloped nations to enter into the international economic order. It was to provide aid to those nations through traditional loans, interest-free credits and grants.

There are essentially two complimentary imperatives related to foreign aid whether from international aid organizations, national governments or NGOs. One variety is an "ethical imperative" and the other as the "economic efficiency imperative." The former represents a moral/ethical mandate that those who have much must help those who have little. In cases of extreme deprivation of human necessities those with needed resources *must* give, at least from their surplus. Ancient Christian teachings, which are frequently reiterated in Catholic Social Teachings, hold that there is a social mortgage on the property of the wealthy.[1] To withhold surplus abundance from the impoverished is virtually stealing from them.[2]

The post-World War II agenda of the victors followed both imperatives. Peace, it was recognized, could not be maintained if the inherent rights of human beings were denied on a large international scale. And extreme poverty deprives people of their

[1]Encyclical Letter of Pope Francis, *Laudato Si'*93 (2015).

[2]Encyclical Letter of Pope Paul VI, *Populorum Progressio* 23 (1967).

most basic needs and rights. The provision of significant financial and non-financial aid would be the answer to the problem of underdevelopment.

4.2 Factual Background—Economic Development

Economic development as a human right has been the subject of scholarship and actions within the UN, but it has never really materialized as a concrete right.[3] The end of the colonial era left many nations free, but impoverished. European colonialism occasionally transferred some progressive institutions to the nations colonized, such as a limited rule of law, transportation infrastructures and civil service systems. Beyond doubt, however, colonial powers primarily exploited the human and natural resources of non-European colonies. The remnants of adverse colonial policies continue to plague the world, perhaps most notably in the existence of post-colonial nation states that conform to boundaries established to facilitate European administration or just the extent of conquest.[4] Peoples of very different ethnic, tribal, cultural, linguistic and religious backgrounds have been shoehorned into states that have little experience with diversity. Often, ancient rivals and enemies have been forced into a single political entity.[5] Despite heroic aspirations by the leaders of the international order following World War II, regional wars, economic exploitation, and even genocide continue into the twenty-first century.

At the same time, however, economic development has occurred on a very large scale throughout the world. When the developed nations following the war committed themselves to aiding the underdeveloped to advance economically, there were thought to be one billion people living with much wealth (the rich) and five billion living in poverty (the poor).[6] Those figures are reversed today. Now about five billion people live in countries that have developed or have at least begun the process of becoming self-supporting and hopefully will be able to sustain that process.[7] The process of economic development of course does not follow a linear model. It is subject to the international economic situation at any given time. When "bubbles burst" in the economies of rich nations, the consequences are experienced by those that have less mature economies. More significantly, there are "traps" that keep undeveloped nations in that state and can drag nations that had begun the process of development back into poverty.[8]

The good news, of course, is that five sixths of the world's population live in nations where opportunities for economic advancement exist. They are part of the

[3]*See*, *e.g.*, Declaration on the Right to Development, G.A. Res. 41/128, Annex U.N. Doc. A/Res/41/128/Annex (Dec. 4, 1986).

[4]Moyo [1, p. 31].

[5]*Id.*

[6]Collier [2, p. 3].

[7]Sachs [3, p. 51].

[8]Collier, *supra* note 6, at 17–73.

"rich world" or have reasonable expectations of moving in that direction. The bad news is that about one billion people still live in poverty with little or no prospect of escaping that situation. "If economic development is a ladder with higher rungs representing steps up the path to economic well-being, there are roughly one billion people around the world, one sixth of humanity, who live as the Malawians do: too ill, hungry, or destitute even to get a foot on the first rung of the development ladder."[9]

4.3 The Aid Dilemma

Dambisa Moyo identifies three categories of aid: "Broadly speaking there exist three types of aid: humanitarian or emergency aid …, charity-based aid, which is dispersed by charitable organization to institutions or people on the ground; and systematic aid[,]payments made directly to governments through government-to-government transfers … or transferred via institutions such as the World Bank."[10] Most of this article deals with the efficacy of systematic aid. No one seriously questions the need for humanitarian aid or the benefits of charity-based aid, although aid from both sources may be squandered or plundered.

The first wave of international foreign aid to deal with poverty was in the form of loans and grants to impoverished nations. Unconditional aid, as well as aid provided for specific construction or infrastructure projects, was virtually all wasted or stolen by corrupt governments. The reaction to the problem of corruption, was to continue to provide financial aid to governments but with conditions intended to bring about financial stabilization and restructuring. Experience taught that conditions were readily agreed to but then ignored by the recipient nations.[11] Aid continued to pour into nations that simply refused to comply with conditions imposed by donors. Moreover, conditionality drew the ire of many of the nations receiving aid. They felt slighted and cried that this practice was simply a new form of colonialism. Some of the most corrupt tyrants of the poorest nations complained bitterly to the United Nations and other international bodies and their complaints had influence.[12] There certainly was no readily single correct solution to the problems faced by failed or underdeveloped nations.

The main problem with both unconditional and conditional aid is that they did not get aid to the people whose lives where effected. Too often the aid came in the form of money provided to the governments of underdeveloped nations where corruption and incompetence were common place. And the stipulations frequently provided that donors (the experts) receive contracts to perform designated studies or projects. Too

[9]Sachs, *supra* note 7, at 18.

[10]Moyo, *supra* note 4, at 7.

[11]*Id.*

[12]For example, several of the most corrupt African leaders helped to block the creation of an OECD Multilateral Agreement on Investment by insisting that they be treated the same as governments that seriously worked toward improving the plight of their people. Collier, *supra* note 6, at 155.

much of aid money therefore has gone to corrupt or incompetent governments or to generally well-meaning "experts" from the developmental aid industry.

Private financial institutions also extended credit to developing nations. The expectation that nations could not default on their debts prompted large banks to start lending to governments without the types of restrictions that the IMF and World Bank imposed. These loans were in lieu of traditional aid and the only condition was repayment. The resulting debts produced financial crises in Latin America and Asia in the last quarter of the twentieth century. This situation, however, has occurred repeatedly in Africa. At times, for example, African nations have been paying more to service their debts than the amounts of foreign aid they received. This resulted in what has been characterized as a "negative aid flow," a flow from poor countries receiving aid to creditors from rich countries.[13] The heavy debt burden resulted in significant loan forgiveness programs, which often resulted in new loans followed by more defaults.[14]

The provision of aid was also side-tracked and distorted by the Cold War throughout much of the late twentieth century.[15] The democracies of the West focused more on the menace of Communism than on the potential benefits of increased international economic cohesion. The Cold War drained extraordinary economic resources from developmental aid and into military aid. This period was largely a global struggle over human rights. The "free world" was aligned against the tyranny of Communism which denied basic human rights to its citizens and established economic systems that were at best grossly inefficient. The so-called "second world" of industrialized socialist nations under the sway of the Soviet Union sometimes met its citizens most basic material needs, although not always and everywhere, but it subordinated the rights of citizens to the power of the state. Too often during this time aid to underdeveloped nations was used to arm the recipient nations and draw them into the role of surrogates for the great powers in regional wars. The emphasis on military aid also laid the foundation for decades of military dictatorships in underdeveloped nations.

As already noted, this article touches on both human rights and economic development, but with some emphasis on the latter. It examines the relationship between international financial aid as it has been employed in the Post-World War II era and the concept of "sustainable human development" which implicates both economic development and human rights. The notion of sustainable human development has had significance in the evolution of Catholic Social Doctrine, as well as secular scholarship and praxis, but with Catholic emphasis on "integral" development. The social doctrine will be further developed later in this work.

First, however, I will explore some of the more prominent contemporary secular scholarship about the state of international development policies. The primary focus of this portion of the paper will be on economic development not because it is the

[13]Moyo, *supra* note 4, at 22.

[14]*See Reckless in Lusaka: Zambia's Looming Debt Crisis Is a Warning for the Rest of Africa*, Economist, Sept. 15, 2018, at 18, https://www.economist.com/leaders/2018/09/15/zambias-looming-debt-crisis-is-a-warning-for-the-rest-of-africa.

[15]Moyo, *supra* note 4, at 14.

most critical element of integral human development, but because it seems to be the most important first step on the road to development in the contemporary world. Economic growth after all leads to the expansion of higher values such as education, literacy, improved health and hygiene, and opportunities for greater individual freedom and personal development. It should be noted that from a Catholic perspective, moral, ethical, cultural and spiritual development are more significant than economic advances as such. The most economically advanced nations in the world after all suffer from types of psychological and spiritual decay that seem rare in underdeveloped societies. Freedom from want in the rich world has morphed into a stridently materialistic consumerism, hedonism and alienation. The developing world can hopefully learn from the experiences of rich counties and avoid the pitfalls of over-abundant and inequitably divided wealth. An agenda that simply fosters replication of the cultural values of the "rich" nations of the world would likely debase aspects of the cultures of many developing nations.

International development policies are also largely based on outdated notions of which nations are "rich" and which are "poor." By many measures, for example, China and India are still "developing." When measured by GDP per population, they have not yet achieved the status of "developed."[16] Yet China is rapidly becoming one of the wealthiest nation on earth. The World Bank reported:

> With a population of 1.3 billion, China is the second largest economy and is increasingly playing an important and influential role in development and in the global economy. China has been the largest contributor to world growth since the global financial crisis of 2008.
>
> Yet China remains a developing country (its per capita income is still a fraction of that in advanced countries) and its market reforms are incomplete.
>
> Rapid economic ascendance has brought on many challenges as well, including high inequality; rapid urbanization; challenges to environmental sustainability; and external imbalances. China also faces demographic pressures related to an aging population and the internal migration of labor.
>
> Significant policy adjustments are required in order for China's growth to be sustainable. Experience shows that transitioning from middle-income to high-income status can be more difficult than moving up from low to middle income.[17]

India also has a robust growing economy but is still considered a developing country.[18] The point is that some nations with great wealth and healthy economies may still be "developing," which provides them with preferences in the international economic regime. Their problems with poverty are very real because of the unequal distribution of the nation's wealth, but by most measures these are major economic powers in the world. Internal poverty requires sound forms of wealth redistribution and growth promotion by national governments, rather than foreign aid and preferential international trade policies.

---

[16] United Nations, Country Classification, www.un.org/en/development/desa/policy/wesp_current/2014wesp_country_classification.pdf (last visited Sept. 6, 2018).

[17] World Bank, The World Bank in China: Overview, http://www.worldbank.org/en/country/china/overview (last visited Nov. 4, 2018).

[18] United Nations, Country Classification, *supra* note 16.

The nations of the "bottom billion," by contrast, have little hope of meaningful economic growth. Their poverty is devastating and seems to be permanent. Prominent international development experts have identified the several "traps" that keep the poorest nations in poverty. They include civil wars and other conflicts, dependence on natural resources, being landlocked with unfriendly neighboring countries, and government corruption.[19] Jeffrey Sachs identifies poverty itself as a trap: "When poverty is very extreme, the poor do not have the ability—by themselves—to get out of the mess."[20]

A major question for the world's development community (some would say development industry[21]) is obviously how to specifically help those nations of the bottom billion. There is much evidence that most foreign aid has produced little results. It is estimated that over $1 trillion dollars have been given as financial aid to underdeveloped countries. Dambisa Moyo paints a grim picture of the situation:

> [H]as more than US$ 1 trillion in development assistance over the past several decades made African people better off? No. In fact, across the globe the recipients of this aid are worse off; much worse off. Aid has helped make the poor poorer, and growth slower. Yet aid remains a centerpiece of today's development policy and one of the biggest ideas of our times.[22]

Other prominent scholars share this skeptical view of the benefits of financial aid. Paul Collier's view is not quite as negative, but he does not believe that aid has been a great success. He states that traditional aid to the "bottom billion" nations has helped but "[a]id has been a holding operation preventing things from falling apart."[23] The impoverished nations were somewhat less poor than they would have been without aid, but aid did not put them on the path to sustainable economic development.

What do the experts recommend? While there is a consensus that aid has not worked for the countries of the bottom billion, there are divergent views about why and what should be done to remedy the problems. Along the continuum of competing points of view, two stand out as opposites.[24] Jeffrey Sachs believes that the problem has been inadequate support from the international agencies, national governments of rich nations, and NGOs. He sees the bottom billion caught in a "poverty trap."[25] Sachs believes that the UN's Millennium Development Goals (now the 17 Sustainable Development Goals[26]) provide the remedy, although they clearly did not achieve their stated goals on the original 2015 timetable. To Sachs the amounts of aid provided proved to be inadequate. He believes that a new comprehensive plan, built on the

---

[19] Collier, *supra* note 6, at 17–64.

[20] Sachs, *supra* note 7, at 56.

[21] Collier, *supra* note 6, at 4, identified the "development *biz*," which is made up "by the aid agencies and the companies that get the contracts for their projects." Those in the development biz like the status quo and oppose changes to development policies based on historic evidence of failure.

[22] Moyo, *supra* note 4, at 186.

[23] Collier, *supra* note 7, at 100.

[24] Banerjee and Duflo [4, pp. 3–4].

[25] Sachs, *supra* note 7, at 56.

[26] Transforming our World: The 2030 Agenda for Sustainable Development, UN General Assembly Resolution, GA/RES/70/1 (Sept. 25, 2015).

Sustainable Development Goals and geared to the specific needs of individual nations, will succeed.[27] It is essential for his plan to work, however, for the rich nations and donors to provide adequate resources, which had not been the case with the original Millennium project. The bottom billion have a moral claim on the rich (the ethical imperative), who can readily afford to provide the needed resources. The bottom line for Sachs is that aid is essential to give those nations caught in the poverty trap what is needed to escape and join the nations that are on the road to economic independence. What is needed is a "big push," a very significant infusion of aid money.

William Easterly[28] and Dambisa Moyo[29] sit on the other end of the continuum. Aid, they believe, as it has been planned and administered is a primary cause of the problem. Virtually all the problems that plague the nations of the bottom billion—malnutrition, child mortality rates, illiteracy, malaria, unclean water, lack of proper sanitation, HIV/AIDS—are unresolved despite more than a trillion dollars in aid. The fact that so much aid has been provided for so many years without improving the situation of the poorest countries is itself evidence that traditional aid does not work.[30] Easterly's conclusions, however, are not simply impressionistic. He provides empirical evidence that the so-called "big push" approach to developmental aid did not work.[31] For example, several undeveloped nations have succeeded in rising out of abject poverty without significant aid from the donor class, e.g., China, India, Hong Kong, Korea, Singapore, and Taiwan, while many who received it failed to do so.[32]

Easterly divides the movers and shakers of development into planners, who decide what to supply to underdeveloped nations, and searchers, who attempt to meet the demands of those in poor nations. He identifies the difference between planners and searchers as follows:

> A Planner thinks he already knows the answers; he thinks of poverty as a technical engineering problem that his answers will solve. A Searcher admits he doesn't know the answers in advance; he believes that poverty is a complicated tangle of political, social, historical, institutional, and technological factors. A Searchers hopes to find answers to individual problems only by trial and error experimentation. A Planner believes outsiders know enough to impose solutions. A Searcher believes only insiders have enough knowledge to find solutions, and that most solutions must be homegrown.[33]

Moyo's critique is similar to Easterly's:

> The donors [of aid] have also made a lot of mistakes. Many times they have assumed they are the ones who know what countries in Africa need. They want to be the ones to choose where to put this money, to be the ones to run it, without any accountability. In other cases, they

[27]Each nation needing financial aid should develop a poverty reduction strategy or plan. Sachs, *supra* note 7, at 270.

[28]Easterly [5].

[29]Moyo, *supra* note 4.

[30]Easterly, *supra* note 28, at 38–41.

[31]*Id.* at 37.

[32]*Id.* at 27.

[33]*Id.* at 6.

> have simply associated with the wrong people and money gets lost and ends up in people's pockets.[34]

The experts do not necessarily attribute malice to the aid problem. There is universal support for aid in the cases of natural disasters and extreme humanitarian needs. And the "planners," to use Easterly's term, are well-intentioned. They just refuse to see that their plans have failed and that more of the same is not likely to bring about better results. Part of the problem is that the development community is dominated by elite experts who insist on top-down solutions. Their plans are technocratic and implementation has failed. Collier attributes the problem in large part to the "development biz"[35] which is highly invested in older models of international development where large amounts of money were given with or without conditionality to governments.

The divide exemplified by Sachs and Easterly/Moyo can well be characterized as the difference between those who seek grand top down policies, shaped and executed by experts, and bottom up piece meal policies relying on market forces ("searchers" in Easterly's term). Other significant experts tend to fall in between the extremes but tend towards Easterly's approach. They favor a more nuanced approach that measures success at the micro level. Collier, as already noted, sees multiple traps that stifle the development of the bottom billion rather than simply a "poverty trap." They include conflict (civil wars), natural resource traps, corruption, and geographic location, i.e., being land locked. Each trap comes with its own complexities. A nation trapped in conflict may actually require military intervention from wealthy nations and it may take a decade or more to change the circumstances enough to ensure stable peace.[36] Nations dependent economically on natural recourses (oil, minerals, diamonds, etc.) benefit from dramatic increases in prices, but the benefits can be short lived and squandered on corrupt governments and they also incentivize conflict to capture the new wealth.

Some experts have a socialistic bias, but most recognize that free markets and private capital must play a significant role in successfully transitioning from undeveloped to the status of sustainable development. Collier believes that part of the solution is that the winners of the race to develop economically—India, China, and other Asian nations—should lose preferential trade status with respect to the poorest nations, mainly in Africa. To him international trade is essential where possible to improve the economic status of nations where bottom up investments are made in the people of poor nations, not the government. Intranational trade does not foster long term growth in agricultural and incipient industrial development. In areas where the nations of the bottom billion should have a relative comparative advantage such as low-cost unskilled labor they cannot compete with their largely Asian neighbors. International trade policy should, therefore, provide some preferred status for the bottom billion nations.

Moyo's remedy would be for aid to continue, but with a concrete cutoff date, e.g., five years. This would give developing nations the aid they need but with the

---

[34]Moyo, *supra* note 4, at 149.

[35]*See* text accompanying note 22, *supra*.

[36]Collier, *supra* note 6, at 133.

clear understanding that during the period of continued aid the recipient nations must make the adjustment to an aid free environment. These nations must learn to rely on their own resources and the human capital of their own people.

4.4 International Human Rights

While the Bretton Woods institutions were the creation of the world's most powerful nations and focused on financial and economic matters, the creation of the United Nations provided a forum for all the world's nations to participate in the establishment of a peaceful world order. The UN took the lead in defining and promoting internationally recognized human rights. The Charter of the United Nations states "We the people of the United Nations [are] determined [to] reaffirm faith in fundamental human rights, in the dignity and worth of the human person, [and] in the equal rights of men and women [...]."[37] This commitment was primarily implemented by the adoption of the Universal Declaration of Human Rights[38] in 1948. Other significant documents were the International Covenant on Civil and Political Rights[39] and the International Covenant on Economic, Social and Cultural Rights[40] which were adopted in 1966. The rights set forth in the Declaration and Covenants are comprehensive and they are largely derived from recognition of the dignity of every human being. The monstrous crimes against humanity by supposedly civilized nations violated all sense of intrinsic inalienable human dignity. The Declaration's rights are, however, largely aspirational. Few, if any, nations fully comply with the vision adopted by the United Nations. A world in which full compliance with the Universal Declaration existed would be one in which sustained integral development was ubiquitous. Education would be universal and largely free. Work would be available with humane working conditions and fair remuneration. Invidious discrimination of all types would be banned. Marriages and family would be protected. The rights of citizens to select their political leaders and to participate in governmental and non-governmental organizations would be protected. The list goes on and together they would lay the foundation for an ideal, perhaps utopian, world order. Unfortunately, the ideal has not been realized.

2018 is the seventieth anniversary of the adoption of the Universal Declaration, and it is clear that applying the principles has been difficult. In a speech to the Council of Europe, Archbishop Paul Gallagher, the Vatican Secretary for Relations with States, identified three contemporary challenges to implementation of the declaration.

---

[37] U.N. Charter pmbl.

[38] Universal Declaration of Human Rights, G.A. Res. 217A.

[39] International Covenant on Civil and Political Rights, G.A. Res. 2200A (XXI) (1966) (entry into force 23 Mar. 1976).

[40] International Covenant on Economic, Social and Cultural Rights, G.A. Res. 2200A (XXI) (1966) (entry into force 3 Jan. 1976).

> [First, in] Western societies a greater breakdown of the social fabric [resulting in] the growth of inequalities, the impoverishment of some sectors of the population, job insecurity, as well as the drastic downsizing of social protection systems.
>
> A second challenge to the universality of human rights derives from the growing cultural pluralism that we experience within our societies. It is certainly not a new phenomenon. Already in 1948, the drafters of the Universal Declaration were confronted with the need to integrate different cultural and religious perspectives. Over the decades, there has been a recurrent criticism of those who wanted to see in the proclamation of human rights a legacy merely of Western culture.
>
> The third challenge arises from the instability of the international order and the growing threats to peace. Here, it is not a question of a theoretical objection to the universality of human rights, but rather the troublesome spread of systematic and very serious violations of them, which continue to challenge the international community.[41]

In short, universal human rights are challenged by the growing inequality and poverty in rich nations, the clash of cultures that is a product of increasing diversity, an undue emphasis on Western culture, and the reality of war and other forms of inhuman treatment around the world.

4.5 Sustained Development Versus Integral Development

For historical reasons the quest for international economic development and human rights were seated in different organizations: economic development in the Bretton Woods institutions and human rights in the United Nations. International law and policy related to these two goals, therefore, have tended to develop independently. "Sustained economic development" focuses on the economy. The furtherance of human rights is indirectly related to economic development. As noted earlier, economic progress lays the foundation for the development of higher values such as education, health care and inclusion. The quest for both economic growth and the furtherance of human rights, however, have by and large traveled on different tracks: different organizations; different rules, legal structures, and court systems. In short, economic and other human rights interact but are not well integrated.

Catholic Social Teachings, by contrast, have always treated economic rights as an integral part of the quest for human rights. The right to private property, associational rights, and the right to a living wage, for example, are rooted in the dignity of the human person. Most significantly, development must not be just sustainable, it must be integral. The formulation articulated so clearly by Pope St. Paul VI is "sustainable *integral* development."

[41] P. R. Gallagher, 'Speech to the Council of Europe in Strasbourg on the 70th Anniversary of International Declaration of Human Rights, www.zenit.org/articles/archbishop-gallagher-marks-70th-anniversary-of-international-declaration-of-human-rights/.

4.6 Religious Influence in the Human Rights Debate

At this point, let me introduce the contribution of Catholic and other Christian religions to the development of human rights. The major powers following the Second World War—The United States, England, and the Soviet Union—were not particularly interested in the human rights project.[42] It was the smaller nations at the UN that insisted on a "Bill of Rights." Many of those nations had political parties that where unknown in the "Big Three." They were members of the Christian Democratic and Christian Social Parties. As a result, for example, Mary Ann Glendon writes that the rights declared to be fundamental were clearly influenced by the two social encyclicals written prior to the War, *Rerum Novarum*[43] and *Quadragesimo Anno.*[44]

4.7 Brief Introduction to Catholic Social Doctrine

It is healthy to view Catholic Social Teachings regarding economic, political, social and cultural developments in the context of the successes and failures of the secular world order. A more thorough analysis than this would, I believe, demonstrate how well the Church has understood the secular issues involved in the context of globalization. It would also show that the Church's recommendations for change, while seldom calling for precise methods (they are left to the appropriate secular authorities), make great practical sense. Catholic Social Doctrine, in short, is well informed in practical matters as well as guided by Christian inspiration and Catholic tradition.

That said; let me shift now to the development of Catholic Social Doctrine during the relevant era. I will very briefly discuss a bit of the earlier development of the social teachings for context.

The modern era of Catholic Social teaching began with Pope Leo XIII's 1891 encyclical, *Rerum Novarum.*[45] Leo addressed the social conditions of his time, particularly the social consequences of the industrial revolution. His primary concern was the condition of the working classes. Leo critiqued both the evils of unconstrained capitalism and the threat of socialism. While finding the working conditions created by industrial capitalism to be brutal and little better than slavery, he found socialism's denial of private property rights to be even more ominous. Men and

[42]Glendon [6, pp. 69–84].

[43]Encyclical Letter of Pope Leo XIII, *Rerum Novarum* (1891). The title in the text uses the custom of identifying encyclicals by the first few words of the Latin version of the document. The English title (The Condition of Labor), however, is far more descriptive of Pope Leo's purpose in writing the document.

[44]Encyclical Letter of Pope Pius XI on the Fortieth Anniversary of *Rerum Novarum, Quadragesimo Anno* (1931).

[45]Encyclical Letter of Pope Leo XIII, *Rerum Novarum, supra* note 43.

women had a natural right to the fruits of their own labor, i.e. private property. To address the evils of the industrial workplaces, workers had a natural right to organize to resist the power of the employers. These natural rights—to own private property and to organize to bargain collectively—were rooted in the overarching principle that every person was endowed by God with inalienable natural rights.

On the fortieth anniversary of *Rerum Novarum*, Pope Pius XI, published the second social encyclical, *Quadragesimo Anno*.[46] Pius said that the "social" encyclicals, following the model provided by Leo, should identify the major social issues of the day and apply Catholic principles. Pius wrote at a time when fascism was in control of Italy and National Socialism was rising in Germany. He was most concerned about the totalitarian state. At the same time that political power was being concentrated in the state, economic power was being concentrated in managers. "Owners" were losing control over the use of their property (capital). Pius accurately predicted that "there is [first] the struggle for dictatorship in the economic sphere itself; then, the fierce battle to acquire control of the state, so that its resources and authority may be abused in the economic struggles. Finally, the clash between States themselves."[47] Pope Pius had accurately anticipated World War II.

Pope Pius's great contribution to the social teachings was the principle of subsidiarity:

> It is a fundamental principle of social philosophy, fixed and unchangeable, that one should not withdraw from individuals and commit to the community what they can accomplish by their own enterprise and industry. So, too, it is an injustice and at the same time a grave evil and a disturbance of right order to transfer to the larger and higher collectivity functions which can be performed and provided for by the lesser and subordinate bodies.[48]

In all social spheres, decisions should be left to the lowest appropriate body. Higher, more-concentrated centers of authority have an important role when circumstances require, but they must not improperly usurp the authority of lower social institutions.

Pope St. John XXIII shared the goals of the United Nation's human rights and development projects. He brought the social teachings into the Post-World War II world and expanded the reach of the teachings to the whole world. He also reflected on the linkage between economic development and human rights generally: "[t]he nations that enjoy a sufficiency and abundance of everything may not overlook the plight of other nations whose citizens experience such domestic problems that they are all but overcome by poverty and hunger, and *are not able to enjoy basic human rights*."[49] The expansion of a nation's and the world's wealth in and of itself is surely not adequate development if the bulk of the people's human rights are denied by poverty.

---

[46]Encyclical Letter of Pope Pius XI on the Fortieth Anniversary of *Rerum Novarum*, *Quadragesimo Anno*, *supra* note 44.

[47]*Id.* at 108.

[48]*Id.* at 79.

[49]Encyclical Letter of Pope John XXIII, *Mater et Magistra* 157 (1961).

St. John's second social encyclical, *Pacem in Terris*,[50] largely mirrors the Universal Declaration of Human Rights. Unlike the declaration, however, the Pope in the distinctively Catholic tradition follows the enumeration of rights with an admonition about duties. As one example, he states that "[the] right to a decent standard of living [carries with it] the duty of living becomingly."[51] And one primary duty of all is to respect the rights of others. As the Pope put it, there must be "Reciprocity of Rights and Duties between persons."

Pacem in Terris identifies the advances that had taken place since *Rerum Novarum*: The lives of the working classes had improved substantially; women "demand rights befitting a human person both in domestic and in public life"; and colonialism was coming to an end. The conquest of Nazism and Fascism produced great international optimism about the future. Pope St. John, while never a utopian, shared that enthusiasm. He knew that globalization was happening and expected that international organizations, particularly the United Nations, would usher in an era of peace and justice.

For the moment, let me go out of chronological order to save St. Paul VI's encyclical, *Populorum Progressio*[52] for special attention later. It began a significant new strain within the social teachings related specifically to development.

On the hundredth anniversary of *Rerum Novarum*, Pope St. John Paul II[53] could explain that what his predecessor, Leo XIII, had foreseen with regard to socialism had come to pass. One hundred years after *Rerum Novarum* was written, the Soviet brand of socialism had collapsed. The most robust effort to build a society without private property rights was a human disaster of immense proportions. The collectivization of agriculture in Eastern Europe resulted in the massive starvation, executions and forced migration of Central and Eastern European peasants. The building of the Soviet industrial base was financed through the exports of food produced by the starving farmers. And the resulting industrial structure was inefficient and corrupt. Maoist policies in China paralleled this European experience. Moreover, the other major variety of socialism in the Twentieth Century, German National Socialism (NAZISM), was even more brutish. What Leo had identified through intuition and Catholic understanding about human nature, St. John Paul had experienced in fact as a native of Poland. It was surely providential that he could write about the collapse of the system that had denied his own nation freedom and impoverished his fellow citizens for so many years. He concluded:

> Socialism considers the individual person simply as an element, a molecule within the social organism, so that the good of the individual, is completely subordinated to the functioning of the socioeconomic mechanism. Socialism maintains that the good of the individual can be realized without reference to his free choice, to the unique and exclusive responsibility which he exercises in the face of good or evil. Man is thus reduced to a series of social relationships, and the concept of the person as the autonomous subject of moral decision

---

50 Encyclical Letter of Pope John XXIII, *Pacem in Terris* [Peace on Earth] 11–27 (1963).

51 *Id.* at 29.

52 Encyclical Letter of Pope St. Paul VI, *Populorum Progressio* [On the Development of Peoples] (1967).

53 Encyclical Letter of Pope St. John Paul II, *Centesimus Annus* 13 (1991).

> disappears, the very subject whose decisions build the social order. A person who is deprived of something he can call 'his own', and of the possibility of earning a living through his own initiative, comes to depend on the social machine and those who control it.[54]

In any case, in *Centesimus Annus* St. John Paul could start assessing the world after the fall of communism. Had the world found *the* way? Liberalism (capitalism) had never been fully embraced in the Church's social magisterium. Had its victory over socialism, however, given the Pope reason to embrace it without reservations? As already noted, the social teachings have never accepted utopian ideologies. Such ideologies, regardless of the economic theories they incorporate, are doomed to failure. Human limitations, e.g. imperfect knowledge, vices, self-interest, will defeat the utopian quest. Heroic virtue is simply too rare among humans and no one is perfectly virtuous. Experience and the social sciences confirm the religious view that humans are limited by their own nature, although the cause may be identified as "bounded rationality," "personality disorders," or "opportunistic behavior" depending on the discipline, rather than "original sin."

St. John Paul did not simply celebrate the demise of the Soviet Union, and the economic system it represented. Rather, he asked and answered the obvious question about capitalism. It had succeeded in the competition with socialism but is it invariably the best provider of human economic welfare. His answer was that a *free economy*[55] *working within a sound juridical framework*[56] is good, perhaps the best to which humans can aspire. "It would appear that, on the level of individual nations and of international relations, the free market is the most efficient instrument for utilizing resources and effectively responding to needs. … It is also necessary to help these needy people to acquire expertise, *to enter the circle of exchange*, and to develop their skills in order to make the best use of their capacities and resources."[57] An economy where the markets operate without constraint and profits are its sole purpose, however, does not reflect Catholic values.

The Pope identified numerous problems in the cultures associated with capitalism, perhaps most notable among them being "consumerism." "It is not wrong to want to live better; what is wrong is a style of life which is presumed to be better when it is directed toward 'having' rather than 'being,' and which wants to have more, not in order to be more but in order to spend life in enjoyment as an end in itself. It is therefore necessary to create lifestyles in which the quest for truth, beauty, goodness and communion with others for the sake of common growth are the factors which determine consumer choices, savings and investment."[58] The cultures of the developed nations are simply too materialistic. Their citizens seek to have things that do not satisfy physical or spiritual needs, and which do not help them to become more human. Possessing "more" clearly satisfies some cultural and psychological needs in the consumerist society, but other real psychological and spiritual needs are not met.

---

[54] *Id.* at 13.

[55] *Id.* at 42.

[56] *See id.* at 35.

[57] *Id.* at 34 (emphasis added).

[58] *Id.* at 36.

It is ironic that societies where citizens have a super abundance of material goods can be marked by a substantial degree of alienation. The phenomenon of alienation from God and self is quite evident in wealthy, consumerist societies. Moreover, the costs to the environment and to those whose real material needs are not satisfied are great in a radically materialistic world. Stated directly, unchecked consumerism is destructive of both the individual and society.

St. John Paul II also emphasized the significance of the virtue and principle of solidarity to the development enterprise. "[Solidarity] then is not a feeling of vague compassion or shallow distress at the misfortunes of so many people, both near and far. On the contrary, it is *firm and persevering determination* to commit oneself to the *common good*; that is to say to the good of all and of each individual because we are *all* really responsible *for all*."[59] Again we see the moral/ethical imperative. Let me leave this discussion of the writings of St. John Paul with his focus on solidarity because it has the most direct bearing on the topic at hand: sustainable integral development.

In the tradition of the social teachings we should be considering the changes that have occurred in the world as well as the ways those changes have influenced the social teachings, particularly as they are reflected in Pope Benedict XVI's first social encyclical, *Caritas in Veritate*.[60] Let me first share some observations about the major economic events that had occurred between the time of *Centesimus Annus* and *Caritas in Veritate*. I will then share some reflections on the impact of those events on the social teachings.

The past twenty-five years have beyond doubt seen great expansions of wealth throughout the world. The principles of capitalism have driven this growth in places like China (ironically), India, Brazil, and other Asian and Latin American nations. This experience confirms the potential for markets to promote economic growth, but it also confirms the fact that markets do not necessarily *distribute* resources equitably. This is no great insight and this unfortunate reality has consistently informed the social teachings. The emerging economic powers have dramatic pockets of wealth and deplorable poverty elsewhere. The goal first identified by Pope Leo in 1891—distributive justice—remains unsatisfied by the modern international economic structure. And, of course, many nations have been unable to benefit from the modern economic order. Pope Benedict continued to emphasize this inequitable distribution of wealth, both among nations and within nations. He accurately reports that the gap between rich and poor is growing in the wealthiest nations and between nations.

There is, moreover, substantial evidence that market failures continue and on an extraordinary level. Enormous wealth has been lost through defects in the markets for capital. The burst of the "housing bubble" in 2008 sent shock waves throughout the world's developed economies. This experience has also demonstrated that important market structures, particularly those for capital, are not appropriately self-correcting. When dramatic adjustments do occur, the costs across national and even international economies are unacceptably high. Markets can be distorted by limited knowledge, manipulation, speculation and regulation in ways that set prices well beyond any

[59]Encyclical Letter of Pope St. John Paul II, *Sollicitudo Rei Socialis* [On Social Concern] 38 (1987).
[60]Encyclical Letter of Pope Benedict XVI, *Caritas in Veritate* [Charity in truth] (2009).

reasonable measure of value. When the reckoning came in the financial markets for housing, the wealth of millions had been diminished or lost. While the wealth involved may not have been "real," the consequences for so many real people have been great and at times overwhelming.

The fraud and ignorance that led up to the current economic crises suggests a need for more regulatory oversight, but it is important to note that the problem was in part the result of regulatory failures. In the United States there are multiple state and federal agencies with responsibility over the financial and banking industries. In fact, the financial regulatory bodies have been less noted for inefficiency and corruption than those in other sectors of the economy. Yet the great crash of 2008 was caused by factors that were either not understood by regulators or deliberately overlooked. The crash has a serious taint of scandal for those in the private sector and those regulating that sector. The point is that government regulation, no matter how well informed and innocent it may be, has to be considered a part of the problem as well as part of the solution when dealing with complex economic matters. Catholic Social Teaching's principle of subsidiarity incorporates this caution. In economic reasoning, neoclassical economists have long considered regulation to be inefficient and public choice theory better explains the political distortions inherent in regulation.

One major legal text on regulation describes a life cycle of regulation.[61] In brief, the cycle begins when a market failure is observed, and regulation is imposed. The regulatory body is eventually subject to capture by the industry it regulates, which results in regulatory failure. The perception that a regulator is captured or otherwise failing eventually leads to deregulation, which then returns us to the problems of market failure. The cycle repeats itself. The fact that regulation, like the market, is subject to failure is not an argument against regulation. It is simply a call for care. Too much faith in either markets or regulators will eventually result in failures. Neither economists, politicians, nor the Church for that matter, have a precise formula for striking the proper balance. Economists can help to better understand the causes and nature of market failures and the Church can best aid the process, as it does, by reminding those who shape policy that the goal is to mitigate poverty, material and spiritual, and to respect the nature of the human person, with both his and her dignity and flaws.

Another notable change over past years is actually a continuation of what had gone before. Globalization is becoming more evident in all respects; economic, social, and cultural. Nation states have less ability to control the economic and cultural actors of the world. Economic development is less a function of international foreign aid than it is of decisions made by multinational business entities. The mobility of factors of production and technological advances make regulation at the national level less significant. The international community, however, is not well equipped to assume responsibility in this level of oversight, nor are nations ready to cede this authority to international bodies. It is very clear in *Caritas in Veritate* that Pope Benedict well understands this phenomenon. This has been a major concern of all Popes, at least since Pope Paul VI. Popes John XXIII and Paul VI appreciated fully the process of

[61] Shapiro and Tomain [7].

globalization and many of its implications. Paul captured the urgency of the issue with the tag line, "development is the new name for peace." Internationalist policies that do not recognize the interdependence of nations and peoples, he cautioned, will fail. Pope Benedict acknowledges the extraordinary significance of Paul's encyclical, and, for that matter, the significance of his entire papal magisterium to our social understanding today.

Caritats in Veritate, I am sure, was a particularly difficult encyclical to produce because the world's economic order was shaken just as the document was to be released. The "new things" of 2008 were *very* new. Pope Benedict XVI, of course, continued the application of timely Christian principles to the problems of the real world. Some of the social problems remain unchanged. There was still too much poverty and the demands of "distributive justice" remained unsatisfied. Pope Benedict was not content to rely on the old formulation of liberals, i.e., the markets will create growth, which can then be distributed equitable through fiscal and welfare policies. The processes of growth and distribution must somehow be better aligned.

Caritas in Veritate suggests a provocative solution: markets should be infused with gratuitousness. Economic markets cannot be solely driven by the logic of profits. Within the structure of markets and business organizations, there must be room for gift. It is not clear how this change would be incorporated into the operation of market-based transactions. It seems clear at one level that this type of change would be dependent on the Church's mission of evangelization. Each person must understand his or her responsibilities to all and make decisions in whatever capacity they function to foster the common good. That is a great challenge of the Christian message.

What I believe is very encouraging about Benedict's message is that it attempts to better integrate the logic of Christianity into the logic of business and government. They must work together. This accepts the reality that markets still seem to work best at promoting development, and that regulation is subject to some of the same limitations that limit the broader social utility of economic markets.

In *Caritas in Veritate* Pope Benedict also calls for greater diversity in the nature of business enterprises. This implicitly enlists market forces to discipline business. There are in fact many organizational models in the world of finance and business. Among them are firms that do seek to foster the common good, not simply by generating profits and selling goods or services. If some are committed to a principle of gratuitousness, that fact may well be enough in the minds of some consumers and investors to engage their services, buy their products or invest in their shares. The market could shed its touted moral neutrality and draw capital to firms that work for the common good. The mission of the Church would be as always to help people, in this case as consumers and investors, to understand the moral and social consequences of their decisions. The purpose of the market would be to minimize the costs of finding out which firms have opted to promote the common good. The diversity of business organizations advocated by Pope Benedict would surely help to determine if markets can become simultaneously instruments of economic growth and equitable distribution of that growth.

Given the continuing reality of a scandalous gap between rich and poor—the "old" problem—which has been exaggerated by recent economic crises, the Church's reservations about markets are reasonable. Prudence and experience with international organizations committed to development suggest that the imposition of a radical "new" economic order will meet resistance. By contrast, changes that are applied incrementally and which focus on benefits to national actors are more likely to succeed in the long run. Catholic Social Teachings have always required the exercise of prudence. To be sure, there are absolute principles—the dignity of the person, the value of life, service to the poor—but praxis requires prudence and moderation. Ultimately, however, it will be the changing of hearts that will bring about a more peaceful and just world order. That continues to be the challenge for the Church in its teachings regarding the social order and from the Church to those who will listen.

The core of Pope Francis's contribution to the social teachings is an emphasis on the natural environment. Sustainable integral development must account for the degradation of the environment as well as other human needs. He builds on St. John Paul's call for a "human ecology":

> The destruction of the human environment is extremely serious, not only because God has entrusted the world to us men and women, but because human life is itself a gift which must be defended from various forms of debasement.[62]

4.8 Pope Paul VI—*Populorum Progressio*

Let me now introduce the most significant social encyclical relevant to the current topic, Pope St. Paul VI's magisterial *Populorum Progressio*.[63] It was the first encyclical to focus exclusively on international development as such. We have already seen that St. John XXIII made the scope of the social teachings international. John saw the post-War era as a time of change and hope. The international community had cooperated to codify human rights and colonialism was dying.

Just a few years later, his successor, Pope Paul VI, had a soberer view. "Development [he wrote] is the new name for peace." To him, development could not be limited to economic advances, it had to be more fulsome. In his words, "[development] cannot be limited to mere economic growth. In order to be authentic, it must be complete; integral that is, to promote the good of every man and of the whole man."[64] While he envisioned development to address all aspects of what humans and societies need to fulfill their potential, he understood that some level of economic advances was a necessary first step towards the more comprehensive individual and social advancement. He stressed the duty of the rich to share their resources with the poor, both

---

[62]Encyclical Letter of Pope Francis, *Laudato Si'* [On Care of our Common Home] 5 (2015).

[63]Encyclical Letter of Pope Paul VI, *Populorum Progressio* [On the Development of Peoples] (1967).

[64]*Id.* at 15.

within their own nation and among nations. He emphasized what has come to be identified as the "universal destination of goods" which limited the unqualified right to private property.

St. Paul VI focused on the role of the individual in the development of society. All people must utilize their intelligence and initiative (gifts from God) to improve themselves and their society. Inequalities, however, in underdeveloped nations leave the poor "deprived of nearly all possibility of [taking] personal initiative and of responsibility …"[65] for their own development and contribution to the development of their society [The Poverty Trap]. To do that, they need education and access to the scientific, technological, and physical resources that allow personal growth. They need the support of rich nations and individuals, as well as intermediary organizations, to assume their responsibility and play a rightful role in the material, cultural, social, and spiritual development of their countries.

To summarize St. Paul's message: It is the duty of the world's wealthy nations to provide for the necessities—food, shelter, clean water, health care, etc.—needed by impoverished nations. That is a moral imperative. The rich—international organizations, nations, and NGOs—must also provide the poor with the resources needed by them to define their own progress. Ultimately, each person in underdeveloped nations must use the resources and culture of their nation to shape the development of their countries. Individuals must use their intellect, skills, and talents to improve themselves and contribute to social development. But, again, the rich must free them from extreme want and contribute the resources, including most notably education, to liberate the initiative and responsibility of citizens who can then control their own development as individuals and as nations.

4.9 Foundational Principles of Catholic Social Doctrine

The Catholic social teaching tradition has produced many principles: among them the primacy of labor over capital; the dignity of and right to work; the preferential option for the poor; the right to private property; the universal destination of goods; the right of association, and the right to religious freedom. St. John Paul, however, identified three foundational principles of Catholic Social Doctrine—Dignity, Solidarity, and Subsidiarity.[66] Later iterations added the Common Good to the list of critical principles. All of the other identified principles are derived from these core principles. Dignity informs the Universal Declaration of Human Rights and all Catholic Social Doctrine. And it is a dignity that is inherent in the human person and is inalienable. Solidarity, in the context of this paper, relates to what I characterize as the ethical/moral imperative to aid the people of countries that are part of the bottom billion. It is the "I am my brother's keeper" rule. St. John Paul II identifies solidarity as critical to the establishment of peace. He updated earlier iterations of the mantra

[65] *Id.* at 9 (quoting *Gaudium et Spes* 63).

[66] Apostolic Exhortation of Pope St. John Paul II, *Ecclesia in America* 55 (1999).

about peace from peace is the fruit of justice and peace is the fruit of development (Paul VI) to peace is the fruit of Solidarity (JP II). He also identified solidarity *in practice* as a virtue. It is not an abstract, idealistic principle, but a virtue that must be practiced. It is only when men and women see themselves in universal solidarity with all humans and respond to the needs of others that stable peace is attainable.

The principle of subsidiarity is the "how to," the most practical of the principles. It requires that decision making be relegated to the lowest social institution competent to address whatever issue is at stake. The virtue it implicates most is prudence. This is where Catholic teaching and economic development come together. The "new" economic development models advocated by Easterly, Moyo, Collier, and others, seem to center on getting aid to the people who are living the struggle. Give them the way to raise themselves out of their condition and they will control the nature of development in their own cultures. This model implicitly relies among other things on entrepreneurship and markets. Naturally there are things that only governments can achieve, e.g., infrastructure development. But even for these major financial projects, the people who are most effected must have input. And corruption must be prevented. The bottom line is that the principle of subsidiarity must be respected and donors as well as recipients must make sound prudential judgements when allocating and using funds.

The common good is the goal of all social activities. It runs counter to what many believe to be the extreme individualism of modern developed societies. At whatever level economic, social, and cultural policy decisions are made, the ultimate goal must be the common good, i.e., the good of each person and all persons. Self-interest may be the great motivator, but the common good must moderate purely selfish interests.

4.10 Conclusion

Can Catholic social doctrine be reconciled with modern thinking about economic aid? Recall that Catholic teaching does not provide exact policy solutions to complex social problems. That belongs to secular experts. The social doctrine does, however, inform the decision-making processes. Since the major question among experts in development policies has to do with the nature of foreign aid, let us use the social doctrine to help inform that debate. Virtually all secular scholars embody a commitment to human dignity and solidarity. The Church's teachings and secular development experts are aligned in this respect. Something must be done for those peoples and societies that are greatly in need of necessities and also the resources to begin and maintain the process of economic growth. Aid must be provided by the rich of the world to those in need. This is the moral imperative taught by most religions and humanistic philosophies. At the very least, aid must be provided to meet major natural disasters and dire need for necessities. Even these forms of aid, however, should conform to the principle of subsidiarity and the exercise of prudence. Resources for substantial natural disasters and human crises must naturally come from the "rich." International agencies such as the U.N. and World Bank, rich developed nations, and major NGOs must provide the resources to meet extreme needs. Implementation of the aid policy, however, can often best be effectuated by intermediate and local governments, private agencies and individuals. The principle of subsidiarity calls for donors and those administering the aid to utilize the human resources closest to the problem.

With regard to the debate between the developmental aid experts, the principle of subsidiarity also seems to put Catholic teaching on the side of the "bottom up" advocates. The "big push" advocates favor a policy that has failed in the past. Sachs may be right that the wealthy nations simply did not provide adequate resources to push the bottom billion over the development hump by 2015. And he is surely right that the rich in developed nations, like the United States, can afford to provide substantially greater aid from their collective surplus. The idea that national policies will make international foreign aid a high priority, however, may be unreasonable. Given the history of failed aid programs, donor fatigue may limit the ability of the aid community to finance a really big push. Moreover, Collier believes that traditional aid is subject to the principle of diminishing returns. The amounts of financial aid are close to the point where the marginal returns from greater influxes of aid will be nil.[67]

Collier's more nuanced list of "traps" moreover suggest that no one-size-fits-all approach is tenable. Aid policies must address the specific barriers that are unique to each nation. Allowing the underdeveloped nations to themselves establish the policies to be applied in the implementation of a "big push" aid program is problematic. The governments or circumstances may render sound national policies impractical.

In addition to calling for a greater emphasis on subsidiarity (the bottom up approach), the social teachings most significant contribution to the aid dilemma is their focus on *integral* development. Economic advances are extremely important for the healthy development of the peoples of the bottom billion nations, as well as other nations that are still developing. Development, however, must advance all the elements of what makes humans unique, social, cultural, and spiritual as well as material and economic. Catholic social doctrine has always kept economic development within a framework that places human rights above economic efficiency. For example, while acknowledging the beneficial role that markets play in the development of nations and peoples, the Church has always rejected a purely utilitarian or profit-motivated approach. The primary goal is not to maximize efficiency or profits, but to provide individuals with the rights and responsibilities to shape their own integral development within their own cultures, and then to contribute to the development of their communities and societies.

[67]Collier, *supra* note 6, at 100.

References

1. Moyo, D. (2009). *Dead aid: Why aid is not working and how there is a better way for Africa.*
2. Collier, P. (2007). *The bottom billion: Why the poorest countries are failing and what can be done about it.*
3. Sachs, J. D. (2015). *The end of poverty: Economic possibilities for our time.*
4. Banerjee, A. V., & Duflo, E. (2011). *Poor economics: A radical rethinking of the way to fight global poverty.*
5. Easterly, W. (2006) *The white man's burden: Why the West's efforts to aid the rest have done so much ill and so little good.*
6. Glendon, M. A. (2013). The influence of catholic social doctrine on human rights. *Journal Catholic Social Thought, 10.*
7. Shapiro, S., & Tomain, J. (2003). Regulatory law and policy: Cases and materials (3rd ed.).

Chapter 5
Common but Differentiated Responsibilities for Developed and Developing States: A South African Perspective

Zuzana Selementová

Abstract In the international context, as well as in international law, *development* serves as a criterion to differentiate between states. As a result, states are commonly divided into broad categories of *developed* and *developing* countries. The notion of *common but differentiated responsibilities* (CBDR) is predicated on such differentiation in international environmental law and allows the imposition of disparate obligations on developed or developing states. Until the adoption of the Paris Agreement in December 2015, the principle of CBDR was applied in the international climate change regime based on the UN Framework Convention on Climate Change. The Paris Agreement, ratified by South Africa on 1 November 2016, brings new perspectives to the international process of addressing climate change. It modifies the principle of CBDR, and introduces the concept of *nationally determined contributions*, specific for and binding on each country.The present chapter outlines and analyses the methods of differentiation between developed and developing states against the backdrop of the principle of CBDR, from a South African perspective. The chapter opens by outlining the definitions and criteria at play to distinguish between developed and developing countries. The most commonly used tools, terms, and indices describing levels of development include GNI/GNP, the Human Development Index, the Gini coefficient, and categories used within the United Nations and by international financial institutions, including the World Trade Organisation, the International Monetary Fund, and the World Bank. Despite well-defined criteria, no clear and precise definition of a developing or a developed state emerges. The second section of this chapter then proceeds to present a practical application of the differentiation based on the level of development used in the UN Climate Change regime. The chapter approaches the theoretical understanding of the two aspects of the principle of CBDR, namely, the *common* and the *differentiated* responsibilities. The effects of the principle of CBDR in the UN Framework Convention on Climate Change, and its Kyoto Protocol, are examined, and the categories of Annex I, Annex II, and non-Annex I countries are presented. The change brought by the Paris Agreement, which has led to the more equitable distribution of rights and duties between developed and developing states, is further analysed. Last, South Africa's imple-

Z. Selementová (✉)
LL.M. (Cape Town), Valouch, Attorneys-at-Law, Prague, Czech Republic
e-mail: zuzana.selementova@gmail.com

P. Szwedo et al. (eds.), *Law and Development*, Kobe University Monograph Series in Social Science Research, https://doi.org/10.1007/978-981-13-9423-2_5

mentation of its Paris Agreement obligations regarding its nationally determined contributions is discussed and evaluated.

Keywords Climate change · Development · Common but differentiated responsibilities · Paris Agreement · Nationally determined contributions

5.1 Introduction

Disillusionment in the aftermath of World War II led countries from all over the world to initiate closer cooperation aimed at avoiding similar disasters in the future. The global North was broadly divided into two camps, and, in the South, the transformation from colonial domains into sovereign states was under way.[1] The differences between the industrial North and poorer southern hemisphere became increasingly apparent, and the impact of global inequality more significant. The differentiation of parties of the United Nations into developed and developing states had commenced.

This chapter focuses on the role the concept and understanding of development played in the differentiation of states, and how the differentiation between developed and developing states influenced the diversity of state commitments aimed at addressing climate change. The introductory part of the chapter analyses the possible definitions at play, the criteria used to distinguish between the two categories, and how such criteria apply to South Africa. Then the chapter summarises the advent of a concept within international environmental law—namely, the concept of common but differentiated responsibilities (CBDR). This principle is presented as defined in the Rio Declaration, the UN Framework Convention on Climate Change (UNFCCC), and its Kyoto Protocol. Lastly, developments in the notion of CBDR in light of the Paris Agreement are discussed with a focus on the newly introduced nationally determined contributions and their implementation in South Africa.

5.2 Definition of Developed and Developing States

In connection to closer cooperation of states in the post-WWII period, there was an urge to take account of the disparity in levels of wealth and economic status of participating states. To identify the capacity and prospects of states, their levels of development were used as a criterion of differentiation. Based on the level of development, states were either bound to obligations or entitled to international assistance, mostly of an economic nature, hence the need to differentiate developed and developing states in some consistent manner. The following part of this chapter questions the terms *developed* and *developing*, summarises the differences between those categories, and analyses whether there may be a definition for developed or developing states.

---

[1] Stokke [1, p. 3].

5.2.1 Differentiation Under the United Nations

The first instance of differentiating states according to their level of development probably took place within the UN context. At the time, development was understood mostly to be matter of economic development and level of industrialisation. A principal aim of the United Nations is to promote economic development (cf., the preamble, and, among others, articles 1(3) and 55(a), UN Charter). The United Nations focused on helping underdeveloped countries to improve their economic and political development through financial aid and technical assistance.[2] Lack of capital was seen as a main constraint for poorer countries in modernising and developing their own infrastructure and public governance to plan and implement future development.[3] Thus the *Expanded Programme of Technical Assistance* was established in 1949, and countries of the global North, led by the United States, were encouraged to share knowledge, technical background, education, and finance with countries with less developed economies.

The terms *developing* and *developed* are since then greatly used in the statistics and data analysis of the United Nations and its agencies. The major programme dedicated to promoting and monitoring global development is the United Nations *Development Programme*, created by merging with the original *Expanded Programme of Technical Assistance* and *Special Fund* in 1966.[4] The most common indicator of a state's development is its economic status expressed through Gross National Product (GNP) or Gross National Income (GNI) indices, sometimes also expressed as GNP or GNI per capita. GNP per capita and its growth rates became accepted as a universal indicator that readily describes economic and human development.[5] However, an index based only on economic development appeared insufficient to effectively express disparities between states and the overall level of development.

5.2.2 Human Development Index

Following the need for a more general development indicator, in 1990, the United Nations Development Programme introduced a new statistical model, the Human Development Index (HDI), to report on state development. The HDI combines economic information of a state's national income per capita, with information about life expectancy at birth, and the level of education (determined through *expected* and *mean* years of schooling). The higher the HDI, the more convenient living conditions are thought to be in the country in question. As part of monitoring global development levels, the United Nations annually publish the *Human Development Report*. Human

[2]Ibid., 6.

[3]Ibid.

[4]United Nations, *United Nations Special Fund*, https://atom.archives.unesco.org/united-nations-special-fund;isaar (last accessed 17 September 2018).

[5]Hicks and Streeten [2, p. 567].

development classifications for states in the 2016 Human Development Report rely on cut-off points, namely, a HDI score of 0.550 or lower suggests low levels of human development, a HDI score of 0.550 and 0.699 suggests a medium level of human development, a HDI score between 0.700 and 0.799 suggests a high level of human development, and a HDI score of 0.800 or greater suggests a very high level of human development.[6] In 2016, South Africa was ranked in the report at 119th position with a HDI score of 0.666, thus placing it in the category of states with *medium* levels of human development.

In 2014, the UN Secretariat's Department of Economic and Social Affairs published its *World Economic Situation and Prospects* report (WECP) that aims to present new trends in the world economy. In its statistical annex, the classification of countries for statistical purposes is presented. All states are divided into three broad categories, namely: developing economies, economies in transition, and developed economies.[7]

Based on the resolution of the United Nations adopted in the 1970s,[8] the United Nations Economic and Social Council and the Committee for Development Policy recommended the acknowledgement of a further category—namely, that for *least developed* countries. Currently, the term *least developed* designates countries with the lowest HDI that meet three criteria: an income criterion showing the level of poverty—this is based on GNI per capita observed for the last three years; a *Human Assets Index* based on four indicators: the ratio of undernourished population, mortality rates for children under the age of five, the ratio of population enrolled into secondary education, and the rate of adult literacy; and, last, an Economic Vulnerability Index that includes indicators which may represent weaknesses present in each country, such as instability of economic production, instability of international trade, or the number of victims of natural disasters.[9] Given the fact that the aims of the United Nations include the eradication of poverty and the inclusion of less developed countries within the world economy, least developed countries can profit from the United Nations *Capital Development Fund*, which promotes financial inclusion in local markets. The category of *least developed* countries is, however, not adopted in the methodologies of the World Bank and the International Monetary Fund.[10]

Apart from the category of the *least developed* countries, the United Nations also distinguishes *Landlocked Developing Countries* and *Small Island Developing States*. Landlocked developing countries often belong among the poorest developing countries due to a combination of factors including their remoteness from foreign markets and usually, their very limited natural resources.[11] In total 16 out of 31 *landlocked*

---

[6]United Nations, *Human Development Report 2016: Human Development for Everyone*, 2016, 207.

[7]United Nations, *World Economic Situation and Prospects 2017*, 2016, United Nations, 1.

[8]United Nations, *Resolution 2768 (XXVI) of 18 November 1971.*

[9]Lenzi [3].

[10]Ibid., 2.

[11]United Nations, *United Nations Landlocked Developing Countries*, http://unohrlls.org/about-lldcs/ (last accessed 17 September 2018).

developing countries are currently ranked among the *least developed* countries.[12] *Small Island Developing States*, endangered by the impact of climate change on their low-lying coastal areas,[13] were recognised as a vulnerable group of developing countries with specific economic, social, and environmental conditions.[14] Despite the specific situation of the three groups of *less developed* countries, underlined by the existence of the United Nations Office of the High Representative for the Least Developed Countries, Landlocked Developing Countries and Small Island Developing States, these states are for statistical purposes included in the category of states with low, medium, high, or very high human development.

As a criterion of development, the HDI can also be complemented by the indicator for levels of inequality. Such supplementation may better express the complexity of the term development and emphasise other factors than solely the economic. The consequent inequality-adjusted HDI may then express inequality in distribution of HDI among the population of a country, and thus, provide fuller insights into the social development of a state.[15]

5.2.3 Gini Coefficient

Disparities *between* states are underlined by the disparities at play *within* each state. Inequalities in wealth distribution within a nation may be expressed by the Gini coefficient. Whilst the dispersion measurement presented in 1912 by the Italian sociologist and statistician Corrado Gini does not provide information on the general level of economic development of a country, it does demonstrate the level of inequality of its distribution within a given population. The values of the Gini coefficient vary from 0 to 1, whereby the value of 0 means a perfectly equal income or wealth situation among all *units* within an economy (for instance, between all households) whereas values approaching 1 represent increasing levels of inequality.[16] Thus, the Gini coefficient cannot be used on its own to differentiate between poor and wealthy states per se.

Despite the connection between economic status and overall human development, the Gini index does not correlate to economic, social or technical development. High values are usually evidence of an unhealthy economic situation in the country where

---

[12]United Nations, *World Economic Situation and Prospects 2017*, 2016.

[13]Glazewski and Du Toit [4, p. 3–8].

[14]United Nations, *United Nations Small Island Developing States*, http://unohrlls.org/about-sids/ (last accessed 17 September 2018).

[15]United Nations, *Human Development Report 2016: Human Development for Everyone*, 2016, 206.

[16]For example, in European countries, the Gini coefficient usually varies between 0.25 and 0.35, indicating decent results for societies without extreme inequality in wealth distribution. *See* World Bank Development Research Group, *GINI Index, World Bank Estimate*, https://data.worldbank.org/indicator/SI.POV.GINI?end=2016&locations=AF-BY-BR-CZ-ZA-IE&start=1981&type=points&view=chart (last accessed 17 September 2018).

wealth is accumulated only among a few, and even when GNI values are on the rise, this might not improve the situation in the population. The coefficient can however serve as a complementary factor that may be taken into consideration when gauging whether a state is developing. When evaluating a country for the purposes of categorising it as developed or developing, the Gini coefficient is not commonly used given that a poor (i.e., developing or less developed) country might actually present an equal distribution of its limited means.

5.2.4 *The Influence of Financial Institutions*

The division of the world's countries into *developed* and *developing* for statistical purposes is not an end in itself; its principal purpose is to provide insights into how to define most equitably different conditions for international commitments of individual states, and for the allocation of financial support provided to the states most in need. In relation to this, three international financial institutions are the most pertinent, namely, the World Trade Organisation, the International Monetary Fund, and the World Bank. Aid provided to less developed countries through financial institutions is mostly through the funding of projects and the provision of loans and grants, usually on a long-term basis.

5.2.4.1 The World Trade Organisation

The World Trade Organisation (WTO) was founded after WWII to support international economic cooperation and to progressively remove barriers to free trade at the inter-state level. The WTO relies on categories of *developed* and *developing*—with a subcategory of *least developed countries*—but states are free to self-designate as regards the categories of *developed* or *developing states*. Their decision can be challenged by the WTO community if necessary. Classification as *developing* or *least developed states* brings advantages and opportunities, usually in benefiting from longer transition periods or access to financial schemes.[17]

5.2.4.2 The International Monetary Fund

The International Monetary Fund (IMF), an international organisation ultimately parented within the UN context, has its own methodology to distinguish between countries. In its global biannually published survey on the world economy, the World Economic Outlook report, the IMF uses several strictly economic criteria to distinguish between states. The criteria include, among others, GNI per head, export

[17] *See* World Trade Organisation, *Development in WTO*, https://www.wto.org/english/tratop_e/devel_e/d1who_e.htm (last accessed 17 September 2018).

diversification, and the degree of integration of states into international financial systems.[18] Based on these criteria, the IMF recognises the categories of *advanced economies*—generally corresponding to the so-called developed states—*emerging markets*, and *developing economies*. Crucially, the IMF also claims that there is no core definition of the categories, and that the criteria and their relative importance evolve in time.[19]

5.2.4.3 The World Bank

Last, the World Bank (covered by the World Bank Group, which is also connected, albeit tangentially, to the UN system) also used to differentiate on the basis of the terms *developed* and *developing* for states to allocate financial aid and to analyse received data. Based on the GNI per capita, the World Bank placed states into the categories of *low*, *lower-middle*, *upper-middle*, and *high-income* groups.[20] In its reports, *lower* and *middle* income countries were referred to as *developing* countries. Thus, almost two thirds of the states with the lowest GNI per head were labelled as such. However, with the development of the global economy, and faced with several changes in global approaches towards human development (particularly, sustainable development), the World Bank no longer uses the terms *developed* and *developing* in its reports to designate states.[21] A main reason has been the very high levels of heterogeneity between developing countries and their current rapid development. The criteria thus became somewhat void of meaning as some of the countries might have very high per head GNI (for example Singapore) or the rate of their development might vary dramatically (including countries in southeast Asia).[22] The World Bank was also encouraged in its decision to stop using these terms during the transition from *Millennium Development Goals* (of sustainable development) to the *Sustainable Development Goals*. As a part, albeit tangential, of the broader UN firmament, the World Bank is expected to promote sustainable development and to respect international law including norms and principles of international environmental law.[23] According to the World Bank's latest report, the implementation of *Sustainable Development Goals*, and the monitoring of progress, emphasise the sustainability of development for every single country and highlight the ultimate interconnection of the whole world. In such conditions, differentiation between *developed* and *developing* countries will no longer be used.[24]

---

[18] International Monetary Fund, *World Economic Outlook 2016*, https://www.imf.org/external/pubs/ft/weo/2016/02/weodata/index.aspx (last accessed 3 November 2018).

[19] International Monetary Fund, *World Economic Outlook—FAQ*, https://www.imf.org/external/pubs/ft/weo/faq.htm#q4b (last accessed 17 September 2018).

[20] Khokhar and Serajuddin [5].

[21] World Bank, *World Development Indicators*, 2016, 7.

[22] Gupta [6, p. 124].

[23] Birnie et al. [7, p. 80].

[24] World Bank, *World Development Indicators*, 2016, 7.

5.2.5 *South Africa as a Developing Country*

In most of the statistics and international rankings (including of the WTO and World Bank), South Africa is classified as a *developing* country. However, thanks to the current state of its economy, which in 2016 had a GDP per capita of USD 7585.80 and a GNI per capita of USD 4300, it is also a country with middle income. According to the United Nations, its HDI ranks South Africa among countries with *middle* human development. Despite increasing industrial and social developments in the country, the South African Gini index remains the worst in the world with the value of 0.63 in 2014. In the context of climate change, discussed in the second half of this chapter, South Africa belongs to the *non-Annex I* countries, i.e., among the developing countries.

5.2.6 *Conclusions on the Disparity Between Developed and Developing States*

Following the analysis in the foregoing, there are several ways of understanding the term *development*, and multiple terms and criteria used to distinguish between different levels of development in different countries. The level of development as a differentiating criterion can be precarious if the assessment of development only covers the economic situation, but it can be more meaningful when it also takes into consideration *social* development or observes the level of *inequality* in the country. The most well-known categories of states based on their level of development include terms such as states with *low, medium, high*, or *very high* human development, as introduced by the Human Development Report, or *advanced markets*, *emerging markets*, and *developing economies*, as per the WTO, from a more economic point of view. The criteria for the various categories were also presented in the foregoing. Some criteria only include economic development (assessed by GNI/GNP), participation in international trade, or the economical vulnerability of a given state, whilst other criteria also consider social development and the well-being of the population, including factors such as access to education and longevity.

Despite the well-defined criteria at play, no universal definitions of what constitutes a *developing* or a *developed* state have emerged, and certainly no such definitions that are precise and clear. Both terms *developed* and *developing* in relation to states present a certain simplification that is used to differentiate states on a non-formal level. This might also be due to the imprecise definition of development. No matter how well-adjusted the HDI or other indices become, they remain statistical and descriptive tools used for different purposes. They, in and of themselves, do not promote further development and improved economic or social conditions in states.

According to the existing criteria discussed in the foregoing, developed states are usually independent, maintain a high level of per head income, and provide their citizens with good infrastructure, a high standard of living supported by decent health care, and a high rate of literacy. No doubt, such levels of development are predicated on factors including advanced level of industrialisation, which, at the same time, has and continues to contribute to severe environmental degradation. Developing states are usually dependent on financial support from more developed countries, as their industry is in the process of developing. The overall population of lesser developed countries has not attained high living standards as their states are unable to provide adequate infrastructure, accessible health care, and education. Birth and death rates are usually higher than in developed states, and the overall environmental conditions are worse, often due to the negative environmental impact of more industrialised countries or to local pollution consequent to laxer environmental regulation of industry. Based on such criteria, the differentiation of states as *developed* and *developing* may be better understood as a shorthand insight to facilitate discussion. As such, these terms will also be used in this chapter.

Even though considerable disparities between countries persist that still roughly correspond to the historic *global North versus global South* dichotomy,[25] labelling less developed states with the term developing country seems somewhat outdated. The World Bank abandoned this term in 2016[26] and now focuses instead on the promotion of sustainable development in the global context so that it includes economic but also social and environmental development in an equitable manner.

Efforts to assist less developed states with their development and to mitigate negative social and environmental effects caused by industrial states on the territories of less developed countries led to the development of the concept of CBDR. This notion is based on differentiation between more and less developed states, and on their common aim of addressing environmental issues. The development of the principle, and its practical use in international agreements dealing with climate change will be discussed in the following section.

5.3 The Concept of Common but Differentiated Responsibilities

The concept of common but differentiated responsibilities (CBDR) was for the first time expressly articulated in the Rio Declaration on Environment and Development in 1992 (Rio Declaration) as a principle of sustainable development. However, the general idea of differentiation between states appeared in international documents since the 1960s, and the preferential treatment of developing countries was part of UN policy linked to the eradication of poverty.[27] Principle 7 of the Rio Declaration stipulates that 'states shall cooperate in a spirit of global partnership to conserve, protect and restore the health and integrity of the Earth's ecosystem'. Furthermore, considering their different contributions to the depletion of the environment, states

[25]Honkonen [8, p. 9].

[26]World Bank, *World Development Indicators*, 2016.

[27]Matsui [9, p. 73].

have common but differentiated responsibilities. In the wording of that provision, developed states acknowledge their leading role in the international quest of implementation of sustainable development, especially due to the pressure their nations exert on the global environment and due to their technical and financial capabilities.

5.3.1 Theoretical Introduction

The concept of CBDR acknowledges the disparity in levels of development in the world and complies with the fundamental principle of state sovereignty and of equity in international law.[28] The CBDR combines two elements: *common responsibilities* and *differentiated responsibilities*. Common responsibilities underline the general idea of sustainable development and stress the necessity of global cooperation as a response to the interconnection of all ecosystems and as the only possible way of their effective protection. The obligation of cooperation appears in many international binding and non-binding documents, such as the Stockholm Declaration on Human Environment,[29] the Rio Declaration,[30] and the UNFCCC that will be analysed in detail.[31] Similarly, the notion of CBDR has developed from its initial proclamation in a soft-law instrument (namely, the Rio Declaration) into a more concrete concept amounting to a principle of international environmental law that is regularly included in environmental treaties, including the UNFCCC.[32]

The element of *common responsibilities* was given effect in different ways. For instance, the United Nations General Assembly established a fund to assist developing countries in effective preparation for and participation in the United Nations Conference on Environment and Development. Thus, during negotiations of the UNFCCC assistance was provided to developing states. Even though the extent of the assistance was sometimes considered insufficient,[33] the joint effort and commitment to attaining equity was evident.[34] The CBDR thus demands all states to cooperate and emphasises the equal role of every country.

The second element of CBDR—*differentiated responsibilities*—refers to different obligations regarding the protection of the environment assumed by states to achieve the common goal. The differentiation is based on two grounds.[35] The first concerns the relative contribution of states to environmental degradation. The devas-

[28] Sands et al. [10, p. 285].

[29] Stockholm Declaration on Human Environment, preamble, principle 24.

[30] Rio Declaration, preamble, principles 5, 7, 9, 12–14, 18, 19, 27.

[31] UNFCCC preamble, arts. 3–6, 11–12.

[32] Abeysinghe and Arias [11, p. 237].

[33] UNESCO Commission on Sustainable Development, Overall Progress Achieved Since the United Nations Conference on Environment and Development: Report of the Secretary General: Addendum: International Legal Instruments and Mechanisms, 7–25 April 1997, E/CN.17/1997/2/Add.29.

[34] Matsui [9, p. 77].

[35] See Footnote 32; Matsui [9, p. 78].

tation of the planet and pressure on natural resources on the part of developed states have hitherto been far more significant than that of developing states. The responsibility of developed states for the environmental degradation they have caused and continue to cause can be also partially addressed by recourse to the polluter-pays principle.[36] The second ground considers the capacity of states to act. It acknowledges that industrialised countries command more advanced technology, know-how, and financial resources that can enhance common efforts of environmental protection or combating climate change.[37]

The CBDR differentiation brings into international treaties divergent standards for developed and developing countries that may be of two kinds. The differences between states may be either substantial or procedural. Substantial differences place specific obligations on different groups of states, usually alleviating the burden from developing states, whether procedural differences include different commencement dates for the application of core provisions, usually giving developing states wider timeframes to implement agreed measures or fulfil necessary conditions. The differentiated approach aims at more equity and solidarity in a disparate and divided world. Together with the common responsibilities, the notion of CBDR applies to various international treaties[38] relating to climate change.

5.3.2 CBDR in the Context of the Climate Change Legal Regime

The concept of common but differentiated responsibilities had played a major role during discussions at the United Nations Conference on Environment and Development in Rio de Janeiro in 1992. The concept of CBDR applied already during the preparations of the conference, and, together with the concept of sustainable development, was included in the outcomes of the conference—the Rio Declaration, the UNFCCC, and the Convention on Biological Diversity. In the spirit of CBDR, the Rio Declaration as well as the other documents are also important as strong statements made *collectively* by developing and developed states on how the protection of environment and its balance with development should be pursued equitably.[39] Sustainable development and concerns regarding climate change are examples of global issues that require the international community as a whole to address collectively. However, not all countries have the same impact on the current state of the environment, nor do they have the same levels of resources. Consequently, states negotiated the inclusion of the CBDR concept in the legal regime addressing climate change.

[36] Sands et al. Principles of international environmental law 286.

[37] Sands et al. [10, p. 286].

[38] Ibid., 288.

[39] Birnie et al. [7, p. 113].

5.3.2.1 The United Nations Framework Convention on Climate Change

According to the opening statement of the UNFCCC, the 'change in the Earth's climate and its adverse effects are a common concern of humankind'. Thus, they need to be addressed jointly by the international community. The obligation of co-operation is mentioned throughout the UNFCCC.[40] In its preamble, parties further note that developed states are historically responsible for greater emissions of greenhouse gas (GHG),[41] and that, although cooperation should apply as widely as possible,[42] all countries will contribute according to their capabilities and social and economic conditions, with special regard to the needs of developing countries.[43] Furthermore, states in the preamble recognise that 'standards applied by some countries may be inappropriate and of unwarranted economic and social cost to other countries, in particular developing countries', and that the principle of CBDR shall apply.

Considering that the notion of CBDR seeks to apply different regimes to different states, classification of states is necessary. The UNFCCC classifies all states into three categories,[44] namely, parties included in its Annex I, parties included in its Annex II, and parties that are not included in either annex. Broadly, most of the countries included in Annex I are what may be deemed *developed* countries, including Australia, Canada, and Germany. Annex I, however, also includes countries with economies in transition, including Lithuania, the Czech Republic, and Poland. The UNFCCC refers to states listed in Annex I as *developed* countries. Annex II includes only the well-developed industrialised countries that were at the time of UNFCCC negotiations part of the Organisation for Economic Co-operation and Development (OECD). Developing countries were not listed in any of the annexes and are commonly referred to with regard to UNFCCC obligations as *non*-Annex I countries. The UNFCCC differentiates countries based on whether they are listed in Annex I or not. Following the concept of CBDR, rights and obligations differ in their substance as well, procedurally, in the flexibility of time given to states to implement their obligations.

Considering that the economic and social development of states led to their inclusion or exclusion in the annexes, it may be concluded that disparate levels of development have led to different obligations. That said, all parties to the convention have some common rights and duties,[45] including to develop national inventories on anthropogenic GHG emissions and provide reports on implementation of the convention;[46] to implement programmes containing measures to mitigate and adapt to

[40] UNFCCC, preamble, arts. 3(5), 4(1)(c)–(e), 5(c).

[41] Ibid., preamble.

[42] Ibid., art 3(1).

[43] Ibid., preamble.

[44] Matsui [9, p. 82].

[45] UNFCCC, art. 4 (commitments).

[46] Ibid., art 4(1)(a).

climate change;[47] to promote and cooperate regarding the use of technologies;[48] or to exchange information.[49] Substantial differences in the commitments of different countries are stipulated in the UNFCCC. Annex I states have committed themselves to limits of GHG emissions and to the protection of GHG sinks and reservoirs.[50] Their reports under the UNFCCC—known as *national communication*—must also include information on implementation of national policies and other measures, and information on transfer of technologies and financial resources. Their approach should show their leading role in changing the trends in long-term production of emissions and in mitigation and adaptation to climate change.[51] Annex I states also commit in a non-binding way[52] to return their CO_2 emissions to 1990 levels by 2000.[53] An example of the concept of CBDR at play is evident in the fact that no such commitments were undertaken by developing states. Moreover, developing states were encouraged to advance their economic development,[54] as it is thought to help them alleviate poverty, which should be their main priority, given that it is among the aims of the UN system. Developed countries have further committed to providing financing to help developing countries with their sustainable development that respects the objectives of the UNFCCC.[55]

Developing countries were, in general, strongly supported through the UNFCCC. Not only were they not burdened with most obligations that applied to developed states, but the regime applicable to them was much more flexible in terms of time frames. Developed countries were expected to report back on their progress with the United Nations within six months after the entry into force of the UNFCCC, whereas developing countries were expected to do so in three years, while the least developed countries were only to do so 'at their discretion'.[56]

Differentiation in rights and duties is also afforded to parties to the UNFCCC whose economies are in transition to a market economy, as they should be allowed a 'certain degree of flexibility'.[57] The UNFCCC further retains the distinction of *least developed* countries and countries that are *particularly vulnerable to negative impacts of climate change*.[58] The convention stresses the necessity of due consideration of specific needs of the disadvantaged groups of states: including small island countries,

[47]Ibid., art 4(1)(b).

[48]Ibid., art 4(1)(c).

[49]Ibid., art 4(1)(h).

[50]Ibid., art 4(2)(a).

[51]Ibid.

[52]See Footnote 13.

[53]UNFCCC, art. 4(2)(b).

[54]Ibid., art 4(7).

[55]Ibid., art 4(3).

[56]Ibid., art 4(5).

[57]Ibid., art 4(6).

[58]Ibid., preamble, art. 3(2), 4(4).

landlocked countries, countries susceptible to natural disasters, or countries with areas with fragile ecosystems.[59]

It may be reasonably concluded that the UNFCCC fully incorporates the concept of CBDR. To that end, it classifies all parties to the UNFCCC into three groups: Annex I, Annex II, and *non*-Annex I countries. Each group enjoys and is bound by different rights and duties, with a special preferential regime being provided to developing countries and vulnerable countries. The UNFCCC thus underlines the greater responsibility of developed states for the pressure placed on natural resources by their industrialisation and for their capacity to address climate change, and the common responsibility of all countries to address the adverse consequences of economic development.

5.3.2.2 The Kyoto Protocol

The UNFCCC initiated global efforts to address climate change. But as a *framework convention*, it contains the scope for the further development of the regime it establishes, primarily, through binding and more technical protocols or agreements. One such subsequent instrument is the Kyoto Protocol, which was adopted in 1996 to set binding requirements on emission reduction. The Kyoto Protocol builds on the UNFCCC, and as such includes and develops the principle of CBDR.[60] It also recognises the principle responsibility of developed states for the elevated levels of carbon dioxide and other GHGs and, as a result, imposes on them regulations regarding GHGs.[61] The protocol follows the differentiation of states as it was stipulated by the UNFCCC—that is to say, all countries remain divided in three categories, with the focus being on Annex I countries, and some relief being made available for such Annex I countries with economies in transition.[62]

Core obligations from the Kyoto Protocol bind only Annex I countries. Based on the principle of CBDR, Annex I countries have committed to reduce their GHG emissions by at least five per cent, compared to 1990 levels in the first commitment period that extends from 2008 to 2012.[63] As the development needs of developing countries are promoted by the Kyoto Protocol, states are obliged to cooperate to facilitate technology transfer of environmentally friendly technologies and know-how, in particular to developing states.[64] The protocol obliges developed countries to provide financial assistance as one of the consequences of the principle of CBDR.

---

[59] Ibid., art 4(8).

[60] Kyoto Protocol, preamble, art. 10 (citing UNFCCC, art 3).

[61] The list of GHGs is included in Kyoto Protocol, annex A.

[62] Kyoto Protocol, art 3(6).

[63] Ibid., art 3(1).

[64] Ibid., art 10(c).

5.3.2.3 Unsustainability of CBDR?

Even though the concept of CBDR is founded upon a principle of equity that can be attained by differentiation, some authors criticise the concept of CBDR and argue that the *double standard* it introduces is undesirable. An exposition on some of the negative perceptions surrounding this notion follows.

First, lower environmental standards in developing countries permitted by operation of the concept of CBDR can lead to the creation of *environmental havens* for multinational corporations that intend to maximise their income to the detriment of the environment.[65] As a result, the total amount of GHG emissions is not diminished, due to the transfer of industrial production from developed to developing countries, and the environmental impact also accrues to the already more vulnerable countries. The legal conditions—including emission regulation—in the developing countries are insufficient for effective environmental protection, law enforcement is less robust, there are high levels of illiteracy in the local communities, and their ability to protect their rights is poor.

Second, despite the fact that developed countries have accepted their historical responsibility for their adverse environmental impact and that they have better access to technologies and financing, some developing countries are actually developing fast, and their emissions are rising significantly. Some commentators argue that as the impact of developing countries on the environment also intensifies, they should accept greater responsibility and commitments in addressing climate change.[66] Considering some of the economic criteria discussed earlier, some of the countries historically considered as *developing* are actually nowadays fairly developed (for instance, Singapore).[67] Last, due to the transboundary and interconnected nature of global environmental issues and challenges, the potentially steady growth of the economies of large developing countries such as China or India, would make the whole concept eventually less effective and therefore less tenable.[68]

In the view of this author, these criticisms are valid. Furthermore, scientific research emphasises the need for global solutions to the transboundary and supranational problem that is climate change. Accordingly, the concept of CBDR has undergone significant changes in light of the latest agreement contracted within the framework of UNFCCC, which was signed at the Conference of Parties in Paris on 12 December 2015.

5.3.2.4 The Paris Agreement

The Paris Agreement is the second international legal agreement that builds upon the UNFCCC. It recognises the concept of CBDR as a core principle of the agree-

[65]Gladwin [12, p. 10].

[66]Gupta [6, p. 121].

[67]Ibid.

[68]Ibid.; Abeysinghe and Arias [11, p. 242].

ment,[69] together with the principles of *sustainable development* such as promotion of social development, the right to development, and the principle of *intergenerational equity*.[70] Unlike its predecessors, the agreement does not divide states into annexes per their economic development, but takes a different approach. The Paris Agreement stresses the common responsibilities for the goal of combating climate change. Parties to the agreement devote to jointly hold the increasing global average temperature of the planet to 'well below 2 °C' but with efforts to limit the temperature raise to 1.5 °C above pre-industrial levels.[71] Such temperature targets should 'significantly reduce risks and impacts of climate change'.[72]

In conformity with the *Sustainable Development Goal* of eradicating hunger and poverty, the agreement obligates states to increase their ability to adapt to the negative effects of climate change, and to mitigate its consequences in their pursuit to secure sufficient food production.[73] Countries also have committed to maintain consistent financing to minimise GHG emissions and to help create climate-resilient development.[74]

Crucially, although the agreement respects the principle of CBDR and confirms the need to support developing countries, rights and duties from the Paris Agreement bind *all* countries regardless of their level of economic development. To promote the objectives of the UNFCCC and to strengthen global efforts to reduce GHG emissions, the agreement introduces the notion of nationally determined contributions (NDC).[75] Every country, irrespective whether its economy is developed or developing, must 'prepare, communicate and maintain'[76] its national contributions as its response to climate change. The NDCs must be ambitious and progressive over time,[77] and the maximum amounts of GHG emissions should be reached as soon as possible and consequently diminish in the future. Even developing countries are encouraged to, in future and according to national circumstances, focus on emission reduction or limitation targets.[78] Countries shall take domestic measures to achieve their NDCs.[79] The participation of all countries will, with respect to their capabilities and the concept of CBDR, enable regular monitoring and global approach.[80] In the reporting regarding the NDCs, emphasis is placed on 'environmental integrity, transparency, accuracy, completeness, comparability and consistency'.[81]

---

[69] Paris Agreement, art 2(2).

[70] Ibid., preamble.

[71] Ibid., art 2(1)(a).

[72] Ibid.

[73] Ibid., art 2(1)(b).

[74] Ibid., art 2(1)(c).

[75] Ibid., art. 3.

[76] Ibid., art. 4(2).

[77] Ibid., arts. 3, 4(3).

[78] Ibid., art. 4(4).

[79] Ibid., art. 4(2).

[80] Under Article 4(9), parties must report nationally determined contributions every five years.

[81] Paris Agreement, art. 4(13).

Notably, the distinction between developed and developing countries is maintained, but no definitions of the categories are offered. Therefore, the designation and position of countries are not immutable and static in relation to a predefined category; rather, countries are encouraged to shift towards more ambitious mitigation targets without becoming complacent.[82]

Apart from the distinction between developed and developing countries, the Paris Agreement retains the UN classification and refers to the *least developed countries* and *small island countries* as 'countries that are particularly vulnerable to adverse effects of climate change' and whose needs should be considered.[83] On the contrary, the agreement neither mentions nor refers to states with economies in transition. This is the result of the subsequent progression of countries from the former post-Soviet republics (and its satellite states in eastern Europe), which have either joined the European Union and are now deemed to fall within the *developed* countries designation, or their transformation was generally less efficient, they are not part of the EU, and they are in the group of *developing* countries.[84]

This evolution of the role that the differentiation of states plays in the latest international climate change agreement seems satisfying. With respect to the NDCs that apply to all parties, the Paris Agreement does not strictly classify countries to differentiate the substance of their latest obligations. However, preferential treatment is still available to developing states, as different national circumstances should be considered. With regard to the concept of CBDR, developed states are obligated to provide developing states with financial assistance.[85]

The concept of NDCs thus implements a tool that enables proper participation of all stakeholders on the common goal with respect to their capabilities. It also minimises the problem with disproportionate heterogeneity within the group of developing states, as each state suggests its own targets. Even though the Paris Agreement upholds the concept of CBDR, its modification arguably leads to a more equitable distribution of rights and duties between developed and developing states. The adopted approach however also has its shortcomings as the motivation of states to determine ambitious goal-directed targets is limited. Despite the fact that more robust regulation would be beneficial to the environment, the adopted agreement should be welcomed, especially in respect of difficult Paris Agreement negotiations, as a compromise with specific requirements and clear goals that requires *developing* states to play a more active role in the combat of climate change.

[82]Voigt and Ferreira [13, p. 67].

[83]Paris Agreement, art. 9(4).

[84]Voigt and Ferreira [13, p. 65].

[85]Paris Agreement, art. 9(1).

5.3.3 South Africa and the Paris Agreement

The Paris Agreement requires that parties communicate their nationally determined contributions. The NDCs are made available in a public register held by the Secretariat. So far, 177 out of 181 parties that ratified the Paris Agreement, including South Africa, have submitted their NDCs. South Africa became party to the agreement on 22 April 2016 and ratified it on 1 November 2016. The agreement entered into force on 1 December 2016.[86] South African NDCs were submitted to the interim register on 1 December 2016.[87] Under the Paris Agreement, South Africa remains a *developing* state, which is mirrored in its NDCs. For South Africa as a developing state, eradication of poverty and elimination of inequality remain priorities.[88] According to the 2012 National Development Plan, this goal should be achieved by 2030. The country is currently profoundly dependent on coal, which represents a cheap energy source that helps to cover increasing demand for energy. In the short term, the shift towards a low-carbon economy is less of a priority than social development.[89] However, South Africa has committed itself to comply with the GHG emission goals expressed in Article 4 of the Paris Agreement, whereby states should aim their emissions to reach their peak as soon as possible in order for them to consequently implement rapid reductions. South Africa aims to achieve this between 2025 and 2030.

National policy regarding climate change is summarised in the National Climate Change Response White Paper. South African NDCs focus on adaptation and to a lesser extent on mitigation. Regarding adaptation, six main goals are defined.[90] As for mitigation, emission projections for the period between 2025 and 2030 are likely to range between 398 and 614 million tonnes of CO_2-equivalent ($MtCO_2$ eq.). In 2012, South Africa's total GHG emissions were 464 $MtCO_2$ eq.[91] Based on this statistic, in 2012, South Africa was the fifteenth largest global GHG emitter with the total of one per cent of global emissions.[92] Its current GNI ranks the country within the group of *medium income* states, along with Brazil or India. Considering the commitments of developing states with similar characteristics and current levels of GHG emissions, the South African target of maximal level of emissions, which allows for an increase of more than 30%, does not seem too ambitious, especially when considering the total amount of GHG emissions produced.

---

[86] United Nations, *The Paris Agreement: Ratification Status*, http://unfccc.int/paris_agreement/items/9444.php (last accessed 5 October 2018).

[87] South Africa, *South Africa's Intended Nationally Determined Contribution*, 2016.

[88] Ibid., 2.

[89] Ibid.

[90] Ibid.

[91] USAID, *Greenhouse Gas Emissions in South Africa*, 2012.

[92] Mace [14, p. 34].

5.4 Conclusion

The differentiation of countries based on socio-economic criteria has a long tradition that developed under the auspices of the United Nations. Economic criteria, such as GNI or GNP, are used most often, but they can only provide limited insights based on general information concerning economic development. More detailed information can be retrieved from the Human Development Index, which combines economic and social development aspects represented by a population's living conditions, longevity, and access to education and healthcare. Apart from those of *developed* and *developing* countries, special categories of the *least developed* countries, particularly vulnerable countries, *landlocked countries*, or *small island countries* are also in use. Moreover, the classification of states for the statistical purposes of international financial institutions was also discussed. Further to the review of different practices concerning terms pertaining to the development levels of states, it is evident that there neither are any universal nor any exact definitions of what constitutes a *developed* or a *developing* country.

Following clarification of these basic, albeit imprecise, terms, the notion of CBDR was discussed. The concept comprises two elements—common responsibilities and differentiated responsibilities. The former derives from the principle of cooperation and solidarity between states, whilst the latter stresses the historical responsibility of developed states for the impact that their development has hitherto had on the environment, and their easier access to technologies and financial resources. The concept of CBDR balances these two responsibilities and is included in many international instruments, both binding and non-binding. The concept of CBDR is fully incorporated in the global climate change regime that was initiated by the UNFCCC.

The UNFCCC differentiates between developed and developing states without offering any definitions. However, state parties are divided into two major categories, with developed states being listed in (the more onerous) Annex I whilst developing states being known as non-Annex I countries. Concerning this broad grouping of state parties, there are differences at play in relation to their substantive rights and obligations, as well as procedural matters, including timeframes.

The purpose of the Kyoto Protocol was to strengthen the commitments of Annex I countries without imposing new duties on non-Annex I parties. This situation changed significantly with the adoption of the Paris Agreement in 2015. The agreement presented a new—common to all states—tool for state participation in addressing global climate issues—the nationally determined contributions. Each party to the agreement is required to determine its own targets and contributions to the common responsibility to maintain global average temperatures well below two degrees Celsius. The agreement thus allows for a more individualised approach at the discretion of each state.

Last, South Africa's Intended Nationally Determined Contribution was presented and evaluated.

In sum, the notion of CBDR remains functional under the Paris Agreement. Due to the lack of definitions as to what constitutes a *developed* or *developing* state, the agreement holds the potential of encouraging parties to take more efficient and more ambitious measures to adapt to and mitigate the impacts of climate change.

References

1. Stokke, O. (2009). *The UN and development: From aid to cooperation*. Indiana University Press.
2. Hicks, N., & Streeten, P. (1979). Indicators of development: The search for a basic needs yardstick. *World Development*.
3. Lenzi, T. (2017). *Recognition and application of the least developed country category by UN development system organizations*. United Nations Committee for Development Policy.
4. Glazewski, J., & Du Toit, L. (2013). *Environmental law in South Africa*. Butterworth Publishers (Pty.) Ltd, South Africa; UNFCCC art 4(8).
5. Khokhar, T., & Serajuddin, U. (2015). *The World Bank*.
6. Gupta, J. (2006). International law and climate change: The challenges facing developing countries. *Yearbook of International Environmental Law*.
7. Birnie, P., et al. (2009). *International law and the environment*. Oxford University Press.
8. Honkonen, T. (2009). *The common but differentiated responsibility principle in multilateral environmental agreements: Regulatory and policy aspects*. Kluwer Law International.
9. Matsui, Y. (2004). The principle of "common but differentiated responsibilities. In N. Schrijver & F. Weiss (Eds.), *International law and sustainable development: Principles and practice*. Martinus Nijhoff Publishers Leiden.
10. Sands, P., et al. (2012). *Principles of international environmental law*. Cambridge University Press.
11. Abeysinghe, A. C., & Arias, G. (2013). CBDR as a principle of inspiring actions rather than justifying inaction in the global climate change regime. In O. Ruppel, C. Roschmann, & K. Ruppel-Schlichting (Eds.), *Climate change: International law and global governance*. Nomos Verlagsgesellschaft Baden-Baden, Germany.
12. Gladwin, T. N. (1987). Environment development and multinational enterprise. In C. S. Pearson (Eds.), *Multinational corporations, environment, and the third world: Business matters*. Duke Press Policy Studies.
13. Voigt, C., & Ferreira, F. (2016). Differentiation in the Paris Agreement. *Climate Law*.
14. Mace, M. (2016). Mitigation commitments under the Paris Agreement and the way forward. *Climate Law*.

Chapter 6
Must Investments Contribute to the Development of the Host State? The *Salini* Test Scrutinised

Dai Tamada

Abstract The *Salini* test, established in the *Salini* case, is composed of four conditions for identifying what constitutes an *investment* under Article 25(1) of the ICSID Convention. This test, however, is among the most controversial topics in investor-State arbitration, as it has been accepted by many tribunals, whilst, at the same time, has been widely criticised by many other tribunals. Among the four conditions, the most criticised is the fourth; namely, the contribution of a transaction to the *economic development* of the host State. Post-*Salini* tribunals have been divided into two camps: one, which accepts the *Salini* test per se, and another, which criticises, modifies, or outright rejects any such economic development condition. So far, these two trends in the arbitral jurisprudence have yet to be reconciled and, thus, it would be premature to identify a definitive conclusion as to whether the *Salini* test holds as it is, or has been modified or entirely rejected by post-*Salini* tribunals. That said, the *Salini* test, particularly the development condition, presents a precious opportunity to reconsider the relationship between *investment* and *development*, both of which, at varying degrees, represent key aspects of the international legal system pertaining to the resolution of investment disputes. At the same time, through the prism of this relationship, there is scope to introduce variations to the notion of *development*, namely, that of *sustainable development*. This contribution aims at outlining the principal contours of the argumentation that seeks to introduce this notion in international investment law and arbitration.

Keywords Investor-State arbitration · ICSID · Definition of investment · The *Salini* test · Economic development · Sustainable development

---

D. Tamada (✉)
Graduate School of Law, Kobe University, 2-1 Rokkodaicho, Nadaku, Kobe 657-8501, Japan
e-mail: tamada@port.kobe-u.ac.jp

P. Szwedo et al. (eds.), *Law and Development*, Kobe University Monograph Series in Social Science Research, https://doi.org/10.1007/978-981-13-9423-2_6

6.1 Introduction

In investor-State arbitration, a seemingly simple question that has been posed and which remains widely debated is whether foreign *investment* must contribute to the *development* of the host State. Needless to say, the notion of *investment* is pivotal in international investment agreements (IIAs) and investor-State arbitration, since their main purpose is the protection of *investment*. However, what constitutes an *investment* is not always clearly defined in IIAs or the ICSID Convention. *First*, States may freely define the notion of investment in their IIAs. However, IIAs normally contain non-exhaustive lists as to what constitutes *investment*, including all manner of assets. Against this broad definition, or lack of definition per se, scholars have long attempted to limit the scope of investment, by excluding, for example, types of assets such as portfolio investments and indirect investment.[1] In actual investment cases, in any event, the definition issue may be resolved pursuant to the definition provision specific to each IIA and the specific context of each IIA. *Second*, to the contrary, the 1965 Convention on the Settlement of Investment Disputes between States and Nationals of Other States (ICSID Convention) contains no definition of *investment* and, as a result, should an investor attempt recourse to an ICSID tribunal, it would have to inevitably address the definition issue, should this be posed. In that sense, the definition issue under the ICSID Convention is of broader significance than that of IIAs. In addition, this issue appears as that of jurisdiction *ratione materiae*, since Article 25(1) of the ICSID Convention allows tribunals to establish jurisdiction solely on *investment*, as follows:

> The *jurisdiction* of the Centre shall extend to any legal dispute *arising directly out of an investment*, between a Contracting State (or any constituent subdivision or agency of a Contracting State designated to the Centre by that State) and a national of another Contracting State, which the parties to the dispute consent in writing to submit to the Centre. When the parties have given their consent, no party may withdraw its consent unilaterally (emphasis added).

The definitional issue has been raised in terms of objections to the jurisdiction of the ICSID tribunals. In response to this, the tribunal in the *Salini* case formulated the so-called *Salini* test, composed of four conditions for the purposes of determining whether a transaction amounts to an *investment* within the context of the ICSID Convention. This chapter focuses on the content of the *Salini* test, with particular attention to its fourth condition, which requires that for a positive finding of *investment* that it ought to contribute to the development of the host State. In other words, unless an asset or operation contributes to the host State's development, it cannot constitute investment under the ICSID Convention, and, consequently, cannot justify the jurisdiction *ratione materiae* of the ICSID tribunal. Inevitably, this leads one to consider and re-analyse the relationship between investment and development. As the drafting history of the ICSID Convention lends little support for clarifying the integrity of the *Salini* test, including its fourth condition,[2] the analysis takes arbitral

[1] Sornarajah [1].

[2] Fellenbaum [2].

practice as its starting point, hence the focus on the pre- and post-*Salini* cases, and the *Salini* case itself in subsequent sections.

6.2 The *Salini* Test: Background, Implications and Acceptance

*6.2.1 Pre-***Salini** *Cases Relating to the Definition of Investment*

It would be incorrect to claim that the *Salini* tribunal clarified, for the first time in the history of the ICSID Convention, the conditions of investment.[3] The tribunal in *Fedax v. Venezuela* (1997)[4] had already shown certain criteria of investment, where the issue before the tribunal had been whether an acquisition of promissory notes, issued by the Venezuelan state in connection with the contract, constitutes investment.[5] The tribunal stated as follows:

> The basic features of an investment have been described as involving a certain duration, a certain regularity of profit and return, assumption of risk, a substantial commitment and *a significance for the host State's development*. [...] And most importantly, there is clearly *a significant relationship between the transaction and the development of the host State*, as specifically required under the Law for issuing the pertinent financial instrument. It follows that, given the particular facts of the case, the transaction meets the basic features of an investment (emphasis added).[6]

This finding is worth being analysed from several perspectives. *First*, the *Fedax* formula is based on the scholarly opinion of Professor Schreuer,[7] and is composed of five elements, which are almost identical to the *Salini* test, apart from the element of 'regularity of profit and return'. Several tribunals in the pre-[8] and post-*Salini* cases followed the *Fedax* formula, rather than the *Salini* test in relation to the post-*Salini* cases. *Second*, according to the *Fedax* tribunal, the promissory notes satisfy the condition of 'significance of the host State's development', even though the financial

---

[3]Kang [3, pp. 159–160].

[4]*Fedax N.V. v. Venezuela* is one of them. *Fedax N.V. v. Venezuela*, ICISD Case No. ARB/96/3, Award on Jurisdiction (11 July 1997).

[5]The tribunal explains the 'promissory note' as follows: '[a] promissory note is by definition an instrument of credit, a written recognition that a loan has been made. In this particular case the six promissory notes in question were issued by the Republic of Venezuela in order to acknowledge its debt for the provision of services under a contract signed in 1988 with Industrias Metalúrgicas Van Dam C. A.; Venezuela had simply received a loan for the amount of the notes for the time period specified therein and with the corresponding obligation to pay interest'. Ibid., para. 37.

[6]Ibid., para. 43.

[7]Ibid., endnote 63; Schreuer [4].

[8]*Consortium R.F.C.C. v. Kingdom of Morocco*, ICSID Case No. ARB/00/6, Decision on Jurisdiction (16 July 2001), para. 65.

instrument—in that case, the promissory notes—was generally regarded as borderline. *Third*, crucially, the *Fedax* formula does not express the conditions under the ICSID Convention Article 25(1), since it regarded Article 25(1) as only requiring consent of the contracting States, which is expressed in a particular IIA.[9] Consequently, the jurisdictional requirements under the ICSID Convention and under a particular IIA are integrated into one whole, and this is why the *Fedax* formula should be understood as containing the criteria of investment under both instruments.[10]

A further pre-*Salini* case is *CSOB v. Slovakia* (1999)[11] in which a near-identical issue was raised to the tribunal, and identical reasoning was advanced by the tribunal. *First*, the tribunal had to address whether a loan constitutes investment under the ICSID Convention *and* the BIT. The tribunal answered affirmatively that '[t]his is so, if only because under certain circumstances a loan may contribute substantially to a State's economic development'.[12] *Second*, as to the definition of investment, the tribunal integrated the ICSID Convention and the BIT as a whole, in the same ways as the *Fedax* tribunal. As shall be addressed in subsequent sections of this chapter, the *Salini* tribunal isolated the ICSID investment from the BIT investment for the first time,[13] which is the reason that the *Salini* case is regarded as the leading case on the definition of investment *under the ICSID Convention*. *Third*, notably, the *CSOB* tribunal relied on the preamble of the ICSID Convention to deduce the development condition.[14]

6.2.2 *The* Salini *Test*

In *Salini v. Morocco* (2001),[15] the tribunal had to consider whether a construction contract with regard to a highway qualified as investment under the ICSID Convention. On this, the tribunal stated as follows:

---

[9] *Fedax v. Venezuela*, *supra* note 4, para. 21. The tribunal, quoting the opinion of Mr. A. Broches, stated that 'the requirement that the dispute must have arisen out of an 'investment' [under Article 25(1) of the ICSID Convention] may be *merged into the requirement of consent* to jurisdiction' (emphasis added).

[10] Although the relationship between the ICSID Convention and IIAs, concerning the definition of *investment*, has been widely discussed, the present analysis does not touch upon this aspect.

[11] *Ceskoslovenska Obchodni Banka, A.S. (CSOB) v. The Slovak Republic*, ICSID Case No. ARB/97/4, Decision of the Tribunal on Objections to Jurisdiction (24 May 1999).

[12] Ibid., para. 76.

[13] Gaillard and Banifatemi [5, p. 107].

[14] *CSOB v. Slovakia*, *supra* note 11, para. 64. The tribunal stated that '[t]his language [economic development] permits an inference that an international transaction which contributes to cooperation designed to promote the economic development of a Contracting State may be deemed to be an investment as that term is understood in the Convention'.

[15] *Salini Construttori S.p.A. and Italstrade S.p.A. v. Morocco*, ICSID Case No. ARB/00/4, Decision on Jurisdiction (23 July 2001).

> The doctrine generally considers that investment infers: contributions, a certain duration of performance of the contract and a participation in the risks of the transaction (*cf. commentary by E. Gaillard, cited above, p. 292*). In reading the Convention's preamble, one may add the contribution to the economic development of the host State of the investment as an additional condition.[16]

This part of the decision contains the *Salini* test, composed of four conditions of investment, namely: the contribution of money or assets; a certain duration; the element of risk; and a contribution to the economic development of the host State. Several points should be mentioned to facilitate an understanding of the *Salini* test. *First*, the *Salini* test is applicable only within the context of the interpretation and application of the ICSID Convention. Consequently, non-ICSID tribunals are not necessarily required to apply the *Salini* test as a question of law.[17] *Second*, the *Salini* test is based on an *objective* approach,[18] independent from the *subjective* perception of investment by the contracting Parties as may be expressed in individual IIAs. Therefore, different to the situation in the pre-*Salini* cases, the *Salini* test concentrates on the definition of investment only under the ICSID Convention, setting aside the definition under any IIA. *Third*, it seems that the development condition was transplanted from the preamble of the ICSID Convention.[19] However, this was inspired more directly by an academic opinion of Georges Delaume, who had suggested a flexible test of investment by proposing a definition of investment based on 'the expected—if not always actual—contribution of the investment to the economic development of the country in question'.[20] *Fourth*, the tribunal indicates some flexibility on the development condition, by stating that 'one may add' it to other three conditions. This suggests that it is not a mandatory, but an optional condition, depending on the tribunal's evaluation in each case. In addition, the *Salini* tribunal did not make clear whether the four conditions must be examined individually or in combination. The tribunal seems to have chosen the latter, by stating that 'these various criteria should be assessed *globally* even if, for the sake of reasoning, the Tribunal considers them individually here' (emphasis added).[21] Consequently, the development condition should not be examined independently from the other three conditions. *Fifth*, what is important is how to apply the development condition in actual cases. In the *Salini* case, that condition was not seriously discussed by the tribunal, which simply concluded that:

> […] the contribution of the contract to the economic development of the Moroccan State cannot seriously be questioned. In most countries, the construction of infrastructure falls

[16]Ibid., para. 52.

[17]Although non-ICSID tribunals have also adopted the *Salini* test, their decisions are not being analysed as part of this contribution and will be so in a different opportunity.

[18]The *Salini* tribunal stated that 'ICSID case law and legal authors agree that the investment requirement must be respected as *an objective condition* of the jurisdiction of the Centre [ICSID]' (emphasis added). *Salini v. Morocco*, *supra* note 15, para. 52.

[19]Emmanuel Gaillard and Yas Banifatemi, *supra* note 13, p. 98.

[20]Delaume [6, p. 801]. English translation is based on the following article. Ibid., pp. 115–116.

[21]*Salini v. Morocco*, *supra* note 15, para. 52.

> under the tasks to be carried out by the State or by other public authorities. It cannot be seriously contested that the highway in question *shall serve the public interest.* Finally, the Italian companies were also able to provide the host State of the investment with *know-how in relation to the work to be accomplished* (emphasis added).[22]

The *Salini* tribunal makes it clear that the contract on the construction of infrastructure serves the *public interest* of the host State and, because of this, satisfies the development condition. This reasoning is reminiscent of *Consortium R.F.C.C. v. Morocco* (2001), in which the tribunal admitted the existence of a contribution in entirely identical words to those stated in the *Salini* case,[23] namely that:

> [s]'agissant enfin de *la contribution du marché au développement économique de l'Etat marocain*, celle-ci ne peut sérieusement être discutée. La construction des infrastructures relève, dans la plupart des pays, des tâches de l'Etat ou d'autres collectivités publiques. Il ne peut être sérieusement contesté que *l'autoroute en cause servira l'intérêt public*. Enfin, le Consortium était également à même d'apporter à l'Etat d'accueil de l'investissement *un savoir-faire en relation avec l'ouvrage à réaliser* (emphasis added).[24]

This reasoning, identical to that in the *Salini* case, suggests that, insofar as an operation serves the *public interest*, it can be deemed to contribute to the development of the host State.

*6.2.3 Post-*Salini *Cases that Espouse the Development Condition*

The *Salini* test has been widely accepted and applied as a four-prong test that includes the development condition in the following post-*Salini* cases: *Joy Mining v. Egypt* (2004),[25] *Bayindir v. Pakistan* (2005),[26] *Jan de Nul v. Egypt* (2006),[27] *Helnan v. Egypt* (2006),[28] *Saipem v. Bangladesh* (2007),[29] *Kardassopoulos v. Georgia* (2007),[30] and

---

[22]Ibid., para. 57.

[23]This is due to the same three arbitrators, namely, Robert Briner (president), Bernardo Cremades and Ibrahim Fadlallah, being present in both cases.

[24]*Consortium R.F.C.C. v. Morocco*, *supra* note 8, para. 65.

[25]*Joy Mining Machinery Limited v. Egypt*, ISCID Case No. ARB/03/11, Award (30 July 2004), para. 53.

[26]*Bayindir Insaat Ticaret Ve Sanayi AS v. Islamic Republic of Pakistan*, ICSID Case No. ARB/03/29, Decision on Jurisdiction (14 November 2005), para. 130.

[27]*Jan de Nul N.V. and Dredging International N.V. v. Arab Republic of Egypt*, ICSID Case No. ARB/04/13, Decision on Jurisdiction (16 June 2006), para. 91.

[28]*Helnan International Hotels v. Egypt*, ICSID Case No. ARB/05/19, Decision on Objection to Jurisdiction (17 October 2006), para. 77.

[29]*Saipem S.p.A. v. Bangladesh*, ICSID Case No. ARB/05/07, Decision on Jurisdiction (21 March 2007), para. 99.

[30]*Ioannis Kardassopoulos v. Georgia*, ICSID Case No. ARB/05/18, Decision on Jurisdiction (6 July 2007), para. 116.

Millicom v. Senegal (2010).[31] In *Joy Mining v. Egypt* (2004), for example, the tribunal adopted almost the same conditions as the *Salini* test, where it stated that:

> Summarizing the elements that an activity must have in order to qualify as an investment, both the ICSID decisions mentioned above and the commentators thereon have indicated that the project in question should have a certain duration, a regularity of profit and return, an element of risk, a substantial commitment and that *it should constitute a significant contribution to the host State's development*. To what extent these criteria are met is of course specific to each particular case as they will normally depend on the circumstances of each case (emphasis added).[32]

In the above decision, the tribunal adopted five conditions, relying on the opinion of Professor Christoph Schreuer.[33] One added condition was 'a regularity of profit and return', which had already appeared in the *Fedax* formula. As to the development condition, the qualification *significant* was added to the contribution that requires a quantitatively considerable amount of contribution, which was lacking in the *Salini* test.[34] Following *Joy Mining v. Egypt*, the *Salini* test was further accepted, with slight modifications, by other tribunals. In *Helnan v. Egypt* (2006), the tribunal followed the *Salini* test and, with regard to the development condition, stated that '[a]s for the contribution to the development of the EGYPT's [sic] development, the importance of the tourism industry in the Egyptian economy makes it obvious'.[35] In *Saipem v. Bangladesh* (2007), in the same sense, the tribunal relied on the *Salini* test, but referred to it as the four 'elements'.[36] Having applied the four conditions to the case, the tribunal concluded that 'Saipem has made an investment within the meaning of Article 25 of the ICSID Convention',[37] although it is not clear whether the tribunal applied the development condition to this case disjunctively yet along with the other condition.[38]

---

[31] *Millicom International Operations B.V. and Sentel GSM S.A. v. Republic of Senegal*, ICSID Case No. ARB/08/20, Decision on Jurisdiction (16 July 2010), para. 80.

[32] *Joy Mining v. Egypt*, *supra* note 25, para. 53. The tribunal did not clarify whether five elements were based on the *Salini* test, even though it referred to the *Salini* case. *Ibid.*, para. 51.

[33] Ibid., footnote 18; Schreuer [7].

[34] *Malaysian Historical Salvors Sdn Bhd (MHS) v. Government of Malaysia*, ICSID Case No. ARB/05/10, Award (17 May 2007), para. 114.

[35] *Helnan v. Egypt*, *supra* note 28, para. 77.

[36] *Saipem v. Bangladesh*, *supra* note 29, para. 99.

[37] Ibid., para. 111.

[38] The tribunal states that 'for the purpose of determining whether there is an investment under Article 25 of the ICSID Convention, it will consider the entire operation. In the present case, the entire or overall operation includes the Contract, the construction itself, the Retention Money, the warranty and the related ICC Arbitration'. Ibid., para. 110. There is no mention by the tribunal to the economic development of the host State.

6.2.4 *Interim Evaluation*

The *Salini* test, composed of four conditions, was invented for the purpose of identifying whether a transaction amounts to an investment within the context of Article 25(1) of the ICSID Convention. It has been accepted and applied widely in several post-*Salini* cases. Consequently, it is possible to provisionally conclude that 'the case law is *progressively evolving* towards a greater recognition of the *Salini* criteria' (emphasis added),[39] and, more simply, that the *Salini* test constitutes '*un courant jurisprudential*'[40] within the context of ICSID dispute resolution. Moreover, it should be pointed out that, in many of the cases mentioned earlier, there was little need for tribunals to examine severely or individually whether the development condition had been met, since the operation or property in question was easily categorised as investment.

6.3 Criticism of the *Salini* Test

Most crucially, it should be noted that the *Salini* test, particularly in connection to the development condition, has been criticised and rejected by several tribunals. For example, although the *Saipem* tribunal adopted and applied the *Salini* test, as mentioned earlier, it observed that '[t]he need for the last element [contribution to the host State's development] is sometimes put in doubt'.[41] It is thus necessary to analyse the reasons behind the criticism that the development condition has attracted.

6.3.1 *Text Takes Priority Over the Preamble*

Initial criticism is based on the interpretation methodology in the *Salini* test, which gives undue weight to the preamble of a treaty. The preamble of the ICSID Convention provides, in its first sentence, that the Contracting States consider 'the need for international cooperation for *economic development*, and the role of private international investment therein' (emphasis added) and, as mentioned earlier, the term *economic development* in the *Salini* test has been inducted from this preamble.[42]

According to this criticism, even though the preamble refers to *economic development*, this cannot be directly incorporated into the interpretation of a treaty term or provision, namely Article 25(1) of the Convention.[43] The customary rule of treaty

[39]Emmanuel Gaillard and Yas Banifatemi, *supra* note 13, p. 124.

[40]*L.E.S.I. S.p.A. et ASTALDI S.p.A. c/ République algérienne démocratique et populaire*, CIRDI No. ARB/05/3, Décision (12 Juillet 2006), para. 72.

[41]*Saipem v. Bangladesh, supra* note 29, footnote 22.

[42]More clearly, *CSOB v. Slovakia, supra* note 11, para. 64.

[43]Fellenbaum [8].

interpretation, as reflected in Articles 31 and 32 of the Vienna Convention on the Law of Treaties (VCLT), dictate that the ordinary meaning of the terms of the text itself is the starting point of the interpretative exercise, and this takes priority over the general object and purpose of a treaty.[44] In *Saba Fakes v. Turkey* (2010),[45] for example, the tribunal stated that 'the criteria of (i) a contribution (ii) a certain duration, and (iii) an element of risk, are both necessary and sufficient to define an investment within the framework of the ICSID Convention. […] These three criteria derive from the ordinary meaning of the word "investment"'.[46] As to the economic development condition, then, the tribunal observed that it was:

> not convinced […] that a contribution to the host State's economic development constitutes a criterion of an investment within the framework of the ICSID Convention. Those tribunals that have considered this element as a separate requirement for the definition of an investment, such as the *Salini* Tribunal, have mainly relied on the preamble to the ICSID Convention to support their conclusions. The present Tribunal observes that while the preamble refers to the "*need for international cooperation for economic development,*" *it would be excessive to attribute to this reference a meaning and function that is not obviously apparent from its wording*. In the Tribunal's opinion, while the economic development of a host State is one of the proclaimed objectives of the ICSID Convention, *this objective is not in and of itself an independent criterion for the definition of an investment* (emphasis added).[47]

This understanding was accepted by another tribunal in *Quiborax v. Bolivia* (2012).[48]

6.3.2 Redundant Due to the Other Three Conditions?

The development condition is criticised because it can be fully covered by the previous three conditions. In *LESI-Dipenta v. Algeria* (2005),[49] for example, the tribunal omitted the development condition and applied the remaining three conditions to the case, by stating that:

> (iv) [i]t would seem consistent with the objective of the Convention that a contract, in order to be considered an investment within the meaning of the provision, should fulfill the following three conditions:
>
> (a) the contracting party has made contributions in the host country;
>
> (b) those contributions had a certain duration; and
>
> (c) they involved some risks for the contributor.

[44] de Figueiredo [9].

[45] *Saba Fakes v. Republic of Turkey*, ICSID Case No. ARB/07/20, Award (14 July 2010).

[46] Ibid., para. 110.

[47] Ibid., para. 111.

[48] *Quiborax S.A., Non Metallic Minerals S.A. and Allan Fosk Kaplún v. Plurinational State of Bolivia*, ICSID Case No. ARB/06/2, Decision on Jurisdiction (27 September 2012), para. 212.

[49] *Consorzio Groupement L.E.S.I. – DIPENTA v. People's Democratic Republic of Algeria*, ICSID Case No. ARB/03/8, Award (10 January 2005).

> On the other hand, it is not necessary that the investment contribute more specifically to the host country's economic development, *something that is difficult to ascertain and that is implicitly covered by the other three criteria* (emphasis added).[50]

Similar reasoning was advanced by other tribunals, including *LESI-Astaldi v. Algeria* (2006)[51] and *RSM v. Central African Republic* (2010).[52] According to those tribunals, it is difficult to establish that the development condition was met and, furthermore, it is covered by the previous three conditions. The details of such reasoning will be discussed in subsequent sections.

6.3.3 Development as an Expected Consequence of Successful Investment

The most substantive criticism against the *Salini* test, and, in particular against the development condition, is based on the view that the contribution to the economic development of the host State is a *consequence* of investment, not an *a priori requirement* for qualifying as investment. This understanding was rapidly espoused by several tribunals around 2010, while its origin may be located earlier in *Pey Casado v. Chile* (2008),[53] in which the tribunal had stated that:

> L'exigence d'une contribution au développement de l'Etat d'accueil, difficile à établir, lui paraît en effet relever davantage du fond du litige que de la compétence du Centre. Un investissement peut s'avérer utile ou non pour l'Etat d'accueil sans perdre cette qualité. Il est exact que le préambule de la Convention CIRDI évoque la contribution au développement économique de l'Etat d'accueil. *Cette référence est cependant présentée comme une conséquence, non comme une condition de l'investissement*: en protégeant les investissements, la Convention favorise le développement de l'Etat d'accueil. Cela ne signifie pas que le développement de l'Etat d'accueil soit un élément constitutif de la notion d'investissement. C'est la raison pour laquelle, comme l'ont relevé certains tribunaux arbitraux, cette quatrième condition est en réalité englobée dans les trois premières (emphasis added).[54]

It is stated here that the contribution to the host State's economic development is a *consequence* of investment, not a *condition* for investment. This means that, even if, at the early stage of investment, an operation cannot bring any benefit to the host State, it nonetheless constitutes investment within the context of ICSID Convention proceedings. This basic understanding has been accepted, albeit with some variation as to the underlying reasoning.

---

[50] Ibid., [Section: Questions of law], para. 13(iv).

[51] *L.E.S.I. – ASTALDI v. Algeria*, *supra* note 40, para. 72(iv).

[52] *RSM Production Corporation c. La République centrafricaine*, CIRDI Affaire No. ARB/07/02, Décision sur la compétence et la responsabilité (7 decembre 2010), para. 56.

[53] *Victor Pey Casado et Fondation «Présidente allende» c. République du Chili*, CIRDI affaire No. ARB/98/2, sentence arbitrale (8 mai 2008).

[54] Ibid., para. 232.

6.3.3.1 Successful Investment

First, at the outset of an investment, there is only an expectation of future success and, thus, any possible contribution to the economic development of the host State is not yet certain. The tribunal in *Quiborax v. Bolivia* (2012)—adopting the first three conditions approach and eschewing the development condition—explained this as follows:

> The Tribunal appreciates that the element of contribution to the development of the host State is generally regarded as part of the well-known four-prong Salini test. Yet, such contribution may well be *the consequence of a successful investment*; it does not appear as *a requirement*. If the investment fails, it may end up having made *no contribution* to the host State's development. This does not mean that it is not an investment. For this reason and others, tribunals have excluded this element from the definition of investment (emphasis added).[55]

Furthermore, the tribunal in *KT Asia v. Kazakhstan* (2012) adopted this reasoning in denying the development condition.[56] This is predicated on the simple assumption that only when an investment is successful, can there be some contribution to the development of the host State. However, even when an investment was not successful, thus not productive, there must be an investment, independent of whether its operation had been successful.

6.3.3.2 Expected Contribution or Desirable Consequence?

According to the foregoing, the key factor in establishing whether a transaction constitutes an investment should be found in its *expectation* of a successful result. It should be recalled, in this context, that the development condition, included in the *Salini* test, had originally been inspired by a scholarly opinion of Georges Delaume, according to which an investment should be identified on 'the *expected—if not always actual*—contribution of the investment to the economic development of the country in question' (emphasis added).[57] This means that, if there is an *expectation* of contribution this is enough for qualifying as an investment, even if it does not result in any actual benefit or merit to the host State. For example, if an investment contract for the drilling of several potential oil fields was concluded and the project had commenced, there must already be an investment at this moment, even if it will not successfully result in a finding of a productive oil field in the host State. In line with this argument, the tribunal in *Saba Fakes v. Turkey* (2010) held that:

> [t]he promotion and protection of investments in host States is *expected* to contribute to their economic development. Such development is *an expected consequence*, not a separate requirement, of the investment projects carried out by a number of investors in the aggregate. Taken in isolation, certain individual investments might be useful to the State and to the

[55] *Quiborax v. Bolivia*, *supra* note 48, para. 220.

[56] *KT Asia Investment Group B.V. v. Republic of Kazakhstan*, ICSID Case No. ARB/09/8, Award (17 October 2012), para. 171.

[57] Georges Delaume, *supra* note 20, p. 801.

> investor itself; certain might not. Certain investments *expected to be fruitful* may turn out to be economic disasters. They do not fall, for that reason alone, outside the ambit of the concept of investment (emphasis added).[58]

Such reasoning was also adopted by the tribunal in *Electrabel v. Hungary* (2012),[59] which, with regard to the development condition, observed that: 'the economic development of the host State is one of the objectives of the ICSID Convention and *a desirable consequence* of the investment, but it is not necessarily an element of an investment' (emphasis added).[60]

6.3.3.3 The Expectation Approach

According to the above *expectation-related* approach, the existence of investment must be admitted only where there is *expected contribution* to or a *desirable consequence* of the development of the host State. In other words, a presumption of contribution suffices for identifying an investment. This understanding gives rise to further issues. *First*, that there is an accurate manner by which to identify, characterise or consider the expectation seems doubtful. In *Electrabel v. Hungary* (2012), the tribunal explains the nature of *expectation* by stating that '[t]he expectation of profit and return which is sometimes viewed as a separate component of an investment must rather be considered as included in *the element of risk*, since every investment runs the risk of reaping no profit at all'.[61] Thus, the expectation approach results in a conclusion that the development condition may be subsumed by the risk condition. *Second*, the tribunal's examination of expectation must be based on a presumption. If we require an actual/existing consequence of investment, in the forms of benefit, merit, or advantage, this leads to a 'post hoc evaluation' of investment activities.[62] The *expected contribution* suggests, on the contrary, that the tribunal is not completely required to identify the existence of a contribution, but it will be sufficient to determine that an investment aims at contributing, or is expected to contribute, to the economic development of the host State. *Third*, based on the above understanding, it appears reasonable to think that the development condition, if applicable, should be examined, not at the jurisdictional phase, but at the merits phase. It should be recalled that the *Salini* test was elaborated as a jurisdictional test, by which ICSID tribunals are required to examine the existence of jurisdiction *ratione materiae*. Against this presupposition, the expectation approach appears to require the application of the

---

[58] *Saba Fakes v. Turkey, supra* note 45, para. 111.

[59] *Electrabel S.A. v. The Republic of Hungary*, ICSID Case No. ARB/07/19, Decision on Jurisdiction, Applicable Law and Liability (30 November 2012).

[60] Ibid., para. 5.43.

[61] Ibid.

[62] In *Alpha v. Ukraine* (2010), the tribunal stated that 'the contribution-to-development criterion [...] invites a tribunal to engage in a post hoc evaluation of the business, economic, financial and/or policy assessments that prompted the claimant's activities. It would not be appropriate for such a form of second-guessing to drive a tribunal's jurisdictional analysis'. *Alpha Projektholding GMBH v. Ukraine*, ICSID Case No. ARB/07/16, Award (8 November 2010), para. 312.

development condition at the merits phase. In *Pey Casado v. Chile* (2008), in fact, the tribunal pointed out that:

> L'exigence d'une contribution au développement de l'Etat d'accueil, difficile à établir, *lui paraît en effet relever davantage du fond du litige que de la compétence du Centre* (emphasis added).[63]

6.3.4 Vagueness and Broadness of the Notion of Development

It is undeniable that, even if one were to reject the expectation approach, the terms *contribution* and *development/economic development* are too vague and extremely broad, possibly allowing the term *investment* to extend to any kind of asset or operation. In other words, if the development condition is not applied strictly, it may not serve the function of setting an outer-limit of the scope of the term *investment*.

6.3.4.1 Flexible Condition

Even if one were to maintain the development condition, it may not have any significance in the actual case of application, since its threshold is too low to exclude certain categories of investments. In *Patrick Mitchell v. Congo* (2006), for example, the annulment tribunal took the position that the development condition, if accepted, requires only a quite small amount of contribution, by stating as follows:

> The ad hoc Committee wishes nevertheless to specify that, in its view, the existence of a contribution to the economic development of the host State as an essential – although not sufficient – characteristic or unquestionable criterion of the investment, *does not mean* that this contribution must always be *sizable or successful*; and, of course, ICSID tribunals do not have to evaluate the real contribution of the operation in question. It suffices for the operation to contribute *in one way or another* to the economic development of the host State, and this concept of economic development is, in any event, *extremely broad but also variable* depending on the case (emphasis added).[64]

This understanding corresponds to the arbitral practice in which ICSID tribunals quite flexibly applied the development condition. For example, the nature of investment was admitted not only with regard to construction contracts (*Salini v. Morocco*), but also to promissory notes (*Fedax v. Venezuela*) and loans (*CSOB v. Slovakia*). As is clear here, the pre-*Salini* tribunals adopted a loose criterion of 'contribution' and, consequently, the development condition was applied as a low threshold.

Conversely, however, some tribunals have *strictly* applied the development condition. In *MHS v. Malaysia* (2007), for example, the tribunal examined whether a

---

[63] *Pey Casado c. Chili*, *supra* note 53, para. 232.

[64] *Mr. Patrick Mitchell v. Democratic Republic of Congo*, ICSID Case No. ARB/99/7, Decision on the Application for the Annulment of the Award (1 November 2006), para. 33.

contract on the cargo salvage operation contributes to the development of Malaysia, by using the *significant* contribution criterion.[65] Based on this, the tribunal concluded that the contract does not satisfy the development condition, since 'the Contract did not benefit the Malaysian *public interest* in a material way or serve to *benefit* the Malaysian economy in the sense developed by ICSID jurisprudence, namely that the contributions were significant' (emphasis added).[66] This finding should be considered exceptional,[67] since the tribunal itself emphasised the 'unusual' character of the case.[68] In that case, an interesting issue was raised—namely, whether there could be a contribution to the *historical and cultural* development of Malaysia, had the salvage operation been successful. On this issue, however, the tribunal denied the *significant* contribution to the *economic* development of the host State, stating that:

> [t]o the extent that the Claimant had provided *gainful employment* to these Malaysians, the Tribunal accepts that the Contract did benefit the Malaysian public interest and economy *to some extent*. However, this benefit is not of the same *quality or quantity* envisaged in previous ICSID jurisprudence. The benefits which the Contract brought to the Respondent are largely *cultural and historical*. These benefits, and any other direct financial benefits to the Respondent, have not been shown to have led to *significant* contributions to the Respondent's *economy* in the sense envisaged in ICSID jurisprudence (emphasis added).[69]

Here, the tribunal understood the development condition as requiring *significant* contribution to the *economic* development of the host State,[70] excluding contributions of 'cultural and historical' significance alone. Pursuant to this qualification, it may be said that the investment arbitral jurisprudence is progressively evolving towards requiring an economic, as opposed to a purely legal, concept of investment.[71]

6.3.4.2 Subjective Condition

Second, as a consequence of its vagueness, the development condition is deemed as being substantially 'subjective', depending on the tribunal's case-by-case evaluation.[72] To respond to this issue, some tribunals considered alternatives. In *RSM v. Central African Republic* (2010), for example, the tribunal observed that 'the criterion of the contribution to the development is *too subjective* and it must be replaced by the criterion of *the contribution to the economy*, which itself is considered as

---

[65] *MHS v. Malaysia*, *supra* note 34, paras. 124 and 130.

[66] Ibid., para. 131.

[67] E.g. Chierici [10, p. 161].

[68] *MHS v. Malaysia*, *supra* note 34, para. 124. The tribunal describes the circumstances of the case as 'unusual situations'.

[69] *MHS v. Malaysia*, *supra* note 34, para. 132.

[70] The tribunal observed quite clearly that '[t]he *economic impact* of the benefits of the Contract must be assessed to determine whether there was an "investment"' (emphasis added). Ibid., para. 138.

[71] Emmanuel Gaillard and Yas Banifatemi, *supra* note 13, p. 124.

[72] As to the need of an industry-specific evaluation, particularly with regard to the entertainment sector, *see* Engfeldt [11].

presumed included in the three other criteria' (emphasis added).[73] Here, the tribunal proposes to replace the term *development* with the term *economy*. Similarly, the tribunal in *Phoenix v. Czech Republic* (2009)[74] highlighted the difficulties stemming from the subjectivity of the development condition:

> [t]he contribution of an international investment to the development of the host State is impossible to ascertain […]. A less ambitious approach should therefore be adopted, centered on the contribution of an international investment to *the economy* of the host State, which is indeed normally inherent in the mere concept of investment as shaped by elements of contribution/duration/risk, and should therefore in principle be presumed (emphasis added).[75]

Even if we replace the term *development* with that of *economy*, the problem is not necessarily resolved, since the latter is arguably wider in scope, and does not seem to shed more light on what kind of asset or operation would produce at least some benefits or merits to the host State's economy. For example, any kind of transaction or operation may bring know-how, development of human capital, and other benefits to the host State and its population. In this sense, any investment is possibly presumed to contribute to the host State's economy in one way or another.

6.3.5 *Other Conditions Have Been Added*

Several tribunals have added further conditions to the *Salini* test, thus increasing it to five or six conditions. These additional conditions pertain to the investor's good faith establishment of investment, and the legality of investment under the host State's domestic law. In *Electrabel v. Hungary* (2012), for example, the tribunal had stated that:

> subject to the wording of the provision in the treaty for dispute resolution, the *legality of the investment* and the investor's *good faith* may be relevant as elements of the definition of an investment or as a bar to the exercise of jurisdiction or to investment protection on the merits (emphasis added).[76]

6.3.6 *Interim Evaluation*

Provisionally, it can be concluded that the *Salini* test has attracted much criticism, particularly with regard to the development condition. Overall, this could be seen

---

[73] *RSM c. La République centrafricaine*, *supra* note 52, para. 56. In original: 'le critère de la contribution au développement est trop subjectif et qu'il doit être remplacé par le critère de la contribution à l'économie, lui-même considéré comme présumé inclus dans les trois autres critères'.

[74] *PHOENIX Action, Ltd. v. The Czech Republic*, ICSID Case No. ARB/06/5, Award (15 April 2009).

[75] Ibid., para. 85.

[76] *Electrabel v. Hungary*, *supra* note 59, para. 5.43.

as an attempt of arbitral tribunals to depart from the *Salini* test in its original formula. This tendency and its implications can be summarised as follows: *First*, some tribunals totally neglected the development condition, and did not apply it in cases before them. Others, however, attempted to modify it by requiring—more onerously insofar as the investor is concerned—that there be *significant* contribution to the *economic* development of the host State for a transaction to be considered an investment for the purposes of redress under the ICSID Convention. *Second*, the essential question is *not* whether the development condition in the *Salini* test should be maintained. As discussed in the foregoing, even if one were to maintain it as a low threshold for the determination of an investment under the ICSID Convention, it would appear useless and meaningless in any such exercise. *Third*, criticism against the development condition appear rather technical, than substantive, in the sense that they do not touch upon the essential problem of how one is to conceive *development*, or, alternatively, *economy*, under the ICSID Convention and, more broadly, under international norms relating to investment. This shall be analysed in the following section.

6.4 Development-Friendly Definition of Investment

6.4.1 IDI Resolution (2013)

Although the development condition in the *Salini* test has been criticised, this condition is still supported by those who seek to emphasise the importance of the notion of *development* in the field of international law relating to investment. A 2013 Resolution of the *Institut de droit international* (IDI),[77] for instance, provides in Article 10 that:

> The definition of investment is determined according to the applicable international instruments, in compliance with the rules of interpretation mentioned in Articles 1-2 and 4 above.
>
> Given the fact that investment arbitration can be initiated by investors solely on the basis of a treaty, *special weight must be given to the requirement that the investment contribute to the development of the host State*, as may appear in the relevant instrument (emphasis added).

It is evident that IDI espouses a development-friendly definition of investment,[78] thus accepting the development condition of the *Salini* test. It is necessary, however, to evaluate IDI's intention carefully. *First*, IDI in referring to the validity of recourse to a *development* element, states that this is so to the extent 'as may appear in the relevant instrument'. This suggests that IDI regards the development element not as a universal mandatory condition applicable from the outset, but as potentially being applicable where such an element has previously been incorporated in the IIA

[77] Resolution of Institut de droit international: 'Legal Aspects of Recourse to Arbitration by an Investor Against the Authorities of the Host State under Inter-State Treaties' (Rapporteur: M. Andrea Giardina), Session de Tokyo—2013 (13 September 2013).

[78] Acconci [12, pp. 69–90].

applicable to the parties. *Second*, the Resolution requires States only to give 'special weight' to the development element, leaving unclear whether States shall accept it when they conclude IIAs.

6.4.2 Vestige of Droit International du Développement

Some have argued that the International Centre for Settlement of Investment Disputes (ICSID), given its institutional frame and general purpose, should function in a way that addresses the issue of *poverty*, by promoting the economic development of the poorest countries.[79] Were one to see the World Bank and ICSID as mechanisms to promote the development of the poorest countries, it would appear entirely appropriate to understand that investments, in order to benefit from the protection of ICSID, ought to positively contribute to the economic development of host States.[80]

However, there are some issues to be addressed before espousing a development-friendly approach. *First*, international investment law and arbitration do not maintain a distinction between developed countries (home State) and the developing countries (host State) in the protection of investment. In the current situation, however, ICSID tribunals are faced with different situations, namely North-North and South-South relations of investment, in which the traditional differentiation between the developing countries and the developed countries has decreased in significance.[81] *Second*, the above development-friendly approach to investment protection is reminiscent of the New International Economic Order (NIEO), which, through resolutions of the UN General Assembly, purported to modify international investment law at that time, particularly with regard to expectations of compensation in cases of expropriation. The ultimate purpose was to bring some economic in the relationship between developing countries (the 'Global South') and developed countries (the 'Global North'). In the event, however, this one-sided movement, supported only by the developing countries, could not succeed. This suggests that the healthy development of international investment law must be based on a win-win basis between both sides; the capital-exporting countries and the capital-importing countries. If one insists only on the development-friendly side of the ICSID Convention, through the development condition of the *Salini* test, it must fail, because of the imbalance of interests.

---

[79]It is said that '[t]he function of the ICSID Convention perfectly fits within the mission of the World Bank to alleviate *poverty* and reduce the gap between developed and developing countries by *favouring the growth* of the latter. […] the analysis on the extent of ICSID jurisdiction cannot be detached from the role played by economic development of the host state, […] in the light of the institutional frame in which the Centre has been devised'. Stefano Chierici, *supra* note 67, p. 160.

[80]Ibid., pp. 175–176.

[81]Pia Acconci, *supra* note 78, p. 89.

6.4.3 Intersection with the Sustainable Development Concept

As arbitral trends remain fluid, it is too early to identify an emerging trend in arbitral jurisprudence, and generally in international investment law, that emphasises the importance of the *sustainable development*. It seems useful, however, to briefly look at what is argued, and to evaluate whether there is room for incorporating it into the definition of investment. *First*, most importantly in relation to our analysis, some authors promote the sustainable development concept by changing interpretations of existing IIAs,[82] irrespective of any modification of the treaty text itself.[83] In this respect, this line of argument can be intersected and addressed with the discussion surrounding the *Salini* test, since it relates only to the interpretation of the term *investment*. *Second*, as mentioned earlier, when the *Salini* tribunal applied the development condition in that case, it relied on the notion of *public interest*, by observing simply that 'the highway in question *shall serve the public interest*' (emphasis added). This reasoning allows us to consider the possibility of opening the door, through the notion of 'public interest', to the adoption of the sustainable development-friendly definition of investment. According to some, the sustainable development concept, in the context of investor-State arbitration, takes the form of the principle of good governance,[84] which is composed of the notions of transparency, anti-corruption,[85] due process and the rule of law. Needless to say, these all are reconcilable with the notion of *public interest*[86] and thus will be easily incorporated into the notion of *development* in the *Salini* test.

6.5 Conclusions

From around 2010, the arbitral jurisprudence tends to slowly depart from the *Salini* test, by criticising, modifying, or rejecting the development condition.[87] On the one hand, it might be possible to say that, setting aside this condition, there remains consensus among arbitrators and scholars to accept the *Salini* test. In that sense, the *Salini* test is possibly still alive and will be applied in future cases as a prototype of the notion of investment.[88] On the other hand, however, there is inconsistency in tribunal practice with regard to the notion of investment, which indicates a 'drifting' notion of

[82] See, for instance, Berner [13].

[83] Sacerdoti [14].

[84] Bonnitcha [15].

[85] The issue of corruption, in particular the corrupt investment, has been provoked in the investment cases. Tamada [16].

[86] Pia Acconci, *supra* note 78, p. 88. In this context, the principle of integration has been discussed and proposed to be introduced into the investor-State arbitration. Crockett [17].

[87] Emmanuel Gaillard and Yas Banifatemi, *supra* note 13, p. 119.

[88] Sungjin Kang, *supra* note 3, p. 187.

investment.[89] One should understand, from the above, the presence of difficulties in defining the notion of investment, particularly when one is to take into consideration the element of *development*.

A crucial point to be resolved is whether the development condition in the *Salini* test should be maintained, and, if so, in which form and to what effect. Unfortunately, arbitral tribunals have not yet been harmonised into a solid consistent jurisprudence in this regard. It is noteworthy, however, that the development condition in the *Salini* test relies on the notion of *public interest* which leaves for us—jurists, practitioners, and so on—the possibility to discuss the scope of *development* under the ICSID Convention and, more widely, the scope and significance of *sustainable development* in international investment law.

References

1. Sornarajah, M. (2011). The definition of foreign investment. In A. H. Qureshi & Z. Gao (Eds.), *International economic law: Critical concepts in law. Vol. IV. International investment law* (pp. 153–161).
2. Fellenbaum, J. (2012). Putting the needle to the Salini Bubble? In I. A. Laird & T. J. Weiler (Eds.), *Investment treaty arbitration and international law* (Vol. 3, pp. 115–117).
3. Kang, S. (2012). Definition of "Investment" under ICSID convention: Did we go beyond *Salini*? In I. A. Laird & T. J. Weiler (Eds.), *Investment treaty arbitration and international law* (Vol. 5).
4. Schreuer, C. (1996). Commentary on the ICSID convention. *ICSID Review - Foreign Investment Law Journal, 11,* 355–358.
5. Gaillard, E., & Banifatemi, Y. (2016). The Long March towards a Jurisprudence Constante on the Notion of Investment: Salini v. Morocco, ICSID Case No. ARB/00/4. In M. Kinnear, et al. (Eds.), *Building international investment law: The first 50 years of ICSID.*
6. Delaume, G. (1982). Le Centre international pour le règlement des différends relatifs aux investissements (CIRDI). *Journal du Droit International, 109.*
7. Schreuer, C. H. (2001). *The ICSID convention: A commentary* (p. 140).
8. Fellenbaum, J. (2011). *GEA v. Ukraine* and the Battle of Treaty Interpretation Principles over the Salini Test. *Arbitration International, 27*(2), 266.
9. de Figueiredo, R. C. (2017). The notion of investment and economic development under the ICSID Convention. In C. Baltag (Ed.), *ICSID Convention after 50 years: Unsettled issues* (p. 130).
10. Chierici, S. (2012). The definition of "Investment" in Article 25(1) ICSID Convention: A possible role of the neoclassical growth model and party autonomy. *The global community yearbook of international law and jurisprudence* (Vol. 1).
11. Engfeldt, H. J. (2014). Should ICSID Go Gangnam Style in Light of Non-Traditional Foreign Investments Including Those Spurred on by Social Media? Applying an Industry-Specific Lens to the Salini Test to Determine Article 25 Jurisdiction. *Berkeley Journal of International Law, 32*, 62–63.
12. Acconci, P. (2013). The "Unexpected" development-friendly definition of investment in the 2013 resolution of the *Institut de droit international. Italian yearbook of international law* (Vol. 23).
13. Berner, K. (2016). Reconciling investment protection and sustainable development: A plea for an interpretative U-Turn. In S. Hindelang & M. Krajewski (Eds.), *Shifting paradigms in international investment law: More balanced, less isolated, increasingly diversified* (pp. 202–203).

[89]Yala [18].

14. Sacerdoti, G. (2016). Investment protection and sustainable development. In S. Hindelang & M. Krajewski (Eds.), *Shifting paradigms in international investment law: More balanced, less isolated, increasingly diversified* (p. 39).
15. Bonnitcha, J. (2017). The principle of good governance in the reasoning of investor-State arbitral tribunals. In M.-C. C. Segger & J. C. G. Weeramantry (Eds.), *Sustainable development principles in the decisions of international courts and tribunals 1992–2012* (pp. 586–593).
16. Tamada, D. (2015). Host states as claimants: Corruption allegations. In S. Lalani & R. P. Lazo (Eds.), *The role of the state in investor-state arbitration* (pp. 103–122). Brill/Nijhoff.
17. Crockett, A. (2017). The integration principle in ICSID awards. In M.-C. C. Segger & J. C. G. Weeramantry (Eds.), *Sustainable development principles in the decisions of international courts and tribunals 1992–2012* (pp. 552–553).
18. Yala, F. (2005). The notion of "Investment" in ICSID Case Law: A drifting jurisdictional requirement? Some "Un-Conventional" thoughts on Salini, SGS and Mihaly. *Journal of International Arbitration, 22*(2), 125.

Chapter 7
Water: The Common Heritage of Mankind?

Franck Duhautoy

Abstract Historically, two models of access to water have coexisted: a natural resource, common good to be used free of charge, and a private economic good with an exchange value and thus generating a market. These two models, sometimes concomitant, draw their roots in a remote past. To enable social and economic development, they are present today in various national legal systems. Nowadays, under the supervision of legal authorities, water resources are also often described as being the *common heritage* of a nation with great freedom to use. Such notion of *heritage* aims at safeguarding the interests of future generations to water by promoting a sustainable development approach. Meanwhile, originating in the law of the sea, the notion of *common heritage of mankind* had initially triumphed in relation to outer space natural resources before it being challenged in some domestic legal orders that grant exploitation permits for outer space natural resources in a manner similar to the grant for the exploitation of water resources. For many, this is necessary to ensure the future development of humanity beyond the finite resources of our 'little' finite planet.

Keywords Common good · Private interests · Common heritage of mankind · Sustainable development · Space law

7.1 Introduction

Mankind is posing threats to its wellbeing, its development, and perhaps even to its survival.[1] We are exceeding planetary boundaries in many regards: excessive emissions of greenhouse gases that are precipitating global warming, ocean acidification, stratospheric ozone depletion, excessive nitrogen and phosphorus contamination as the result of heavy use of chemical fertilisers, excessive land use at the expense of other species, destruction of biodiversity (NB., we are experiencing Earth's sixth

[1] For some lessons from the past, see: Diamond [1].

F. Duhautoy (✉)
University of Warsaw, Centre of French Civilisation, ul. Dobra 55, 00-312 Warsaw, Poland
e-mail: franck.duhautoy@netcourrier.com

P. Szwedo et al. (eds.), *Law and Development*, Kobe University Monograph Series in Social Science Research, https://doi.org/10.1007/978-981-13-9423-2_7

great extinction wave), aerosol loading (microscopic particles in the atmosphere affecting climate and living organisms), industrial chemical pollution, introduction of novel entities (including radioactive materials, nano-materials, and micro-plastics) and overuse of freshwater.[2] The latter constitutes the essential substratum for life as we know it. Abundant water is a necessity to ensure human survival and the economic development of many sectors, including agriculture, agri-food, chemistry, textile, pharmacy, and many others. Effective protection of water resources is predicated on knowledge of its legal status. Contrary to what Adam Smith had thought, water goes beyond simple use value, and may also possess exchange value.[3]

However, who *owns* the water? Attempting to answer this inevitably brings to mind a well-known verse of Dante Alighieri (1265–1321) relating to his entry into Hell, guided of the Latin poet Virgil (70–19 BC): 'Abandon all hope, you who enter here'.[4] Indeed, enduring different social and political climates and domestic legal orders, throughout the vagaries of history, the status of water traverses between appropriation, common use, individualism, and common heritage. To confine in precise legal rules, such a flowing natural resource proves to be particularly thorny task. However, to question the existence of water appropriation is fundamental given that, one could argue, markets are constructs and not natural occurrences per se. Not to mention that, even such water resources placed out of commercial circulation (*extra commercium*) that are therefore free of use, may generate value from the services required for their extraction, transport, purification, and so on. Such activities—requirements for social or economic development—may be carried out by public or private entities. Legal history indicates that, concerning water resources, the private good[5] and common good free of use dichotomy is particularly old. It remains relevant to, and may even coexist within, the same domestic legal order. The current stresses on freshwater resources due to the growth of human populations, coupled by the deterioration of their quality, has led academics and policymakers to favour the commodification of such resource.[6] Others, citing human rights considerations, resist such logic. Is there a legal way to go beyond this dichotomy in order to associate economic efficiency and access to a resource so fundamentally necessary for all human life? After having

---

[2]Sachs [2].

[3]See: Smith [3]. Adam Smith referred to water as an example to differentiate use and exchange values. For him, in spite of their essential value to human beings, water resources generate almost no capital because of their abundance. According to him, water is the exact opposite of diamonds, in that the latter have no actual use value yet possessed enormous exchange value. In fact, Adam Smith reasoned like a Scotsman surrounded by a very wet nature. It goes without saying that water is not everywhere so abundant and can, therefore, have an exchange value alongside that of use.

[4]Dante Alighieri, Divine comedy, inferno, Canto III, 9 (1307): "*Lasciate ogne Speranza, voi ch'intrate*".

[5]Some jurists describe private appropriation as '*strange*' concerning something as indispensable as freshwater. See: Valérie Varnerot, *L'étrange pérennité du droit de propriété sur les eaux souterraines. A propos de la décision du TGI (Tribunal de grande instance) d'Angers en date du 12 juillet 2001* [*The strange durability of the right of ownership over groundwater. About the decision of the TGI (High Court) of Angers dated July 12, 2001*], Revue juridique de l'environnement [RJE], 2002/2, at 135.

[6]Water markets already exist in some countries including the United States and Chile.

noted the historical existence of these two models (water common good/private good) within different legal systems and domestic orders (1), it will be possible to note how this dichotomy may be transcended by means of the *matrix concept* of common heritage, as a condition of future human and economic development (2).

7.2 Water, a Development Between Free Use and Appropriation

The legal nature of water is particularly fluid. Some will even say evanescent. Confining in precise legal rules such a moving natural resource proves to be particularly delicate. Indeed, it is difficult to think of a flowing resource contained by law predicated on static logic around land ownership. Consequently, on Earth, water resources—so essential for human and economic development—engage different statuses. As far as we go back in the past, they can be considered as *commons* (1) or *private goods* (2) with the intermediate category of *res nullius*.

7.2.1 The Wellbeing of All Under the 'Res Communis' and 'Res Nullius' Pair

Considered vital to human beings, some resources are not regarded as economic goods per se.[7] By their crucial nature, they are recognised as non-appropriable as their use is common to all.[8] In Roman times, air, sea and fresh water were often described as common goods (*res communes*).[9] The same was true for flowing water[10]

[7] As stated by the French civilist Jean Carbonnier (1908–2003), there must be a possibility of appropriation to lead from a thing to an economic good. See: Carbonnier [4].

[8] Examples from the French Civil Code: Code Civil [C. CIV.] art. 714 (Fr.): 'There are things that belong to no one and whose use is common to all. Police laws regulate the way to enjoy it', or from the Quebec Civil Code: art. 913 (para. a) (Que.): 'Some things are not susceptible to appropriation; their use, common to all, is governed by laws of general interest and, in some ways, by the present code'.

[9] Aelius Marcianus, *Digesta* [Dig.] 1.8.2.1. Marcian is a Roman jurist of the late 2nd century-early 3rd century AD. The *Digest* is a methodical collection of the decisions of the most famous Roman jurisconsults. Its realisation was decided by the Byzantine Roman emperor Justinian (527–565 AD). This anthology of doctrinal opinions had a practical use given that they constituted the material of the law of that time. The *Digest*, having received official value, could therefore be cited before the judges across the Empire. Nowadays, a collection of doctrinal opinions is less relevant for practical use.

[10] Justinian's *Institutes* [JI] 2.1.1. Justinian's *Institutes* created in 533 AD were used as a manual for jurists in training and were given the authority of law. It is largely based upon the *Institutes* of Gaius, a Roman jurist of the second century AD.

or for man-made canals into which a public river flowed.[11] It was even possible that stagnant waters to be considered in the same way.[12] The consequence was a freedom of use of such resources.[13] Indeed, as explained by the Roman jurist Gaius (109–180 AD), ownerless things are deemed as belonging to the whole population.[14] A right to access water sources exists even when such sources are located on private properties: 'many rightly believe in the number of rustic easements the right to draw water, to water his cattle ... in the properties of landowners'.[15] This Roman conception of water as a common good has inspired present domestic legal orders routed in the *Romano Civilis* legal tradition. The result is some legal effectiveness for the human and economic development objectives of those States concerned.

In medieval and modern France, water as a common good existed with free use, including rights of access to water on private lands by means of rural/pastoral easements. This right went so far that the rights-holder of an easement to a fountain not located on his property did not even have to contribute to its maintenance.[16] Use of rivers was also public.[17] In consequence the landowner could not build something interfering with common access.[18] The French jurist Charles Loyseau (1566–1627) summed up very well this situation. He described the things common to all as belonging to no one with regard to property, and open to all regarding their use, on condition not to hinder their universality.[19]

What is more, freshwater as a common good is also seen in different religious legal systems. The Quran and Talmud refer to public wells open to all travellers.[20] Free use is also present in customary rights of the 20th century as among the Toubou Gounda (Circle of Bilma, Niger) where it is possible to find universal wells.[21] In the Ewe of Ghana, river and stream resources are conceived as common goods (*res*

---

[11]Ulpian, Dig.43.12.1.8. Ulpian (170–224 AD) is a prominent Roman politician and jurist of his time.

[12]Ulpian, Dig.43.14.1.6.

[13]Ulpian, Dig.39.2.24pr. 'The use of public rivers is common'; JI.2.1.4: 'The use of the banks of a river, according to the right of the people, is public, like the use of the river itself'.

[14]Gaius's *Institutes* [GI], *Alia Fragmenta, De Rebus*, pr.: 'Public things are not supposed to have masters, they belong to all'. Gaius was a famous Roman jurist of the 2nd century AD. His works were composed between the years 130 and 180 AD. His writings were recognised as of great authority, and the emperor Theodosius II (408–450 AD) named him as one of the jurists whose opinions were to be followed by judicial officers in deciding cases.

[15]JI.2, 3, 2.

[16]See: De Boutaric [5, p. 306].

[17]See: Coutumes du bailliage de Troyes avec les commentaires de m. Louis le grand [Customs of the bailliage of Troyes with the comments of m. Louis le grand] 314 (Montalant, Paris 4ème édition 1737).

[18]See: De Boutaric [6, p. 558–559].

[19]See: Loyseau [7].

[20]For example, Talmud Bavli Beitza 39 a. The Talmud also indicates: 'Rivers and streams forming springs, these belong to every man' (Talmud Bavli Shabbat, 121 b).

[21]See: Capitaine Couturier, Coutumiers Juridiques De L'afrique Occidentale Française [Legal Customaries of French West Africa] 205 (Larose Paris 1932), *reprinted in* Ramazzotti [8, p. 268].

communes). As a result, any person may draw there freely.[22] This effectiveness of the right of use greatly influences local human and economic development.

When declared *res nullius* (i.e., nobody's thing), water, without any owner, may consequently be appropriated. The Quebec Civil Code (article 913, b) refers to an appropriable resource, if not initially intended for the public and placed in a reservoir; a situation formerly mentioned by John Locke (1632–1704).[23] To a water *usus* for all, it adds a *fructus* for such person who isolates the resource. Watercourse riparian landowners take advantage of a usufruct but they do not have the *abusus* (i.e., the right to degrade/destroy/dispose of) of the water resource because the bare ownership belongs to the authorities, the nation, or even mankind.[24] A riparian right does not allow one to degrade the resource. It is a dismemberment of the property right uniting *usus* for everybody (servitude of public utility) and usufruct for such person who isolates the resource. Roman law describes *res nullii* waters as limited to the surpluses (the fruits according to the French Civil Code). The Digest—a rescript[25] of Antoninus Pius (138–161 AD) and Lucius Verus (161–169 AD)—prescribes that owners bordering a public source can enjoy it, in proportion to their domain, but without harming the community.[26] In the name of the common interest and of future uses, the substance of the resource must not be diminished. In the same vein, Pierre Biarnoy de Merville (1670–1740) specifies that the lord holder of a riparian right should not harm the rest of the population (custom of Normandy).[27] Similarly, in the French Civil Code (article 644), the use of the resource as a usufruct must be without harming it. If not, there could accusations of abuse of right or of abnormal neighbourhood conduct.

The Islamic legal system also acknowledges riparian rights. Lakes, streams, and springs on private land are considered as restricted public goods. This gives owners privileges (priority of drawing, greater quantity) but without exclusivity. They may not forbid anyone to drink or for his basic needs, however, owner permission is required for agricultural or industrial uses.[28]

Ultimately, the riparian right is an original dismemberment of the right of ownership associating one's *usufructus* without denying the *usus* to all members of the community. It is possible here to speak of a right of collective use referring to the notion of *res communis*, as a right based on the existence of public utility easements. Within the latter, Roman law recognised the right of aqueduct (*aquae ductus*) as

---

[22]Kludze [9], *reprinted in* Ramazzotti [10, p. 117].

[23]Locke [11].

[24]Cf., French Environemental Code, Code De L'environnement [C. ENV.] art. L 210-1 (Fr.) according to which, 'Water is part of the common heritage of the nation'.

[25]In the Roman Empire, a *rescript* is an imperial response having executive force to a question of law from a provincial governor, magistrates or even a private individual.

[26]Papyrius Justus, Dig.8.3.17.

[27]See: article 206: Pierre Biarnoy De Merville, La Coutume De Normandie Réduite En Maximes Selon Le Sens Littéral, Et L'esprit De Chaque Article [The Custom of Normandy Reduced in Maximes According to the Literal Sense, and the Spirit of Every Article] 236 (Henry Charpentier, Paris 1707).

[28]See: Faruqui et al. [12].

'the right to drive water through the land of others'.[29] The ultimate goal is to ensure the survival of everyone while ensuring economic development by allowing for the exploitation of the available surplus.

7.2.2 Appropriation as an Economic Good/Advantage

Free access is occasionally denounced as leading to wasteful use, which poses challenges to a balanced development. Some may argue that a full appropriation regime (i.e., whereby the *usus/fructus/abusus* accumulate to one), accompanied by free markets, is more sustainable. One's property right over a good could often involve an exclusive, perpetual, and enforceable power.[30] Geographical or seasonal water scarcity, the increasing need to upgrade costly infrastructure, could lead to commodification. Sensitive to the 'tragedy of the commons',[31] partisans to the extension of the capitalist market to all aspects of the environment consider that the protection of natural resources requires private appropriations that avoid exploitation being at the expense of nature. This could engender a more balanced development.

In *The Laws*, Plato (428–348 BC) attests to the existence of property rights on water in ancient Greece, possession of which was placed under the protection of the authorities.[32] In Rome, certain wells, ponds or springs were owned as they were considered accessories to private land.[33] Waterways of variable flow, lakes, and artificial pools could also be owned.[34] Under the Principate (27 BC–286 AD), a landowner possessed the *abusus* and could therefore exhaust the water, even that under ground (*ius utendi et abutendi*).[35] This could even lead to diverting sources and thus depriving the neighbour's well of water without any possibility of appeal for him.[36] In the Middle Ages, many wills refer to water legacies for the benefit of a whole community. Thus, in 1247, Thomas Vézian bequeathed his well to the city of Montpellier

[29]Ulpian, Dig.8.3.1pr.

[30]See an example from the French Civil Code, CODE CIVIL [C. CIV.] article 544 (Fr.): 'Property is the right to enjoy and dispose of things in the most absolute manner, provided that they are not used as prohibited by law or by the regulations'. Also, Protocol I to the European Convention of Human Rights art. 1: 'Every natural or legal person is entitled to the peaceful enjoyment of his possessions. No one shall be deprived of his possessions except in the public interest and subject to the conditions provided for by law and by the general principles of international law'.

[31]Hardin [13].

[32]Plato, Laws, book VIII, chapter XI.

[33]Ulpian, Dig.39.2.24.12 (use of the water of a well leaving to dry that of the neighbour), Dig.10.3.4.1: 'We ask if we could form an action to share a well between two people? Mela thinks that this action can take place if the soil on which the well is seated is common'. Therefore, a partition is not possible if the well is exclusively located in a property.

[34]Ulpian, Dig.43.12.1.3 (private waterways because of non-continuous flows).

[35]Pomponius, Dig.8.1.15pr. Sextus Pomponius is a Roman jurist from the middle of the 2nd century AD.

[36]Ulpian, Dig.39.3.1.12, Ulpian, Dig.39.2.24.12.

(South of France) in order to allow everyone to draw from.[37] *A contrario*, this indicates the existence of water appropriations. During the French *Ancien Régime*, the jurisconsult Francois Bourjon (died in 1751), from the custom of Paris, wrote: 'one on whose ground finds a source of water, can dispose of it at his pleasure; it is his good, it is his thing'.[38] Other works confirm this legal situation: '[w]ith regard to particular fountains, which spring from an inheritance, they unquestionably belong to the owner of the inheritance; he can divert the water, make it flow elsewhere than by its natural slope, use it entirely for his needs, without the neighbours being able to complain about it'.[39] An acquisitive prescription can even be refused (judgment of the Besançon Parliament of 5 April 1710).[40] The current French Civil Code pursues this appropriative logic on underground resources (article 552) and on other springs (article 642) if the latter do not result in flows of water. The source can even be transferred independently of the land.[41]

Water appropriations exist also in the customary law aspects of various legal systems. In Libya, an extremely arid territory, wells are often privately owned and are considered land/ground accessories. They are transferable by testamentary means (by will) and, in relation to land where the owners of the water and of the flora are different, the former must receive compensation (often in fruits) for the use of his water resources.[42] In some States, the chronology of seizure is a prerogative opposable to newcomers (cf., the rule of priority appropriation). The initial users (and their descendants) may use the resource anywhere they can lead it. For instance, a few dozen farmers in the Imperial Valley (California) take advantage of the Colorado water as of rights derived by their ancestors. This has turned an arid valley into one of the major agricultural production centres in the United States, and indeed the world. With the rule of priority appropriation, in a period of droughts, holders of the oldest rights take precedence over recent permits.

Water appropriations generate markets. In ancient Rome, access easements were used as real rights (i.e., rights in *rem*) held by the owner of the dominant land over a subservient one.[43] In the Middle Ages, in the south of France, the *Carpentras archives* reveal the acquisition (1313) of a spring by Pope Clement V (1305–1314). There appears a property right with *abusus* and not a simple *res nullius* - usufruct.[44] In the 17th century, the jurist Louis Le Grand, in relation to the custom of Troyes (north-

---

[37] Montpellier Municipal Archives, EE 305, August 3, 1247.

[38] See: Bourjon [14].

[39] See: De Boutaric [15, p. 563].

[40] See: De Boutaric [16], p. 564).

[41] For the transferable character of such rights, see: Cour d'appel [CA.] [regional court of appeal] Nancy, Oct. 12, 1955. For the independence from the ground, see: Cour d'appel [CA.], Grenoble, March 17, 1992, Juris-Data n° 1992-042253.

[42] See: Dante Caponera, Report (N°. 21) To the Government of Libya on Agriculture 198–200 (FAO, N°. 7530 Nov. 1952), *reprinted in* Ramazzotti [17, p. 154].

[43] Ulpian, Dig.8.3.1.1, Dig.43.20.1.16.

[44] See respectively: Communal Archives Carpentras, DD 18, f° 7v-11v.; DD 18, f° 12-15v.; DD 17, n° 264 § DD 18 f° 8v-9. About the many adventures of this purchase, see: Valérie Theis, *Histoire d'eau. Les conflits sur l'approvisionnement en eau de Carpentras (XIVème – XVème siècles)* [*Water*

central France) refers to purchases of water servitudes.[45] Currently, in France, the owner of a low-flow spring may not prevent the inhabitants of a commune, a village or even a hamlet from access to it, however, the owner can claim compensation, unless they have acquired or prescribed its use.[46] Nowadays, the States of Arizona, California and Nevada organise water banks contracting transfers. Owners of access rights can sell them without losing their prerogatives on them.[47] The goal is simply to adjust supply and demand through a pricing system. Some jurists, economists and politicians consider that solutions to environmental problems may lie in the development of a totally free market on natural resources.[48] It is also a way of circumventing the rule of *beneficial use*, which, in those federated states, considers that a holder of usage rights may lose it if he does not exercise it. However, market or water bank terms should not disguise the fact that water rights remain controlled by States or local authorities. Thus, in Australia, public authorities set the volumes allocated to holders of water permits (often farmers) or the terms and limits of transfers. In Chile, the role of the State is, however, limited to distributing permits granting rights of water use[49] which may then be sold or mortgaged like any asset. Such freedom goes very far as the administration does not intervene when the related use or the place of extraction evolve. Unlike the western part of the United States where the rule of beneficial use prevails, unused rights are not extinguished.[50] It is worth noting that from the 1970s, the development of Chile was particularly inspired by the economic liberalism of the Chicago School of Economics.

7.3 Common Heritage: A Development by the Union of Opposites

The notion of *common heritage* defined that territorial areas, natural or cultural resources should be protected from excessive exploitation, in the interest of future generations who are thus granted rights as owners of heritage properties. For the French environmentalist, Jean Lamarque, building a notion of common heritage would allow 'the evolution towards a property right conceived as the exercise of a

story. Conflicts over the water supply of Carpentras (14th–15th centuries)], Médiévales [MED.], autumn 2007 (53), at 23.

45Coutumes du bailliage de Troyes avec les commentaires de m. Louis le grand [Customs of the bailliage of Troyes with the comments of m. Louis le grand] 314 (title X, article 179, I, § 33) (Montalant, Paris 4ème édition 1737)

46CODE CIVIL [C. CIV.], art. 642, para. 3 (Fr.).

47See: Dan Tarlock [18].

48Cf., the theory of 'Free Market Environmentalism' which claims that property rights, free markets, and tort law are the best way to preserve the environment, by internalising pollution costs and durability of resources. The University of Montana is at the centre of this school of thought.

49Indeed the 1981 Water Code specifies that this resource belongs to the State.

50For Water markets in Chile, See: Petit [19].

social function'.[51] In this sense, it would become possible to marry common use and appropriation without questioning the latter, a way to avoid the risk of having to grant financial compensation to the present owners. This heritage of water resources may be done under the guise of the interests of the nation or mankind (3. 1.) but could also be a problem for the outer space exploration (3. 2.).

7.3.1 The Promotion of the Notion of Common Heritage

Despite historical evidence demonstrating the legal status of water resources as *res communis* and as a private good, questions remain. In economics, goods and services are divided according to criteria of exclusion and rivalry.[52] Neither public goods (non-exclusive/not readily susceptible to competitive), nor private goods (exclusive/susceptible to competition) that could deprive poor people of a vital resource, water is a resource accessible to all but in a situation of rivalry. One solution would be to promote a common heritage on the water endowing the property with a social function. In France, '[w]ater is part of the common heritage of the nation'.[53] Such a vision of protection and transmission to future generations is thus privileged, reinforcing the legitimacy of the French State to intervene. The preservation, enhancement, and development of water resources are described as being 'of general interest'.[54] As for its management, it must be 'sustainable' and 'well-balanced'.[55] The latter gives priority to the primary needs of people: drink, health, public health (*salubrité publique* in the original French text), and civil security.[56] Then come the requirements of the natural environment (including its fauna and flora), agriculture, industry, energy production and other human activities (transport, tourism, and recreation including water sports).[57] The practice of considering resources or rights the patrimony of the nation can be observed in various other internal legal orders such as that of Quebec.[58]

---

[51] Jean Lamarque, *La loi du 3 janvier 1992 sur l'eau* [*The law of 3 January 1992 on water*], 485, Cahiers juridiques de l'électricité et du gaz [CJEG] 80, 85 (1993).

[52] See writings of Paul Samuelson, Nobel Prize laureate in Economics 1970.

[53] Code De L'environnement [C. ENV.] art. L. 210-1 (Fr.).

[54] C. ENV. art. L. 210-1 (Fr.).

[55] C. ENV. art. L. 211-1, para. I (Fr.).

[56] C. ENV. art. L. 211-1, para. II (Fr.).

[57] C. ENV. art. L. 211-1, para. II (Fr.). This notion of well-balanced management has not been taken up by EU law. On this topic, See: Conseil d'Etat, Rapport Public [20]. The European Union seems to be lagging behind France concerning water priority to people compared to the needs of economic activities.

[58] Act affirming the collective character of water resources and aimed at strengthening their protection, adopted on 11 June 2009, assented 12 June 2009, art. 1: 'Being of vital interest, surface water and groundwater, in their natural environment, are resources that are part of the common heritage of the Quebec nation'. On the basis of article 913 of the Quebec Civil Code, it is asserted that the use of water is common and may not be appropriated.

A common heritage of the nation limits private appropriation because, in this situation, two holders for the *abusus* exist (a legal one and a patrimonial). The legal owner may not destroy his property because that aspects of it are not his to destroy, and must be passed on to future generations. The term *heritage* is found in Roman law, which saw in it, not a pecuniary value but an object to be transferred/bequeathed.[59] During the Middle Ages, control over property was based on the customary notion of *seizure,* designating a power to enjoy a thing but, under no circumstances, an absolute or exclusive right to that thing. It allowed that person's enjoyment of use of a thing without prohibiting its use by others. Thus, a piece of land would see successive farmers then, after the harvest, widows and disabled people using the right of gleaning to eventually end in grazing rights for all the villagers.[60] Development occurred collectively given that on the same land simultaneous appropriations co-existed, each taking advantage of a particular aspect of another. This medieval mentality partly originates in religion. Indeed, in the Christian logic of that time, the ultimate owner is God. Human beings take advantage of freedoms or rights over things such as water, only in relation to their peers. Saint Thomas Aquinas (1225–1274) considered that God, as supreme suzerain, had the *dominium* on natural things, while his terrestrial vassals only benefited from a use on these (a form of usufruct).[61] Without the *abusus* right, development must be sustainable since human beings had to preserve such fundamental resources such as water. Therefore, on Earth, there cannot be any exclusivity of appropriation over such resources. Moreover, the *gift* of water was a widespread practice of Christian charity. Jean Pitard (1228–1315), successively surgeon of the French kings, including Louis IX ('Saint Louis') (1226–1270), Philippe III (1270–1285) and Philippe IV ('the Fair') (1285–1314), had sunk a well in Paris for the benefit of the neighbourhood (and of his soul).[62] By sacralising individual property rights elevated to a natural and imprescriptible *human right*, article two of the French Declaration of the Rights of the Man and the Citizen (1789) seemed to have settled all these subtleties of simultaneous appropriation. Its article 17 insists that: 'property being an inviolable and sacred right, no one can be deprived of it'. However, in the public interest,[63] the present notion of common heritage resurrects the dual holder logic with a regime that unites private and patrimonial appropriations under the supervision of the State or of conservation easements transferred to

[59] See: Véronique Inserguet-Brisset, Propriété Publique Et Environnement [Public Property and Environment] 256 (LGDJ 1994).

[60] A landless poor farmer thus had pasture to feed a few cows and sheep.

[61] Thomas Aquinas, Summa Theologiae, Secunda Secundæ Partis, quæstio 66, especially art. 1 and 2.

[62] Aurelle Levasseur, '*La police de l'eau dans la ville médiévale (XIIIème-XVème S.). Fondements, mise en oeuvre et protection d'un devoir de l'eau*' [*The water police in the medieval town (13th–15th centuries). Fundamentals, implementation and protection of a duty of water*], in Mergey and Mynard [21].

[63] However, the public interest is a flexible notion that allows governments to adapt to societal changes.

an NGO.[64] As had been the case prior to 1789, the legal owner tends to become a mere user of his property accountable for the way he uses it. This often involves zoning logic by means of administrative easements having the objective of limiting pollution around water catchment areas as indicated by the French Code of Public Health.[65] To take a sustainable development approach would lead to a decline in the exclusiveness of the private owner.

The 2004 French Environmental Charter, which is an instrument of constitutional value and, therefore, containing normative principles, affirms in its introduction that: '[t]he environment is the common heritage of human beings'. On planet Earth, it is hard to imagine a natural environment without the (even minute) presence of water. Consequently, albeit indirectly, such resource is here defined as common heritage, the beneficiaries of which is not the French nation per se, but every member of mankind. A normative *common heritage of mankind* already exists (cf., pertaining to the high-seas seabed and subsoil-related, and to outer space) with four normative principles: non-national appropriation,[66] international management, equitable sharing of earnings between States,[67] and peaceful use.[68] However, to designate water per se as a common heritage of mankind generates many legal difficulties. Indeed, unlike other things having received such designation, water resources do not concern a specific area.[69] Moreover, the notion of common heritage of mankind has generally so far only been normatively affirmed in relation to territories located beyond the jurisdiction or, otherwise, control of States.[70] Designating water as the common heritage of mankind would give rise to an extremely delicate problem. It would deprive private owners of some of their prerogatives, but also States of their territorial sovereignty

---

[64] A conservation easement is an operational legal concept of private law corresponding to a voluntary transfer by a landowner of part of his property rights for environmental reasons. This assignment is usually in favour of some NGO. This service of environmental servitude is particularly present in the United States. It can be a means to protect the interests of future generations.

[65] Code De La Santé Publique [CSP], art. L. 1321-2 (Fr.).

[66] Treaty on Principles Governing the Activities of States in the Exploration and Use of Outer Space, including the Moon and Other Celestial Bodies, art. 2. This international treaty, signed on 27 January 1967, came into force on 10 October 1967. As of 15 September 2018, the number of States Parties stood at 106.

[67] Agreement Governing the Activities of States on the Moon and Other Celestial Bodies, art. 11, para. 5 (for the international regime), art. 11, para. 7, d (for the equitable sharing by all States Parties). As of 15 September 2018, only 18 states are parties to this treaty (also known as Moon Agreement).

[68] The United Nations Convention on the Law of the Sea (UNCLOS), art. 141. This international treaty, signed on 10 December 1982, came into force on 16 November 1994. As of 15 September 2018, the number of parties stood at 168 (167 states and the European Union). The USA has not ratified UNCLOS.

[69] Besides the moon and the celestial bodies, the spaces concerned by this designation are the deep seabed, defined as the 'Zone', circumscribed by the outer extremities of the continental shelves.

[70] Sylvie Paquerot, Le Statut Des Ressources Vitales En Droit International: Essai Sur Le Concept De Patrimoine Commun De L'humanité [The Status of Vital Resources in International Law: Essay on the Concept of the Common Heritage of Humanity] 23 (Bruylant, Collection mondialisation et droit international, Bruxelles 2002).

over this resource in relation to the principle of non-appropriation.[71] This seems hardly conceivable in a world where most major economic powers but also States controlling upstream sources have refrained from ratifying the New York Convention on the Sharing of International Watercourses.[72] Moreover, in such event, although mankind would possess heritage interests/rights, it lacks legal personality per se, therefore there are important practical questions of legal standing, representation, and enforcement that arise. Mankind *sui juris* is not a subject of international law.[73]

Pursuing human and economic development on such an imprecise basis seems, therefore, hard to imagine, let alone to achieve. However, some organisation possessing legitimacy—e.g., some global NGO that enjoy wide acceptance and support by States—could potentially represent mankind given that the water cycle is transboundary and supranational by its very nature, and its effective management is predicated of international cooperation, and could, therefore, justifiably be universal. Perhaps it is time for the United Nations galaxy to ramify in such direction?

7.3.2 The Implications of the Notion of Common Heritage for the Pursuit of Human Activities in Outer Space

The Outer Space Treaty (1967)[74] set the prerequisites for subsequent space treaties regulating the development outer space human activities. Its article 1 states that, 'the Moon and other celestial bodies… shall be the province of all mankind'. Consequently, these territories *belong* to us all. Arguably, this designation slowed down space exploration. It is also stated in that instrument that '[o]uter space, including the moon and other celestial bodies, is not subject to national appropriation by claim of sovereignty, by means of use or occupation, or by any other means' (art. 2). The consequence of this norm is free access for any country. Such limitation of national appropriation has been reinforced in the Moon Agreement (1979), which is the reason that major developed States have refused to ratify this treaty.[75] In fact, States lacking

[71]Marie Cuq, L'eau En Droit International. Convergences Et Divergences Dans Les Approches Juridiques [Water in International Law. Convergences and Divergences in Legal Approaches] 79 (Larcier, Bruxelles 2013).

[72]Convention on the Law of the Non-Navigational Uses of International Watercourses (May 1997, entry into force in August 2014). As of 15 September 2018, only 36 states have ratified it. China or the USA have not done so, as States very rich in water resources (Canada, Russia, Brazil) or which control the upstream sources (Turkey, Israel, Ethiopia).

[73]Daillier et al. [22].

[74]Treaty on Principles Governing the Activities of States in the Exploration and Use of Outer Space, including the Moon and Other Celestial Bodies. UNTS 8843. As of 15 September 2018, outer space powers including the United States, Russia, China, France, United Kingdom, India, and Japan were parties to this international convention.

[75]See Sara Bruhns § Jacob Haqq-Misra, *A Pragmatic Approach to Sovereignty on Mars*, Vol. 38 Space Pol'y 57, 57, 59 (November 2016) with regard for the reasons that major developed States have refused to ratify the 1979 Moon Agreement.

the technology for space exploration and to exploit celestial bodies have used the above two treaties to prevent great space powers to exclusively and fully capitalise on their abilities. The Moon Agreement also states that 'the moon and its natural resources are the common heritage of mankind'.[76] The latter—a notion in international law—holds that defined territories and certain intangible cultural or natural matters or objects should be held in trust for future generations. It means that they must be preserved from over-exploitation by individuals, States, and corporations. The great innovation of the Moon Agreement, compared to the Outer Space Treaty, is to require an equitable sharing of benefits from the moon or other celestial bodies by all States parties.[77] Also, while the Outer Space Treaty tells nothing about a private individual or a company willing to operate in outer space, the Moon Agreement prohibits private companies from requiring a title deed.[78]

Arguably, this desire to affirm extra-terrestrial resources as the common heritage of mankind is as an obstacle to human colonisation of outer space. Indeed, without the recognition and the support of at least a sovereign State, what means do pioneers in the field possess, if they lack the protection of their government to espouse their cause and defend their property rights on celestial resources?[79] Investors, associations, pioneers, all need an effective authority to define and confirm what they own, capable of enforcing that ownership, and defending it against others. Without this, it would be incredibly risky for individuals or corporations to seek to explore some extra-terrestrial territory to exploit its natural resources. What would only seem amenable for ownership would be whatever equipment from Earth we would bring to celestial bodies. In international outer space conventions, rights of withdrawal, management, exclusion, and alienation have been erased and the property right is limited to that of access.[80] Human expansion beyond our 'small' planet surely suffers from this legal situation.

In order to encourage private interests to invest in outer space, it is advisable to substitute the status of common heritage of mankind for that of *res nullius* (for the water so necessary to first pioneers as for all the minerals). To guarantee this enhancement, it could be necessary to resort to the doctrine of *terra nullius*. This notion in international law, originating in Roman law, is used in relation to territory not yet subject to the sovereignty or control of any state. Norway has relied on it to claim sovereignty over Svalbard.[81] If future technical progress leads to an effective appropriation of celestial objects, the notion of *terra nullius* could be adopted to facilitate their enhancement.

---

[76]Agreement Governing the Activities of States on the Moon and Other Celestial Bodies, art. 11, 1.

[77]Agreement Governing the Activities of States on the Moon and Other Celestial Bodies, art. 11, 7, 4.

[78]Agreement Governing the Activities of States on the Moon and Other Celestial Bodies, art. 11, 3.

[79]See Pop [23] with regard to the protection of celestial ownership without state sovereignty.

[80]See Butler [24] with regard to the stripping of the most important property rights in international space law.

[81]Svalbard is an archipelago in the Arctic Ocean ranging from 74° to 81° north latitude, and from 10° to 35° east longitude. It is about midway between continental Norway and the North Pole.

Also, the doctrine of *discovery* remains current.[82] For example, China invoked it to claim sovereignty over the seabed of the South China Sea.[83] However, all major space powers have ratified the Outer Space Treaty (1967) banning all national sovereignty over celestial bodies (art. 2). A solution to circumvent this has then appeared in the American Space Act signed into law by President Obama on 25 November 2015. It instructs the executive branch to 'promote the right of U.S. citizens to engage in commercial exploration for and commercial recovery of space resources free from harmful interference, in accordance with the international obligations of the United States and subject to authorization and continuing supervision by the Federal Government'.[84] The aim is therefore to guarantee private property rights to celestial resources but, is this guarantee compatible with article 2 of the Outer Space Treaty (prohibition of national appropriation)? Under international law, property rights require a superior authority, such as a State entity, entitled to attribute and enforce them. May, or indeed could, a State ensure title to property in a territory on which it lacks sovereignty? It should be noted that, in international law, States exercise jurisdiction over their territory but also over their nationals (vis-à-vis other States). Thus, even in a territory outside sovereign reach, as soon as a natural or legal person conducts an activity, the personal competence of the State over which that person has nationality applies. This one must respect domestic law but also international commitments of its State of origin. With the American Space Act, there is no affirmation of State sovereignty per se; just a declaration of operation and exploitation. Following registration in the Registration Convention,[85] pioneers will work for their activities and will use local water with state permits. On 1 August 2017, a Luxembourg law authorising also the exploration and use of space resources entered into force. Article 1 of this legislation states that: '[s]pace resources are capable of being appropriated' with, as consequences, setting up public-private financial partnerships and issuing exploration and exploitation permits.

Outside international and domestic public law options, there is the possibility of commercial governance under the auspices of a self-regulation in which private entities tend to comply including dispute resolution procedures.[86] Organising a *private* legal order could lead to great adaptability as, if necessary, a commodification of water. It is possible to draw inspiration from historical solutions made in the context of State absence. After the collapse of the Roman Empire and the decline of its legal infrastructure, emerged a *lex mercatoria,* a system of self-enforcing property rights,

[82] The US Supreme Court cites this doctrine as a basis of property ownership as recently as 2005. See, City of Sherrill v. Oneida Indian Nation of N.Y., 544 U.S. 197, 203 n. 1 (2005).

[83] William J. Broad, *China Explores a Frontier Two Miles Deep,* N. Y. TIMES, September 11, 2010, at A1.

[84] Commercial Exploration and Commercial Recovery, 51 U.S.C. § 51302, a, (3) (2017).

[85] The Convention on Registration of Objects Launched into Outer Space was adopted by the United Nations General Assembly in 1974 and came into force in 1976. Under it, a State retains jurisdiction over a space object it has registered.

[86] See Salter [25] with regard to the argument that the law would result from specific bargains build by commercial entities.

and legal rules on commercial dispute resolution.[87] While the court had no formal enforcement power, most traders would comply with merchant court decisions as, otherwise, a defector would be considered an unsafe trading partner.[88] No one would have wanted to continue to have a commercial connection with him.

The question of common heritage of mankind over outer space exemplifies the *res communis/res nullius* debate. Is ownership possible over outer space resources? If mankind is the owner, it must be necessary to share, otherwise the rule of *'first in time, first user'* may apply as is the case in the field of radio frequencies. A further problem arises: to manage licences or permits of exploitation, a register will be necessary but ought this be national, or international (such as that for satellites)? The future of our civilisation might be to use the notion of common heritage over finite resources of our 'little' planet in order to ensure their sustainability, while, at the same time, resolutely applying the logic of *res nullius* to all resources (water or otherwise) of outer space. This would be a way to attract the necessary investments. In fact, for all these questions, we must be very modest. After all, future pioneer societies would probably establish their own rights with little regard to increasingly distant homelands.[89]

References

1. Diamond, J. (2005). *Collapse: How societies choose to fail or succeed* (2nd ed., 2011). Viking Press.
2. Sachs, J. D. (2015). *The age of sustainable development* (pp. 185–193). Columbia University Press.
3. Smith, A. (1776). *An inquiry into the nature and causes of the wealth of nations* (p. 37). Woodstock, Ontario: Devoted Publishing 2016.
4. Carbonnier, J. (2000). *Droit civil, tome 3, les biens* (Civil Law, Vol. 3, Property, p. 83). PUF, collection Thémis.
5. De Boutaric, F., (1775). *Traité des droits seigneuriaux et des matieres feodales* [*Treaty of seigneuriale rights and feudal matters*] (p. 306). Les libraires associés.
6. De Boutaric, F., (1775). *Traité des droits seigneuriaux et des matieres feodales* [*Treaty of seigneuriale rights and feudal matters*] (pp. 558–559). Les libraires associés.
7. Loyseau, C. (1608). *Traité des seigneuries* [*Treaty of the seigneuries*] (p. 313). Paris: Abel Angelier.
8. Ramazzotti, M. (1996). *Readings in African customary water law* (p. 268). FAO Rome: FAO legislative study.
9. Kludze, A. (1973). *Ewe law of property* (p. 137). London: SOAS.
10. Ramazzotti, M. (1996). *Readings in African customary water law* (p. 117). FAO Rome: FAO legislative study.
11. Locke, J. (1690). *Two treatises of government book II chapter V Sect. 29*. Awnfham Churchill, Amen-Corner.

---

[87]See Benson [26] with regard to the spontaneous birth of a *lex mercatoria* in the Middle Ages protecting property rights.

[88]See Milgrom et al. [27] with regard to the merchant law and enforcement system.

[89]Couston [28].

12. Faruqui, N. I., Biswas, A. K., & Bino, M. J. (2003). (DIR.), *La gestion de l'eau selon l'islam [Water management according to islam*] (pp. 132–133) (Editions Karthala, Les Presses de l'Université des Nations unies, Centre de recherches pour le développement international, Paris).
13. Hardin, G. (1968). The tragedy of the commons. *Science, 13,* 1243.
14. Bourjon, F. (1770). *Le droit commun de la France, et la coutume de paris réduits en principes (tome second) [The common law of France, and the custom law of Paris reduced in principles (second volume)]* (p. 10). Paris: Grangé, Cellot.
15. De Boutaric, F. D. (1775). *Traité des droits seigneuriaux et des matieres feodales [Treaty of seigneuriale rights and feudal matters*] (p. 563). Les libraires associés.
16. De Boutaric, F. D. (1775). *Traité des droits seigneuriaux et des matieres feodales [Treaty of seigneuriale rights and feudal matters*] (p. 564). Les libraires associés.
17. Ramazzotti, M. (1996). *Readings in African customary water law* (p. 154). FAO Rome: FAO legislative study.
18. Dan Tarlock, A. (2005). *Water transfers: A means to achieve sustainable water use*. In Edith Brown Weiss Laurence Boisson De Chazournes & Nathalie Bernasconi-Osterwalder (Eds.), *Fresh water and international economic law* (pp. 52–53). Oxford University Press.
19. Petit, O. (2017). La nouvelle économie des ressources et les marchés de l'eau: une perspective idéologique [The new resource economy and water markets: An ideological perspective]. In Max Falque (sous dir.), *L'eau, Entre Reglementation Et Marche* [*Water, between regulation and market*] (pp. 114–121). Paris: Editions Johanet.
20. Conseil d'Etat, Rapport Public. (2010). *L'eau et son droit* [*Council of state, public report 2010, water and its right*] (p. 336). Paris: La Documentation française, Collection Études et documents du Conseil d'État.
21. Mergey, A., & Mynard, F. (2017). (sous dir.), *La police de l'eau. Reglementer les usages des eaux: un defi permanent* [*The police of water. Regulating water uses: A permanent challenge*] (pp. 52–53). Paris: Editions Johanet.
22. Daillier, P., Forteau, M., & Pellet, A. (2009). *Droit international public* [*Public international law*] (p. 443) (par. 261) (LGDJ 8ème éd.).
23. Pop, V. (2000) Appropriation in outer space: The relationship between land ownership and sovereignty on the celestial bodies. *Space Policy, 16*(4), 275, 280–281.
24. Butler, D. A. (2017). Who owns the moon, mars and other celestial bodies: Lunar jurisprudence in corpus juris spatialis. *The Journal of Air Law and Commerce, 82*(3), 505–510.
25. Salter, A. W. (2017). Ordering the cosmos: Private law and celestial property rights. *The Journal of Air Law and Commerce, 82*(2), 311–314.
26. Benson, B. L. (1989). The spontaneous evolution of commercial law. *South Econ J 55*(3), 644, 647–648.
27. Milgrom, P. R., North, D. C., & Weingast, B. R. (1990). The role of institutions in the revival of trade: The law merchant, private judges, and the champagne fairs. *Economical Policy 2*(1), 1, 9–10.
28. Couston, M. (2017). Que faut-il prévoir pour les cinquante ans à venir du droit spatial? 2ème partie. Le droit à l'exploitation des ressources planétaires [What is to be expected for the next fifty years of space law? Part 2. The right to exploit planetary resources]. *Revue française de droit aérien et spatial [RFDAS] 283*(3), 291, 305.

Chapter 8
Private-Sector Transparency as Development Imperative: An African Inspiration

Richard Peltz-Steele and Gaspar Kot

Abstract Access to information (ATI) is essential to ethical and efficacious social and economic development. Transparency ensures that human rights are protected and not overwhelmed by profiteering or commercial priorities. Accordingly, ATI has become recognised as a human right that facilitates the realisation of other human rights. But ATI as conceived in Western law has meant only access to the state. In contemporary development, private actors are crucial players, as they work for, with, and outside the state to realise development projects. This investment of public interest in the private sector represents a seismic shift in social, economic, and political power from people to institutions, akin to the twentieth-century creation of the social-democratic state. Contingent on state accountability, Western ATI law has struggled to follow the public interest into the private sector. Western states are stretching ATI law to reach the private sector upon classical rationales for access to the state. In Poland, hotly contested policy initiatives over privatisation and public reinvestment have occasioned this stretching of ATI law in the courts. Meanwhile, in Africa, a new model for ATI has emerged. Since the reconstruction of the South African state after Apartheid, South African ATI law has discarded the public-private divide as prohibitive of access. Rather than focusing on the nature of a private ATI respondent's activity as determinative of access, South African law looks to the demonstrated necessity of access to protect human rights. This chapter examines cases from South Africa that have applied this new ATI model to the private sector in areas with development implications. For comparison, the article then examines the gradually expanding but still more limited Western approach to ATI in the private sector as evidenced in Polish ATI law. This research demonstrates that amid shifting power in key development areas such as energy and communication, Polish courts have been pressing ATI to work more vigorously in the private sector upon theories of attenuated state accountability, namely public ownership, funding, and function. We posit that Poland, and other states in turn, should jettison these artifices of state

R. Peltz-Steele (✉)
University of Massachusetts, North Dartmouth, USA
e-mail: rpeltzsteele@umassd.edu

G. Kot
Jagiellonian University, Kraków, Poland
e-mail: gaspar.kot.kot@doctoral.uj.edu.pl

P. Szwedo et al. (eds.), *Law and Development*, Kobe University Monograph Series in Social Science Research, https://doi.org/10.1007/978-981-13-9423-2_8

accountability and look instead to the South African model, since replicated elsewhere in Africa, for direct access to the private sector. ATI law should transcend the public-private divide, and the nations of the North and West should recognise human rights as the definitive rationale for ATI in furtherance of responsible development.

Keywords Access to information · Comparative law · Poland · Privatisation · South Africa · Sustainable development

8.1 Introduction

Transparency is a sine qua non of social and economic development. Now enjoying broad recognition as a principle of human rights, access to information—'ATI', also known as freedom of information or the right to know—is the lynchpin of democratic accountability. ATI ensures that resources are developed and managed ethically, for the betterment of people, and not perverted to wasteful, corrupt, or injurious aims. In this capacity, ATI is an ancillary human right, or 'enabler' right. Its indispensable purpose is to facilitate the realisation of core human rights, such as representative government and sustainable development.

However, the contemporary human right of ATI did not spring wholly formed from the head of Zeus. In fact the heritage of ATI tracks the gradual recognition of the core human rights that ATI facilitates. In the twentieth century, ATI law charted a course through the classically, if not fully accurately, conceived evolution of human rights from civic and political life, to social and economic sustenance, and to collective needs. Correspondingly, ATI norms in a given legal system tend to reflect the phase of human rights development that predominated in the system's constitutional design. For example, in the United States, where modern ATI law originated in the early twentieth century under a 1789 Constitution, the federal ATI is largely statutory, applies to a limited range of state action, and focuses to a fault on political participation as its raison d'être for purposes of judicial construction. In contrast, European courts in recent decades have inclined to construe ATI to facilitate the social and economic ideals constituted in pan-European governance.

ATI's legal journey has not ended. Just as Africa is pioneering human rights development in the collective vein, African states also are experimenting with a more robust model of ATI. South Africa developed an ATI model that extends transparency into the purely private sector. Now replicated in other African states, this innovation was born of experience with Apartheid, for which the private sector bore culpability hand in hand with the public sector. In both sectors, transparency is an antidote to the unethical and immoral practices that allowed Apartheid to thrive for so long. In the post-Apartheid constitutional system, the extension of ATI across the public-private threshold is not unlimited, but a function of necessity. Transparency may overcome the presumption of commercial secrecy in economic enterprise when a requester can assert a countervailing need of sufficient magnitude. Thus much better than the Western model, African ATI represents a balance of values.

In this chapter we examine ATI in the private sector as a means to promote ethical practices in sustainable social and economic development. We begin with the balancing test in South Africa, where this innovative application of ATI law was conceived and is beginning to bear fruit. Reflected in case law, recent experience suggests a vast potential for African ATI to promote social and economic development in South Africa and on the continent. Then, for contrast, we examine ATI in the private sector in Poland. We focus on Poland for this study because it is simultaneously an exemplar of contemporary European access norms and of a legal system struggling to maintain trajectories of social and economic development in the wake of the global financial crisis. As a former Soviet state, Poland comes to the table with an experience of radical privatisation already under its belt. Now Poland appears poised to experiment with public reinvestment, further loosening the classical boundary between public and private sectors. The Polish courts have been expansive in construction of ATI law to penetrate the private sector. But the ATI regime remains tied to the classical Western model, which requires a public 'hook', such as public funding or function, to cross the public-private threshold.

We propose that as Western democracies such as Poland increasingly blur the line between public and private sectors in the interest of development, they should take a page from the book of African ATI. Profiteering, waste, and corruption are all capable of thriving in public and private sector alike. South Africa discovered the importance of sunshine as disinfectant in both sectors only upon an untold cost in human suffering. Accordingly, power shifts between public and private sector—whether public-to-private, as in US prisons and Irish water, or private-to-public, as in Polish electricity and Parisian water—demand an ATI system capable of transcending the public-private threshold. This chapter suggests that access should be predicated on requesters' demonstrable human needs rather than on flimsy theories of a respondent's quasi-public role. Such a reenvisioning of ATI would work to bolster ethics and efficacy in sustainable development.

8.2 Access to the Private Sector in South Africa

8.2.1 Advent of a New Rule of Law in Africa

The Apartheid regime in South Africa employed secrecy as a weapon.[1] In response, transparency and accountability were clarion demands of reformers after the regime crumbled in 1991.[2] Because private actors had born equal culpability in perpetrating Apartheid, reformers focused on transparency as a supervening objective, overriding the classical distinction between public and private sectors.[3] That is, ATI must be

[1] Calland [6], Darch and Underwood [8].

[2] Calland, *Illuminating the Politics*, *supra* note 1, at 4–5; Ngabirano [20], Roling [29].

[3] Adeleke [1].

guaranteed both vertically, as against the state, and horizontally, as between private actors, to ensure the realisation of human rights.[4] Previous research has demonstrated the soundness of this approach as a departure from the classical liberal model of ATI.[5] As enabler of human rights attainment, ATI frees a flow of information to level the distribution of power in society—whether between individuals and a burgeoning administrative state, as in the twentieth-century United States, or, for example, between black laborers and corporations that profited from Apartheid.

The 1993 interim constitution in South Africa stepped out timidly with an ATI right only as against the state, and then only 'in so far as such information is required for the exercise or protection of any of his or her rights'.[6] In short order, though, negotiation over the permanent 1996 constitution yielded a much more liberal approach.[7] Transplanting the necessity qualifier, article 32 of the new constitution declared, '(1) Everyone has the right of access to—(a) any information held by the state; and (b) any information that is held by another person and that is required for the exercise or protection of any rights'.[8] A paragraph (2) required implementing legislation 'to give effect to this right', allowing 'for reasonable measures to alleviate the administrative and financial burden on the state'.[9]

Many factors influenced the advent of ATI in horizontal application. The European Data Protection Directive had been adopted in 1995 and advanced the notion that personal privacy, or personal integrity, justified a horizontal imposition of rights against the private sector for access to personally identifying information.[10] European advisers played a part in the development of the new South African constitution[11]; extrapolation to the protection of human rights besides privacy is not a great leap.[12]

At the same time, expanded ATI in the new South African constitution cannot be viewed apart from the document's unprecedented commitment to socio-economic development. ATI was recognised for its auxiliary capacity to facilitate access to housing, healthcare, food, water, social security, education, and anti-discrimination, as well as the possibility of land restitution and the collective right to a clean envi-

[4]See Liebenberg [16].

[5]Calland [7], Roberts [28].

[6]S. Afr. (Interim) Const., 1993, § 24.

[7]O'Regan [21].

[8]S. Afr. Const., 1996, § 32(1).

[9]*Id.* § 32(2).

[10]Directive 95/46/EC of the European Parliament and the Council on the Protection of Individuals with Regard to the Processing of Personal Data and on the Free Movement of Such Data, 1995 O.J. (L 281) 31, http://eur-lex.europa.eu/LexUriServ/LexUriServ.do?uri=OJ:L:1995:281:0031:0050:EN:PDF.

[11]See Lange [15].

[12]See Klaaren et al. [14].

ronment.[13] Responsive to the abuses of Apartheid, ATI constitutionalised fairness in administrative process through transparency.[14]

In 2000, the constitutionally required implementing legislation took shape in the Promotion of Access to Information Act (PAIA).[15] Notwithstanding a constitutional challenge, the PAIA operationally superseded ATI claims that had been brought directly under the 1996 constitution.[16] Though influenced by ATI laws in the common law cohort of Australia, Canada, Ireland, New Zealand, and the United States,[17] the PAIA marked a significant departure by effecting the constitutional guarantee of direct access to the private sector.[18] Public bodies include quasi-public entities through a disjunctive power-or-function test.[19] Defining a 'private body', the PAIA includes natural persons and partnerships, insofar as they are engaged in 'any trade, business or profession', and 'any former or existing juristic person'.[20]

The PAIA spells out procedures for access to private bodies apart from access to public bodies, though the provisions play out in parallel. Like the later African Model Law, the PAIA burdens the requester 'to identify the right the requester is seeking to exercise or protect and provide an explanation of why the requested record is required for the exercise or protection of that right'.[21] Public bodies acting in the public interest may assert private persons' rights and act as requesters.[22]

A private body under the PAIA—so in essence, any business—affirmatively must compile and maintain an access manual that lists contact information and describes categories of information already publicly available, information available through other legislation, and 'description of the subjects on which the body holds records and the categories of records held on each subject'.[23] The PAIA authorises denial of access by private respondents upon grounds[24] that track those that pertain to public bodies[25] and include the privacy of a third-party natural person, trade secrets and commercially sensitive information, breach of confidentiality obligation to a third

[13] Asimow [2]; O'Regan, *supra* note 7, at 14; Open Democracy Advice Ctr., Right to Access Information Training Manual 14 (2011), http://www.r2k.org.za/wp-content/uploads/2012/12/rti-training-manual-dec-2012.pdf.

[14] Asimow, *supra* note 13, at 395; Calland, *Illuminating the Politics*, *supra* note 1, at 6; O'Regan, *supra* note 7, at 14.

[15] Promotion of Access to Information Act, No. 2 of 2000, § 9(b) (S. Afr.) [hereinafter PAIA].

[16] *Inst. for Democracy in S. Afr. v. Afr. Nat'l Cong.* [2005] ZAWCHC 30, 2005 (5) SA 39 (C), [2005] 3 All SA 45 (C), ¶¶ 14–19.

[17] Roling, *supra* note 2, at 10.

[18] Burns [5].

[19] PAIA, § 1.

[20] *Id.*

[21] *Id.* §§ 50(1), 52(2)(d). Because a requester must assert a rationale under this unusual provision, the usual ATI principle of interest neutrality must be forfeit.

[22] *Id.* § 50(2).

[23] *Id.* § 51(1)–(3).

[24] *Id.* §§ 63–69.

[25] Roling, *supra* note 2, at 21–22.

party, risk to safety of person or property, legal privilege, and research integrity.[26] Most exemptions are subject to a public-interest override when disclosure would reveal illegality or 'imminent and serious public safety or environmental risk', or the public interest in disclosure 'clearly outweighs' the harm exemption seeks to avert.[27]

Following the example of its 1995 predecessor, the PAIA was accompanied by the formation of an independent civil society organisation to support implementation, the Open Democracy Advice Centre (ODAC).[28] Still today, ODAC strives vigorously for social and economic development and its ethical attainment, employing the PAIA and complementary whistle-blower protection law. It must be said, though, that PAIA compliance in South Africa has been consistently poor.[29] ODAC has documented trending secrecy in public and private sectors, as well as efforts to intimidate requesters and commodify information.[30] Darch and Underwood cautioned that failure of African states to fulfil their duties fails to account for profound public demand and need for information.[31] As a result, 'the freedom of information idea may be under wider critical examination in African countries than the data in the global surveys indicate'.[32] Examining the efforts of civil society organisations to press for accountability, researchers have located transparency obstacles in unduly complex procedures, insufficient pre-judicial enforcement mechanisms, and an enduring political culture of secrecy.[33]

Compliance notwithstanding, ODAC's stated priorities suggest the extant potential of the PAIA to advance development through transparency in housing, planning, land and property disposition, social welfare, procurement, energy, environment, public spending, municipal minutes and resolutions, information policy, and public participation in legislation and rulemaking.[34] Regarding ethics in development practice, ODAC has reported mixed success, with more work to do, using PAIA to investigate public-private partnerships, procurement corruption, private land ownership, utility pricing, medical malpractice, industrial pollution, utility infrastructure, genetic engineering, and human displacements—the latter such as occasioned by the 2010 World Cup.[35]

At the African continental level, the ATI has followed an evolutionary track from European model to South African influence. Developed in the early 1980s, the African Charter on Human and Peoples' Rights enumerates a 'right to receive information' next to, but distinctly from, the freedom of expression.[36] The African

[26] PAIA, §§ 63–69.

[27] *Id.* § 70.

[28] Ngabirano, *supra* note 2, at 209–10.

[29] See Darch and Underwood, *supra* note 1, 237–42.

[30] McKinley [17].

[31] Darch and Underwood, *supra* note 1, at 243.

[32] *Id.*

[33] Bentley and Calland [3].

[34] McKinley, *supra* note 30, at 12–13.

[35] *Id.* at 20–92.

[36] African Charter on Human and People's Rights art. 9.

Commission of Human and People's Rights has cited the right as acting in tandem with the freedom of expression to serve purposes of both self-fulfilment and political involvement.[37] ATI is found in other pan-African instruments[38] and in sectoral devices of the South African Development Community regarding anti-corruption, mining, fishery and forest management, wildlife conservation, transport and communication, and cultural information and sport.[39]

Implementing the African Charter, the African Commission adopted the 2002 Declaration of Principles on Freedom of Expression in Africa, which articulates the 'Freedom of Information' in a detailed article IV, following the South African example in extension to the private sector. Explicitly recognising that information is held by public authorities in public trust, the article asserts a right to ATI in 'public bodies' and in 'private bodies which [information] is necessary for the exercise or protection of any right'. The same article also spells out what today are characterised as data protection rights of access and correction vis-à-vis both public and private sectors, leaving no doubt as to the deliberately horizontal implication of the ATI right.

To facilitate the recognition of ATI in domestic law, the African Commission in 2013 adopted a model ATI law.[40] The Pan-African Parliament, the inter-governmental legislative body of the African Union, called on countries to adopt the African Model Law and to review existing ATI laws to ensure compliance with pan-African norms.[41] The model law is premised upon the familiar presumption of public access and duty of government to respond to requests, subject to narrowly drawn exemptions in the public interest.[42] The product of a two-and-a-half-year drafting process coordinated by the Centre for Human Rights at the University of Pretoria,[43] the African Model Law represents a thorough compilation of best practices in contemporary ATI law.[44]

---

[37]Phooko [26].

[38]Media Inst. of S. Africa, Draft Law on Access to Information in Africa, https://misaswaziland.com/draft-law-on-access-to-information-in-africa/ (last visited Sept. 18, 2018); *see* African Charter on Democracy, Elections, and Governance art. 19(2) (2007); African Charter on Statistics princ. 1 (2009) (transparency); African Charter on Values and Principles of Public Service and Administration art. 6 (2011); African Union Convention on Preventing and Combating Corruption art. 9 (2003); Protocol to the African Charter on Human and Peoples' Rights on the Rights of Women in Africa ('Maputo Protocol') art. 2(2), 4(2)(f), 5(a), 14(2)(a), 18(2)(b) (2003).

[39]Lasseko Phooko, *supra* note 37, at 179.

[40]Afr. Comm'n on Hum. & Peoples' Rts. [ACHPR], Model Law on Access to Information for Africa (2012) [hereinafter African Model Law], http://www.achpr.org/files/instruments/access-information/achpr_instr_model_law_access_to_information_2012_eng.pdf (adopted 2013).

[41]Pan-African Parliament, *Midrand Declaration on Press Freedom in Africa* (May 15, 2013), https://africacheck.org/wp-content/uploads/2014/06/Midrand-Declaration-on-Press-Freedom_FINAL_En-3-1.pdf.

[42]See African Model Law, *supra* note 40, § 2.

[43]*A New Model Law on Access to Information for Africa*, FREEDOMINFO.ORG, Apr. 12, 2013, http://www.freedominfo.org/2013/04/african-model-access-law-issued-by-rights-panel/.

[44]Though in sum the African Model Law is exemplary, there remain points of contention. For example, the model might afford respondent authorities too much latitude to refuse requests as

Just as elsewhere in the world, existing ATI laws in Africa approach the private sector principally through an array of policy choices that rationalise access upon entanglements with public money or power.[45] The African Model Law describes this mechanism by defining a class of private respondents as 'relevant public bod[ies]',[46] a confusing label if 'welcome' distinction.[47] The definition reaches the private sector coextensively with public control, financing, or function.[48]

Unlike anywhere else in the world, the African Model Law extends its reach to the private sector, adopting a variation of South Africa's conditional language. Apart from public bodies and relevant private bodies, a 'private body' is defined exhaustively to include natural persons, businesses, or any other 'juristic person' (such as an estate).[49] ATI is afforded as against a private body 'where the information may assist in the exercise or protection of any right'.[50] The express 'general principles' of the model law articulate the same right of ATI as against public, relevant private, and private bodies, to be effected 'expeditiously and inexpensively', only adding the rights-protective requirement for the latter class of respondents.[51] Variations of such direct, conditional access to the private sector are now known in at least five other African countries.[52]

An academic observer rated private-sector accountability the 'key strength' of the African Model Law, especially for its potential to combat environmental pollution and threats to public health attributable to extractive industries.[53] At the same time, Western commenters have wrung their hands over potential overreach to the detriment of the free market.[54] Critics focused on impact on small business and individuals, who would be bound to designate information officers and submit to compliance oversight, as well as media outlets, whose confidential sources and investigative journalism might be compromised. The African Model Law does restrain itself by excluding purely private bodies from some expectations, such as proactive disclosure requirements, the obligation to transfer record requests to more appropriate respondents, internal compliance training, and planning and reporting requirements.[55]

'manifestly vexatious'. African Model Law, *supra* note 40, § 37; see also Mutula and Wamukoya [19] (quasi-public bodies).

[45]Mutula and Wamukoya, *supra* note 44, at 334.

[46]African Model Law, *supra* note 40, § 1.

[47]Darwala et al. [9] (on behalf of Commonwealth Human Rights Initiative, New Delhi).

[48]African Model Law, *supra* note 40, § 1.

[49]African Model Law, *supra* note 40, § 1.

[50]*Id.* § 12(1)(b).

[51]*Id.* § 2(a)–(b).

[52]Peltz-Steele [24], *Access,* at 930 (Kenya, Rwanda, Sierra Leone, South Sudan, Tanzania).

[53]Hartshorn [10].

[54]E.g., Bertoni and Sánchez (n.d.) [on behalf of Centro de Estudios en Libertad de Expresión y Acceso a la Información, University of Palermo (Argentina) Law School].

[55]See African Model Law, *supra* note 40, §§ 6–9, 17, 62(2)(d), 65, 57.

8.2.2 South African ATI and the Private Sector

The 1996 South Africa Constitution and the 2000 PAIA, section 50—'any information that is held by another person [private body] and that is required for the exercise or protection of any rights'—raise two key substantive questions: (1) what rights are 'any rights'?; and (2) when is access 'required', or necessary? Today there is a small body of section 50 case law, mostly in business contexts unrelated to development. At the same time, a small body of public-sector access cases in development contexts suggest future applications for section 50. Questions of direct access to the private sector are only now coming to the fore in the judiciary. But together, these bodies of precedent sum a profound potential of ATI to further development through private-sector accountability.

The 'rights-required' test ostensibly posits two questions, though neither is binary, and the two are inextricably relative. The more intensely a 'right' is implicated—say, a fundamental human right, such as the right to life—the less demanding is the 'required' connection to vindicate that right. Inversely, the less intense the right—say, the right to demand performance on a contract—the more tightly the sought-after disclosure must exclusively and demonstrably ensure vindication of the right. The dynamic is not unlike the 'necessity' analysis of European human rights law, or the strict scrutiny of US constitutional law. But here the analysis tests the burden of ATI law, initiated by the private requester, on the social and economic freedom of another, the private respondent.

Guidance on the 'rights' question comes from the oft-cited *Cape Metropolitan Council v. Metro Inspection Services (Cape Metro)* in the Supreme Court of Appeal (SCA).[56] Interpretation of the 'required' question was refined by a line of high court cases—of which the Cape's *Van Huyssteen v. Minister of Environmental Affairs and Tourism* and *Nortje v. Attorney General* are representative—and then treated accordingly in two key SCA precedents, *Clutchco v. Davis*[57] and *Unitas Hospital v. Van Wyk*.[58]

Certainly 'any right' includes any fundamental right,[59] but case law has taken 'any' literally, generating a range of enforceable interests. *Cape Metro* involved a contract dispute between the council and contract levy collector Metro, amid allegations of fraud in claims for commissions.[60] Metro asserted 'rights' (1) to enforce 'a contractual or delictual claim for damages', and (2) 'to equality or to protect its busi-

[56] *Cape Metro. Council v. Metro Inspection Serv. W. Cape CC* [2001] ZASCA 56.

[57] *Clutchco (Pty.) Ltd. v. Davis* [2005] ZASCA 16, [2005] 2 All SA 225 (SCA), 2005 (3) SA 486 (SCA), ¶ 10.

[58] *Van Huyssteen v. Minister of Envtl. Affairs & Tourism* 1996 (1) SA 283 (C) (High Ct. E. Cape Prov. Div. June 28, 1995), *reprinted in* 1 COMPENDIUM OF JUDICIAL DECISIONS ON MATTERS RELATED TO ENVIRONMENT: NATIONAL DECISIONS 59, 71 (1998) [hereinafter COMPENDIUM], http://www.right2info.org/resources/publications/case-pdfs/south-africa_van-huyssteen-and-others-nno-v-minister-of-environmental-affairs-and-tourism-and-others.

[59] E.g., *Shabalala v. Attorney-Gen. of Transvaal* (CCT23/94) [1995] ZACC 12, 1995 (12) BCLR 1593, 1996 (1) SA 725 (fair trial).

[60] *Cape Metro. Council*, [2001] ZASCA 56, ¶ 6 (applying interim constitution); *see id.* ¶ 26.

ness reputation and good name'.[61] Relying upon precedent, the court reaffirmed that '"rights" in [ATI] in the interim Constitution included *not only* fundamental rights as set out in the … the interim Constitution'—and moreover, that the same principle carried over into ATI in the 1996 constitution.[62] Common law contract enforcement suffices. Later, though, the court pinned its decision on reputation, ruling that disclosure would help Metro to clear its name.[63] Producing language oft quoted as to the 'required' analysis, the court opined, 'Information can only be required for the exercise or protection of a right if it will be of assistance in the exercise or protection of the right'.[64] The court made no fuss over the leap from 'required' to the seemingly much weaker, 'of assistance'.

When disclosure is 'required' was the preoccupation of a series of cases under the 1993 interim constitution. Because the interim constitution used the rights-required test for *all* ATI claims, provincial case law on public-sector access from 1993 to 1996 informs the rights-required problem for private-sector access since 1996. The asserted right in *Van Huyssteen* was administrative fairness, which is constitutionally guaranteed. The decision confirmed that 'required' cannot be construed strictly. The case involved land trustees seeking access to environmental ministry records about a steel mill proposed for construction on neighbouring wetlands. The trustees feared pollution. The court concluded that the trustees 'reasonably require[d]' access to ministry records to be able to make their case and thereby vindicate the right to fair administrative process.[65] The *Van Huyssteen* court relied on discussion in the earlier *Nortje*,[66] in which criminally accused defendants won access to police records.[67] Considering where 'required' lies in a range from 'desire[]' to 'need[]',[68] the *Nortje* court concluded that witness statements 'would ordinarily be reasonably required by an accused person in order to prepare for trial in a criminal prosecution', criminal defence being a right 'beyond question'.[69]

The *Nortje-Van Huyssteen* line of cases received SCA imprimatur in *Clutchco*[70] and *Unitas Hospital*.[71] In both cases, requesters sought to apply the PAIA to private respondents, and both requesters ultimately failed. The court acknowledged up front in *Clutchco*: 'In extending the fundamental right of access to information to records

---

[61] *Id.* ¶ 24.

[62] *Id.* ¶ 27 (emphasis added) (citing *Van Niekerk v. Pretoria City Council* 1997 (3) SA 839 (T) at 844A-846G).

[63] *Id.* ¶ 29.

[64] *Id.* ¶ 28.

[65] *Van Huyssteen*, 1996 (1) SA 283 (C), *reprinted in* COMPENDIUM, *supra* note 58, at 71 (citing interim constitution).

[66] *Nortje v. Attorney Gen.* 1995 (2) SA 460 (C).

[67] *Van Huyssteen*, 1996 (1) SA 283 (C), *reprinted in* COMPENDIUM, *supra* note 58, at 70 (citing *Nortje*, 1995 (2) SA 460 (C) at 474F–475A).

[68] *Id.* (citing *Nortje*, 1995 (2) SA 460 (C) at 474F–475A).

[69] *Id.* (citing *Nortje*, 1995 (2) SA 460 (C) at 474F–475A).

[70] *Clutchco (Pty.) Ltd. v. Davis* [2005] ZASCA 16, [2005] 2 All SA 225 (SCA), 2005 (3) SA 486 (SCA), ¶ 10.

[71] *Unitas Hosp. v. Van Wyk* 2006 (4) SA 436.

held by private bodies, the Constitution and the statute have taken a step unmatched in human rights jurisprudence'.[72] Arising from straightforward commercial relationships, neither case bore overtones of development or public accountability, though that was not a causal factor in either analysis. Rather, the failure of both requesters might best be attributed to the existence of a parallel access system, causing the court to construe the PAIA strictly.

Clutchco arose out of an internecine struggle over control of a family company.[73] Davis, a son estranged from the company but a thirty-percent shareholder, sought access to company books for the asserted purpose—a 'right'—of valuing his shares after refusing a buy-out.[74] The Companies Act did not authorise access to the detailed books as Davis desired, so he resorted to the PAIA.[75] The court did not reject the PAIA as overridden by the Companies Act, but the legislature's failure to provide detailed access pressed the court to seek a 'substantial foundation' for PAIA access.[76] The court explained: 'In enacting PAIA Parliament could not have intended that the books of a company, great or small, should be thrown open to members on a whiff of impropriety or on the ground that relatively minor errors or irregularities have occurred'.[77]

The court assumed *arguendo* that Davis's right held water, though never analysed it on the merits.[78] Suggesting that Davis's personal reputation might be tied up with his valuation claim, the court quoted *Cape Metro* approvingly with regard to reputation as a viable rights theory.[79] But the court found fault with Davis's 'required' claim. Citing the *Nortje* line, the court revisited the 'reasonably required' range, from mere desire, to assistive, to indispensable, and to 'dire necessity', locating legislative intent at 'more than "useful"' and shy of 'essential'.[80] To articulate 'required', a requester must 'lay a proper foundation for why that document is reasonably "required" for the exercise or protection of his or her rights'.[81] '"[R]easonably required" in the circumstances is about as precise a formulation as can be achieved, provided that it is understood to connote a substantial advantage or an element of need'.[82] Because 'an experienced accountant and auditor' had failed to agree that disclosure would support the claim by Davis,[83] he could not meet the PAIA standard.[84]

[72] *Clutchco*, [2005] ZASCA 16, ¶ 10.

[73] *Id.* ¶¶ 2–9.

[74] *Id.* ¶¶ 3, 7–8.

[75] *Id.* ¶¶ 14–16.

[76] *Id.* ¶ 17.

[77] *Id.*

[78] *Id.*

[79] *Id.* (quoting *Cape Metro. Council*, [2001] ZASCA 56).

[80] *Id.* ¶ 11 (quoting precedents).

[81] *Id.* ¶ 12.

[82] *Id.* ¶ 13.

[83] *Id.* ¶ 18.

[84] *Id.* Later high court cases have divided on cases that are factually distinguishable. *Compare Loest v. Gendac* 2017 (4) SA 187 (GP) (finding better foundation in requester's contract-based claim to

In *Unitas Hospital*, the court acknowledged the relativity of 'required' analysis.[85] Van Wyk's husband died in intensive care after surgery at Unitas Hospital.[86] Van Wyk suspected nursing malpractice and moreover suspected that a hospital assessment report had documented the problem.[87] Thus in anticipation of a negligence claim, Van Wyk asked for the report under the PAIA.[88] Upon Van Wyk's 'right' to claim tort damages,[89] arguments focused on what the report would show. The lower court sided with Van Wyk, reasoning that even if the report would not evidence negligence, she would 'know this early and therefore avoid unnecessary litigation'.[90]

The SCA reversed. Acknowledging the 'reasonably required' standard of *Clutchco*, the court observed that negligence litigation would allow Van Wyk to avail of discovery.[91] Pre-litigation discovery under section 50 'would encourage … "fishing expeditions"', the court worried.[92] That is not to say that 'reliance on s 50 is automatically precluded merely because the information sought would eventually become accessible under the rules of discovery',[93] but the prospect of litigation is a factor in 'required' analysis.

Indeed, the SCA later confirmed the viability of the PAIA as a pre-litigation discovery tool in *Claase v. Information Officer of South African Airways (Pty.) Ltd.*[94] A retired pilot, Claase sought access to SAA records in a bid to prove non-compliance with the terms of his retirement contract.[95] The court lamented that 'disregard of the aims of the [PAIA] and the absence of common sense and reasonableness has resulted in this court having to deal with a matter which should never have required litigation'.[96] Reasoning that access 'would be decisive', 'bring[ing] a short sharp end to the dispute' without a need for litigation, the court ordered access and awarded Claase punitive costs.[97]

In sum, the 'reasonably required' formulation made for lasting precedent, not for its semantic significance, but for its consignment of a multi-factor analysis. An inverse function of the magnitude of the 'rights' claim, a case for 'required' must be constructed upon evidentiary foundation in documents and expert testimony, and

access books for valuation, nevertheless defeated on 'required' analysis for incompatibility with remedies under Companies Act), *with Fortuin v. Cobra Promotions CC* 2010 (5) SA 288 (ECP) (viewing valuation claim as legitimate pre-litigation discovery).

[85] *Unitas Hosp.*, 2006 (4) SA 436, ¶ 6.

[86] *Id.* ¶ 7.

[87] *Id.* ¶¶ 8–9.

[88] *Id.* ¶ 3.

[89] *Id.* ¶ 14.

[90] *Id.* (quoting lower court opinion).

[91] *Id.* ¶ 19.

[92] *Id.* ¶ 21.

[93] *Id.* ¶ 22.

[94] *Claase v. Info. Officer of S. Afr. Airways (Pty.) Ltd.* [2006] SCA 163 (RSA).

[95] *Id.* ¶¶ 2–3.

[96] *Claase*, [2006] SCA 163 (RSA), ¶ 1.

[97] *Id.* ¶ 11.

must navigate the shoals of parallel disclosure systems, such as the Companies Act and litigation discovery.

8.2.3 African ATI and Development

We have identified five reported ATI cases in South Africa with important implications for development accountability—specifically in areas of election law, truth and reconciliation, environmental law, and sport for development. Together these cases demonstrate that collective rights concomitant with social and economic development, such as the right to a healthy environment, can satisfy the 'rights' inquiry to empower citizens with access to the private sector. The cases furthermore articulate fact scenarios in which access may be argued as promotive of ethical development, or remonstrative of the unethical, well sufficiently to meet the 'required' standard of the ATI law.

8.2.3.1 Elections

Civil-society record requesters failed to gain access to the contribution records of major political parties in *Institute for Democracy in South Africa (IDASA) v. African National Congress (ANC)*.[98] Nevertheless, the bid of requesters IDASA, et al., to combat corruptive money in politics provides a roadmap for potential ATI litigation to secure civil and political rights.

With much wrangling, the respondent political parties in *IDASA* were held purely private bodies for the particular purpose of fundraising, so the ATI claim properly arose under PAIA section 50.[99] Because electoral integrity is essential to democracy, the requesters were able to assert manifold constitutional 'rights' theories.[100] The court rejected as non-justiciable 'rights' arising from the organisation of government and faulted requesters for failure to articulate a 'rational connection' between contribution-record access and the freedoms of expression and association.[101] But two 'rights' held water: the constitutional 'free[dom] to make political choices', including party organisation, and the 'right to free, fair and regular elections for any [constitutional] legislative body'.[102]

Tracking the 'reasonably required' approach of *Clutchco*, the requesters relied on political scientists to build a foundation proving the essentiality of contribution

---

[98] *Inst. for Democracy in S. Afr. v. Afr. Nat'l Cong. (IDASA)* [2005] ZAWCHC 30, 2005 (5) SA 39 (C), [2005] 3 All SA 45 (C).

[99] *IDASA*, [2005] ZAWCHC 30, ¶ 32.

[100] *Id.* ¶ 36 (citing S. Afr. Const., 1996, §§ 1(d), 16, 18, 19(1)–(2), 41(1)(c), 152(1)(a), 195(1)).

[101] *Id.* ¶¶ 39–40 (citing S. Afr. Const., 1996, §§ 1(d), 16, 18).

[102] S. Afr. Const., 1996, § 19(1)–(2).

transparency to inform and empower the electorate.[103] Experts proffered sectoral transparency systems in other countries. The court was unimpressed. Nowhere else, the court observed, did transparency arise from general ATI legislation or constitutional litigation.[104] Moreover, the requesters could not close the 'required' loop by explaining how contribution-record access would protect electoral rights.[105] The court was unconvinced that anyone 'require[s] such information *now*'.[106] Indeed, the requesters were undone by their own words in a position paper touting litigation as leverage to prompt sectoral legislation.[107]

If the *Clutchco* requester failed because his request was too narrow, eclipsed by the Companies Act, the *IDASA* request was too broad. The *IDASA* requesters would have had the PAIA occupy the field of campaign-finance regulation, constitutionally pre-empting legislative policymaking. To mind its lane, ATI in the private sector must neither undermine nor pre-empt a parallel access system. Despite the requesters' failure, *IDASA* established that political rights can support a section 50 claim. The requester must then delineate with care a scope of 'required' access mindful of parallel avenues. ATI can thus facilitate the maintenance of accountable democratic governance, a precondition to social and economic development.

8.2.3.2 Truth and Reconciliation

Truth and reconciliation naturally complement the post-Apartheid motivation behind constitutional ATI. The right to truth is recognised worldwide as a precondition to social development, and the role of commercial actors in past atrocities must be reconciled with prospective economic development. In this vein, Hlatshwayo, a researcher, sought access to historical records of the private manufacturer Mittalsteel in *Mittalsteel South Africa Ltd. v. Hlatshwayo*.[108] The time in question, from 1965 to 1973, predated the 1989 privatisation of Mittalsteel, which had been South Africa's largest steel producer as the state-controlled 'ISCOR'.[109] The SCA studiously underplayed the shadow of Apartheid, but it lay at the heart of Hlatshwayo's investigation into ISCOR labor[110]: a troubling mix of 'racial despotism', the 'cheap black labour system', and Afrikaner nationalism in the 'apartheid company state'.[111]

Mittalsteel was obliged as a former public body to respond to Hlatshwayo under the PAIA, the SCA concluded.[112] So the researcher was not obliged to articulate a

[103] *IDASA*, [2005] ZAWCHC 30, ¶¶ 42–43.
[104] *Id.* ¶ 45.
[105] *Id.* ¶ 47.
[106] *Id.* ¶ 48 (original emphasis).
[107] *Id.* ¶ 49.
[108] *Mittalsteel S. Afr. Ltd. v. Hlatshwayo* [2006] SCA 94, ¶ 2 (RSA).
[109] *Id.* ¶¶ 1, 23–27.
[110] *Id.* ¶ 2.
[111] Hlatshwayo [11].
[112] *Mittalsteel S. Afr. Ltd. v. Hlatshwayo* [2006] SCA 94, ¶ 28 (RSA).

'rights-required' foundation. Nevertheless, such historical inquiry furthers the human right to truth, which has motivated entities such as the South African History Archive to be a frequent user of the ATI law. The court's treatment-in-time of Mittalsteel ensures that privatisation is not an escape from accountability. Hlatshwayo's case moreover suggests the viability of PAIA section 50 as a vehicle to retrospective accountability for the many corporate actors that did exploit labour and profit from Apartheid.

8.2.3.3 Environment

Two ATI cases have involved civil-society advocacy for environmental protection: *Trustees for the Time Being of Biowatch Trust v. Registrar: Genetic Resources* in the Gauteng high court,[113] and *ArcelorMittal South Africa Ltd. (Arcelor) v. Vaal Environmental Justice Alliance (VEJA)* in the SCA.[114]

Though playing out against public-sector respondents, *Biowatch* involved privately owned information with important implications for agricultural development and public health. The court awarded watchdog Biowatch, along with intervenor ODAC,[115] presumptive access to a public registry of genetically modified organisms (GMOs).[116] From private-sector biotech, heavy-hitter Monsanto led intervening *amici* in opposing access.[117] Biowatch feared contamination of native maize by insecticide-resistant GMOs.[118] The corporate intervenors vigorously asserted commercial confidentiality.[119] Without ruling on the merits, the court allowed that the registrar could subsequently, after due consideration, deny access insofar as required to protect commercial confidentiality, '—if he were honestly and *bona fide* of the opinion that such a refusal is justified'.[120]

Biowatch demonstrates how the rights-required balance of ATI law tracks the balancing of interests at stake in social and economic development. It is not difficult to imagine a subsequent PAIA request, grounded in constitutional environmental guarantees or administrative fairness, lodged directly against a private entity such as Monsanto.[121] Biowatch instructs that commercial secrecy merits deference, because absolute transparency would be counter-productive to investment. At the same time, the PAIA remains as an investigative tool in the event native crops are genetically compromised. The ATI law thereby promotes commercial research in the public

[113] *Trs. for Time Being of Biowatch Tr. v. Registrar: Genetic Res.* [2005] ZAGPHC 135, ¶ 69.

[114] *Co. Sec'y, ArcelorMittal S. Afr. Ltd. v. Vaal Envtl. Justice Alliance* [2014] ZASCA 184, 2015 (1) SA 515 (SCA).

[115] *Id.* ¶ 11.

[116] *Trs. for Time Being of Biowatch Tr.*, [2005] ZAGPHC 135, ¶ 69.

[117] *Id.* ¶¶ 7–10.

[118] *Id.* ¶¶ 17–21.

[119] *Id.* ¶¶ 39–40.

[120] *Id.* ¶ 41.

[121] *See* S. AFR. CONST., 1996, §§ 24, 33.

interest while also limiting commercial activity at the point of injury or exploitation at public expense.

In a second environmental case, VEJA won access to historical and strategic information from steel producer Arcelor (progeny of ISCOR and Mittalsteel) about its waste disposal practices, particularly one 'comprehensive strategy document'.[122] The court began with a solicitous statement on collective rights:

> First, the world, for obvious reasons, is becoming increasingly ecologically sensitive. Second, citizens in democracies around the world are growing alert to the dangers of a culture of secrecy and unresponsiveness, both in respect of governments and in relation to corporations. In South Africa, because of our past, the latter aspect has increased significance.[123]

The court furthermore characterised the case as an 'entanglement' of economic development and environmental conservation, both constitutional priorities that must be balanced.[124]

For 'rights', the court allowed VEJA to rely on the constitutional right to a healthy environment; restraint would derive from the rights-required analysis.[125] VEJA was held to be a 'genuine advocate[] for environmental justice'.[126] The court rejected Arcelor counterarguments, including that VEJA was on a fishing expedition, that VEJA would effect itself as a shadow regulatory authority, and that VEJA should have availed of access under sectoral environmental law rather than the PAIA.[127] Distinguishing *Clutchco*'s analysis of the Companies Act, the court found VEJA's aims complementary rather than circumventive of environmental regulation because constitutional policy calls for 'collaborative corporate governance in relation to the environment'.[128] Rebuffing Arcelor's objection to private accountability, the court invoked South African history to explain the constitution's deliberate articulation of horizontal rights[129]: 'Corporations operating within our borders, whether local or international, must be left in no doubt that in relation to the environment in circumstances such as those under discussion, there is no room for secrecy and that constitutional values will be enforced'.[130]

VEJA established environmental protection as a cognisable right for ATI purposes. Moreover, through section 50 rights-required testing, *VEJA* plays out the *Biowatch* balancing of development interests, suggested there by disclosure-and-exemption analysis. The SCA in VEJA plainly allowed ATI as a horizontal right and enabler of collective rights, and thereby a means to corporate accountability. Where the *IDASA* requesters were too bluntly ambitious, VEJA navigated 'rights-required' on a tight

---

[122] *Co. Sec'y, ArcelorMittal S. Afr. Ltd. v. Vaal Envtl. Justice Alliance* [2014] ZASCA 184, 2015 (1) SA 515 (SCA), ¶¶ 2, 9.

[123] *ArcelorMittal*, [2014] ZASCA 184, ¶ 1.

[124] *Id.* ¶¶ 3–4.

[125] *Id.* ¶ 41 (quoting S. Afr. Const., 1996, § 24), ¶¶ 49–50.

[126] *Id.* ¶ 53.

[127] *Id.* ¶¶ 58–60.

[128] *Id.* ¶¶ 53, 60–74, 83; *see id.* ¶ 80.

[129] *Id.* ¶ 78.

[130] *Id.* ¶ 82.

course, aiming narrowly for foreseeably revelatory records known already to exist. This roadmap is instructive for future section 50 claims, whether in furtherance of civil-political, environmental, or other rights.

8.2.3.4 Sport

Finally one high court case directly implicated development in relation to the 2010 FIFA World Cup in South Africa: *M&G Media Ltd. v. 2010 FIFA World Cup Org. Comm. S. Afr. Ltd.*[131] Because the 2010 tournament marked the quadrennial mega-event's debut on the African continent, media watchdogs and academic researchers were keen to determine whether organisers and corporate sponsors made good on abundant promises of favourable development impact. To that end, the Johannesburg-based weekly *Mail & Guardian* (M&G) sought access to procurement records of the quasi-public organising committee.[132] Most of the lengthy court opinion was preoccupied with whether the respondent was a public or private body, owing to its oddly hybrid constitution. Ultimately, the court equivocated, but opted for an efficient ruling: M&G was entitled to have its request fulfilled either way.[133]

On the section 50 analysis, invoking *Cape Metro*, the court emphasised 'any' before 'rights' in the PAIA, construing legislative 'intention to ensure … the broadest possible interpretation'.[134] M&G relied on the freedom of expression.[135] The court acknowledged the media 'duty as public watchdog, and the information they require in order to discharge this obligation',[136] citing South African, European, UK, and Canadian case law,[137] and analogising to 'the special position of journalists', who receive prophylactic latitude in defamation law even to publish falsity.[138]

On the 'required' analysis, the court invoked reasonableness.[139] The court in one breath sought only 'some connection between the requested information and the exercise or protection of the right',[140] and in the next construed 'required [to] exercise or protect[]' as 'will enhance and promote'.[141] Generously to media, the

[131] *M&G Media Ltd. v. 2010 FIFA World Cup Org. Comm. S. Afr. Ltd.* 2011 (5) SA 163 (GSJ), ¶¶ 1–3.

[132] *Id.*

[133] *Id.* ¶ 163.

[134] *Id.* ¶ 334.

[135] *Id.* ¶ 337; S. AFR. CONST., 1996, § 16(1)(a).

[136] *M&G Media Ltd.*, 2011 (5) SA 163 (GSJ), ¶ 338.

[137] *Id.* ¶ 341.

[138] *Id.* ¶ 343. *But see* Nairobi Law Monthly Co. v. Kenya Elec. Generating Co., Pet. No. 278 of 2011 (High Ct. Nairobi, Const. & Hum. Rts. Div. May 13, 2013) (construing private-sector access provision in Kenyan law and rejecting requester reliance on constitutional role of journalist per se, because such bootstrapping would yield unbridled access to private sector upon any investigative claim).

[139] *M&G Media Ltd.*, 2011 (5) SA 163 (GSJ), ¶¶ 350–351.

[140] *Id.* ¶ 353.

[141] *Id.* ¶ 355.

court recognised that a requester who does 'not usually know [a record's] contents ... cannot be expected to demonstrate a link between the record and rights with any degree of detail or precision'.[142] Media's watchdog role was specially implicated to investigate 'the most significant sporting event in the world', more than the 'corner fish-and-chips shop'.[143] Thus, the court concluded, access could expose 'corruption, graft and/or incompetence'.[144] M&G proffered no facial evidence of wrongdoing; nevertheless, the court was satisfied by the need to hold the respondent accountable to claims that procurement 'created opportunities for small businesses and previously disadvantaged communities'.[145] '[T]he public has a "right to know" that this in fact so'[146]; inversely, '[t]he consequences of inaccurate reporting may be devastating'.[147] The court moreover rebuffed the respondent's claim of competitive commercial exemption.[148]

Ample doubts surround the development efficacy of the 2010 World Cup, and that story is only a piece of the global debate over the socioeconomic impact of sport mega-events and corruption in international sport governance. The *M&G* case is therefore crucially instructive. Even as mere high court precedent, *M&G* demonstrates the potential of ATI to promote development and combat corruption in a contemporary world in which the power and cachet of governments is dwarfed by the resources and influence of transnational corporations, both for-profit and ostensibly non-profit.

8.3 Access and the Private Sector in Poland

8.3.1 Polish ATI and the Private Sector

Poland has had a tumultuous modern relationship with privatisation. Liberation from the Soviet Union naturally resulted in a radical wave of privatisation in the 1990s, as Poland reshaped its economy into a free market. The run-up to full membership in the European Union, attained in 2004, dampened officials' enthusiasm for privatisation, as Poland revamped social services and regulatory systems to be compatible with European norms. Thereafter, Donald Tusk, prime minister from 2007 to 2014, sought aggressively to reinvigorate privatisation and simultaneously to enhance European integration, moving Poland toward the Eurozone. In 2015, the Law and Justice party (PiS) became the first winner of an outright majority in parliamentary election since 1989 and again applied the brakes to privatisation. Though economically conserva-

[142] *Id.* ¶ 353.
[143] *Id.* ¶¶ 355–356.
[144] *Id.* ¶ 360.
[145] *Id.* ¶¶ 383–385.
[146] *Id.* ¶ 384.
[147] *Id.* ¶ 387.
[148] *Id.* ¶¶ 408–413.

tive in ideology, PiS staked out a middle ground between the free market and state control in 'strategic sectors', namely finance, energy, and media.[149] PiS touts both privatisation and public reinvestment as necessary to strike the right balance. The likely result of this agenda will be a new breed of public/private-hybrid corporations controlling social and economic services that are essential to development.

However dramatic its swings in the short term, Polish experience with privatisation is a microcosm of the vagarious western European experience in the long term. In scarcely 70 years, Europe has vacillated from the advent of the social-democratic state and centralisation of the continental economy to an unprecedented turn-of-the-century privatisation crusade and austerity authorities' recent passion for privatisation—even amid a burgeoning movement for water re-municipalisation. On the accountability side of the coin, the freedom of information also has transformed—from its mere implication as ancillary to political expression in post-World War II human rights instruments, through a phase of rejection in the European human rights court, to widespread contemporary acceptance in the same court, in national constitutions, and in international legal norms.

Like its EU cohort, Poland binds itself to the ATI guarantees—however much, or little, they in fact guarantee—of the Universal Declaration of Human Rights, the International Covenant on Civil and Political Rights, and the European Convention on Human Rights and Fundamental Freedoms.[150] The Constitution of the Republic of Poland recognises ATI generously, both as ancillary to the freedom of expression and as an express right.[151] Article 61 guarantees 'the right to obtain information on the activities of organs of public authority as well as persons discharging public functions' and private entities insofar as they are entrusted with state funds or property.[152] The article prescribes legislative enactment of access and authorises legislative limitations on access 'solely to protect freedoms and rights of other persons and economic subjects, public order, security or important economic interests of the State'.[153] Article 51 states principles of data protection, including rights of consent, minimisation, access, and correction of information about oneself. In a development vein, article 74 contains ecological and environmental protection guarantees that include 'the right to be informed of the quality of the environment and its protection'.

---

[149] Pacula [22].

[150] See Tarnacka [31].

[151] KONSTYTUCJA RZECZYPOSPOLITEJ POLSKIEJ [RP] Z DNIA 2 KWIETNIA 1997 R. [CONSTITUTION OF THE REPUBLIC OF POLAND OF APR. 2, 1997] art. 14, 54, http://www.sejm.gov.pl/prawo/konst/angielski/kon1.htm (official English translation).

[152] *Id.* art. 61, sec. 1 ('Such right shall also include receipt of information on the activities of self-governing economic or professional organs and other persons or organizational units relating to the field in which they perform the tasks of public authorities and manage communal assets or property of the State Treasury.'). The article also requires access to the records and meetings of 'collective organs of public authority formed by universal elections, with the opportunity to make sound and visual recordings'. *Id.* art. 61, sec. 2.

[153] *Id.* art. 61, sec. 3–4. Legislative access is specified for enactment through rules of procedure in the respective houses of parliament. *Id.* art. 61, sec. 4.

In interpreting the freedom of expression, the Supreme Court of Poland has signaled that constitutional protection exceeds that of the European human rights regime. Regarding the right of access to information, the court in 2000 reiterated the constitutional bar on access restrictions in the absence of a codified state interest in secrecy.[154] Inversely, the court articulated a national interest in affording media the widest possible access to information held by public bodies, including the right to obtain information in oral, written, or any form, and by inspection of records that result from the activity of public bodies.[155]

Poland codified ATI in the Act of September 6, 2001 on Access to Public Information (ATPIA), which entered force in 2002.[156] Broader than the constitution, the ATPIA affords access to all persons, not only citizens.[157] A 'person' includes the natural and juridical, the foreign and stateless, and organisational units without legal personality, such as social organisations.[158] Adhering to the modern ATI principle of interest neutrality, a person is not required to articulate any prerequisite legal or factual interest to obtain specific information.[159] The statute echoes the constitutional characterisation of public information, embracing information created by public authorities sensu *largo*, as well as entities executing public functions and using state or municipal property.[160] Because the constitution does not explicitly catalogue the entities bound by the ATI right, the *ratione materiae* defines the *ratione personae*.[161] Therefore information not produced by covered entities but related to them can be public information. The content of records, not their creation, nor their location, controls their access disposition.[162]

The ATPIA expands on the function test of the constitution to reach otherwise private entities. These quasi-public ATI respondents might not be part of the state authority structure, but they exercise authority normally reserved to the state, because they implement public tasks.[163] These are tasks that serve not only the needs of a

---

[154] Wyrok Sąd Najwyższy [SN] z 1 czerwca 2000 r. [Supreme Court Judgment of June 1, 2000], III RN 64/00, http://www.sn.pl/sites/orzecznictwo/Orzeczenia1/III%20RN%2064-00.pdf.

[155] *Id.*

[156] Ustawa z dnia 6 września 2001 r. o dostępie do informacji publicznej (Dz. U. 2001 Nr 112 poz. 1198, with amendments), *translated in* LEGIS. ONLINE, https://www.legislationline.org/documents/id/6757 (OSCE Off. for Democratic Institutions & Hum. Rts. last visited Sept. 11, 2018) [hereinafter ATPIA].

[157] *Id.* art. 2.

[158] Wyrok Wojewódzki Sąd Administracyjny [WSA] w Warszawie z 11 lutego 2004 r. [Warsaw District Administrative Court Judgment of Feb. 11, 2004], III SAB 391/03, http://orzeczenia.nsa.gov.pl/doc/9C8EB0684A.

[159] ATPIA art. 2(2); TOMASZ R. ALEKSANDROWICZ, KOMENTARZ DO USTAWY O DOSTEPIE DO INFORMACJI PUBLICZNEJ [COMMENTARY ON THE STATUTE ON ACCESS TO PUBLIC INFORMATION] 121 (2006).

[160] ATPIA art. 4.

[161] Pawlik [23].

[162] Wyrok Najwyższy Sąd Administracyjny [NSA] z 3 kwietnia 2014 r [Supreme Administrative Court Judgment of Apr. 3, 2014], I OSK 2994/13, http://orzeczenia.nsa.gov.pl/doc/1AA23834FB.

[163] *Zakres stosowania przepisów dostępowych* [*Scope of Application of Access Rules*], *in* GÓWNE PROBLEMY PRAWA DO INFORMACJI W ŚWIETLE PRAWA I STANDARDÓW MIEDZYNARODOWYCH,

limited number of people, but the public good, that are carried out on an ongoing basis, and that are implemented to effect publicly available benefits.[164] Whether an entity performs public tasks, and thus whether it must disclose public information, is determined by analysing its activity.[165] As to the alternative test for access via public funding, the ATPIA follows public money and property into its private-sector management.[166]

As the constitution authorises, ATPIA access may be limited by statute. The ATPIA itself defers to collateral access systems,[167] which include the Public Procurement Act.[168] That act introduced the principle of transparency for the award of a public contract, extending public inspection to award procedures, offers, expert opinions, statements, information from meetings, notifications, applications, and other records submitted by authorities and contractors. Contractors may apply to restrict access to information protectable in law, such as trade secrets. Similarly, the Protection of Classified Information Act[169] controls access to information held secret by other statutes, such as upon a doctor's or lawyer's duty of confidentiality.[170] The ATPIA defers to personal privacy[171] and the Protection of Personal Data Act.[172] And the ATPIA exempts 'entrepreneur's secrets', when not related to public functions and

EUROPEJSKICH I WYBRANYCH PAŃSTW UNII EUROPEJSKIEJ [THE MAIN PROBLEMS OF THE RIGHT TO INFORMATION IN LIGHT OF INTERNATIONAL LAW AND STANDARDS, EUROPEAN AND SELECTED EUROPEAN UNION COUNTRIES] 22–23 (Grzegorz Sibiga ed., 2014).

[164] Uchwała NSA z 11 kwietnia 2005 r [NSA Resolution of Apr. 11, 2005], I OPS 1/05, http://orzeczenia.nsa.gov.pl/doc/571022A55E.

[165] Pawlik, *supra* note 161, at 3; *Zakres*, *supra* note 163, at 23.

[166] Pietras [27].

[167] ATPIA art. 1(2); Wyrok WSA w Warszawie z 5 września 2013 r [WSA Judgment of Sept. 5, 2013], VIII SA/Wa 433/13, http://orzeczenia.nsa.gov.pl/doc/41D1B89D6E.

[168] Prawo zamówień publicznyc z 29 stycznia 2004 r (Dz. U. 2004r. Nr 19, poz. 177, with amendments).

[169] Ustawa o ochronie informacji niejawnych z 22 stycznia 1999 r (Dz. U. 2005r Nr 196, poz. 1631, uniform text).

[170] ATPIA art. 5(1); *see* Ustawa o radcach prawnych z 26 maja 1982 r [Advocates' Profession Act of May 26, 1982] art. 6 (Dz. U. 2018 Nr 1184, 1467, uniform text); Ustawa o radcach prawnych z 6 lipca 1982 [Legal Counsels' Profession Act of July 6, 1982] art. 3 (Dz. U. 2018 poz. 138, 723, 1467, uniform text); Ustawa z dnia 5 grudnia 1996 r. o zawodach lekarza i lekarza dentysty [Medical Profession Act of Dec. 5, 1996] art. 40 (Dz. U. 2018, poz. 617, 650, 697, uniform text).

[171] ATPIA art. 5(2).

[172] Ustawa z dnia 10 maja 2018 r. o ochronie danych osobowych [Protection of Personal Data Act of May 10, 2018] (Dz. U. 2018 poz. 1000) (implementing Regulation (EU) 2016/679 of the European Parliament and of the Council of 27 April 2016 on the protection of natural persons with regard to the processing of personal data and on the free movement of such data, which repealed Directive 95/46/EC).

when secrecy is not waived, without defining the term.[173] Courts have construed the provision *per analogiam* to commercial secrets[174] in the Unfair Competition Act.[175]

8.3.2 Polish ATI and Development

The Polish courts have had ample occasion to apply the ATPIA to quasi-public entities. The court of first instance in ATI cases, the Supreme Administrative Court (NSA) has applied the ATPIA to partially state-owned enterprises. Through the function and funding formulas of the ATPIA, the NSA has moreover extended ATI to privately owned entities in the key development sectors of energy, transportation, and telecommunication. Owing to the constitutional and statutory design, the courts' approach to ATI has been grounded in analysis of an otherwise private actor's public tasks or funding. From this starting point, the courts have applied ATI liberally. The rhetoric in the court opinions suggests broad conceptualisation about the importance of a free flow of information to the provision of vital services to the public. At the same time, the courts remain beholden to the constitutional and statutory focus on the function and funding of the otherwise-private respondent entity. Typically of the classical Western model of ATI, then, access in Poland remains a function of the respondent's role, rather than of the public requester's need.

8.3.2.1 State Ownership

In its resolution of April 11, 2005, the NSA construed 'use of public property' in the ATPIA to include property owned by the state, by a municipality, by an entities of the public finance sector, or by a bank or commercial law company, in which the state holds more than half of shares in the share capital.[176] In a ruling in 2016, the court added that even an indirect dominant position, as the state achieved through ownership of an intermediary company as a shareholder, triggered application of the ATPIA.[177]

[173] ATPIA art. 5(2).

[174] Wyrok SN z 6 czerwca 2003 r. [SN Judgment of June 6, 2003], IV CKN 211/01 (LEX nr 585877); Wyrok WSA w Krakowie z 18 grudnia 2006 r. [WSA in Kraków Judgment of Dec. 18, 2006], II SAB/Kr 87/06, http://orzeczenia.nsa.gov.pl/doc/C4D7263C27; Wyrok WSA w Poznaniu z 1 marca 2011 r. [WSA in Poznań Judgment of Mar. 1, 2011], II SAB/Po 1/11, http://orzeczenia.nsa.gov.pl/doc/B2BF568588.

[175] Ustawa z dnia 16 kwietnia 1993 r. o zwalczaniu nieuczciwej konkurencji (Dz. U. 2003 Nr 153 poz. 1503, with amendments).

[176] Uchwała NSA z 11 kwietnia 2005 r. [NSA Resolution of Apr. 11, 2005], I OPS 1/05, http://orzeczenia.nsa.gov.pl/doc/571022A55E.

[177] Wyrok NSA z 28 października 2005 r. [NSA Judgment of Oct. 28, 2016], I OSK 603/15, http://orzeczenia.nsa.gov.pl/doc/89D128A548.

8.3.2.2 Energy

In its judgment of August 18, 2010, the Supreme Administrative Court (NSA), which is the court of first instance in ATI cases, decided that companies in the electric power industry are public utilities that perform public tasks within the meaning of the ATPIA.[178] The court explained that 'public task', as used in the ATPIA, is broader than 'public authority task', as stated in the constitution. The statutory term broadens the *ratione personae* scope to mean that public tasks can be performed by entities which are not authorities, and even which have not been specifically charged with public tasks by statute. First, the performance of public tasks always is connected with the realisation of citizens' basic rights. Because of the importance of electricity for development and standard of living, the generation and distribution of electricity by utility companies are public tasks. Second, public tasks are characterised by universality and usefulness for the general public, as well as promotion of goals enumerated in the constitution or the ATPIA. Delivery of electricity is necessary to attain the common good of the people, which is referenced in article 1 of the constitution. Therefore electric power companies are obliged to obey the ATPIA upon requests for information on 'public matters', as stated in the statute's article 1.1.

8.3.2.3 Transportation

In its judgment of October 17, 2013, the NSA held a transportation company obliged to disclose information on public matters under the ATPIA.[179] The court found that the private provider of a municipal transportation service was executing public tasks and also using public property, as it received subsidies for discounted tickets. Either of those conditions requires compliance with the ATPIA, the court reasoned. First, the court referenced statutes that oblige local governments to secure public transportation for the general public to reason that regular transportation services are public tasks, whether provided by a public or private entity.[180] The trending 'phenomenon of so-called "privatization"' does not vary the ATPIA analysis, the court opined. Second, the NSA held that an entity entrusted with 'even a small part of public property' is bound to accountability under the ATPIA. The law allows local government to finance transportation services, and the mere reimbursement of costs invites the ATPIA to follow the money.

---

[178] Wyrok NSA z 18 sierpnia 2010 r. [NSA Judgment of Aug. 18, 2010], I OSK 851/10, http://orzeczenia.nsa.gov.pl/doc/529C4D0B34.

[179] Wyrok NSA z 28 października 2013 r. [NSA Judgment of Oct. 17, 2013], I OSK 952/13, http://orzeczenia.nsa.gov.pl/doc/FBB404C78B.

[180] E.g., Ustawa z dnia 8 marca 1990 r. o samorządzie gminnym [Act on Municipal Local Government of Mar. 8, 1990] (Dz. U. 2018, poz. 994, 1000, 1349, uniform text).

8.3.2.4 Telecommunication

In its judgment of May 28, 2013, the NSA held that Orange Polska S.A. (Orange), a private-sector telecom conglomerate, performs public tasks and is therefore obliged to respond to ATPIA requests on public matters.[181] Orange Polska S.A. was once Telekomunikacja Polska, a wholly state-owned enterprise derived from a communist-era predecessor in 1991. The company underwent a transition of privatisation around the turn of the century, ultimately vesting majority ownership in France Télécom, which rebranded itself as Orange. While Orange is the largest provider in Poland, the NSA's reasoning pertains equally well to a small entrepreneur.

In sum the court reasoned that access to communication, including telephone and internet, is both socially necessary and vital to the functioning of the state. First, the NSA recognised the nature of the contemporary 'information society', in which access to telecommunication services, especially mobile telephony and internet, is fundamentally important. Thus meeting this citizen need, the court reasoned, is as essential socially and economically as the provision of electricity. Telecommunication providers therefore must comply with the ATPIA in making decisions about infrastructure development for both wireless and landline networks. In the instant case, Orange was asked for information about its strategic decisions on locating and constructing telecommunication network infrastructure.

Second, by statute, Poland recognised Orange as a provider and operator of publicly available telecommunications services. The Telecommunications Act obliges a telecommunications entrepreneur to perform tasks and duties of defence, state security, and public safety and order, as specified by statute and regulation.[182] The NSA furthermore grounded its 'public task' analysis in provisions of the Real Estate Management Act[183] and the Spatial Planning and Development Act,[184] which regulate the construction and maintenance of public communication facilities and equipment, regardless of private or public control.

8.4 Analysis and Conclusion

Researchers have recognised the peculiar capacity of ATI as 'an enabler right', capable of facilitating other human rights, from the civil-political to the collective.[185] The

[181]Wyrok NSA z 28 maja 2014 r. [NSA Judgment of May 28, 2014], I OSK 2380/13, http://orzeczenia.nsa.gov.pl/doc/F7EE820FB6.

[182]Prawo telekomunikacyjne 16 lipca 2004 r. [Telecommunications Act of July 16, 2004] art. 176 (Dz. U. 2014, poz. 243, item 1503, with amendments).

[183]Ustawy z dnia 21 sierpnia 1997r. o gospodarce nieruchomościami, art. 6 ust. 1 (t.j. Dz. U. z 2010r. Nr 102 poz. 651 ze zm.).

[184]Ustawy z dnia 27 marca 2003r. o planowaniu i zagospodarowaniu przestrzennym, art. 2 pkt 5 (t.j. Dz. U. z 2012r. nr 647 ze zm.).

[185]Article 19, *Open Development: Access to Information and the Sustainable Development Goals* 9 (July 2017), https://www.article19.org/data/files/medialibrary/38832/Open-Development--Access-to-Information-and-the-SDGs-2017.pdf; *see also* UNESCO, Keystones to Foster Inclusive

International Council on Human Rights recognised that human rights merit protection regardless of whether threats against them emerge from the public sector or the private sector.[186] Joining these observations, researchers in ATI law—notably Darch and Underwood,[187] Calland,[188] and Roberts,[189] building on Hohfeld[190]—have concluded that ATI does its human rights work by altering distributions of power in society.

Both Calland and Roberts have championed the idea of ATI as a *power* dynamic, because it empowers a requester of information as against a holder of information. Roberts described the emergence of transparency as a norm in the twentieth-century United States in response to the proliferation of bureaucracy in the administrative state.[191] The pluralisation of public service provision through a range of hybrid, privatised, and private actors later in the twentieth century marked a shift in power away from people and to the private sector, threatening a second wave of 'democratic deficit'[192] or 'information poverty'.[193] Socio-economic freedom is especially vulnerable to monopolistic or oligopolistic power in the provision of infrastructure, such as transportation and telecommunication, because consumers have no market alternative.[194]

ATI in the private sector is the antidote. Rather than stopping arbitrarily at the public-private divide, ATI should persist as a function of necessity. In the public sector, access is presumptive, because public ownership of government is a defining characteristic of democracy. Beyond the divide, the public interest in transparency does not vanish, but diminishes inversely with the strengthening social and economic freedom of private actors. ATI therefore restores balance. Development seeks the same balance: to promote private-sector growth while simultaneously furthering the public good. The relationship is complementary, not zero-sum.

In the development context, South African law demonstrates how ATI can transcend the classical public-private divide and, through the 'rights-required' analysis, deploy transparency to bolster ethics and efficacy in development. *IDASA* estab-

---

KNOWLEDGE SOCIETIES: ACCESS TO INFORMATION AND KNOWLEDGE, FREEDOM OF EXPRESSION, PRIVACY, AND ETHICS ON A GLOBAL INTERNET: FINAL STUDY 29, http://unesdoc.unesco.org/images/0023/002325/232563E.pdf.

186 INT'L COUNCIL ON HUMAN RIGHTS (ICHR), BEYOND VOLUNTARISM: HUMAN RIGHTS AND THE DEVELOPING INTERNATIONAL LEGAL OBLIGATIONS OF COMPANIES (2002), http://www.ichrp.org/files/summaries/7/107_summary_en.pdf, cited in Siraj [30].

187 Darch and Underwood, *supra* note 1, at 140–41.

188 Calland, *supra* note 1.

189 Roberts, *supra* note 5.

190 Hohfeld [12, 13]; see also Siraj, *supra* note 187, at 214 [citing JANET DINE, COMPANIES, INTERNATIONAL TRADE AND HUMAN RIGHTS (1995); TIM DUNNE & NICHOLAS J. WHEELER, HUMAN RIGHTS IN GLOBAL POLITICS (1999); JEDRZEJ GEORGE FRYNAS & SCOTT PEGG, TRANSNATIONAL CORPORATIONS AND HUMAN RIGHTS (2003)].

191 Roberts, *supra* note 5, at 245–55.

192 *Id.* at 269.

193 Bentley and Calland, supra note 33, at 341.

194 Mulgan [18].

lished the pertinence of ATI to the rule of law itself as a guarantee of representative democracy, even if through a dedicated statutory framework. *Mittalsteel* revealed an important role for ATI in truth and reconciliation, a proposition with as ready implication in Polish experience with communism as in the South African experience with Apartheid. *Biowatch* and *VEJA* point to the role of ATI in environmental protection, a priority recognised expressly in the Polish constitution. *M&G* applied ATI to the tidal fiscal force of football, which governments in Europe no less than in Africa have sought to enlist in the cause of economic development. While plenty of interpretive work remains to be done—not to mention strengthening implementation on the ground—the driving force in these cases is the necessity of access to protect human rights.

Meanwhile in Poland, as in Europe and much of the world, ATI remains stubbornly tethered to the classical twentieth-century divide between public and private sectors. Accountability through access is a defining feature of the public sector, while the purely private sector is left to the accountability of mere market forces. Yet the Polish state strives to stimulate development and to fulfil the promises of human rights by enlisting the private sector in various permutations of public entanglement. The Polish legislature and courts, after the Western model, press ATI law through public interest into the private sector along avenues such as funding and function. State ownership offers an inviting entry point, but access stops abruptly at the arbitrary halfway line. The courts have recognised the essentiality of energy, transportation, and telecommunication to the realisation of democracy and human rights, extending ATI in tandem with 'public matters' and pushing back against the opacity of privatisation. This advancement signals the overriding importance of the public interest in access analysis. Still, though, the focus of Western ATI remains fixed on *state* accountability.

Access avenues such as funding and function are artifices. The common thread driving access toward the private sector is necessity. To ensure meaningful development within a democratic framework, ATI must do more than hold governments to account. Power to disaffect human rights rests increasingly in the private sector. A resulting democratic deficit cries out for rebalance through ATI. Accordingly, the legal approach to ATI must shift from means to ends. The public-private divide is not a stopping point for access, but a point of burden shifting, where presumptive access inverts to presumptive secrecy. The latter presumption still must yield to human rights upon demonstrated necessity. In this vein, African ATI law is charting a new course, one worthy of attention as the nations of the North and West map out their own agendas for responsible development.

Acknowledgements The authors wish to acknowledge previous research that contributed to this chapter and to thank the journals that supported that work: Peltz-Steele [24, 25].

References

1. Adeleke, F. (2013). Constitutional domestication of the right of access to information in Africa: Retrospect and prospects. In F. Diallo, & R. Calland (Eds.), *Access to information in Africa: Law, culture and practice* (pp. 83, 89).
2. Asimow, M. (1996). Administrative law under South Africa's interim constitution. *The American Journal of Comparative Law, 393,* 394.
3. Bentley, K., & Calland, R. (2014). Access to information and socio-economic rights: A theory of change in practice. In M. Langford & B. Cousins (Eds.), *Socio-economic rights in South Africa: Symbols or substance?* (p. 361).
4. Bertoni, E., & Sánchez, G. (n.d.). Draft model law for African Union States on access to information: Comments and recommendations. http://www.palermo.edu/cele/pdf/investigaciones/AU-Draft-Model-Law-CELE.pdf.
5. Burns, Y. (2000). Introduction. In *The Constitutional Right of Access to Information, Conference Proceedings*, September 4, 2000 (p. 5) http://www.kas.de/wf/doc/kas_4936-1522-2-30.pdf?040625152235.
6. Calland, R. (2009). Illuminating the politics and practice of access to information in South Africa. In K. Allan (Ed.), *Paper wars: Access to information in South Africa* (Vol. 1, p. 4). http://foip.saha.org.za/static/paper-wars-access-to-information-in-south-africa.
7. Calland, R. (2014). Exploring the liberal genealogy and the changing praxis of the right of access to information: Towards an egalitarian realisation, *Theoria, 61,* 70–71.
8. Darch, C., & Underwood, P. (2010). *Freedom of information and the developing world: The citizen, the state and models of openness* (pp. 233–235).
9. Darwala, M., Nayak, V., Nalule, C., & Choraria, V. (2011). *Draft model law for African Union Member States on access to information: A preliminary analysis with recommendations for change*, August 2011 (p. 6). http://www.humanrightsinitiative.org/programs/ai/rti/international/AUmodelATIlaw-CHRIprelimcritique-Aug11-Delhi-VrindaCVenkatN.pdf.
10. Hartshorn, J. V. (2014). *Can the model law on access to information for Africa fulfil expectations?* Paper at European Consortium for Political Research Conference on Regulatory Governance, Barcelona (pp. 10, 12). http://reggov2014.ibei.org/bcn-14-papers/66-212.pdf.
11. Hlatshwayo, M. S. (2003). *The politics of production and forms of worker response at the ISCOR Vanderbijlpark works, 1965–1973* (p. 53) (Unpublished M.A. thesis, University of the Witwatersrand). Available at Academia.edu, https://www.academia.edu/24723973/THE_POLITICS_OF_PRODUCTION_AND_FORMS_OF_WORKER_RESPONSE_AT_THE_ISCOR_VANDERBIJLPARK_WORKS_1965-1973.
12. Hohfeld, W. N. (1917). Fundamental legal conceptions as applied in judicial reasoning. *The Yale Law Journal, 26,* 710.
13. Hohfeld, W. N. (1920). *Fundamental legal conceptions as applied in judicial reasoning and other legal essays* (p. 5).
14. Klaaren, J., Currie, I., & Smith, A. (2000). Analysing foreign access to information legislation from a South African viewpoint. In *The Constitutional Right of Access to Information, Conference Proceedings*, September 4, 2000 (pp. 29–30). http://www.kas.de/wf/doc/kas_4936-1522-2-30.pdf?040625152235.
15. Lange, M. (2000). Welcoming remarks. In *The Constitutional Right of Access to Information, Conference Proceedings*, September 4, 2000 (pp. 7–8). http://www.kas.de/wf/doc/kas_4936-1522-2-30.pdf?040625152235.
16. Liebenberg, S. (2014). Socio-economic rights beyond the public-private law divide. In M. Langford & B. Cousins (Eds.), *Socio-economic rights in South Africa: Symbols or substance?* (pp. 63, 66–72).
17. McKinley, D. T. (2012). *The right to know, the right to live: Open data in South Africa* (p. 7). https://opengovernmentafrica.files.wordpress.com/2013/04/info-needs-report.pdf.
18. Mulgan, R. (2000). Comparing accountability in the public and private sectors. *Australian Journal of Public Administration, 59,* 87–88.

19. Mutula, S., & Wamukoya, J. M. (2009). Public sector information management in east and southern Africa: Implications for FOI, democracy and integrity in government. *International Journal of Information Management, 29,* 333–334.
20. Ngabirano, D. (2013). The Uganda freedom of information campaign: Stuck in the mud? In Diallo, F., & Calland, R. (Eds.), *Access to information in Africa: Law, culture and practice* (pp. 191, 208–209).
21. O'Regan, K. (2000). Democracy and access to information in the South Africa Constitution: Some reflections. In *The Constitutional Right of Access to Information, Conference Proceedings*, September 4, 2000 (pp. 11–12). http://www.kas.de/wf/doc/kas_4936-1522-2-30.pdf?040625152235.
22. Pacula, P. (2016). Poland seeks to boost state control of economy. *EU Observer*, February 24, 2016. https://euobserver.com/beyond-brussels/132421.
23. Pawlik, K. (2018). Przedsiębiorca w procedurze dostępu do informacji publicznej [Entrepreneur in the procedure of access to public information]. *Studenckie Zeszyty Naukowe* [*Sci. J. Students*], *21,* 37–38. http://journals.umcs.pl/szn/article/view/6782/5157.
24. Peltz-Steele, R. J. (2018, Forthcoming). Access to information in the private sector: African inspiration for U.S. FOIA reform. *Villanova Law Review, 63,* 907.
25. Peltz-Steele, R. J. (2017). Accountability in the private sector: African ambition for right to information in India, *Research Journal Social Sciences, 25,* 203.
26. Phooko, M. L. (2013). An actionable constitutional right of ATI. In F. Diallo & R. Calland, R. (Eds.), *Access to information in Africa: Law, culture and practice* (pp. 171, 177).
27. Pietras, S. M. (2011). Podmioty zobowiązane do udzielenia informacji publicznej w rozumieniu art. 4 ustawy z dnia 6 września 2001 r. o dostępie do informacji publicznej [Entities obliged to public information in the meaning of ATPIA]. *Ius Novum*, 108–119. https://iusnovum.lazarski.pl/fileadmin/user_upload/dokumenty/czasopisma/ius-novum/2011/Ius_Novum_4_6_2011_Pietras.pdf.
28. Roberts, A. (2001). Structural pluralism and the right to information. *The University of Toronto Law Journal, 51,* 243, 265.
29. Roling, S. (2007). *Transparency & access to information in South Africa: An evaluation of the promotion of access to Information Act 2 of 2000* (Dissertation) (p. 3). http://www.publiclaw.uct.ac.za/usr/public_law/LLMPapers/roling.pdf.
30. Siraj, M. (2010). Exclusion of private sector from freedom of information laws: Implications from a human rights perspective. *Journal of Alternative Perspectives in the Social Sciences, 211,* 215–216.
31. Tarnacka, K. (2009). *Prawo do informacji w polskim prawie konstytucyjnym* [*The right to information in Polish constitutional law*] (p. 13).

Chapter 9
Between Economic Development and Human Rights: Balancing E-Commerce and Adult Content Filtering

Adam Szafrański, Piotr Szwedo and Małgorzata Klein

Abstract Notwithstanding its many positive attributes, the internet also poses serious risks for the human rights of some of the most vulnerable users: children. As is the case with their peers in the developed world, minors in developing countries also face the threat of online adult content exposure. Efforts to address this have been under way in the United Kingdom, Poland, and United States (cf., Utah) relying on different regulatory methods. Whilst, both, self-regulation and State regulation may comply with international requirements on the freedom of services and the freedom of expression, they must still be scrutinised properly. The present contribution shall examine regulatory means in relation to addressing the issue of child exposure to adult content in the developed and developing parts of the world. In sum, statutory regulation appears more suited to serving the interests of developing countries than soft law and self-regulatory approaches, as public and mandatory measures may bring greater transparency and may usually make it possible to challenge individual decisions or abstract regulations before national courts.

The original version of this chapter was revised: The affiliation of the author Małgorzata Klein has been corrected. The correction to this chapter is available at https://doi.org/10.1007/978-981-13-9423-2_14

This research is partly based on our article titled *Comparative Perspectives of Adult Content Filtering: Legal Challenges and Implications*, published in the Catholic University Law Review, Vol. 68, Issue 1.

A. Szafrański
Faculty of Law and Administration, University of Warsaw, ul. Krakowskie Przedmieście 26/28, 00-927 Warsaw, Poland
e-mail: adam.szafranski@uw.edu.pl

P. Szwedo (✉)
Faculty of Law and Administration, Jagiellonian University, ul. Gołębia 24, p. 3, 31-007 Kraków, Poland
e-mail: piotr.szwedo@uj.edu.pl

M. Klein
Faculty of Geography and Regional Studies, University of Warsaw, ul. Krakowskie Przedmieście 30, 00-927 Warsaw, Poland
e-mail: gosia.przepiorka@gmail.com

P. Szwedo et al. (eds.), *Law and Development*, Kobe University Monograph Series in Social Science Research, https://doi.org/10.1007/978-981-13-9423-2_9

Keywords Developing countries · Children's rights · Adult content · Freedom of services · Regulation

9.1 Introduction: Growing Internet Access in Developing Countries

The importance of internet access for development is evident. It is stressed by Sustainable Development Goals (SDGs); Goal 9 which calls on States to '[b]uild resilient infrastructure, promote sustainable industrialization and foster innovation.' Target 9.c. calls on States to 'significantly increase access to information and communications technology and strive to provide universal and affordable access to the internet in least developed countries by 2020'.[1]

The United Nations' Broadband Commission for Digital Development in 2015 published a report on global internet access entitled 'The State of Broadband 2015: Broadband as a Foundation for Sustainable Development'.[2] Based on the data presented in that report and on statistics concerning internet user volumes in each country, the following table has been prepared to illustrate the levels of internet access in the developing world (Fig. 9.1).

For now it is China who is the global leader in internet penetration, according to user numbers. In 2015 more than half of the Chinese population had internet access,

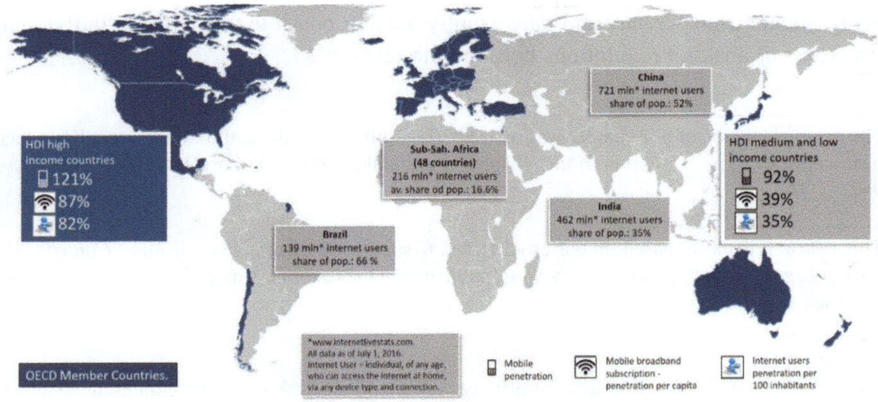

Fig. 9.1 Internet access in the world

[1]Resolution adopted by the United Nations General Assembly on 25 September 2015, 70/1, *Transforming our world: the 2030. Agenda for Sustainable Development.*

[2]ITU, UNESCO, *The State of Broadband 2015, Broadband as Foundation of Sustainable Development*, available at http://www.broadbandcommission.org/documents/reports/bb-annualreport2015.pdf, visited 18 September 2018.

namely, there were 706 million users, of which 11% were under age.[3] Moreover, the penetration of internet use in developing countries is forecast to rise—for instance, by 2018 84% of the Chinese population between the ages of 12 and 17 will likely have internet access.[4] According to data presented by Mander, 27% of global internet users are between the ages of 16 and 24, but in developing countries the figures for that age group are even higher, reaching 39% for India, 36% for Vietnam, 34% for China and 33% for Brazil.[5]

According to the Barbosa et al. study on internet risk and safety in Brazil, new internet users are mostly children—53% of the parents in families who took part in the study survey were not internet users. The same study found that 'the proportion of Brazilian parents/guardians who were internet users and accessed the internet via mobile phones was much lower than the proportion of their children, 6 and 18%, respectively'.[6]

Still, it is sub-Saharan Africa, with an expected population of 1.5 billion by 2050, that has the biggest potential of becoming the latest new-user champion. Even though in 2012 only 9.6% of sub-Saharan Africa's population had internet access, with investment in undersea cables, faster internet services are becoming available through mobile phones. It is particularly important given that the number of young people in Africa aged 9–18 who are mobile phone users has been skyrocketing regardless of their financial status or location. Suffice it to say that in 2008 there were 246 million mobile phone subscribers in sub-Saharan Africa. That number doubled by mid-2010.[7]

Figures indicate that even though today the societies of developing countries are still far behind when it comes to internet penetration, the situation is quickly changing and within approximately 5 years, a billion new users reaching adulthood from the developing States will become connected. By 2020 there should be c. 4 billion people online.[8] The remaining 3 billion will need to overcome some greater challenges, such as creating online content in their native tongues, financing the broadband network in more remote and therefore less profitable for the provider parts of the world, and accessing affordable devices. All the same, these challenges will only slow down the growth of the online global community—not stop it. This tendency is supported by the growing availability of mobile phones and developments in telecommunications technology including Long-Term Evolution (LTE). Global figures on mobile cellular phones already exceed 7 billion.[9] In 2015 the UK Office of Communications (Ofcom)

[3]Statista, *Projected internet user penetration in China from 2014 to 2018, by age*, available at http://www.statista.com/statistics/369636/china-internet-user-penetration-by-age-forecast/ ,visited 18 September 2018.

[4]*Ibidem.*

[5]Mander [1].

[6]Barbosa et al. [2].

[7]Porter et al. [3].

[8]ITU, UNESCO, *The State of Broadband 2015*, fn. 2 *supra*, at 14.

[9]*Ibidem*, at 16.

reported that in 2015 that for the first time, smartphones had overtaken laptops as the most popular device for getting online.[10]

Internet access brings many benefits to the developing world; one could mention better access to health information through telemedicine,[11] easier education by e-learning,[12] administration through e-government instruments,[13]limiting corruption, and increasing transparency and accountability through electronic management systems.[14] M-commerce and e-commerce are probably among the most important advantages of the internet which give economic operators from developing countries an opportunity to be more competitive in the global trading system.[15] Also, for that reason, Sustainable Development Goal target 17.10 calls for the promotion of a 'universal, rules-based, open, non-discriminatory and equitable multilateral trading system', and target 9.c (mentioned earlier) calls for universal and affordable internet access. Nevertheless, internet access is Janus-like and comes with certain risks, including increased risk of adult content exposure to children due to insufficient restrictions and regulation in those countries.

9.2 Adult Content Exposure as a Risk

Galloping internet accessibility comes with certain threats, including those concerning children's safety. As one author has put it, the 'internet is Janus-faceted when it concerns children. Within this context, a number of developing countries are facing the challenge of finding the right balance between the promotion of internet access for children and online child safety and protection'.[16] Adult content exposure is one such risk, as it is also in these parts of the world, where different forms of human trafficking and sexual exploitation occur most often, and children and teenagers are common among the victims.[17] Therefore, developing country governments, main actors in development aid, and those who fight against human trafficking and sexual exploitation should not lose those risks from sight, and should pay closer attention to protecting the rights of the youngest consumers in the quickly changing e-commerce markets in the developing world.

The body of research concerning the potentially harmful effects of pornography, albeit growing, remains limited. Its potential of leading to addiction is still an object of research and debate.[18] Some academics challenge the adequacy of the use of term

---

[10]Martellozzo et al. [4, p. 10].

[11]Grimwood [5, p. 524].

[12]Sife et al. [6].

[13](Darha) Ndou [7].

[14]Dutta [8].

[15]World Trade Organisation (WTO) [9].

[16]Berson and Berson [10, p. 194].

[17]Ghosh [11]; Jordan Greenbaum [12].

[18]Duffy et al. [13].

'addiction',[19] but in 2011, the American Society of Addiction Medicine (ASAM) expanded its definition to refer to behaviour 'which is not solely related to problematic substance use […] Research shows that the disease of addiction affects neurotransmission and interactions within reward circuitry of the brain, leading to addictive behaviors that supplant healthy behaviors, while memories of previous experiences with food, sex, alcohol and other drugs trigger craving and renewal of addictive behaviors'.[20] Even if susceptibility to such dependence varies, neuroscience[21] and psychology[22] seem to confirm that pornography watching may lead to addiction[23] termed 'clinically identifiable illness'.[24] According to studies conducted by Voon '[p]eople who are addicted to pornography show similar brain activity to alcoholics or drug addicts',[25] even if 'it's probably too early to put compulsive porn users in a box with people who suffer from drug or alcohol problems'.[26] As addictions start usually in young age, children constitute the most vulnerable group, which requires specific attention and protection.

Moreover, there is sufficient scientific proof to conclude that child access to pornography is harmful. It may negatively skew their sexual understanding and may lead them to 'risky behaviours'.[27] Types of pornography which are increasingly entering the internet mainstream promote aggression and the degradation of women. According to research provided by Bridges & al. 88.2% of pornographic scenes contain physical aggression and 48.7% of them contain verbal aggression. Perpetrators of aggression were usually male, whereas targets of aggression were overwhelmingly female.[28] Pornographic content, especially that contains violence, may cause children 'distress when they accidentally come across online pornography', and is 'particularly harmful for vulnerable groups'.[29]

Indeed, the phenomenon is similar in developing countries. 47% of Brazilian parents who participated in the Barbosa study were concerned about 'a possibility of the child seeing inappropriate content online' and 20% of the children were 'bothered' by seeing pornography online.[30] The negative impact of pornography on children was also confirmed India and Taiwan.[31] It is where different forms of human trafficking and sexual exploitation of children occur most often. Also, according to

---

[19]Ley et al. [14].

[20]American Society of Addiction Medicine (ASAM) [15].

[21]Hilton and Watts [16]

[22]Ford et al. [17].

[23]Cline [18].

[24]Reed [19, p. 249]; Delmocino [20, p. 239].

[25]Withnall [21].

[26]Weir [22].

[27]Horvath [23, pp. 7–11].

[28]Bridges [24].

[29]Hargrave and Livingstone [25, p. 13].

[30]Alexandre Barbosa et al., *Risks and Safety on the Internet*, fn. 6 *supra*, at 15.

[31]Miranda A. H. Horvath, Llian Alys, Kristina Massey, Afroditi Plna, Mia Scally & Joanna R. Adler (2013), *Basically… porn is everywhere*, fn. 26, at 37.

Google, the top six porn-watching countries are all low-income countries: Pakistan, Egypt, Vietnam, Iran, Morocco and India. According to *Pornhub* statistics, massive pornography viewing takes place in India, Mexico and Brazil.[32] Furthermore, Colin Rowntree, co-founder of Boodigo, a porn search engine, informs us that '[w]e are definitely witnessing an increase in "locally [in developing countries] grown" porn'. Cragg (2000), cited by Hargrave and Livingstone, gathered the comprehensive opinion of a group of experts who agreed that viewing pornography is harmful to children. Some specific negative effects of adult content for children include 'addiction to pornography, deviant or criminal sexual behavior, aggression and negative attitudes towards women'.[33]

There are no clear statistics on pornography watching by children in developing countries, nevertheless in the EU, on average 23% of children report seeing naked images in media, mostly on the internet[34] and governments should engage in providing safe internet use.[35] Moreover, much adult-content material is produced in developing countries, such as the Philippines, Mexico, Cambodia, Thailand, Gambia, Nigeria, Kenya, and the Dominican Republic.[36]

9.3 Reaction to the Risk: Adult Content Filtering

Many states, including the US, China and France, even if for different reasons, are already implementing various methods of digital censorship. The debates on adult-content filtering in the UK have already inspired lawmakers in Poland and Utah, and may be expected to motivate regulators in the developing world. Several years ago Little and Preston wrote that: '[i]n many developing countries, the drive to train a new generation in technology skills as a foray into global commerce has produced an epidemic of pornography addiction that parents have no idea how to address. Protecting children from internet pornography is a global problem without a global answer. The borderless nature of the internet makes coordinating responses extremely difficult. Individual countries are scrambling to find solutions'.[37]

American authors insisted that internet regulation could be mostly satisfied by Internet Corporation for Assigned Names and Numbers (ICANN) but they were also critical about a lack of genuine leadership of the US in that respect. This situation has recently changed in the state of Utah, which adopted the Current Resolution on

[32]Pornhub Insights [26].

[33]Andrea Millwood Hargrave, Sonia Livingstone, *Harm and Offence in Media Content*, fn. 28 *supra*, at. 123.

[34]Livingstone et al. [27, pp. 49–50].

[35]Miranda A. H. Horvath, Llian Alys, Kristina Massey, Afroditi Plna, Mia Scally & Joanna R. Adler (2013), *Basically... porn is everywhere*, fn. 26, at 11.

[36]Stolen Innocence [28]; EPCAT [29]; Palet [30]; Gupta [31]; Samuels [32].

[37]Little and Preston [33].

the Public Health Crisis, signed in March 2016.[38] The Resolution has not yet an 'enforcement muscle' and follows a 2013 Joint Resolution Regarding the Impact of Adult Images on Children's Development. Criticised from different standpoints, including that it is based on weak scientific evidence,[39] or that it limits freedom of speech,[40] this has not discouraged Utah lawmakers to take further steps in order to limit the access to pornography especially for children.[41] Utah regulation was inspired by regulatory measures taken in the UK and was also based on economic arguments.[42] The American Academy of Matrimonial Lawyers hints the relationship between interest in pornographic sites and the rise of divorce rates in the US.[43] Internet users in developing countries are increasingly becoming more aware of its harmful content, and seek regulatory tools or technical solutions to protect children from such content.[44]

As UK regulations inspired lawmakers in Poland and Utah it may be legitimately expected that those attempts will inspire developing countries. Purely private initiatives do not seem to be sufficient (Sect. 9.4.1 *infra*). Even larger and more powerful countries have difficulties in controlling illegal online conduct where offenders minimise their dependence on intermediaries, thereby eliminating a government's means of regulating them.[45] What is more, internet censorship may potentially constitute a violation of international trade law regulating freedom of services (Sect. 9.4.2 *infra*). Also, disproportionate censorship may potentially amount to a violation of the freedom of expression (Sect. 9.4.3 *infra*). For that reason legal tools must approach this issue 'with a scalpel rather than a sledgehammer.'[46]

9.4 Mitigating the Risk Through Regulation

'[The] [i]nternet is not a lawless prairie'.[47] It is regulated by private and public legal instruments of national and international origin, at the national and international level. Limiting access to the internet has implications for international trade as it affects the provision services. Liberalisation of trade in services was regulated on an almost universal plane by the General Agreement on Trade in Services (GATS)[48] and,

---

[38] Utah [34].

[39] Utah [35]; Allen [36].

[40] Phillips [37].

[41] Bolton [38].

[42] Ibidem.

[43] Manning [39].

[44] Brent A. Little, Cheryl B. Preston, *Symposium: I Think I Can*, fn. 36 *supra*, at 79–80.

[45] *Ibidem*, at 79.

[46] *Ibidem*.

[47] Hampson [40].

[48] General Agreement on Trade in Services, 15 April 1994, Marrakesh Agreement Establishing the World Trade Organization, 1869 U.N.T.S. 183, (1994).

regionally, by regional economic organisations including the EU and NAFTA. Both layers are oriented towards the successive elimination of trade barriers but remain interlinked with other sub-fields of international co-operation (and corresponding areas of international law), such as that of human rights protection.

Internet access is filtered for a variety of motives including political. It is rigorously monitored, and critical sites based overseas on occasion blocked in many countries, including, China, Iran, Myanmar, North Korea, Syria, Tunisia, Turkey, Uzbekistan, and Vietnam to mention but a few.[49] Further motivation may pertain to what societies perceive as immoral or illegal; examples of such perceptions are numerous and usually concern pornography, gambling, or criminal activities.[50] In the US, moral censorship of online gambling was also based on morality considerations but have also included the protection of children (see Section 4.2 *infra*). The Children's Internet Protection Act requires that public libraries use internet filters as condition for receipt of federal subsidies.[51] The US Supreme Court ruled that regulation is not unconstitutional under the First Amendment.[52]

Other than a diversity of motives, there is also a diversity of internet censorship methods. The first technique is based on website blocking. It may also be effectuated by forbidding Internet Service Providers (ISPs) in the country from allowing access to any site appearing on an official list of banned sites. Another technique effectuated in China relates to filtering through internet search engines; sites which have been blacklisted do not appear in the result lists at all. A more sophisticated method is that of selective filtering, whereby it is not the whole website that is blocked, such as Amazon—only selected subpages. Such selective filtering is less restrictive than the other two methods.

Whereas public institutions regulate some aspects of internet activities, alternative or cumulatively private standards are set. In the UK, with regard to the Internet Watch Foundation, private actors called upon ISPs to get involved in securing the internet for children through self-regulation and Codes of Conduct.[53] In some aspects of economic law 'soft regulations' may be more efficient or desirable than hard law. For many economic operators, being stigmatised by public or business opinion may be more harmful than a regular public sanction. That is why in civic societies NGOs wield considerable power in shaping the public sphere. One such group, 'Save the Children Europe Group', called upon the EU to coordinate work on possible inter-

[49] Erixon et al. [41, p. 4]; Faris and Villeneuve [42, p. 6].

[50] Fredrik Erixon, Brian Hindley, Hosuk Lee-Makiyama, *Protectionism Online*, fn. 47 *supra*, at 4.

[51] Children's Internet Protection Act, § 1701, 114 Stat. 2763A-335.

[52] Supreme Court of the United States, United States, et al., Appellants, v. American Library Association, Inc., et al., No. 02-361. Argued 5 March 2003 and decided on 23 June 2003.

[53] Save the Children Europe Group, *Position paper on child pornography and Internet-related sexual exploitation of Children*, https://www.google.com/url?sa=t&rct=j&q=&esrc=s&source=web&cd=1&ved=2ahUKEwibw6CvicfcAhWFJZoKHSEXDQkQFjAAegQIARAC&url=https%3A%2F%2Fec.europa.eu%2Fjustice%2Fgrants%2Fresults%2Fdaphne-toolkit%2Fen%2Ffile%2F1032%2Fdownload%3Ftoken%3DgvOsFz_E&usg=AOvVaw1uX37WytXXoFIwCTang6H1, visited 18 September 2018, at 24.

net child abuse.[54] Such initiatives resulted in the adoption in 2003 of a Council Framework Decision on combatting the sexual exploitation of children and child pornography, which was later replaced by the 2011/92 Directive. Though the ban of child pornography is a rather well-settled rule, awareness of children's access to pornography is relatively recent in terms of possible regulations. It has rather been perceived as a moral or educational issue. Unprecedented access to internet pornography by minors has shown negative effects for their development and, generally, for society.[55] Despite different moral assessments of pornography as such, regulating child access to adult content becomes a social need. As such the aim of regulation is twofold. Law not only regulates human behaviour but also plays a strong educational function in that respect; it can be a 'whistleblower' signalling possible dangers. One could ask whether technological solutions or private standards alone would be sufficient. Just as smoking bans have further raised awareness about the harmful effects of smoking tobacco, and have helped many people to quit smoking, similarly regulating access to pornography would raise awareness of its potentially negative effects[56] especially on children.[57]

9.4.1 *The Method: Self-regulation v. State Regulation*

The production of child pornography, especially in developing states, is a phenomenon which requires the involvement of the international community. The example of the law in Madagascar, and the implementation therein of the Protocol to the Convention on the Rights of the Child on the Sale of Children, Child Prostitution and Child Pornography, demonstrate that developing countries would likely follow the standards set by developed countries and the international community related to children protection in the internet.[58] Art. 3 para. 1(c) of the Protocol requires that State-Parties penalise '[p]roducing, distributing, disseminating, importing, exporting, offering, selling or possessing for the above purposes child pornography'. This stipulation was introduced into Malagasy Penal Code which provides that: '[t]aking, recording or transmitting a picture of a minor with a view to circulating it, where that image has a pornographic character, is punished' (art. 346).[59] The cited regulation is almost identical to that of the French Penal Code (art. 227-23).[60] Similarly art.

[54] *Ibidem*, at 4.

[55] Greenfield [43].

[56] Kühn and Gallinat [44].

[57] Ybarra and Mitchell [45]; Curtis [46].

[58] *Office of the United Nations High Commissioner for Human Rights (OHCHR)*, Report of the Special Rapporteur on the sale of children, child prostitution and child pornography, Najat Maalla M'jid-Addendum-Mission to Madagascar, A/HRC/25/48/Add.2, 23/12/2013, available at http://ap.ohchr.org/documents/dpage_e.aspx?si=A/HRC/25/48/Add.2, visited 18 September 2018.

[59] Madagascar, Penal Code of 17 June 1972, Journal officiel no. 871, later amended.

[60] Penal Code, resulting from various acts adopted on 22 July 1992, later amended.

347 of the Malagasy Code provides that: '[t]he manufacture, transport, distribution by whatever means and however supported, of a message bearing a pornographic or violent character or a character seriously violating human dignity, or the trafficking in such a message, is punished' clearly copies art. 227-24 of the French Code. Both regulations appear to respond to the needs of the 'pre-digital era' and mostly reflected dissemination of such content via television, printed media or cinemas. It was a source of debate about age classification of films in France.[61]

What is more, recent, and still subject to debate, is the open access of children to online adult (pornographic) content on the internet. Many countries have introduced blocking systems to reduce child pornography traffic on the internet, and to make access to illegal content more difficult. More problematic is the free access to the content that is not illegal *per se*. An example of such regulatory need arises in relation to the protection of children against lawful adult content. Child protection advocates seek to implement default pornographic filtering to all users unless they are adults and signal their intention to unfiltered access to internet content (opt-in). Default filtering or blocking systems were developed more than a decade ago. Their primary goal was to combat illegal child pornography. Comparable systems of blocking legal pornography are relatively new. In the UK a pioneer default filtering method was introduced only recently. Some authors claim that the UK system is the most advanced in Europe.[62] No doubt, it serves as a reference point for other States willing to limit children's access to pornography online. Some commentators however criticise the UK model for over-blocking[63] and, therefore, hampering the development of the internet services sector. Nevertheless, it serves as a foundational reference point in other countries seeking to regulate this problem, namely, in Poland and the US (in relation to Utah). It may be genuinely expected that the UK model may serve as inspiration for other countries, including developing States, seeking to regulate this problem, including Madagascar (briefly mentioned earlier). India, is a further example, which in July 2015 introduced a government order of blocking more than 800 adult content websites but as the ban affected all internet users, it was partly withdrawn. The national debate which also involved the Indian Supreme Court demonstrates that also developing countries seek to balance the freedom to access internet content with public morals and public order.[64]

UK regulation has been developing over the last 20 years. In 1996, the Internet Watch Foundation (IWF) was created. Its aim is to identify pages and internet services containing sexually abusive images and illegal pornography. The Police, the Director of Public Prosecutions, and the most important UK ISPs all played a part in setting up the IWF. Although the IWF is supported by public bodies, it remains a private/sectoral institution. ISPs that joined the organisation have agreed to comply with high standards elaborated by the IWF. The IWF's objective is to oversee the internet, to cooperate with police, prosecutors, and ISPs in order to detect illegal

---

[61] Le Roy [47].

[62] Waglewski [48, Vol. 1, p. 14].

[63] Vincent [49]

[64] Nair [50].

pornography and to prevent abuses in this matter. The activity of the IWF resulted in the largest UK ISP—namely, BT—setting up the *Cleanfeed Content Blocking System*, which since 2004 has worked as a filter of pages marked as suspect by the IWF. The IWF provides a list of pages and the Cleanfeed Content System blocks access to the detected illegal content. BT states on its home page that it was the first telecommunications operator in the world to introduce the blocking system against child pornography and offered other operators free access to the system.[65] The filter does not protect children against all pornographic content, but does block pages with illegal pornography and images of child abuse. According to public opinion, the Cleanfeed Blocking System was perceived as successful, but, above all, it was praised by the UK Government with the express approval of the Prime Minister. As a result of political pressure, other ISPs and children's advocacy groups followed BT's example. Political pressure was quite intense: the Home Office threatened to introduce legislation compelling blocking unless ISPs voluntarily complied. Ultimately governmental plans for legislation were abandoned in 2009 as an Ofcom survey established that already 98.6% of home connections were subject to blocking systems.[66]

The next step in child protection took place in 2014 when a large group of Telecommunication Operators (including BT, TalkTalk, Virgin, and Sky), by means of support from the Prime Minister, embarked to survey over 19 million internet home users in order to know if they were interested in blocking children's access to pornography. Lack of interest was interpreted as a default allowance for the blockade. The free of charge blocking system had to work on all devices connected to the internet: laptops, PCs, mobile phones, and tablets. It must be noted that in the UK governmental support was political but not statutory. The market regulated the matter on its own. Lastly, in 2015 the broadband provider Sky, under its Sky Broadband Shield scheme started to block adult content by default, that is unless users opt-out. BT decided to ask its customers whether they wished to activate parental controls but without obliging them to do so.

For many years governments have relied on the goodwill of the internet industry's ability to self-regulate.[67] Political pressure and civil society movements have led to the establishment of self-regulatory systems with little supervision by public authorities. Polish attempts to regulate the problem have been based on hard law. It can also be more easily introduced in States having less experience in private sector self-regulation and less established democratic traditions. The *Committee on Administration and Digitisation* of the Polish Parliament drafted a resolution calling for the government to design a law concerning default filtering—parental control. In its resolution, deputies called upon the government to draw up an act obliging telecommunications operators to use filtering of pornography in order to protect children. Such approach meant that ISPs are not obliged on a self-regulatory basis, but by

[65] The BT Story, available at http://www.btplc.com/Thegroup/Ourcompany/TheBTstory/index.htm, visited 18 September 2018.

[66] McIntyre [51, pp. 277, 283].

[67] Carr and Hilton [52, p. 306].

binding law. By contrast, the UK system was founded on a self-regulatory model, as it received important political backing. The UK system, although it may raise issues with transparency and possible judicial supervision, it is less strict and is more likely to be adaptable to the changing digital environment. However regulations on internet censorship may constitute a barrier in trade and therefore need to be further evaluated under international trade (Sect. 9.4.2) and human rights (Sect. 9.4.3) standards. Passing this test seems to be more difficult if regulations are statutory and public than private or of soft law character. This evaluation would also be useful for regulatory models to be chosen by developing states in the future.

9.4.2 Freedom of Services

Internet censorship may constitute a violation of the freedom to provide services under international trade law. For that reason different blocking methods have to be evaluated and justified on legitimate grounds stemming from the applicable international norms. Only when they meet such threshold, should they serve as models for developing countries.

Services are the fastest growing sector of the global economy and account for two-thirds of global output, one-third of global employment and nearly twenty percent of global trade.[68] Much of this growth is due to the impact digital developments have had on the services sector. For instance, many traditional goods, such as printed materials and music records and CDs, are now available online and may be downloaded across borders. This situation complicates the goods/services distinction and the applicability of respective WTO agreements. There is scope within WTO law for its integration with other values; this is primarily effectuated through the list of exceptions provided in art. XX of the General Agreement on Tariffs and Trade (GATT)[69] and XIV of the GATS. Both articles contemplate that measures may be 'necessary for the protection of human, animal or plant life or health'. As psychological research has demonstrated exposure to internet pornography among children and adolescents may be harmful (Sect. 9.2 *supra*), one could invoke, as per the Utah 2016 Resolution, public health as grounds for trade restrictive measures. Moreover, the US-Gambling case has shown possible synergies between public morality exceptions and the protection of minors against 'special health and youth protection risks' (US-Gambling, panel report para 3.211, see Sect. 9.4 *infra*). Apart from the 'human health', the 'public morals' grounds within the GATS may be raised. Art. XIV(a) provides that 'nothing in this Agreement shall be construed to prevent the adoption or enforcement by any Member of measures: (a) necessary to protect public morals or to maintain public order'. The importance of this clause becomes more apparent especially in times of a growing services market when an increasing amount of services may be provided online.

---

[68] Brown [53, p. 2].

[69] General Agreement on Tariffs and Trade (1947), 55 U.N.T.S. 194.

The free trade–morality conflict emerged in the area of internet services in the *US-Gambling* case before the WTO Dispute Settlement Body. The case concerned the provision of online gambling services from Antigua and Barbuda to US consumers. One of the arguments raised by the US before the WTO concerned the availability of online gambling to children given that: 'the internet can be used anonymously, the danger exists that access to internet gambling will be abused by underage gamblers. The American Psychiatric Association has similarly warned that "[y]oung people are at special risk for problem gambling and should be aware of the hazards of this activity, especially the danger of internet gambling, which may pose an increased risk to high school and college-aged populations"'.[70] It is not hard to see the parallels between the arguments on the negative effect and dangers connected to online gambling, and the availability of adult content to minors. The possible addiction to online gambling may represent a comparable danger to children as in the case of pornography: '[R]emote gambling also presents special health and youth protection risks in part because it is available to anyone, anywhere—including compulsive gamblers and children—who can gamble 24 h a day with a mere 'click of the mouse.' Isolation and anonymity compound the danger'.[71] The WTO Appellate Body took a position on that issue. This judicial authority plays the highest role in settling international economic disputes and is sometimes called 'The World Trade Court.[72] It found that US regulations are 'measures … necessary to protect public morals or to maintain public order'[73] and are therefore justified. For that reason one could therefore conclude that preventative measures aiming to protect minors from inappropriate content on the internet may be justified under this exception. This conclusion by the Appellate Body provides important guidance for countries wishing to regulate child internet access to adult content, including for 'emerging and developing economies'.

9.4.3 Freedom of Expression

Adult content filtering should be balanced against other fundamental human rights protected under international law. Freedom of expression is guaranteed by universal and regional human rights agreements. The International Covenant on Civil and Political Rights in Article 19(2) provides that '[e]veryone shall have the right to freedom of expression; this right shall include freedom to seek, receive and impart information and ideas of all kinds, regardless of frontiers, either orally, in writing

[70]United States—Measures Affecting the Cross-Border Supply of Gambling and Betting Services, panel report, circulated 10 November 2004, WT/DS285/R, para. 3.18.

[71]*Ibidem*, para. 3.211.

[72]Claus-Dieter Ehlermann, "*Six Years on the Bench of the „World Trade Court"—Some Personal Experiences as a Member of the Appellate Body of the World Trade Organization*, 36 Journal of World Trade, 605.

[73]United States—Measures Affecting the Cross-Border Supply of Gambling and Betting Services, Appellate Body report, adopted 20 April 2005, WT/DS285/AB/R, para. 327.

or in print, in the form of art, or through any other media of his choice'.[74] This *quasi*-universal regulation (currently 168 ratifications) would also have to be taken into account when regulating adult content filtering in different countries. As in other cases of international human rights treaties, they are binding upon states that have ratified it, nevertheless, they were designed to affect the legal status of individuals.

Freedom of expression is also safeguarded in regional instruments including the European Convention on Human Rights (ECHR). Human rights, as expressed in the ECHR, also have some normative implications at the EU level and some persuasive effect for the case law of the Court of Justice of the European Union (CJEU). Article 10 of the ECHR provides that '[e]veryone has the right to freedom of expression. This right shall include freedom to hold opinions and to receive and impart information and ideas without interference by public authority and regardless of frontiers'.[75] A very similar right is expressed in Article 11 of the EU's own Charter of Fundamental Rights.[76]

Until now, the European Court on Human Rights (ECtHR) did not have an opportunity to express its opinion on default filtering. Nevertheless, certain cases may provide guidance in understanding the relevant limits of freedom of speech. An illustrative example is the seizure of the *Little Red Schoolbook* which gave rise to the Handyside case. In this case, UK authorities decided to seize a book entitled 'The Little Red Schoolbook' and to prohibit the distribution of it. The book was addressed to children above the age of 12 and encouraged them to question societal norms on sex, drugs, alcohol, and tobacco. The distributor contested the prohibition decision before UK courts. After exhausting the domestic legal justice system, it was submitted to the ECtHR.[77] The court did not find a violation of article 10 of the ECHR. It stated that the main objective of the judgment was to protect minors and their morals.[78] This limitation was therefore justified. According to article 10 para. 2 of the ECHR the exercise of the freedom of expression may be subjected to such formalities, conditions. and restrictions as are prescribed by law and are necessary in a democratic society for the protection of morals. Therefore, in that case, considerations of public morality justified restrictions to the freedom of expression. In the context of national legal systems, 'in the Handyside case the Court noted that there was no uniform European Concept of 'morality' and made it clear that States would enjoy a wide margin of appreciation in assessing whether measures were required to protect moral standards'[79] Similarly, A. H. Robertson finds that: '[t]here is more

[74]International Covenant on Civil and Political Rights, Adopted and opened for signature, ratification and accession by General Assembly resolution 2200A (XXI) of 16 December 1966, 999 U.N.T.S 171.

[75]Convention for the Protection of Human Rights and Fundamental Freedoms, Sept. 4, 1950, Rome, 231 UNTS 222.

[76]Charter Of Fundamental Rights of The European Union, 18 December 2000, Official Journal of the European Communities, 2000/C 364/01.

[77]Case of Handyside v. the United Kingdom, Judgment, December 7, 1976.

[78]*Ibidem*, para. 52.

[79]Ovey and Robin [54, p. 285].

scope for the margin of appreciation (in morality)'.[80] As had been the case in the US-Gambling dispute settled before WTO Appellate Body, it was stated that the main objective of the judgment was to protect minors and their morals.[81]

Pursuant to article 10 of the ECHR, freedom of expression may be limited if it is necessary in a democratic society. The term 'necessary in a democratic society' establishes a proportionality requirement. In the EU and ECHR legal orders, proportionality is understood in a formal way. The standard is composed of four stages: there must be a legitimate aim for the measure at hand, the measure must be suitable to achieve the aim, the measure must be necessary to achieve the aim, and lastly, the measure must intend the correct balance between restrictions and freedoms or rights.[82] The protection of children against adult content may be categorised as a legitimate aim. When deciding on adult content filtering, it is not only morals that are relevant, but first of all, the rights of children (to be free from harm). The ECHR does not make specific provision for children although they are included by operation of the term 'everyone' throughout the text of the ECHR. There is, however, a separate international agreement ratified by almost every state in the world: the UN Convention on the Rights of the Child. According to article 34, States Parties 'undertake to protect the child from all forms of sexual exploitation and sexual abuse'.[83] It also relates to measures preventing child pornography. However, child sexual abuse may also sensibly consist in child exposure to images, which is inappropriate for their age as it may be detrimental to their sexual and broader development, and may lead to 'risky behaviours'. Therefore default filtering could be justified not only in relation to abstractions such as public morals but also by the need to safeguard child's psychosexual and broader development, and defend its right to a healthy human environment. The second stage is the criterion of adequateness, which is more problematic. Until now, pure technical solutions have been evaluated as ineffective. But even though the UK system may not be perfect, it plays other important roles. First, it has an educational function—it informs children about the inappropriateness of adult content. It overlaps with the educational function of law or regulatory measures as such. It also limits free access to pornography by making it more difficult, if not impossible, as well as prevent incidental access to it. The third stage in the proportionality test is the compulsion and possibility of achieving the same goal by other, less restrictive, means. In fact, parents may now buy or even use free of charge software, which is already in use in schools or libraries. However, many parents do not use such means for reasons including the lack of proper knowledge, awareness and/or computer skills. Easy access to pornography among children is a socially incontestable fact. In Poland 83% of 8 year olds and 91% of 11 year olds use the internet regularly, and 40% of 8 year olds and 65% of 11 year olds do so without parental

[80]Robertson and Merrills [55, p. 152].

[81]Case of Handyside v. The United Kingdom, para. 52.

[82]Christoffersen [56 p. 31]; Khosla [57, p. 298].

[83]Convention on the Rights of the Child, General Assembly Resolution 44/25 of 20 November 1989.

supervision.[84] Given that 75% of US teens own mobile devices[85] it can be assumed a great deal of their online activity takes place not necessarily tied to one place for long spells of times, and therefore less likely to be consistently monitored.[86] According to research cited earlier, in the EU, on average 23% of children report seeing naked images in media, mostly in internet.[87] As pornography watching may negatively impact on child development, and given extensive possession of smartphones which makes it more difficult for parents to monitor access, the necessary balance between restricting access and the limitation of rights (freedom of expression) appears to be duly struck.

The freedom of expression is also incorporated in article 9 para. 2 of the African Charter on Human and Peoples' Rights[88] and in art. 13 of the American Convention on Human Rights.[89] It is not uncommon for courts from different legal orders to have regard to the jurisprudence of their counterparts[90] and to reproduce their reasoning.

9.5 Conclusions: Implications for Developing Countries

There is relative consensus around the need to prevent child pornography. It is a challenge that has highlighted in challenges and possibilities in regulating the world-wide web. In their efforts to do so, developing countries due to their accession to international treaties appear to look to the developed West for standards of regulation. Child protection against exposure to online adult content may follow a similar but slightly different path. Many initiatives are taken by internet companies, such as Google, to provide 'safe search' mode for their users. However, in many developing countries private initiatives may not be sufficient, and there be weaker civil society traditions to put adequate pressure on operators. ISP self-regulation will probably not be adequate and legislative means may be required. Such preventative measures should comply with, and be proportional to, the requirements of applicable norms of international trade and of human rights, including the freedom of expression. Internet regulation may affect the provision of digital services and therefore would require justification. The rationale may stem from relevant exceptions concerning public morals and public health in trade law. As the harmful impact of adult content exposure on child development becomes recognised, children's rights as human

[84]Czapiński and Panek [58]; Batorski [59].

[85]Lenhart et al. [60, p. 9].

[86]Owens et al. [61, p. 100].

[87]Sonia Livingstone, Leslie Haddon, Anke Görzig & Kjartan Ólafsson, *Risks and safety on the internet*, fn. 33 *supra*, at 49–50.

[88]African Charter on Human and Peoples' Rights, 27 June 1981, 1520 UNTS 217.

[89]American Convention on Human Rights, San José, 22 November 1969, 1144 UNTS 123.

[90]Council of Europe (COE), European Court of Human Rights (ECHR), *References to the Inter-American Court of Human Rights in the case-law of the European Court of Human Rights*, Research Report, available at http://www.echr.coe.int/Documents/Research_report_inter_american_court_ENG.pdf, visited 18 September 2018.

rights should serve as justifying grounds to take the measures necessary that may present possible limitations on trade in services, and that may infringe freedom of expression. With expanding knowledge, it is very likely that legislative models will be adapted from developed countries to the developing world. State regulation may also provide judicial control of decisions based on proscribed law, more public control, and more transparency, than what may be possible via self-regulatory soft-law means.

References

1. Mander, J. (2015, March 23). Over a quarter of the world's internet users are aged 16–24. *Globalwebindex*. Available at http://www.globalwebindex.net/blog/over-a-quarter-of-the-worlds-internet-users-are-aged-16-24, visited 18 September 2018.
2. Barbosa, A., et al. (2013). *Risks and safety on the Internet, Comparing Brazilian and European Results*. LSE: EU Kids Online. London, LSE: EU Kids Online, 14.
3. Porter. G., et al. (2012). Mobile phones, Livelihoods and the poor in sub-Saharan Africa: Review and prospect. *Geography Compass, 6*(5), 241.
4. Martellozzo, E., Monaghan, A., Adler, J. R., Davidson, J., Leyva, R., Miranda, A.H., et al. (2018). *I wasn't sure it was normal to watch it*. The impact of online pornography on the values, attitudes, beliefs and behaviours of children. Report for National Society for the Prevention of Cruelty to Children and Children's Commissioner. Available at https://www.nspcc.org.uk/globalassets/documents/research-reports/mdx-nspcc-occ-pornography-report.pdf, visited 18 September 2018.
5. Grimwood, K. (2001, September 8). Telemedicine in developing countries. *British Medical Journal*, 524.
6. Sife, A. S., Lwoga, E. T., & Sanga, C. (2018). *New technologies for teaching and learning. Challenges for higher learning institutions in developing countries*. Available at http://ijedict.dec.uwi.edu/viewarticle.php?id=246/&layout=html, visited 18 September 2018.
7. Valentina (Darha) Ndou. (2004). E-government for developing countries, opportunities and challenges. *Electronic Journal of Information Systems in Developing Countries, 18*(1), 1–24.
8. Dutta, S. (2018). *An uneven path of accountability: A comparative study of MGNREGA in two states of India*. WZB Discussion Paper, No. SP, 2015-201, at 17. Available at https://www.econstor.eu/bitstream/10419/108736/1/820319341.pdf, visited 18 September 2018.
9. World Trade Organisation (WTO). (2013). *E-commerce in developing countries. Opportunities and challenges for small and medium sized enterprises*. WTO, Geneva. Available at https://www.wto.org/english/res_e/booksp_e/ecom_brochure_e.pdf, visited 18 September 2018.
10. Berson, I. R., & Berson, M. J. (2010). *Childhood in a digital world*. Information Age Pubishing, Charlotte, NC.
11. Ghosh, B. (2009, December). Trafficking in women and children in India: Nature, dimensions and strategies for prevention. *The International Journal of Human Rights, 13*(5), 720, 731–733;
12. Jordan Greenbaum, V. (2014, October). *Commercial sexual exploitation and sex trafficking of children in the United States. Current Problems in Pediatric and Adolescent Health Care, 44*(9), 245, 247.
13. Duffy, A., Dawson, L., & das Neir, R. (2016). Pornography addiction in adults: A systematic review of definitions and reported impact. *The Journal of Sexual Medicine, 13*(5), 760–777.
14. Ley, D., Prause, N., & Finn, P. (2014, June). The emperor has no clothes: A review of the pornography' addiction' model. *Current Sexual Health Reports, 6*(2), 94–105.
15. American Society of Addiction Medicine (ASAM). (2018). *ASAM releases new definition of addiction*. Available at http://www.asam.org/docs/pressreleases/asam-definition-of-addiction-2011-08-15.pdf, visited 18 September 2018.

16. Hilton, D. L. Jr., & Watts, C. (2011). Pornography addictions: A neuroscience perspective. *Surgical Neurology International, 2*, 19.
17. Ford, J. J., Durtschi, J. A., & Franklin, D. L. (2012). Structural therapy with a couple battling pornography addiction. *The American Journal of Family Therapy, 40*(4), 336–348. available at http://www.tandfonline.com/doi/abs/10.1080/01926187.2012.685003 visited 18 September 2018.
18. Cline, V. B. (1993). *Pornography's effects on adults and Children.* Morality in Media, New York.
19. Reed, M. D. (1994) *Pornography addiction and compulsive sexual behavior*. In G. Zillmann, J. Bryant, A. C. Huston (Eds.), *Media, children and the family. Social scientific, psychodynamic and clinical perspectives*. New York and London: Routledge, p. 249;
20. Delmocino, D. L. (2002). *Sex on the superhighway: Understanding and treating cybersex addiction.* In P. Carnes, K. M. Adams (Eds.), *Clinical management of sex addiction.* New York-Hove: Brunner-Routledge.
21. Withnall, A. (2013, September 22). Pornography addiction leads to same brain activity as alcoholism or drug abuse, study shows. *The Independent*. Available at http://www.independent.co.uk/life-style/health-and-families/health-news/pornography-addiction-leads-to-same-brain-activity-as-alcoholism-or-drug-abuse-study-shows-8832708.html, visited 18 September 2018.
22. Weir, K. (2014, April). Is pornography addictive? *Monitor on Psychology*. Available at http://www.apa.org/monitor/2014/04/pornography.aspx, visited 18 September 2018.
23. Horvath, M. A. H., Alys, L., Massey, K. Pina, A., Scally, M., & Adler, J. R. (2013). *Basically... porn is everywhere: A rapid evidence assessment on the effects that access and exposure to pornography has on children and young people. Project Report. Office of the Children's Commissioner for England, London, UK*, Middlesex University's Research Repository at http://eprints.mdx.ac.uk/10692/, at 7–11, visited 18 September 2018.
24. Bridges, A. J., Wosnitzer, R., Scharrer, E., Sun, C., & Liberman, R. (2010). Aggression and sexual behavior in best-selling pornography videos: A content analysis update. *Violence Against Women, 16*(10), 1065–1085.
25. Hargrave, A. M., & Livingstone, S. (2006). *Harm and offence in media content. A review of the evidence*. Bristol/Portland: Intellect.
26. Pornhub Insights. (2018, January 6). *Pornhub's 2015 year in review.* Available at http://www.pornhub.com/insights/pornhub-2015-year-in-review, visited 18 September 2018.
27. Livingstone, S., Haddon, L., Görzig, A., & Ólafsson, K. (2018). *Risks and safety on the internet: The perspective of European children: Full findings and policy implications from the EU Kids Online survey of 9–16 year olds and their parents in 25 countries*. EU Kids Online, Deliverable D4. EU Kids Online Network, London, UK. Available at http://eprints.lse.ac.uk/33731/1/Risks%20and%20safety%20on%20the%20internet%28lsero%29.pdf, visited 18 September 2018.
28. Stolen Innocence. (2018). Available at http://www.globalinitiative.net/stolen-innocence-the-online-exploitation-of-children/, visited 30 July 2018.
29. EPCAT. (2018). *Protection of Children against Sexual Exploitation.* Available at https://www.unicef.org/protection/files/FBO_Guide_for_Religious_Leaders_and_Communities_ENG.pdf, visited 18 September 2018.
30. Palet, L. S. (2018). *The rise of porn in the developing world.* Available at http://www.ozy.com/fast-forward/the-rise-of-porn-in-the-developing-world/64784, visited 18 September 2018.
31. Gupta, A. (2009). *Growth of the Porn Industry in India.* Available at http://www.desiblitz.com/content/growth-of-the-porn-industry-in-india, visited 18 September 2018.
32. Samuels, T. (2009, August 30). Africa goes hardcore. *The Guardian.* Available at https://www.theguardian.com/commentisfree/2009/aug/30/pornography-corporate-responsibility-developing-world, visited 18 September 2018.
33. Little, B. A., & Preston, C. B. (2008). Symposium: I Think I Can, I Think ICANN: Regulating the Internet... or Not: ICANN Can: Contracts and Porn Sites–Choosing "To Play Internet Ball in American Cyberspace". *Pacific McGeorge Global Business & Development Law Journal, 21*, 79.

34. Utah. (2016). Current resolution on the Public Health Crisis, signed 29 March 2016.
35. Utah. (2013). *Joint resolution regarding the impact of adult images on children's development*, adopted 14 March 2013.
36. Allen, S. (2018, April 22). Utah's Anti-Porn Law is pure pseudoscience. *The Daily Beast*. Available at http://www.thedailybeast.com/articles/2016/04/22/utah-s-anti-porn-law-is-pure-pseudoscience.html, visited 18 September 2018.
37. Phillips, A. (2016, April 22). *Porn has been declared ‚public health crisis' in Utah. Here's why*. The Washington Post. Available at https://www.washingtonpost.com/news/the-fix/wp/2016/04/22/anti-porn-advocates-are-changing-the-game-and-it-starts-with-utah-declaring-it-a-public-health-crisis/, visited 18 September 2018.
38. Bolton, D. (2016). *Porn could be blocked from the internet in Utah under UK-inspired laws*. Independent, 24 May 2016. Available at http://www.independent.co.uk/life-style/gadgets-and-tech/news/porn-could-be-blocked-from-the-internet-in-utah-under-uk-inspired-laws-a7044621.html, visited 18 September 2018.
39. Manning, J. C. (2006). The impact of Internet Pornography on Marriage and the Family: A review of the research. *Sexual Addiction and Compulsivity, 13,* 131, 141.
40. Hampson, N. C. N. (2011). The Internet is Not a Lawless Prairie: Data Protection and Privacy in Italy. *Boston College International and Comparative Law Review, 34*, 477.
41. Erixon, F., Hindley, B., & Lee-Makiyama, H. (2009). *Protectionism online: Internet Censorship and International Trade Law.* ECIPE Working Paper, 12/2009, http://www.ecipe.org/app/uploads/2014/12/protectionism-online-internet-censorship-and-international-trade-law.pdf, visited 18 September 2018.
42. Faris, R., & Villeneuve, N. (2008). *Measuring global internet filtering*. In R. Deibert, Palfrey, J., Rohozinski, R., Zittrain, J. (Eds.), *Access denied: The practice and policy of global internet filtering*. MIT Press, Cambridge.
43. Greenfield, P. M. (2004). Inadvertent exposure to pornography on the Internet: Implications of peer-to-peer file-sharing networks for child development and families. *Applied Developmental Psychology, 25*, 741, 743–744.
44. Kühn, S., & Gallinat, J. (2018). Brain structure and functional connectivity associated with pornography consumption. The Brain on Porn, *JAMA Psychiatry, 71*, 827. Also available at http://archpsyc.jamanetwork.com/article.aspx?articleid=1874574#References, visited 18 September 2018.
45. Ybarra, M. L., & Mitchell, K. J. (2005). Exposure to Internet pornography among children and adolescents: A national survey. *Cyber Psychology & Behavior, 8,* 473. Also available at http://innovativepublichealth.org/wp-content/uploads/2009/04/cpb.2005.8.pdf, visited 18 September 2018.
46. Curtis, R. D. (2018). Panel on Porn as health crisis defends controversial resolution. *Utah Political News*. Available at http://utahpoliticalcapitol.com/2016/07/28/panel-on-porn-as-health-crisis-defends-controversial-resolution/, visited 18 September 2018.
47. Le Roy, M. (2012, June 30). *Protection des mineurs et oeuvres cinématographiques, un état des lieux.* Cinéma. Available at http://www.inaglobal.fr/cinema/article/protection-des-mineurs-et-oeuvres-cinematographiques-un-etat-des-lieux, visited 18 September 2018.
48. Waglewski, P. (2013). *Rozwiązania prawne regulujące dostęp do bezpiecznego Internetu, wolnego od pornografii na przykładzie wybranych krajów Unii Europejskiej*. Biuro Analiz Sejmowych.
49. Vincent, J. (2018). One in five sites blocked by the UK's over-zealous 'pornography filters'. Available at http://www.independent.co.uk/life-style/gadgets-and-tech/one-in-five-sites-blocked-by-the-uks-overzealous-pornography-filters-9579838.html, visited 18 September 2018.
50. Nair, H. V. (2015, July 8). *Supreme Court says India can't ban porn: CJI says a total ban on sex sites would violate privacy and personal liberty. Daily Mail*. http://www.dailymail.co.uk/indiahome/indianews/article-3153957/Supreme-Court-says-India-t-ban-porn-CJI-says-total-ban-sex-sites-violate-privacy-personal-liberty.html, visited 18 September 2018.

51. McIntyre, T. J. (2013). *Child abuse images and cleanfeeds: Assessing Internet blocking systems*. In I. Brown (Ed.), *Research handbook on Governance of the Internet*. Edward Elgar Publishing, pp. 277, 283.
52. Carr, J., & Hilton, Z. (2009). Child protection and self-regulation in the internet industry: The UK Experience. *Children et Society, 23*, 306. Available at http://onlinelibrary.wiley.com/doi/10.1111/j.1099-0860.2009.00235.x/pdf, visited 18 September 2018.
53. Brown, C. A. (2017). *Non-discrimination and trade in services: The role of tax treaties*. Singapore: Springer.
54. Ovey, C., & Robin, C. A. (2002). *White, European Convention on Humans Rights* (3rd Ed.). Oxford University Press.
55. Robertson, A. H., & Merrills, J. G. (1993). *Human Rights in Europe, A study of the European Convention on Human Rights* (3rd Ed.). Manchester University Press.
56. Christoffersen, J. (2009). *Fair balance: Proportionality, subsidiarity and primarity in the European Convention on Human Rights*. Martinus Nijhoff Publishers.
57. Khosla, M. (2010). *Proportionality: An assault on Human Rights? A Replay. International Journal of Constitutional Law, 8*(2), 298.
58. Czapiński, J., & Panek, T. (Eds.) (2018). Social diagnosis 2013. *Objective and Subjective Quality of Life in Poland, 7*(3).
59. Batorski, D. (2018). *Poles and communication technology—Access conditions and modes of use*. Available at http://ce.vizja.pl/en/issues/volume/7/issue/3.1#art367, visited 18 September 2018.
60. Lenhart, A., Purcell, K., Smith, A., & Zickur, K. (2010). Social media & mobile Internet use among teens and young adults. Pew Internet & American Life Project, *PewInternet*. Retrieved, from http://www.pewinternet.org/files/old-media/Files/Reports/2010/PIP_Social_Media_and_Young_Adults_Report_Final_with_toplines.pdf, visited 31 July 2018.
61. Owens, E. W., Behun, R. J., Manning, J. C., & Reid, R. C. (2012). The impact of internet pornography on adolescents: A review of the research. *Sexual Addiction & Compulsivity, 19*, 1–2, 99–122. https://doi.org/10.1080/10720162.2012.660431, visited 18 September 2018.

Chapter 10
A Comparative Law Approach to the Notion of Sustainable Development: An Example from Urban Planning Law

Ermanno Calzolaio

Abstract 'Sustainable development' is a multifarious and multidisciplinary notion. The research project for this book is concerned with pointing out the balancing of a variety of objectives—including that of economic progress, environmental protection, individual rights, and collective interests—that is often shielded by this notion. In that sense, it surely has normative implications for lawmaking and legal application. However, from a legal point of view, the definitions of sustainable development in legal texts are often too vague and in legal literature it is commonly recognised that there is no accepted legal definition. What is more, a 2015 UN General Assembly Resolution acknowledges that 'there are different approaches, visions, models and tools available to each country, in accordance with its national circumstances and priorities, to achieve sustainable development'. Against this backdrop, the primary aim of the present chapter is to focus on the problems concerning the legal definition of sustainable development. Secondly, this chapter intends to present some methodological reflections on the comparative approach in the process of defining the field of application of the notion of sustainable development. In this respect, it has been argued that an international commitment to sustainable development requires the use of comparative law in order to find, develop and apply solutions to the problems that the imprecise notion of sustainable development engenders. Lastly, this chapter contends that the aims and methods of comparative law transcend the mere assessment of the differences between the rules in force across the various legal systems.

Keywords Sustainable development · Normative effect · Comparative law · Urban planning · Environmental protection

10.1 Introduction

This chapter aims at investigating the concept of 'sustainable development', defined as development which 'meets the needs of current generations without compromis-

---

E. Calzolaio (✉)
University of Macerata, Piaggia Università, 2, Macerata, Italy
e-mail: ermanno.calzolaio@unimc.it

P. Szwedo et al. (eds.), *Law and Development*, Kobe University Monograph Series in Social Science Research, https://doi.org/10.1007/978-981-13-9423-2_10

ing the ability of future generations to meet their own needs' (Brundtland Report). Whilst the notion of sustainable development is deployed across a variety of fields and for a variety of needs, its legal relevance is often questioned; being claimed to be an oxymoron, consisting in the juxtaposition of two words involving arguably antithetical meanings (namely, those of *economic development* and *environmental sustainability*).[1] It is often remarked that even if sustainable development has an evocative conceptual value, from a legal point of view it lacks effectiveness.[2]

Yet, elusive as it may appear, the term is often used in legal texts, both at an international level and in the legislation of the various domestic legal systems. Further to the foregoing, after a short account of the historical background to the emergence of the notion under review (par. 2), a focus on the legal dimensions of sustainable development shall follow, through a survey on the use of the term in statutory provisions, both in the law of the European Union and in the principal European legal systems (par. 3). This shall be followed by an examination of the concrete relevance of sustainable development in the specific field of urban planning law, through a comparative study of recent judgments in the English, French and Italian experience (par. 4). Lastly, some conclusive remarks shall be presented, arguing that sustainable development remains a challenge that jurists need to address (par. 5).

10.2 The Emergence of the Notion of Sustainable Development

The notion of 'sustainable development' marks a new approach within the environment-related literature. Since the late 19th century the main concern of environmental studies has been whether and how to preserve or conserve natural areas, with different suggested options: some have favoured the preservation of natural areas in their original form; others, on the contrary, have stressed the importance of conserving land and resources for later human use. In the 20th century, particularly after WWII, the advent of new concerns required that they be perceived in all their importance; that is to say, in tandem with issues of pollution, non-renewal resource depletion, and population growth.

Against this backdrop, the idea of sustainable development emerged in the mid-1980s 'as an attempt to bridge the gap between environmental concerns about the increasingly evident ecological consequences of human activities and socio-political concerns about human development issues.'[3]

More specifically, in 1987 the World Commission on Environment and Development issued the well-known Brundtland Report. It focused attention on social and economic conditions in developing countries and on their connection to environmental degradation. The report argued that ecological sustainability cannot be achieved if the problem of poverty is not successfully addressed around the world. Sustainable

[1]On this aspect, *see* Cafagno [1].

[2]Ferrara [2].

[3]Robinson [3].

development was defined as development that 'meets the needs of current generations without compromising the ability of future generations to meet their own needs.'[4] That definition essentially rests on two basic pillars: on the one hand, the needs of future generations and of the global poorest people of our planet; on the other, the limits in the use of natural resources and in the capacity of the biosphere to absorb the negative effects of anthropogenic activities.

Since its emergence, the notion of sustainable development has been accompanied by a veil of scepticism. This has largely been due to its vagueness and polysemy, and due to its occasional use to promote *un*sustainable activities. As mentioned earlier, the notion under review has been seen as an oxymoron, considering that economic development may stand in contradiction with the safeguard of environmental issues.[5]

Critics seem not to take in due account that in the Brundtland Report sustainable development is not conceived as 'a fixed state of harmony.'[6] Rather, it is a dynamic process of change, characterised by the need to strike a balance between socio-economic development and environmental protection. Be that as it may, it is undisputable that after thirty years since the publication of the Brundtland Report the precise meaning of sustainable development remains undetermined.

In recent times, the situation is complicated by the fact that there has been a progressive change in the understanding of this notion. Without going into great detail, it is worth noting that in 2002 at the Johannesburg Summit a tripartite definition was adopted which rested on three pillars, namely, economic, social, and environmental, which, however, are treated unequally given the relegated status of the last. This tripartite definition was restated at the 2012 Rio Conference, which led to the signature of the Declaration 'The Future We Want', § 3 of which reads as follows: 'We therefore acknowledge the need to further mainstream sustainable development at all levels, integrating economic, social and environmental aspects and recognizing their interlinkages, so as to achieve sustainable development in all its dimensions'. This formulation may be suggestive of the environmental dimension standing in a lower hierarchical order with respect to the economic and social interests.[7]

The debate around the meaning and the implications of sustainable development has received a new boost as a result of three key events which took place in 2015, namely, the publication of Pope Francis's Encyclical Letter "*Laudato si*'—On care for our common home'; the approval of the UN Sustainable Development Goals and the related 2030 Agenda for sustainable development by the UN General Assembly; and the Paris Agreement on Climate Change in the framework of the Paris Climate Conference. It is beyond of the scope of the present chapter to examine these in details. However, it should be noted that these three crucial events demonstrate that—notwithstanding the critics and the elusiveness of the concept of sustainable

[4]U.N. World Comm'n on Env't & Dev., Our Common Future 8 (1987).

[5]For an in-depth account, see again Robinson, *supra* note 3, at 373.

[6]Cf. U.N. World Comm'n on Env't & Dev, *supra* note 4, at 9.

[7]In this sense, see Montini and Volpe [4].

development—its use persists, from different perspectives, as a tool to polarise the need to take account of the consequences of such uncontrolled development that fails to consider the needs of the poorest and to address ecological and environmental concerns.

10.3 The Use of Sustainable Development in Statutory Provisions

Against the backdrop of the foregoing, any trepidation on the part of jurists in identifying the legal dimension of such a concept is understandable. Scholars agree on the point that the definitions of sustainable development in legal texts are vague, too long and not functional. Consequently, the normative value of the notion of sustainable development is difficult to ascertain, given that a clear and precise definition is lacking.[8]

Yet, many statutory provisions, albeit not exhaustively listed herein, make great use of the term.

As far as European Union law is concerned, it is worth considering that art. 37 of the European Charter of Fundamental Rights prescribes that 'a high level of environmental protection and the improvement of the quality of the environment must be integrated into the policies of the Union and ensured in accordance with the principle of sustainable development'. The Charter has the same normative value as the Treaties, as provided by art. 6 of the Treaty on the Functioning of the European Union (TFEU), according to which 'The Union recognises the rights, freedoms and principles set out in the Charter of Fundamental Rights of the European Union of 7 December 2000, as adapted at Strasbourg, on 12 December 2007, which shall have the same legal value as the Treaties'. Moreover, sustainable development has been considered by numerous initiatives at the EU level, including the Communication from the Commission 'A Sustainable Europe for a Better World: A European Union Strategy for Sustainable Development' adopted in 2011,[9] and many other related documents. Amongst the most recent is the 'New European Consensus on Development—'Our world, our dignity, our future'', signed by all Member States in June 2017.[10] It constitutes a comprehensive common framework for European development cooperation and, for the first time, it is applicable to all EU Institutions and to all Member States per se.

---

[8]See Salardi [5].

[9]*Communication from the Commission A Sustainable Europe for a Better World: A European Union Strategy for Sustainable Development* (*Commission's proposal to the Gothenburg European Council*), COM (2001) 264 final (May 15, 2001).

[10]*New European Consensus on Development—'Our world, our dignity, our future'*, Joint Statement by the Council and the Representatives of the Governments of the Member States: Meeting within the Council, the European Parliament and the European Commission, http://www.consilium.europa.eu/media/24004/european-consensus-on-development-2-june-2017-clean_final.pdf (last visited 11 September 2018).

Moving to the main European legal systems, it should be stressed that an acknowledgement of the notion of sustainable development is often witnessed at a constitutional level. For instance, art. 45 of the Spanish Constitution, albeit not explicit, refers to the notion of sustainable development when it prescribes that public authorities have a duty to ensure rational use of natural resources in line with environmental concerns and with collective solidarity.[11]

In relation to France, the *Charte de l'environnement*—enacted in 2005 by way of constitutional statute (*Loi constitutionnelle n° 2005-205 du 1er mars 2005*)—integrates with the Preamble of the French Constitution to mandate that the French Republic respect human rights and the right and duties set in the *Charte*. Art. 6 of the *Charte* prescribes that public policies must promote sustainable development, recurring to the terminology considered earlier (that is to say, in order to reconcile the protection and valorisation of the environment, economic development, and social progress).[12] It is worth noting that, in this manner, sustainable development has now acquired constitutional recognition in France.[13]

In Germany, the *Grundgesetz* has recently been amended by the addition of article 20a, soon after art. 20 ('*fixing the basic German constitutional principles*'). This provision reads as follows: '[m]indful also of its responsibility toward future generations, the state shall protect the natural foundations of life and animals by legislation and, in accordance with law and justice, by executive and judicial action, all within the framework of the constitutional order.'[14] Again, this wording clearly echoes the language used in sustainable development discourse.

In relation to Switzerland, art. 73 of the Swiss Constitution is explicitly dedicated to sustainable development: '[t]he Confederation and the Cantons shall endeavour to achieve a balanced and sustainable relationship between nature and its capacity to renew itself and the demands placed on it by the population'.[15]

Similar provisions can be found in the Polish Constitution (art. 74) and in the Portuguese Constitution (art. 66).

---

[11]'*Todos tienen el derecho a disfrutar de un medio ambiente adecuado para el desarrollo de la persona, así como el deber de conservarlo. Los poderes públicos velarán por la utilización racional de todos los recursos naturales, con el fin de proteger y mejorar la calidad de la vida y defender y restaurar el medio ambiente, apoyándose en la indispensable solidaridad colectiva. Para quienes violen lo dispuesto en el apartado anterior, en los términos que la ley fije se establecerán sanciones penales o, en su caso, administrativas, así como la obligación de reparar el daño causado*'.

[12]'*Les politiques publiques doivent promouvoir un développement durable. A cet effet, elles concilient la protection et la mise en valeur de l'environnement, le développement économique et le progrès social*'.

[13]The constitutional value of the *Charte* is recognised by the French *Conseil constitutionnet* [CC] [Constitutional Court] decision No. 2014-394, QPC, May 7, 2014. For an in-depth account of the progressive recognition of the concrete legal value of sustainable development by French courts see François-Guy Trébulle, *Droit Du Développement Durable*, JPC 55 ff. (2017).

[14]For an English translation of the German Constitution see https://www.btg-bestellservice.de/pdf/80201000.pdf.

[15]For an English translation of the Swiss Constitution see https://www.admin.ch/opc/en/classified-compilation/19995395/201709240000/101.pdf.

In Italy, there is no explicit reference in the Constitution, even though some authors argue that the principle can be inferred interpretatively.[16] In reality, several ordinary statutes make reference to sustainable development, the most important of which being the '*Codice dell'ambiente*' (i.e., Environmental Code), approved in 2006, considered in the next paragraph. The same could be said for most, if not all, European legal systems, where several norms are dedicated whether expressly or not to sustainable development.

10.4 The Legal Relevance of Sustainable Development in the Field of Urban Planning Law

The survey carried out in the previous paragraph, albeit incomplete, demonstrates that the term 'sustainable development' is well documented in the law and policy of the European Union and in those of the major European legal systems, both at a constitutional level and in ordinary legislation. Against this backdrop, the real issue is whether such wide recognition of the notion of sustainable development in legal texts is merely a formal tribute to a fashionable principle, or, on the contrary, whether it is in fact indicative of its concrete legal relevance.

In addressing such questions, it is necessary to move from general perspectives to an investigation of how the notion under review is deployed in specific areas of law, as this is a concrete manner in which to gauge the normative implications of the notion of sustainable development by its application to a specific area of policy/social activity. To that end, urban planning law is one of the main areas to explore, given that it is at the juncture of many competing interests, including the need to provide housing, to stimulate economic growth, and to address the consequences of the exploitation of the environment.

Our methodological choice of a comparative approach to this question chimes with a 2015 United Nations General Assembly Resolution (namely, the Resolution adopted by the General Assembly at its seventieth session on 25 September 2015 'Transforming our world: the 2030 Agenda for Sustainable Development' (A/Res/70/1)) which acknowledges that 'there are different approaches, visions, models and tools available to each country, in accordance with its national circumstances and priorities, to achieve sustainable development' (p. 15, para. 59). A comparative analysis is well-suited to providing meaningful insights into the implications of the notion under review.

[16] Porena [6].

10.4.1 English Law: The Role of the 'Presumption in Favour of Sustainable Development'

The English system (i.e., that which applies the law of England and Wales, which is itself one of the separate jurisdictions of the United Kingdom) of urban planning law requires that applications for planning permission be determined in accordance to the geographically relevant development plans—which may include the Local Plan and neighbourhood plans made in relation to the relevant area—unless material considerations indicate otherwise.[17] In the development of local and neighbourhood plans, public authorities are under the obligation to take into account the National Planning Policy Framework (NPPF), which is a material consideration in planning decisions.[18] In relation to neighbourhood plans, the independent examiner will consider whether, having regard to national policy, it is appropriate to make the plan.[19] Planning policies and decisions must reflect, and, where appropriate, promote relevant EU obligations and statutory requirements. The NPPF was issued by Government in March 2012 and updated in July 2018.[20] In the part entitled 'Achieving sustainable development' para. 2.7 states that the 'purpose of the planning system is to contribute to the achievement of sustainable development[...] meeting the needs of the present without compromising the ability of future generations to meet their own needs' and para. 2.10 provides that 'at the heart of the Framework is *a presumption in favour of sustainable development*' (emphasis in the original).

A recent case decided by the Court of Appeal (of England and Wales) clarifies the meaning of this presumption.[21] The case concerned the grant of planning permission for 150 dwellings. The Borough Council and the appellant agreed that the proposed development was contrary to the strategic policies of the up-to-date Local Plan and that there was a five-year supply of housing land, both of which assumptions were accepted by the Inspector. However, the Inspector concluded that the proposed development accorded with the three aspects to sustainable development as per the NPPF at para. 7 (NB., NPPF citations in the court decision are in relation to the 2012 version) and therefore satisfied the sustainable development requirement as defined in the NPPF. Subsequently, the Inspector concluded that the NPPF presumption in favour of sustainable development was to be given such weight as to rebut the presumption of refusal arising from the conflict with the Local Plan. In other words, and without entering into details of very technical issues, the presumption in favour

[17] Section 38(6) of the Planning and Compulsory Purchase Act 2004 and section 70(2) of the Town and Country Planning Act 1990.

[18] This is provided in sections 19(2)(a) and 38(6) of the Planning and Compulsory Purchase Act 2004 and section 70(2) of the Town and Country Planning Act 1990.

[19] See section 38B and C and paragraph 8(2) of new Schedule 4B to the 2004 Act (inserted by the Localism Act 2011 section 116 and Schedules 9 and 10).

[20] See the latest version at: https://assets.publishing.service.gov.uk/government/uploads/system/uploads/attachment_data/file/733637/National_Planning_Policy_Framework_web_accessible_version.pdf (last accessed 11 September 2018).

[21] Barwood Strategic Land II LLP v. East Staffordshire Borough Council [2017] EWCA Civ 893.

of sustainable development was interpreted in such manner as to enable to grant permission even though the project of development was not consistent with the local plan. The main outcome of the Court of Appeal's decision is that it clarifies that where a proposed development is in conflict with an up-to-date development plan, and the local planning authority can demonstrate that a five-year supply is unlikely to benefit from the presumption in favour of sustainable development within the meaning of paragraph 14 of the NPPF, there may be no presumption in favour of granting planning permission.

It may be reasonably deduced from this case that sustainable development is a relevant consideration that local authorities must take into account when adopting local plans, and that the presumption in favour of sustainable development, as set by the NPPF, cannot be an argument used by property developers in order to supersede the planning decisions of local authorities.[22] This suggests that not only has sustainable development concrete implications, from a legal point of view, as guidance for specific options to be set in planning schemes, but also that the presumption in favour of sustainable development cannot be used as a way of evading the provisions in the local plans limiting urban development.

10.4.2 The French Experience: The Pre-eminence of Plans of Sustainable Development in Respect of Local Urban Plans

Let us now consider the French experience: very briefly, art. 151-8 of the *code de l'urbanisme* provides that the local plan of urban development ('*Plan Local d'Urbanisme*', PLU) must be coherent with the *project of sustainable development* ('*Projet d'Aménagement et de Développement Durable*', PADD),[23] which is, in its turn, a document issued by the local authority, setting the general objectives of the development of the local area in accordance with the principle of moderation in the use of space and against the urban sprawl.[24]

The specific content and coherence of this obligation has been questioned. In particular, given that the PADD is essentially a generic instrument setting the direction of policy, it is not clear in instances of contradiction between the PLU and the PADD whether judges are entitled to intervene.

---

[22] '*Sustainable development is highly valued in the Framework, and there is a "momentum" in favor of it*' [7].

[23] '*Le règlement fixe, en cohérence avec le projet d'aménagement et de développement durables, les règles générales et les servitudes d'utilisation des sols permettant d'atteindre les objectifs mentionnés aux articles L. 101-1 à L. 101-3*', introduced by the *ordonnance No. 2015-1174* of Sept 23, 2015).

[24] Art. 151-5 Code de l'urbanisme.

This issue was recently settled in an important judgment of the Nantes Court of Appeal in 2016.[25] This case concerned the decision of the local authority to approve a PLU which permitted the expansion of building activities in an area located near the coast, whereas the PADD set the objective of valorising natural patrimony through the localisation of new urban expansions outside the areas located near the coast. An environmental organisation challenged the local authority decision on grounds that the PADD was unambiguous in prohibiting new buildings near the coastal area, and that the local plan contradicted the PADD, compromising the requirement of sustainable development. The Court allowed the appeal and annulled the relevant provision of the PLU as it violated the law [i.e. art. Loi 123-1-5 *Code de l'urbanisme* (Code of Planning)] by approving a PLU in contrast with the provisions of the PADD.

This judgment is considered a clear recognition of local plans of sustainable development as being hierarchically superior to local plans of urban development.[26] It is another example demonstrating that, despite its nebulous character, in practice the notion of sustainable development may play a deciding role to the extent that judges afford it such concrete value.

10.4.3 The Italian Experience: Sustainable Development as a Limit of the Discretionary Powers of Public Authorities

In the Italian legal system, the '*codice dell'ambiente*' (i.e., the environmental code) approved in 2006[27] promulgates a general principle: every human activity concerning the fields covered by its provisions must be in accordance with the principle of sustainable development, in order to guarantee that the needs of present generations do not compromise the quality of life and the possibilities of future generations (art. 3-quater/article 3.4). More specifically, the activity of public administrations must achieve the aim of allowing the best application of the principle of sustainable development. This means that in the exercise of their discretion public authorities must prioritise environment protection. As it has been observed, the implications of these provisions is that the principle of sustainable development is the means by which judges assess the reasonableness of the outcomes of the use of discretionary powers on the part of public authorities.[28]

There is a series of recent key cases of administrative courts (TAR) making clear that the perspective of sustainable development implies that the right of private property itself must be concretely shaped according to the needs of harmonic territorial growth in the light of preserving the integrity of the natural landscape. In this respect, for instance, Italian administrative judges have confirmed the decision of a local

[25] Cour d'appel (CA) (i.e., the regional Court of Appeal) de Nantes, 5ème chambre, Jul 27, 2016, 14NT02815.

[26] In this sense, see de Baleine [8].

[27] D.Lgs. 3 april 2006, n. 152 (It.).

[28] Porena, *supra* note 16, at. 14.

authority not to permit any possibility of expansion to an area where a quarry had been located.[29]

Similarly, a regional statute providing that local plans should be drafted in accordance with the principle of sustainable development has been interpreted to mean that they have to avoid new territorial exploitation, should this be in contrast with the rights of future generations, asserting that the growth of the population does not mean that new buildings can be allowed, given that the interest of preservation of the environment and the landscape has to be prioritised.[30] In another case, it has been asserted that local authorities are entitled to consider environment and landscape issues in assessing every project having an impact on the environment.[31]

It has been argued that sustainable development is shaping anew the very content of private rights, through their instrumentalisation for the achievement of environmental protection objectives. This, however, is an argument that has presently received much criticism and has attracted controversy—that said, in Italy no one could seriously claim that sustainable development discourse is merely confined to the sphere of policy declarations. On the contrary, it assumes a concrete relevance as a parameter in the decisions of public bodies when considering the permission of the exercise of private activities.[32]

10.5 Sustainable Development as a Challenge for Jurists

There is no doubt that sustainable development is quite an elusive and vague notion, lacking precise content and a universal legal definition, therefore, it is unsurprising that jurists may feel disoriented.

Omnis definitio in iure periculosa est (i.e., any legal definition is dangerous), warned the Roman jurist Javolenus. Yet, the problem of 'definition' is a thorny issue from a legal point of view. Technical notions and an apparatus of terms and categories for the concrete application of rules are essential.[33] This need cannot be underestimated and is universally felt. In this respect, it can be useful to allude to Confucian theory that attaches social (and moral) value to the precision/correctness of language in designating things. This theory is expounded in the *Analects of Confucius* under the heading of the 'rectification of names' (*zheng ming*). Master Confucius was once called to assist the ruler of Wei in the administration of his reign. During the journey to his destination, one of his disciples asked: 'The ruler of Wei [is] waiting

[29]Tribunale amministrativo regionale (TAR) (Regional Administrative Court of Appeal) Firenze, sez. I, Jun 12, 2017, No. 790.

[30]Tribunale amministrativo regionale (TAR) (Regional Administrative Court of Appeal) Milano, sez. II, Sept 23, 2016, No. 1696.

[31]Tribunale amministrativo regionale (TAR) (Regional Administrative Court of Appeal) Sardegna, sez. V, Jul 11, 2016, no. 3059.

[32]For an in-depth discussion, see Fracchia [9].

[33]*See* Moccia [10].

for you, in order to administer the government. What will you consider the first thing to be done?'. Confucius replied: 'What is necessary is to rectify names'. But that answer left the poor disciple so confused and dissatisfied that he dared to reply: 'So! indeed! You are wide of the mark! Why must there be such rectification?'. Then the Master severely rebuked his disciple with the following words: 'How uncultivated you are! A superior man, in regard to what he does not know, shows a cautious reserve. If names be not correct, language is not in accordance with the truth of things. If language be not in accordance with the truth of things, affairs cannot be carried on to success'.[34]

What one can conclude, therefore, is that establishing the content of terms should not be an exercise done in a manner than either appeals to teleological dogmatism or to unbridled relativism. To this respect, sustainable development presents a real challenge to jurists. The debate around the elusiveness and vagueness of the notion of sustainable development—understandable and well-grounded as it may be—cannot lead to the conclusion that it has no legal value. The examples in the field of urban planning law illustrate how, on the contrary, it does have concrete implications, to the extent of bringing to the fore the need to re-interpret traditional legal institutions such as that of property rights. Therefore, the challenge is to ascertain the concrete role that the notion of sustainable development plays in a variety of fields where it is used and applied.

To this end, the preceding remarks aim to contribute to that task, and to solicit further reflections, recurring to all the possibilities offered by a comparative approach which appears to be essential in casting light on such a controversial yet fascinating topic.[35] After all, what is at stake is the need to reconcile development and sustainability for our world, and jurists must not fail to play their role in this respect.

References

1. Cafagno, M. (2013). Cambiamenti Climatici tra Strumenti di Mercato e Potere Pubblico. In G. F. Cartei (Ed.), *Cambiamento Climatico e Sviluppo Sostenibile* (p. 105).
2. Ferrara, R. (2005). I Principi Comunitari della Tutela dell'ambiente. *Diritto Amministrativo, 13*, 509.
3. Robinson, J. (2004). Squaring the circle? Some thoughts on the idea of sustainable development. *Ecological Economics, 48*, 370.
4. Montini, M., & Volpe, F. (2016). Sustainable development at a turning point. *Federalismi.it*, 5.
5. Salardi, S. (2011). Sustainable development: Definitions and models of legal regulation. Some legal-theoretical outlines on the role of law. *Rivista Quadrimestrale di Diritto dell'Ambiente, 2*, 76.

[34]The Sayings of Confucius, Bk. 13, v. 3 (James R. Ware trans., Mentor book, new ed. 1980), *quoted in* Moccia, *supra* note 33, at 761.

[35]In the sense that an international commitment to sustainable development requires the use of comparative law, see Dernbach [11].

6. Porena, D. (2016). Il 'Rango' del Principio dello Sviluppo Sostenibile nella Gerarchia delle Fondi del Diritto: Norme Pattizie, Consuetudini Internazionali ed Art. 10 della Costituzione. *Federalismi.it*, 13.
7. Choongh, S., & Cairnes, P. (2018). The element of planning discretion in the context of an up-to-date plan: The implications of the barwood case. *Journal of Planning & Environment Law,* 129.
8. de Baleine, A. D. (2016). Le Règlement du Plan Local d'Urbanisme Doit Être Cohérent avec le Projet d'Aménagement et de Développement Durables. *AJDA* [*L'Actualité Juridique Droit Administratif*], 2108.
9. Fracchia, F. (2010). Sviluppo Sostenibile e Diritti delle Generazioni Future. *Rivista Quadrimestrale di Diritto dell'Ambiente, 1*, 12.
10. Moccia, L. (2007). Basic ways of defining property. In Undefined Editors, *Colloqui in Ricordo di Michele Giorgianni* (p. 759).
11. Dernbach, J. C. (1998). Reflections on comparative law, environmental law, and sustainability. *Widener Law Symposium Journal, 3*, 279.

Chapter 11
Challenges Concerning 'Development': A Case-Study on Subsistence and Small-Scale Fisheries in South Africa

Jan Glazewski

Abstract This chapter examines the notion of 'development'—in particular sustainable development—as it pertains to the plight of subsistence or small-scale fishing communities in the near-shore coastal areas of South Africa. It does so against the backdrop of the South African Roman-Dutch common law, customary law, and the 1996 Constitution, which marked the end to over 300 years of minority rule. The Constitution replaced the Westminster system of parliamentary sovereignty with a constitutional democracy underpinned by a Bill of Rights. The latter includes an environmental right that, among other things, refers to 'sustainable development' as well as the right to equality. The present contribution discusses 'development' against the backdrop and interaction of pertinent United Nations' Sustainable Development Goals, in particular 'No Poverty' (Goal 1), 'Zero Hunger' (Goal 2) and 'Conservation and Sustainable Use of Marine Resources' (Goal 14). The chapter also refers to the 1981 African Charter on Human and Peoples' Rights, which provides for a '... right to a general satisfactory environment favorable to their development'. It concludes that, despite the exhortation in the Preamble of the Constitution to rectify the '... injustices of the past', many challenges remain before the poorer fishing communities can claim to have had the right to development realised.

Keywords South Africa · Environmental right · Food security · Sustainable development · Sustainable development goals · Subsistence and small-scale fishers

11.1 Background

The year 2017 marked the twenty-first anniversary of the adoption of South Africa's landmark Constitution in 1996.[1] This heralded the end of over three hundred years

[1]This final Constitution of the Republic of South Africa, 1996 ('the Constitution') replaced the Interim Constitution of 1994.

J. Glazewski (✉)
Institute of Marine & Environmental Law, University of Cape Town, Rondebosch 7701, South Africa
e-mail: jan.glazewski@uct.ac.za

P. Szwedo et al. (eds.), *Law and Development*, Kobe University Monograph Series in Social Science Research, https://doi.org/10.1007/978-981-13-9423-2_11

of racial laws, and the replacement of a Westminster system of government with a constitutional democracy, including a Bill of Rights, following negotiations after the release of Nelson Mandela in 1990.[2] Expectations of a 'better life for all',[3] were high in the initial years as exemplified in the Preamble of the Constitution which included phrases such as: 'We, the people of South Africa, [r]ecognise the injustices of the past; ... [and intend to] "[i]mprove the quality of life of all citizens ....'

Being situated at the interface of two vast seas—the Atlantic and Indian oceans—and in close proximity to a third—the inhospitable Southern Ocean—[4] South Africa is blessed with a diverse and a well-established fisheries economy enjoying ready access to vast ocean space in excess of a million square kilometres and a variety of marine resources therein.[5] The west coast of the country is characterised by the cold, nutrient-rich waters of the Benguela Current, that originates in the Antarctic region and flows northwards up the west coast of southern Africa towards the equator. In contrast the warmer, fast-flowing but nutrient-poor Agulhas current flows southward from the equator along the east coast of southern Africa.[6]

The diversity of South Africa's fishery stocks is broadly categorised as:

- the demersal or white fish, (predominantly hake) sector—this refers to bottom-dwelling fish which are harvested by trawling and long-ling methods; and
- the pelagic sector (predominantly pilchard and anchovy)—stocks which are captured by purse-sein netting.

These two sectors which tend to be offshore, are by and large, the most lucrative, and, have historically been predominantly fished by the commercial fishing sector. But it is the near-shore rock lobster and abalone industries that are the most relevant for the purposes of this chapter. These have historically been the mainstay of poorer subsistence fishing communities, albeit having also been heavily exploited by the commercial sector, in particular the West Coast rock lobster fishery.[7] The latter is one of South Africa's oldest formal commercial fisheries, dating back to the late-nineteenth century, which expanded rapidly in the early part of the twentieth century, with peak catches occurring in the 1950s when up to 18,000 tonnes were landed annually. Catches declined sharply to 10,000 tonnes in the 1960s and have continued the downward trend to around and even below 2,000 tonnes in recent years, indicating unsustainable exploitation levels. Such severe decline is believed to be driven by a number of factors, including changes in management measures, fishing methods and

[2]Chapter 2 of the Constitution is the 'Bill of Rights'.

[3]The slogan of the previously banned African National Congress at the first free and democratic elections in 1994.

[4]For a general perspective, see McLean and Glazewski [1].

[5]South Africa has claimed a 200 nautical mile Exclusive Economic Zone (EEZ) under its Maritime Zones Act 15 of 1994.

[6]Department of Environmental Affairs, *State of the Oceans and Coasts around South Africa 2014* (2015).

[7]The two predominant rock lobster sectors are the West coast rock lobster (*jasus lalandii)* and the South coast rock lobster; cf., Strydom et al. (fn 4), at 595–599. See also Sowman [2].

efficiency, environmental degradation and overexploitation.[8] Hardest hit have been the poorer fishing communities.[9] The second major resource that has historically been a staple of poorer communities is abalone (*Haliotis midae*) referred to locally as 'perlemoen'. These are caught by divers in shallow subtidal kelp beds, usually less than 10 m deep. Abalone flesh is the most valuable South African seafood per kilogram, and most of the catch is exported. The value of the product has increased the potential for illegal fishing and has created a fisheries management predicament of vast proportions.[10] Records going back to 1953 indicate that catches peaked at nearly 3,000 tonnes in 1965, but have since declined, with a particularly dramatic collapse over the past decade. The Total Allowable Catch (TAC) for commercial exploitation decreased from 693 tonnes in 2000 to less than 240 tonnes for the 2005–06 season. In the case of *WWF South Africa and Minister of Agriculture, Forestry and Fisheries and Others*,[11] the Court held that the setting by the Minister of the TAC for West Coast Rock Lobster for the 2017/18 season at 1,924 tons was irrational and set the decision aside. At the heart of the Court finding of irrationality was the fact the determination of the TAC by the Minister was contrary to sound scientific advice and must take sustainability into account before other considerations.

As mentioned earlier, rampant illegal harvesting and continual decline in the abundance of the abalone resource resulted in a total closure of the commercial fishery during 2008. Immense demand for high-priced abalone internationally, along with weak enforcement capacity within South Africa, has led to the establishment of well-organised illegal abalone harvesting syndicates in recent years. Moreover, an ecological development—namely, the encroachment of rock lobsters on the centre of the most productive abalone region—has further compounded the low stock levels.[12] Recent trends indicate that such fisheries will be rendered commercially extinct unless enforcement and compliance are greatly strengthened in the short term.

Against this backdrop this chapter outlines and assesses the policy and legal measures taken in an attempt to improve the lives of subsistence and small-scale fishing communities that have historically been disadvantaged by the legal structures of apartheid. Historically, South Africa has had one of the highest Gini coefficient scores in the world; the subsistence fishing communities being an example of this lamentable situation.[13] This unsatisfactory situation had resulted from the imposition of over three hundred years of racial discrimination, and the exclusion of the majority of the population from access to land and natural resources. However, despite the advent of the new Constitution, South Africa's Gini coefficient has not improved.

[8]Driver et al. [3], at 325.

[9]Raemaekers et al. [4].

[10]Hauck and Sweijd [6], Steinberg [7].

[11]Unreported case no 11478/18 dated 26 September 2018 (Western Cape High Court).

[12]Cf., Department of Agriculture Forestry and Fisheries, *Status of South African Marine Fishery Resources* (2014).

[13]This index measures the extent to which the distribution of income (or, in some cases, consumption expenditure) among individuals or households within an economy deviates from a perfectly equal distribution.

Against this background this chapter focusses on the plight of the subsistence and small-scale fishing communities, particularly with regard to their reliance on West Coast rock lobster and abalone resources that have provided a source of food security for centuries. These communities are typically scattered in small villages on the arid and inhospitable West coast of South Africa but also on the more populated South and East coast of the country.

11.2 International Context

The interaction of a number of UN Sustainable Development Goals (SDGs), in particular: 'No Poverty' (Goal 1), 'Zero Hunger' (Goal 2), 'Life below Water' (Conservation and Sustainable Use of Marine Resources) (Goal 14), including access to marine resources by small-scale fishers and the markets (Sub-goal 14b), as well as 'Life on Land' (Goal 15), are particularly pertinent to the conservation and sustainable use of South Africa's marine resources, generally, and to small-scale fishing communities in particular. It is suggested that the notion of sustainable development is a cornerstone of environmental law in national jurisdictions.

Moreover, recent times have seen the growing phenomenon of transboundary fisheries crime resulting in increased pressure on coastal marine resources worldwide in the form of overfishing and poaching by locals, outsiders, gangsters, and foreign corporate fishing interests.[14] In South Africa, poaching by both local and foreign syndicates has become particularly rife.[15] Linked to this is the fact that at the regional level, the 1981 African Charter on Human and Peoples' Rights provides for a '... right to a general satisfactory environment favorable to their development'.[16] The Food and Agricultural Organisation of the United Nations (FAO) has recognised the phenomenon of Illegal Unreported and Unregulated (IUU) fishing globally and the notion of transboundary fisheries crime has grown apace.[17] What is more, the white-collar nature of transboundary fisheries crime has been vividly illustrated in the case of *US v Bengis* entailing the illegal harvesting of thousands of tonnes of rock lobster—in excess by over 1,000% of the quota—and smuggling the illegal harvest to the USA where it was marketed over a period of over a decade. During June 2013, the US Southern District Court for New York handed down a restitution order in favour of South Africa for an amount of over USD 29 million for the illegal harvest of tonnes of rock lobster.[18] The problems depicted here are by no means unique to South Africa and are as applicable in traditional fishing villages worldwide, from other countries in Africa to the Mediterranean to North America and Asia.

[14] de Coning and Witbooi [8].

[15] See Raemaekers et al. (fn 9).

[16] See in general Scholtz [9], Chenwi [10].

[17] Pescadolus, www.pescadolus.org.

[18] Glazewski [11].

11.3 The Constitutional Dimension

As briefly discussed in the foregoing, the end of apartheid heralded in a new constitutional order aimed at addressing historical injustices suffered by the majority of the South African population. This part of the chapter accordingly considers the constitutional aspects pertinent to the issue under review.

11.3.1 The Environmental Right and Sustainable Development

The notion of 'sustainable development' forms the basis of South African environmental law. The 'Bill of Rights' chapter of the Constitution contains an *environmental right* which provides for '… an environment that is not harmful to … health or well-being', and goes on to refer to sustainable development in the following terms: 'Everyone has the right to … have the environment protected, for the benefit of present and future generations, through reasonable legislative and other measures that … secure ecologically sustainable development and use of natural resources while promoting justifiable economic and social development'. This right to a decent environment is fleshed out in the framework National Environmental Management Act 107 of 1998 (NEMA), which, among other things, defines *sustainable development* as 'the integration of social, economic and environmental factors into planning, implementation, and decision-making so as to ensure that development serves present and future generations'. The Act goes on to provide for a set of national environmental management principles based on the foundation of sustainable development. This notion is also incorporated in the Marine Living Resources Act 18 of 1998 (MLRA) as outlined below.

What is more, South Africa enjoys a creative and independent judiciary that has embraced environmental rights and the notion of sustainable development in a number of cases such as *Director: Mineral Development, Gauteng Region and Sasol Mining (Pty) Ltd v Save the Vaal Environment and Others*,[19] where the court upheld an NGO's argument that environmental concerns had to be considered by the Director of Mineral Development prior to granting mining authorisation. In that case, the Supreme Court of Appeal stated that:

> Our Constitution, by including environmental rights as fundamental justiciable human rights, by necessary implication requires that environmental considerations be accorded appropriate recognition and respect in the administrative processes in our country. Together with the change in the ideological climate must also come a change in our legal and administrative approach to environmental concerns.

Furthermore, sustainable development was specifically considered in *BP Southern Africa (Pty) Ltd v MEC for Agriculture, Conservation, Environment and Land*

---

[19]*Director: Mineral Development, Gauteng Region and Sasol Mining (Pty) Ltd v Save the Vaal Environment and Others* 1999 (2) SA 709 (SCA) at 719C–D.

Affairs[20] in a matter concerning the refusal to grant authorisation to develop a filling station on a property in a commercial area in Johannesburg owned by the applicant. The court stated:

> The concept of "sustainable development" is the fundamental building block around which environmental legal norms have been fashioned, both internationally and in South Africa [...]. Pure economic principles will no longer determine, in an unbridled fashion, whether a development is acceptable. Development, which may be regarded as economically and financially sound, will in future be balanced by its environmental impact, taking coherent cognisance of the principle of intergenerational equity and sustainable use of resources [...]. By elevating the environment to a fundamental justiciable human right, South Africa has irreversibly embarked on a road, which will lead to the goal of attaining a protected environment by an integrated approach, which takes into consideration, inter alia, socio-economic concerns and principles.[21]

11.3.2 The Marine Living Resources Act 18 of 1998 and Sustainable Development

The constitutional ideal of sustainable development is further fleshed out in a set of foundational principles of the Marine Living Resources Act 18 of 1998 headed 'Objectives and Principles',[22] which include: '[...]the need to conserve marine living resources for present and future generations', the need to ensure their optimal utilisation and ecologically sustainable development,[23] the endorsement of the precautionary approach in marine living resources management,[24] and the need to use marine living resources to promote economic growth and create employment.[25] However, as will be illustrated below, the recent past has seen the resuscitation and emergence of customary rights, that, despite having always been recognised as a source of South African law, had rarely enjoyed much prominence. This has resulted in conflicting claims between customary rights and environmental rights, as shall be examined below.[26]

---

[20] 2004 (5) SA 124 (W).

[21] At 144A–144D.

[22] Set out in Section 2.

[23] Section 2*(a)* and *(b)*.

[24] Section 2*(c)*.

[25] Section 2*(d)*.

[26] Feris [12].

11.3.3 Customary Law and Rights of Indigenous Peoples Under the Constitution

Apart from having to balance environmental rights and the notion of sustainable development against other rights, indigenous peoples' rights or customary law rights may also have implications for environmental and sustainable development considerations. Historically, many coastal communities in South Africa have relied upon marine resources for their survival; so much so that the use of marine resources by communities is arguably not merely a matter of subsistence but also constitutes a part of their culture and custom. Specifically, where there are well-developed rules relating to access to, and use of, marine resources, this can be considered to be a customary right to fish. An example is the oft-cited *Van Breda* case,[27] where the long-standing practice, namely, of not casting nets in front of others to intercept an approaching shoal of fish, was recognised. Customary law—recognised in the Constitution as an independent and original source of law—has resurged in the post-constitutional dispensation, as exemplified in *Alexkor Ltd v The Richtersveld Community*,[28] where the Constitutional Court affirmed customary law as an independent and original source of South African law holding that[29]:

> While in the past indigenous law was seen through the common law lens, it must now be seen as an integral part of our law. Like all law it depends for its ultimate force and validity on the Constitution. Its validity must now be determined by reference not to common law, but to the Constitution. [...] It is clear, therefore that the Constitution acknowledges the originality and distinctiveness of indigenous law as an independent source of norms within the legal system. At the same time the Constitution, while giving force to indigenous law, makes it clear that such law is subject to the Constitution and has to be interpreted in the light of its values. ... In the result, indigenous law feeds into, nourishes, fuses with and becomes part of the amalgam of South African law.

Chapter 12 of the Constitution entitled 'Traditional Leaders' provides that: 'The courts must apply customary law when that law is applicable, subject to the Constitution and any legislation that specifically deals with customary law'.[30]

The Constitution also recognises the right to one's culture, and implicitly custom. This is acknowledged in the Bill of Rights chapter of the Constitution, which provides that:

(1) Persons belonging to a cultural, religious or linguistic community may not be denied the right, with other members of that community

  (a) to enjoy their culture, practise their religion and use their language; and
  (b) to form, join and maintain cultural, religious and linguistic associations and other organs of civil society.

---

[27] *Van Breda v Jacobs* 1921 AD 330.

[28] 2004 (5) SA 460 (CC); 2003 (12) BCLR 1301 (CC).

[29] *Alexkor Ltd v The Richtersveld Community* 2004 (5) SA 460 (CC); 2003 (12) BCLR 1301 (CC) at para 51.

[30] Section 211(3).

(2) The rights exercised in subsection (1) may not be exercised in a manner inconsistent with any provision of the Bill of Rights.[31]

The customary right of a community to fish in a marine protected area was considered in *State v David Gongqoze*.[32] Three members of the Hobeni community were charged with fishing illegally without a permit in a marine protected area,[33] in contravention of the Marine Living Resources Act 18 of 1998 (MLRA). Although the court of first instance, the Magistrates' Court, found the three accused guilty, it noted that:

> [T]here can be no other conclusion than that the absolute ban on fishing and/or harvesting of marine resources in the reserve amounts to a complete extinguishment of the customary rights of the communities of Dewsa Cebe to practice [sic] these customs in that specific geographical area.[34]

However, the court was not able to pronounce on the constitutional validity of the MLRA, as magistrates' courts lack the jurisdictional capacity to do so. Consequently, it convicted all three accused. In a combined appeal and review to the Eastern Cape High Court, the court dismissed the appellants' arguments concluding that the relevant section of the MLRA '[...]is not unconstitutional for not permitting the recognition of customary law rights of access to marine resources'.[35]

On appeal to the Supreme Court of Appeal,[36] the court commenced its judgment by stating that: '[t]his appeal brings customary law, which has not occupied its rightful place in this country, directly to the fore', and continued:

> The central issue is whether the appellants could successfully raise the exercise of a customary right as a defence in criminal proceedings against them, more specifically, whether the exercise of a customary right of access to marine resources rendered their conduct in attempting to fish in the Dwesa-Cwebe Marine Protected Area ... without a permit, lawful.[37]

After a thorough analysis of foreign and local law, the court corroborated the magistrates' court view that the evidence established the existence of a customary right to fish within the waters of the Dwesa-Cwebe reserve.[38] It found that, on a proper construction of the MLRA, the Act did not extinguish the appellants' customary right of access to, and use of, marine resources. Consequently, the appellants' convictions and sentences were set aside. In effect the Supreme Court of Appeal held that, being

[31] Section 31.

[32] The case was initially heard in the Magistrate's Court for the district of Willowvale at Elliotdale (Case no. E382/10) but later went on appeal to the Eastern Cape High Court, and subsequently to the Supreme Court of Appeal.

[33] The Dwebe-Cwebe reserve is in the former 'independent' homeland of Transkei. Section 43(2) of the MLRA (before its amendment in 2014) made it an offence to fish or attempt to fish in any marine protected area, without permission.

[34] Feris [12].

[35] At para 50.

[36] *Gongqose and Others v Minister of Agriculture, Forestry & Fisheries and Others; Gongqose and Others v State and Others* (1340/16 & 287/17) [2018] ZASCA 87 (1 June 2018).

[37] Para 1.

[38] At para 39.

an independent source of law, the customary system may give rise to rights, including rights of access to and use of resources.

Among evidence considered by the court was the crucial deposition of a scholar, which the court summarised as follows:

> A system of customary regulation governs the use of natural resources in the communities around Dwesa and Cwebe. There is historical evidence of fishing and collection of shellfish since at least the 18th century. Members of the communities gained access to these resources by birth, marriage or affiliation to a headman. Access was dependent upon knowledge and skills transmitted from generation to generation as young people accompanied elders on fishing trips. These rules were part of a larger body of customary regulation governing access to local resources including residential, agricultural and grazing land, firewood and building wood, thatching grass and mud for brickmaking. Access to natural resources promotes socio-economic rights and substantive equality. The Dwesa-Cwebe communities are among the poorest in South Africa and the loss of access to marine resources has caused them substantial hardship. The closure of marine resources took place without consulting the communities.[39]

As such the appeal succeeded, and the convictions were set aside.

11.3.4 The Bill of Rights and Food Security

A further right in the Bill of Rights (i.e., Chap. 2 of the Constitution)[40] provides for food security, in a section titled 'Health care, food water and social security', as follows:

(1) Everyone has the right to have access to

 (a) sufficient food and water;

(2) The state must take reasonable legislative and other measures, within its available resources, to achieve the progressive realisation of each of these rights.

While there has not been any case law on food security the leading case on the constitutional right to water is *Mazibuko and Others v City of Johannesburg and Others*,[41] where the appellants challenged the legality of the city's provision of six kilolitres of water per household per month under the 'Free Basic Water Policy' as well as the city's installation of prepaid water meters. The applicants argued, *inter alia*, that the provision of 25 litres of water per person per day (six kilolitres per household per month) was not sufficient and that 50 litres per person per day is what is required for 'dignified life'.[42] The court declined to pronounce on the

[39]At para 31.

[40]Section 27.

[41]2010 (4) SA 1 (CC) (cited hereafter as the *Mazibuko* case). See also *Mazibuko and Others v City of Johannesburg and Others* [2008] 4 All SA 471 (W) and *City of Johannesburg and Others v Mazibuko and Others* 2009 (3) SA 592 (SCA).

[42]Para 51 of the *Mazibuko* case (fn 41).

amount of water required for dignified life, stating that the Constitution requires 'progressive realisation' of the right and does not require that 'sufficient water' be provided immediately.[43] The court also opined that 'it is institutionally inappropriate for a court to determine precisely what the achievement of any particular social and economic right entails and what steps government should take to ensure the progressive realisation of the right'.[44] The applicants' further arguments regarding the reasonableness of the Free Basic Water Policy were rejected by the court as it found that the Policy was not in conflict with section 27 of the Constitution. The judgment has been criticised by a number of authorities including Liebenberg who argues that the court failed 'to give any independent significance to the right of access to sufficient water in s[ection] 27(1)(*b*)... [which is instead]... subsumed within the overarching qualification of reasonableness in s[ection] 27(2)'.[45] This right has not been invoked regarding marine or other natural resources but there is certainly potential to do so.

11.3.5 The Right to Equality Under the Bill of Rights

The right to equality in the Bill of Rights provides the basis for the legal elimination of racial discrimination established under the previous apartheid regime. It has been, arguably imaginatively, invoked in the South African Equality Court to further the rights of traditional fishers in South Africa. The right to equality provides:

(1) Everyone is equal before the law and has the right to equal protection and benefit of the law.
(2) Equality includes the full and equal enjoyment of all rights and freedoms. To promote the achievement of equality, legislative and other measures designed to protect or advance persons, or categories of persons, disadvantaged by unfair discrimination may be taken.
(3) The state may not unfairly discriminate directly or indirectly against anyone on one or more grounds, including race, gender, sex, pregnancy, marital status, ethnic or social origin, colour, sexual orientation, age, disability, religion, conscience, belief, culture, language and birth [...].[46]

The right to equality was invoked in a joint action by a group of traditional fishers before the Equality Court during 2005.[47] The applicants contended that the MLRA

---

[43] At para 57.

[44] At para 61.

[45] Liebenberg [5], at 467.

[46] Section 9.

[47] The Equality Court is provided for in the Promotion of Equality and Prevention of Unfair Discrimination Act 4 of 2000 ('Equality Act') which has been established to further the right to equality, outlined above.

failed to respect the right to substantive equality by not recognising traditional artisanal fishers as a distinct group.[48] The court described the applicant fishers as:

> [...] small-scale fishers who use traditional low-technology methods to catch fish primarily for local sale or barter as a means of making a living. Most of them are members of traditional artisanal fishing communities. These are coastal communities of relatively poor people whose members have, for generations, engaged in traditional artisanal fishing.[49]

The applicants argued that in order to carry out their fishing activities, traditional fishers had to obtain a fishing right under the MLRA.[50] This entailed falling within a policy for the allocation of commercial rights—a complex and bureaucratic process that did not accommodate traditional fishers. Apart from a failure to provide substantive equality for traditional artisanal fishers to access marine resources, it was argued that apart from the right to non-discrimination, other constitutional rights—including the right to choose a trade or occupation freely, the right of access to sufficient food and water, and the right of every child to basic nutrition—had also not been met.[51] After long and protracted litigation concerning, among other things, whether the High Court should hear the equality issue in its capacity as Equality Court, or whether all the issues should simply be heard by the High Court in its capacity as High Court, the Minister entered into a settlement agreement in May 2007 in terms of which the Minister announced 'interim measures to accommodate fishers along the Western and Southern Cape coastline'. In terms of the arrangement, an NGO[52] undertook to identify 1,000 *bona fide* 'artisanal' (subsistence) fishers who were not holders of existing commercial fishing rights allocated in terms of the MLRA, and who could 'demonstrate both historical dependence and reliance' on fishing activities. The Minister, in turn, after considering whether or not they met the criteria, would grant an exemption under the MLRA to these fishers.[53] This was notwithstanding the fact that the Minister's own scientific advice was that the extension of the exemption granted for a further interim period would result in the TAC being exceeded and not being absorbed within the recreational catch allocation. It appeared that the Minister's decision to grant exemptions was taken to protect the affected fisheries from severe hardship, as those who qualified for an exemption would be entitled to apply for a recreational fishing permit.

This politically expedient approach resulted in a further Court application being brought by recreational fishermen in *West Coast Rock Lobster Association and Others v The Minister of Environmental Affairs and Tourism and Others*.[54] The association argued that although the MLRA permits the Minister to exempt certain categories of

[48] *George and Others v Minister of Environmental Affairs and Tourism* 2005 (6) SA 297 (EqC).

[49] At para 14.

[50] Section 18.

[51] At para 15.

[52] Masifundise Development Trust.

[53] Section 81.

[54] *West Coast Rock Lobster Association and Others v Minister of Environmental Affairs and Tourism and Others* [2011] 1 All SA 487 SA.

persons from a provision of the Act, the section in question[55] could not be employed to grant fishing rights. Moreover, the association pointed out that the Minister could not re-categorise subsistence fishers and pretend they were recreational fishers in order to get around the seemingly fully-subscribed rights in the subsistence sector. The court dismissed the appeal on the basis that the appeal was moot; there had been no evidence of a live issue.[56] In the event, the court refused the appeal but did find that there was some force in the attack on the Minister's application of the MLRA, noting that to permit such a wide power of exemption could result in the executive being able to undo the structure, purpose and principles of the legislation. Such judicial intervention no doubt spurred the Department of Agriculture, Forestry and Fisheries (DAFF) to re-examine the lot of subsistence fishers, and to develop a policy and legislative amendments as outlined in subsequent parts of this chapter.

11.4 Subsistence and Small-Scale Fishers: Policy and Legal Considerations

Prior to the new constitutional dispensation, sea fisheries management legislation was primarily aimed at regulating the allocation of quotas in the commercial fishing sector, in particular public and private fishing companies. The statutes also regulated the fishing activities of a mixed bag of small-scale near-shore fishers,[57] typically ranging from middle-class recreational 'week-end fishermen' to poorer people fishing for the pot and/or making a small subsistence living. Previous legislation did not, however, expressly refer to these categories of fishers.

As seen in the previous part of this chapter, the post-constitutional transformational MLRA repealed and replaced previous fisheries legislation, and included a set of progressive foundational principles based on the notion of sustainable development. Moreover, the MLRA formalised the various fisheries sectors by acknowledging and defining three categories of fishers, namely: 'commercial', 'recreational', and (initially) 'subsistence' fishers. The new Act formally defined 'commercial fishing' to mean 'fishing for any of the species which have been determined by the Minister […]' in terms of discretionary powers granted to the Minister.[58] In effect, commercial fisheries comprise local and foreign fishers who require a right and a permit under the MLRA to harvest fish.[59] The Act defines the term 'recreational fishers' as those who fish 'for leisure or sport and not for sale, barter, earnings or gain'.[60] This sector, typically white middle-class males, traditionally targets species such as line fish,

[55]Section 81.

[56]At paras 35 and 40–46.

[57]In the spirit of the new constitutional dispensation the term 'fisherman' has fallen into disuse and has been replaced by the gender-neutral term 'fishers'.

[58]Section 1 definitions read with section 14.

[59]Sections 18 and 13 respectively.

[60]Section 1 Definitions: "recreational fishing".

abalone and rock lobster. As discussed earlier, the latter two species are increasingly under pressure partly from over-fishing and illegal harvesting,[61] and conflicts over rights to fish have arisen between recreationalists and traditional subsistence fishers in this regard, as seen in the West Coast Lobster case referred to earlier.[62]

In relation to traditional fishers, the MLRA had originally defined the term 'subsistence fisher' to mean: 'a natural person who regularly catches fish for personal consumption or for the consumption of his or her dependents, including one who engages from time to time in the local sale or barter of excess catch, but does not include a person who engages on a substantial scale in the sale of fish on a commercial basis'. However, this definition, and other factors in this sector, did not meet the needs and circumstances of this category of fishers. Consequently, a long and protracted policy development initiative, including an intensive public consultation process, commenced in 1998 with the appointment of a Subsistence Fisheries Task Group (SFTG) mandated to facilitate the implementation of the MLRA's subsistence provisions. It released a comprehensive report in 2000, containing detailed recommendations, including the amendment of the MLRA's definition of 'subsistence' fisher, the introduction of a new sub-category of commercial 'artisanal/subsistence', along with the assignment of suitable coastal resources to the subsistence sector and co-management of the sector within a devolved system of management responsibilities.[63] A Subsistence Fisheries Management Unit was established in mid-2002 at national level to implement and oversee this new sector.[64] This initiative eventually resulted in the publication of an extensive and detailed Small Scale Fisheries Policy by the Department of Agriculture Forestry and Fisheries in 2012,[65] with its primary objective being:

> [T]o introduce certain fundamental shifts in Government's approach to the Small Scale fisheries sector. This entails adopting a developmental approach and an integrated and rights-based allocation system which recognizes the need to ensure the ecological sustainability of the resource; identifies Small Scale fishers as a category of fishers for the purposes of the MLRA in law; and provides for community orientation in the management of the marine living resources harvested by these fishers.

In essence the policy was developed to recognise better the circumstances of traditional and artisanal fishers that were excluded from the long-term rights allocation process.[66] As such, the policy aims to accommodate those fishers who rely on fishing for their livelihood and are directly involved in the catching or processing of marine

---

[61] Hauck [13].

[62] Fn 54 above.

[63] SFTG Draft Recommendations for Subsistence Management in South Africa Prepared for the Chief Director, Marine and Coastal Management, Department of Environmental Affairs and Tourism, South Africa (2000). The Draft SFTG Report was presented to MCM in February 2000, and was subsequently accepted by the Minister of the Department of Environmental Affairs and Tourism and became the final Report of the SFTG.

[64] See generally Young [14].

[65] Policy for the Small Scale Fisheries Sector in South Africa GN 474 *Government Gazette* No. 35455 (dated 20 June 2012). The draft regulations were published previously for comment.

[66] See generally Young, fn 64, at 290; Witbooi [15].

resources, have traditionally relied on marine resources near or on the shore, and make use of traditional low-technology or passive fishing gear such as nets. Crucially, fishing rights will only be allocated to communities and not to individuals.[67] The policy also seeks to give effect to the Equality Court orders (discussed earlier) by providing procedures and mechanisms to accommodate small-scale fishers within the allocation of fishing rights. What is more, the definition of 'subsistence fisher', outlined earlier, did not reflect the reality and needs of this sector, was subject to intensive scrutiny, and was accordingly re-visited in the Policy.

In the event, the MLRA was amended in 2014,[68] among other things, to repeal the definition of 'subsistence fisher' and to replace it with a new definition of 'small-scale fisher'. The latter is now defined to mean:

> … [A] member of a small-scale fishing community engaged in fishing to meet food and basic livelihood needs, or directly involved in processing or marketing of fish, who— (a) traditionally operate in near-shore fishing grounds; (b) predominantly employ traditional low technology or passive fishing gear; (c) undertake single day fishing trips; and (d) is engaged in consumption, barter or sale of fish or otherwise involved in commercial activity, all within the small-scale fisheries sector.[69]

The 2014 MLRA Amendment Act introduced further amendments necessary to implement the Small-Scale Policy.[70] These included an amendment to section 19 of the principal Act, now titled 'Small scale fishing", to grant the Minister a discretionary power to "…recognise a community to be a small-scale fishing community, if the community meets requirements contained in the definition of a small-scale fishing community".[71] This includes the allocation of small-scale fishing rights to co-operatives, a category previously not recognised under the MLRA, as well as to trusts, companies and close corporations.[72] The Small-Scale Policy is silent as to which marine species will be allocated, although it contemplates a 'multi-species' approach, and that fishers will be allocated multiple species within an area.[73] In conformity with the dictates of 'full and equal enjoyment of all rights and freedoms' as provided for in the Constitution,[74] a further amendment to section 19 obligates the Minister to establish areas or zones where small-scale fishers may fish, subject to any marine protected areas that may have been established.[75] Crucially, the section goes on to provide that small-scale fishing permits, granted in terms of the Act,[76]

---

[67] Section 6.2.2 of the Small Scale Policy, at 35.

[68] Marine Living Resources Amendment Act, 2014 *Government Gazette* No. 37659 (dated 19 May 2014); in force on 8 March 2016 in terms of Proclamation 229 in *Government Gazette* No. 39790 of that date.

[69] Section 1 of the Amendment Act.

[70] Marine Living Resources Amendment Act 5 of 2014.

[71] Section 19(1) (b).

[72] In terms of s.18(4), only South African persons may acquire or hold fishing rights. A co-operative is now included in the definition in terms of the MLRA Amendment Act.

[73] Section 6.2.3 of the Small Scale Policy, at 35.

[74] As guaranteed in s 9(2) of the Constitution.

[75] Section 19(1)(*a*).

[76] Sections 18 and 13.

are not transferable except with the approval of, and subject to, the conditions determined by the Minister.[77] Unlike recreational fishers, small-scale fishers are entitled to engage in the sale of their excess catch to the degree indicated in the definition.[78] Subsequently, regulations were published to provide for the process and procedures for the allocation of small-scale fishing rights.[79]

11.5 Marine Aquaculture

During October 2014 the potential of the ocean economy, the so-called 'blue economy', was acknowledged at the highest level of South Africa's government with the formal launch of 'Operation Phakisa'.[80] This is a government initiative to unlock the economic potential of South Africa's oceans and among its priority areas is to develop the potential of the marine aquaculture sector. The growth of the industry is anticipated to help meet the increasing demand for fresh seafood, promote further economic development and even assist with replenishing of wild stocks.[81] A number of commercial marine aquaculture operations have been launched in the last decade, including in the abalone sector—rock lobster is not suited to marine aquaculture. There appears to be insufficient attention to the likely effect of this initiative on poorer communities as they struggle for a slice of the commercial marine aquaculture pie.[82]

While the development of a large-scale aquaculture industry has the potential to supplement the availability of luxury seafood species, it should by no means be seen as a quick-fix solution to the critical governance issues driving the collapse of wild stocks. Global experience in aquaculture highlights the need for careful consideration of the social, economic, and environmental impacts on the surrounding environment resulting from the construction, operation, and decommissioning of aquaculture facilities. Potential negative environmental impacts have been shown to arise from the development of infrastructure as well as from production activities such as contamination of the surroundings from operations (including waste products and chemical pollution), the spread of invasive species and/or diseases into nearby habitats, and the genetic contamination of wild species by escaped captive-bred animals. The negative impacts of marine aquaculture depend on a variety of factors including, among others, the species farmed, methods utilised, stocking densities,

[77] In terms of Sections 18 and 13 respectively.

[78] Young (fn 64).

[79] 'Regulations relating to small-scale fishing' Proclamation 229 in *Government Gazette* No. 39790 (dated 8 March 2016).

[80] President Jacob Zuma: Launch of Operation Phakisa: ICT in Education, http://www.gov.za/speeches/president-jacob-zuma-launch-operation-phakisa-ict-education-2-oct-2015-0000; see generally Hallwood [16], van Wyk [17].

[81] Glazewski [18].

[82] See generally Marine Management Organisation, *Social Impacts and Interactions Between Marine Sectors* (MMO Project No: MMO 1060, 2014), at 273.

feed types, husbandry practices, and the hydrography of the site. From the perspective of environmental integrity, land-based marine aquaculture operations are preferable to in situ marine operations.[83] Aside from addressing the economic potential of marine aquaculture the socio-economic effects on poorer communities, including subsistence fishers, should be fully considered.

11.6 Conclusion

This contribution has surveyed the notion of 'development' from the vantage point of the internationally accepted environmental law norm of 'sustainable development' with reference to the plight of subsistence fishers in South Africa, which has been a sector historically marginalised and acknowledged to be among the poorest sectors of South Africa's diverse populace.[84]

In sum, there has been a coordinated multi-pronged legal approach aimed at improving the lot of subsistence fishers, mainly based on constitutional norms, values, and rights. The environmental right, which includes reference to sustainable development, has to be tempered against the right to equality, where the somewhat unconventional legal reliance on 'substantive equality' by the disgruntled subsistence fishing communities has proved effectual. This has been illustrated by the accommodation of subsistence fishers in the policy and legislative process which now, for the first time, recognises customary fishing rights for certain sectors of the South African fishing community. In turn, customary rights have come to the fore as a means of giving expression to constitutional values and precepts. However, this has been a long and protracted process, and it remains to be seen if and how the ideal to redress and heal 'the injustices of the past'—as stated in the Preamble of the Constitution—will improve the lot of small-scale fishers in the long term.

References

1. McLean B., & Glazewski, J. (2018). Marine environments, oceans law and governance. In Strydom H. A., et al. (Eds.), *Fuggle and Rabie's environmental management in South Africa* (3d ed.).
2. Sowman, M. (2006). Subsistence and small-scale fisheries in South Africa: A ten-year review. *Marine Policy, 30,* 60.
3. Driver, A., et al. (2012). *National diversity assessment 2011: An assessment of South Africa's biodiversity and ecosystems, synthesis report.*
4. Raemaekers, S., et al. (2011). Review of the causes of the rise of the illegal South African abalone fishery and consequent closure of the rights-based fishery. *Ocean & Coastal Management, 54,* 433.

[83] Driver et al., (fn 8 above), at 325.

[84] See generally Sowman et al. [19].

5. Liebenberg, S. (2010). *Socio-economic rights: Adjudication under a transformative constitution.*
6. Hauck, M., & Sweijd, N. A. (1999). A case study of abalone poaching in South Africa and its impact on fisheries management. *ICES Journal of Marine Science, 56,* 1024.
7. Steinberg, J. (2005). *The illicit abalone trade in South Africa* (Institute for Security Studies Papers 105) (p. 16).
8. de Coning, E., & Witbooi, E. (2015). Towards a new "fisheries crime" paradigm: South Africa as an illustrative example. *Marine Policy, 60,* 208.
9. Scholtz, W. (2015). Human rights and the environment in the African Union context. In A. Grear & L. J. Kotzé (Eds.), *Research handbook on human rights and the environment.*
10. Chenwi, L. (2018). The right to a satisfactory, healthy and sustainable environment in the African Regional Human Rights System. In J. H. Knox & R. Pejan (eds.), *The human right to a healthy environment.*
11. Glazewski, J. (2014). United States v Bengis (2013): A victory for wildlife law and lessons for international fisheries crime. *International Journal of Marine and Coastal Law, 29,* 273.
12. Feris, L. (2013). A customary right to fish when fish are sparse: Managing conflicting claims between customary rights and environmental rights. *PER/PELJ, 16,* 555.
13. Hauck, M. (1999). Policing marine resources in South Africa. *Acta Juridica,* 211.
14. Young, M. (2013). Achieving equity in the fishing industry: The fate of informal fishers in the context of the policy for the small-scale fisheries sector in South Africa. *PER/PELJ, 16,* 288.
15. Witbooi, E. (2002). Subsistence fishing in South Africa: Implementation of the marine living resources act. *17 The International Journal of Marine and Coastal.*
16. Hallwood, P. (2014). *Economics of the oceans: Rights, rents and resources.*
17. van Wyk, J.-A. (2015). Defining the blue economy as a South African strategic priority: Toward a sustainable 10th province? *Journal of the Indian Ocean Region, 11*(2), 153.
18. Glazewski, J. (2016). Marine aquaculture in South Africa: The policy and legal framework. In N. Bankes et al. (eds.), *Aquaculture law and policy: Global, regional and national perspectives* (p. 386).
19. Sowman, M., et al. (2014). Shifting gear: A new governance framework for small-scale fisheries in South Africa. In M. Sowman & R. Wynberg (Eds.), *Governance for justice and environmental sustainability.*

Chapter 12
Economic and Social Development in the Republic of South Africa's New Model of Mineral Rights: Balancing Private Ownership, Community Rights, and Sovereignty

Wojciech Bańczyk

Abstract The present chapter analyses the evolution of the legal regime relating to mineral ownership and management in the Republic of South Africa, introduced by the 2002 Mineral and Petroleum Resources Development Act as an example of the implementation of the notion of *sustainable development*. The introduction of the new system of state competences in the management of the mineral wealth has challenged the historical balance between the rights of varied subjects involved in the mining sector. Both mining industry investor protection and the economic development of the nation—including that of the local communities affected by mining activities—were taken into account. Also, the non-economic values of environmental protection, infrastructure protection, workers' rights, and community participation were taken into account. The present chapter examines the rationale behind such legislative reform, and its content from the perspective of sustainable development, which, to a great extent, have been provided by extensive judicial review of the new legal regime at play.

Keywords Community interests · Mineral rights · Property rights · State sovereignty · Sustainable development

12.1 Introduction

Minerals located in situ, typically underground, pose significant social, economic, and legal challenges. The issue of their legal status, including issues of ownership and management, is of even greater importance with regard to predominantly mineral-based economies, such as the Republic of South Africa.[1] This is why the new regulatory regime over minerals in South Africa is worth examining. This is particularly

[1] Cawood and Minnitt [1, p. 369].

W. Bańczyk (✉)
Jagiellonian University, ul. Gołębia 24, 31-007 Kraków, Poland
e-mail: wojciech.banczyk@uj.edu.pl

P. Szwedo et al. (eds.), *Law and Development*, Kobe University Monograph Series in Social Science Research, https://doi.org/10.1007/978-981-13-9423-2_12

so should its content not only challenge the common law model of ownership over the mineral wealth, but also impose the notion of sustainable development in the management of minerals and as a restriction to private property, thus making the nation, including local communities—and not the previous holders—the primary beneficiaries of the mineral wealth.

To provide insights into the new law, this chapter first analyses the plurality of the values contained within the mining legislation and the general conflict between them. Subsequently, the meaning of the new law is presented against the backdrop of historical and comparative examples of such legislation. This is followed by a discussion on the legal position of the mining rights-holders under the new law. Last, the article will present judicial consideration of the new law, based on the case regarding primarily the legal position of the holders of rights under previous law.

12.1.1 General Conflicts of the Values Contained in the Mining Legislation

It ought be stated that without stable legal protection of mining investments[2]—particularly over the content and durability of mining rights *per se*—mineral exploration and exploitation, and the consequent enjoyment by any subject including investors of the benefits of such activities, would undoubtedly be plagued by uncertainty and insecurity. Lacking investments, the high costs involved in mining activities would likely lead to minerals remaining unexploited, thus leading to profits for no party. Not to mention, this could also deny local communities the opportunity to benefit from investor-funded development of the local social infrastructure, which sometimes occurs.[3]

What is more, minerals hold significant economic value for all relevant stakeholders, including landowners, mineral extracting and processing operators, people employed across the sector, as well as the state and local communities on whose territory mining activities take place. At the same time, there are specific challenges at play. It is primarily the threat to the natural environment resulting from underground and above-ground operations which may also affect local agriculture, infrastructure, and housing. Moreover, there are worker-related concerns including that workers recruited mainly from local communities might be overexploited, or that foreign labourers might be discriminated against.[4] Proper regulation of mineral extraction must consider such interests.

Additionally, unfair division of rights and profits from mining activities may effectively be against the public interest, should only a certain group take advantage

[2]With reference to the peaceful and stable environment necessary to boost investor confidence, see Munslow and Fitzgerald [2, p. 240]. Long-term security in investment in the form of private ownership of mineral rights is underlined by Cawood and Minnitt, *supra* note 1, at 370.

[3]UNICEF [3, p. 26].

[4]With regard to Sierra Leone, see Human Rights Watch [4, p. 43].

from the mineral wealth, whilst the non-economic cost of such activities accrues to other groups, including local communities. Also, unfairness in the distribution of profits to particular actors only could, potentially, lead to social unrest, either between regions,[5] or social groups,[6] and to escalate into deadly hostilities, such as the diamond war in Sierra Leone.[7] Moreover, a fair division of profits should ensure that those subjects who are affected by the mining activity primarily benefit.[8]

To a great extent, such considerations contributed to the change in South Africa's mineral law. The change attempted to challenge the traditional (derived from common law and rooted in the apartheid system) balance among private ownership, community rights, and sovereignty over minerals, in order to introduce a fairer division of profits resulting from mineral wealth. In that sense, a primary purpose of the development of mineral law is to balance the rights at play, including those of private parties to enjoy unrestricted ownership, and those of the State to regulate.[9]

12.1.2 Specificity in the New Mineral Law of South Africa

The far-reaching legislative change that the 2002 Mineral and Petroleum Resources Development Act (MPRDA)[10] introduced in this field, nevertheless, posed challenges to investor interests and, in time, led to a judicial challenge. Three subsequent court decisions ensued,[11] namely, before the High Court of South Africa (North Gauteng, Pretoria) (HC), the Supreme Court of Appeal of South Africa (SCA), and the Constitutional Court of South Africa (CC), in a case of effectiveness of rights under past legislation. This jurisprudence examines the rationale of the new law, and demonstrates the attempts undertaken to balance the values involved in the applicability of the new law.

The issue under consideration is an example of the practical application of the notion of sustainability to the economic development of the state. This notion is,

[5]Munslow and Fitzgerald, *supra* note 2, at 237.

[6]With regard to the discriminative allocation in the Republic of South Africa as a reason for the MPRDA, see Belinkie [5, pp. 220–22].

[7]With regard to Sierra Leone, see United Nations Environment Programme [6, p. 22, 64].

[8]With regard to the example of Sierra Leone, it is agreed as highly inappropriate that '[t]he financial benefits [of the mining industry] are divided nationally, but negative environmental impacts are mostly localised in rural areas with vulnerable communities'. Brown et al. [7, p. 9].

[9]Mostert [8, p. 1].

[10]Mineral and Petroleum Resources Development Act of 10 October 2002 (South Africa) (cited hereinafter by inline reference to 'MPRDA').

[11]*Agri S. Afr. v. Minister of Minerals & Energy* (2013) ZACC 9, 2013 (4) SA 1, 2013 (7) BCLR 727 (CC) (cited hereinafter by inline reference to 'CC'); *Minister of Minerals & Energy v. Agri S. Afr.* (2012) ZASCA 93, 2012 (5) SA 1, 3 All SA 266, 2012 (9) BCLR 958 (SCA) (cited hereinafter by inline reference to 'SCA'); *Agri S. Afr. v. Minister of Minerals & Energy* (2011) ZAGPPHC 62, 3 All SA 296 (GNP) (cited hereinafter by inline reference to 'HC').

therefore, not only invoked as a general principle, but also operates as the solution for a particular legal problem.

Thus, the research on the abovementioned notion requires and deserves analysis from the perspective of law and development studies. The mineral law, in general, primarily is aimed at the pursuit of economic growth, and it sought to achieve this to a great extent by the stabilisation of well-defined and alienable property rights.[12] However, doubt was cast over this attitude to legislation, as the model legal regime derived from better developed countries was deemed inadequate.[13] This observation was accompanied by the tendency to observe the social and cultural specificity of nations (and, therefore, of their laws), which was accepted by later theories within law and development studies.[14] In that sense, law and development are better understood as amounting to a legal framework for social change.[15]

Such a change proceeded in South Africa in the field of mineral law, as mandated[16] by the Articles 24 and 25 of the Constitution of the Republic of South Africa[17] regarding protection of environment, at first, and then protection of property, including in its regulation also the necessary rejection of past injustices and discrimination in allocation.

The attitude as above led the analysis of law and development towards the sustainability of the latter. This is understood not only from the perspective of environmental protection, as opposed to economic development,[18] but also in relation to the rationale of poverty eradication.[19] All those concerns were present in the analysis of the MPRDA and arguments raised within its judiciary challenge. This makes the example especially worth analysing from the perspective of practical application of the concepts of sustainable development.

12.2 Change to Mineral Law and Implications for Sustainable Development

The MPRDA was established in acknowledgment of the fact that mineral wealth belongs to the nation, and that the state is its custodian (cf., the second line of the

[12]Dawis and Trebilcock [9, p. 23].

[13]de Gaay Fortman and Mihyo [10, p. 157]; Merryman [11, p. 483].

[14]Gopal [12, p. 235].

[15]Merryman, *supra* note 13, 471.

[16]Marais [13, p. 2988].

[17]S. Afr. Const., 1996 (cited hereinafter by inline reference to 'Constitution').

[18]This results from the traditional attitude of sustainable development as a constraint on the present generation to take advantage of temporary control over earth resources. *See* Weiss [14, p. 19].

[19]Barral [15, p. 392]; Munslow and Fitzgerald, *supra* note 2, at 229. *But see* Weiss, *supra* note 18, at 22 (asserting that eradication of poverty might conflict with sustainable development understood only as care to preserve the environment for further generations, because those values are deemed opposing, even though poverty may cause ecological degradation constraint).

Preamble to the MPRDA). Accordingly, it is expressed in the wording of Article 3(1) by means of which '[m]ineral and petroleum resources are the common heritage of all the people of South Africa and the State is the custodian thereof for the benefit of all South Africans'.

12.2.1 System of Ownership of Minerals Vested in the Surface Owner

Article 3(1) of the MPRDA appears as a far-reaching contradiction to the traditional principle of South African mineral law—namely, that the ownership of minerals is vested in the owner of the land (CC, 7). This derives from the common law principle that the surface owner is also the owner of the underlying minerals, according to the principle *cuius est solum, eius est usque ad coelum et ad infernos.*[20] In the system of landowner's ownership of minerals, rights regarding the ownership of minerals may be separated from the ownership of the land, e.g., in the form of cession of an *ad personam* right, or the establishment of a limited real right, which may be necessary in exchange for a capital injection from a third-party to the owner, and that may be required for infrastructural development regarding mining investment (CC, 9). This may particularly be the case when the minerals are located underground, the owner of which may not be interested in mining, e.g., homestead or school land,[21] or may be unable to undertake the high costs of prospecting and mining.[22]

12.2.2 Two Basic Forms of State Intervention into Mineral Ownership and Mining Activities

The bolstering of state rights with regard to mining activities is not uncommon throughout the world. There may, however, be implications of the possible exercise of public influence in at least two varied dimensions.

First, the state may be vested with ownership of minerals ('right to minerals'), regardless of the question of ownership of the relevant land. Such a basic system, which distinguishes between the ownership of the surface and of the subsoil, in which minerals are located, is known as the 'Royalty' regime,[23] which varies from the common law system of landowner ownership over minerals. An example of the Royalty system is reflected in the Polish Geological and Mining Law (PGML).[24]

---

[20]Campbell [16, p. 38].

[21]*Id.* at 38.

[22]Mostert, *supra* note 9, at 10.

[23]Campbell, *supra* note 20, at 39.

[24]Prawo górnicze i geologiczne [Geological and Mining Law], 9 June 2011 (cited hereinafter by inline reference to 'PGML').

According to its Articles 10.1 and 10.5, hydrocarbon and other specified mineral resources, regardless of the territory on which they are located (so long as it is under Polish jurisdiction), belong to the state. Therefore, the ownership of the land does not extend to such resources, but is limited to the space directly beneath the land surface, within the context of the socio-economic utility of the land (cf., Article 143 of the Polish Civil Code).[25] The latter is not clearly outlined and needs to be specified for every piece of land, based on circumstances applicable to each individual case, with consideration of the actual use of that land, its surroundings, geographical positioning, and its intended utilisation.[26]

Complexities arise when the mineral exploitation is likely to affect the land surface. In such cases, the consent of the landowner (under private law) is needed, unless expropriation is possible, should the mining be held to be a public utility.[27] This gives rise to yet more problems, when landowner rights extend to the depth of the deposits. In such circumstances, it is claimed that the ownership of the minerals on the part of the state prevails,[28] and the landowner is, therefore, limited in his enjoyment even of the space directly beneath the surface of his land.

Second, the state is vested with granting the 'right to mine' as an administrative type of consent for particular mining activities. The typical (though broad) scope of this kind of right is stipulated in Article 3(2)(a) of the MPRDA, which establishes the state's (acting through the Minister) exclusive competence to 'grant, issue, refuse, control, administer and manage any reconnaissance permission, prospecting right, permission to remove, mining right, mining permit, retention permit, technical cooperation permit, reconnaissance permit, exploration right and production right'. It is followed by the state royalty (Article 3(4) of the MPRDA).

The right to mine is present, both in the system of landowner ownership of minerals in which the state administratively regulates the exploitation[29] and in the Royalty regime. In relation to the latter, next to the private law right granted to mining entities by the state, so that such entities may perform some of the state's rights (as of an owner of rights to minerals), any mining activity is subject also to administrative consent on the part of the state. This is made clear in Article 13 of the PGML, which separately deals with public law concessions for mining activities, and civil law contract of mining usufruct of the state-owned minerals,[30] but often it may be difficult to draw a distinction.

---

[25] *Kodeks cywilny* [Civil Code], 23 Apr. 1964.

[26] Supreme Court Judgment of 3 Nov. 2004, III CK 52/04 (Poland).

[27] Campbell, *supra* note 20, at 43.

[28] Rakoczy [18, Article 10, section 2].

[29] Campbell, *supra* note 20, at 37.

[30] Rakoczy, *supra* note 30, at Article 13, section 2.

12.2.3 MPRDA 'Right to Mine' Ensuring Sustainable Development in Mining

From the perspective of the MPRDA, the competence to grant the right to mine may be executed only when the sustainable development of the mineral resources is ensured (Article 3(3) of the MPRDA). Such an important function of the notion of sustainable development within a legal act may also well serve the function of sustainable development as a prism through which to interpret other applicable norms, as invoked by V. Barral,[31] as this is justified by a systematic approach to analysing law in accordance with other relevant norms within a system. Sustainability may also be achieved by means of interpretation of the legislation by having regard to its purpose; in fact, this is facilitated by the fact that sustainable development goals are listed among the MPRDA objectives, enumerated in Articles 2–6, which guide the interpretation of the act.[32] Arguably, the new model of mining law promotes non-economic values well. Not only does it make it impossible to undertake mining activities without proper authorisation [33] but it also ensures actual recognition of values important to the MPRDA and reflected in its particular provisions on the subsequent stages relating to the state's prerogative to grant the right to mine.

Environmental concerns primarily are taken into consideration. Articles 17(1)(c) and 23(1)(d) of the MPRDA, in near identical terms, stipulate that the granting of prospecting or mining rights is conditional on the activity not resulting in *unacceptable pollution, ecological degradation*, or *damage to the environment*, which needs to be confirmed by issuing an environmental authorisation.

Other non-economic values also are promoted under the MPRDA. The application for prospecting or mining rights relating to the land occupied by a community may be conditioned by obligations to promote the rights and interests of the community in question, including its participation (Articles 17(4A) and 23(2A) of the MPRDA). The landowner also must be consulted, and the effects of the consultation are to be included within an environmental report (Article 16(4)(b) and 22(4)(b) of the MPRDA). Furthermore, such rights cannot be granted when the land involved in the potential activity is a residential area (Article 48(1)(a) of the MPRDA). Among further conditions on applications for the granting of such rights is, for instance, the requirement that the applicant provides financially and otherwise for a *social and labour plan* (Article 23(1)(e) of the MPRDA), and that condition that the grant does not result in the concentration of mineral resources to the applicant, thus preventing fair competition and equitable access (Article 17(2)(b) of the MPRDA).

---

[31] Barral, *supra* note 19, at 398.

[32] Mostert, *supra* note 9, at 79.

[33] Belinkie, *supra* note 6, at 240.

12.2.4 The MPRDA 'Right to Mine' Compared with Other Rights Involving Mining

Moreover, administrative consent to mining activities has long been present (not only in South African legislation) as a factual requirement to benefit from owning minerals. It is, though, possible for mining activities to be free from any state regulation, and based only on private law ownership of minerals, but such situations are rare. Requiring a highly limited development of administration, such instances are limited to such extremes as 'gold rush' (SCA, 70).

It could be claimed that the notion of 'mineral rights', by which the right to minerals is connected with the right to mine them (SCA, 27), is founded on the right to mine (SCA, 28). In other words, such right to mine is at the heart of mineral rights (SCA, 81). Thus, since the early history of mineral law the exploitation of minerals has been subject to state control (SCA, 29). It is also stated that the value of mineral rights lies in both the quantity and value of the minerals themselves, and also on the possibility to obtain the right to mine (SCA, 71). It should additionally be noted that the property law relationship between the holder of the right to minerals and the landowner (in cases when these are not the same), and the public law relationship between such holder and the state, are separate matters, albeit often not easily practically separable.[34]

Regardless of the true scope of the public law consent in the previous and current legislation, the sheer imposition of Article 3(2)(a) of the MPRDA should not be seen as revolutionary change as such. Article 5(1) of the previous legislation in this field, namely 1991 Minerals Act (MA),[35] established that the 'holder of the right to any mineral ... shall have the right to ... prospect and mine for such minerals ... and to dispose thereof'. The mineral rights-holder was primarily the owner of the land in which the minerals were located (Article 1(ix)(a) of the MA). At the same time, the rights vested in him as such holder were altogether referred to as the right to mine (SCA, 27). However, in Article 5(2) of the MA it was stated that '[n]o person shall prospect or mine for any mineral without the necessary authorisation granted to him ...'. The rights and entitlements resulting from the right to mine (which could not have been obtained without the status of a mineral rights-holder) could then be subject to overturning, or to sterilisation, e.g., when land rich in minerals also has agricultural potential, and the owner could decide which activity, mining or farming, he wishes to pursue (SCA, 27).

At the same time, regarding the right to minerals, the MA also was considered the nearest step towards a system of exclusive private mineral rights ownership, and the greatest limitation of the role of the state in mining by means of limiting its own rights to minerals.[36] This is demonstrated by Article 64 of the MA, which explicitly allows state-owned rights to minerals to be directed to the private sector. However,

[34]Mostert, *supra* note 9, at 15.

[35]Minerals Act 50 of 15 May 1991 (South Africa) (cited hereinafter by inline reference to 'MA').

[36]Cawood and Minnitt, *supra* note 1, at 371.

independently of the scope of the right to minerals, the lack of the right to mine could be seen as depriving the right to minerals of most value, so that eventually only little value (or even explicitly no value) remains in the right to minerals when it is not followed with the right to mine them (SCA, 69–70). At the same time, arguably, it is not the right to mine per se, but the ability to obtain it, which determines the value and market utility of the right to minerals (cf., the concurring opinion to the SCA, 105). Next to the willingness to utilise land rich in minerals differently, or enjoy only a potential to obtain a right to mine, there can also be a value in withholding the minerals from any kind of mining activity, for instance, by keeping them as an economic asset.

12.3 Ownership of Minerals Under the MPRDA

The MPRDA contains no direct reference to the issue of ownership of minerals. However, it expressly refers to how the mineral wealth is the 'common heritage of all the people of South Africa and the State is [its] custodian … for the benefit of all South Africans' (cf., Article 3(1) of the MPRDA). This may suggest that mining activities subject to the MPRDA take place regardless of the question of ownership of minerals, and the right to mine may be granted to anyone, while under past laws it could only be granted to the mineral rights-holder (mineral owner) (CC, 40).

12.3.1 Analysis of the Position of the State as Owner of Minerals Under the MPRDA

Further to the foregoing, it could be claimed that ownership vests in the state. Thus, such an understanding may be traced back to the recognition of an inherent 'internationally accepted right of the State to exercise sovereignty over all the mineral and petroleum resources' (Article 2(a) of the MPRDA). The same concept can be found in: the explanation of the new law invoking the state's *de facto* ownership and its regulatory competences (HC, 52); the notion of minerals 'belonging to the nation' as echoing the Royalty system (SCA, 30); and in connecting the 'power or competence to decide whether to exploit minerals … and to whom they could give their exploitation rights [being] an incidence of ownership, [to] the state [which under the MPRDA] has that power or competence by virtue of its custodianship of mineral resources' (concurring opinion, CC, 81). This is even referred to as *nationalisation* of the mining industry.[37]

This view was, however, not followed by the Constitutional Court of South Africa (CC), which claimed that the role of the state as custodian is limited to being *a facilitator or a conduit* (CC, 68). Also, according to H. Mostert, use of the notion of

[37] Belinkie, *supra* note 6, at 237.

'custodianship' is intentional, and the state is only obliged to administer resources to the benefit of all people.[38]

At the same time, further analysis of the legal character of rights under MPRDA is needed. Although the rights of prospecting, mining, exploration, and production are limited real rights (Article 5(1) of the MPRDA), they are inalienable without the consent of the minister (Article 11(1) of the MPRDA) and are subject to numerous restrictions as to their performance.

12.3.2 Limitation of Holders' Rights in the MPRDA

The aforementioned rights may be granted only upon the financial and technical ability of applicants to conduct mining activities optimally and in accordance with the requirements of the proposed work programme (e.g., Articles 17(1)(a) and 23(1)(a)-(b) of the MPRDA, regarding both right to prospect and right to mine). Upon being granted the right, it must be executed, or, otherwise, the right may be lost. For instance, those endowed with the right to prospect must begin prospecting within 120 days from effectiveness of the right and follow the prospecting programme (Article 19(2)(b)–(c) of the MPRDA). At the same time, those endowed with the right to mine must commence mining within a year from effectiveness of the right and actively conduct mining according to the mining programme (Article 25(2)(b)–(c) of the MPRDA). Lacking an administrative consent, or not fulfilling the duties resulting from such consent, leads to suspension or cancellation of the right (Article 47(1) of the MPRDA). Therefore, we could question, to what extent we can say about the true limited real right character, if it is so severely conditioned by public law limitations, and if it is a limited real right, whether the scope of those limitations does not infringe the international law obligations to protect ownership, e.g., Article 14 of the African Charter on Human and Peoples' Rights, which stipulates that 'the right to property shall be guaranteed …'.

The right of sterilisation of the abovementioned right is to a great extent limited. The retention period may, thus, be granted by the Ministry only upon petition, when prospecting activity is completed, the site has mining potential, but a study of the market proved that the mining of the minerals would be 'uneconomical due to prevailing market conditions' (Article 32(1)(b)–(d) of the MPRDA). Such a petition may be refused, for instance, if mining could take place profitably (Article 33(a) of the MPRDA). At the same time, granting such a retention right incurs a retention fee and the requirement to submit progress reports as to continuous market conditions and as to the efforts undertaken to commence mining before expiration of retention period (Article 35(2)(a)–(b) of the MPRDA). This means that neither retaining a monopoly, leaving minerals unexploited for investment, nor protection of land for different aims is admissible. Thus, if there is no application for a right to mine by the prior holder, the right to mine may eventually be obtained by someone else, and such

[38]Mostert, *supra* note 9, at 133–34.

holder of unused old order rights had a choice to either 'activate' his rights or lose them.[39] This seems to be justified by the public interest in monetising mineral wealth as soon as possible, making it an incentive for the development of the economy of the state. From this perspective, the economic value of minerals is underlined, yet within the parameters of sustainable development in the course of granting the right to mine.

It should be observed that according to the MPRDA, any kind of right connected to mining requires the state's consent and strict compliance with the conditions imposed. Those rules do not provide rights-holders with the freedom characteristic to the holder of an *ad rem* right.

Consequently, the property rights to minerals lack continuity between the previous and current legislation, and this is due to the entirely different regime under the MPRDA, under which the state grants rights to prospect or mine.[40] This, however, is similar to the Royalty regime, as regards the scope of state rights regarding supervision over minerals.

This content of a right seems to align with the values listed in the description of the MPRDA, namely, '[t]o make provision for equitable access to and sustainable development of the nation's mineral and petroleum resources'. To a great extent it is reflected in the further aims in its Preamble, such as the obligation to protect the environment, which includes sustainable development of resources (3), recognition of the need to promote local and rural development of communities affected by mining (4), bringing equitable access to resources (5), commitment to eradicate discriminatory practices in mining industry (6), and the duty to undertake legislation to redress past racial discrimination (7)—the latter in order to execute Article 25(8) of the Constitution (concerning private property rights and the need to redress the results of past racial discrimination).

12.4 Old-Order Rights-Holders in Judicial Challenge to the MPRDA

The coming of the MPRDA into force deprives *old-order* rights—by which rights regarding minerals under past legislation are understood, in particular derived from the ownership of minerals—of any effectiveness. The right vested into rights-holders of old-order rights (rights to mine based on those derived from ownership), extended for five years following the act coming into force (Article 7(1) of Schedule II to the MPRDA). It would also be possible to extend this further only upon conversion into a right to mine, when certain conditions are satisfied, including, the submission of: an approved environmental programme, a social and labour plan, evidence of undertaken mining activities, the mining work programme (Article 7(2)–(3) of Schedule II to the MPRDA). Unused old-order rights, the holders of which did not apply for the right

[39] Marais, *supra* note 16, at 3021.

[40] Mostert, *supra* note 9, at 129.

to mine, could have been converted into new-order rights within one year (Article 8(1) of Schedule II to the MPRDA).

In that sense, the protection of the new economic and social situation introduced by the MPRDA to a certain extent has been at the expense of the old-order rights-holders. The subsequent judicial challenge of the new legislation was an opportunity to rebalance the values of the new regime and the stability of the rights already acquired (under old-order law), particularly as the rights derived from the old regime were far-reaching, given that they had been based on the protection of private property, which is of undeniably broad scope, also due to international law obligations, mentioned earlier.

12.4.1 'Legislating' Old-Order Rights Out of Existence

A compensation claim was raised by *Agri South Africa* against the Ministry of Minerals and Energy, initially before the High Court of South Africa, where the subject matter of the review had been the coal rights of Sebenza, acquired in November 2001. Sebenza had obtained neither a prospecting permit nor mining authorisation under the previous legislation, and it had not performed any mining activities. Upon its liquidation, Sebenza sold its rights to Agri, which as a federal association of commercial farmers sought to challenge the MPRDA (HC, 12, 16–17). The court, based on previous jurisprudence, confirmed the classification of old-order rights as quasi-servitudes allowing for entry to someone else's land, search for minerals, and for the severance and carrying away of such minerals (HC, 26). The court pointed out also that a characteristic feature of old-order rights is the possibility to sterilise or hoard them (HC, 31).

Although the enactment of the MPRDA was within the context of addressing the racially discriminatory property law (HC, 38), it was claimed that old-order rights, as they existed before the MPRDA, 'had been legislated out of existence' (HC, 57, 67), or that they do not exist anymore (HC, 68). Also, the argument that the MPRDA was only a regulatory mechanism to quasi-servitudes in order to prevent sterilisation or hoarding of rights was not confirmed (HC 70). It was stated that sovereignty over all minerals in the country could not be exercised so long as private law mineral rights existed (HC, 71). Subsequently, the inability of Sebenza to cover the costs of conversion due to its financial situation and lack of access to resources in liquidation proceedings was raised (HC, 73). Therefore, it was held that Sebenza was deprived of its rights under Article 25(1) of the Constitution (HC, 77). Also it was held that expropriation under Article 25(2) of the Constitution had occurred, and that the commitment to bring equitable access to mineral resources was a matter of public interest under Article 25(4) of the Constitution (HC, 84, 88). At the same time, it was of no importance that the expropriated right and the right acquired were not identical (HC, 85). In the end, the claim for compensation was upheld (HC, 99).

12.4.2 The 'Right to Mine' as Prioritised Over the Right to Own Mineral Resources

The judgment was appealed and became the subject of adjudication by the Supreme Court of Appeal of South Africa. This court disagreed with the argumentation of the previous court. The main rationale was that it was the *right to mine*, continuously controlled by the state and allocated thereby, which was implemented in the MPRDA, and this is the reason that the old-order rights-holders had not been deprived of any right per se: they had never held it (SCA, 85). The state, thus, was entitled to change the legislation concerning the granting of the right to mine (SCA, 99), which was even deemed a 'gift from the state' (concurring opinion to SCA, 113).

It was further stated that the old-order rights-holders were not deprived of their rights by a time limit to apply for the conversion of their old-order rights to new-order rights, but it was their own failure to apply that led to such deprivation (SCA, 97). At the same time, successful applications conforming to all conditions could lead to the granting of 'broadly the same rights', or even of more extensive rights as new-order rights (SCA, 91, 94, 97). The sheer fact that such an application involved costs and other burdens was considered as unimportant, as the application for the right to mine under the previous regime was also connected with comparable requirements (SCA, 98).

Although, undoubtedly, there is difference in the treatment of the holders of unused old-order rights in comparison with the holders of 'used' old-order rights, this was justified by the necessarily stronger protection of rights to mine acquired under past law that were already being exercised and that required more stable protection (SCA, 73). Also it was held that without the right to mine, old-order rights based solely on ownership were of no value (SCA, 97), and the potential of transforming such rights into new-order rights to mine was held even as prioritising the past holder (SCA, 97).

The SCA judgment suggests that the right to minerals was of no value when unaccompanied by the right to mine minerals. However, despite the obvious interconnection between the two rights, the right to mine may be obtained only upon a valid right to minerals. Although the right to mine undeniably adds value to the right to minerals, it must not be forgotten that the right to minerals is predicated on the protection of ownership-type, and is of undeniable value even without the right to mine, but only based on the potential to acquire one.

12.4.3 Necessity to Observe Social Needs and Non-economic Values Within Private Property

The case was eventually challenged before the Constitutional Court of South Africa where it was subject to review particularly with regard to coherence with constitutional provisions concerning deprivation and expropriation. The analysis began with justification of the new law in overturning disproportionate distribution of wealth in the country, in which 'the architecture of the apartheid system placed about 87% of the land and the mineral resources that lie in its belly in the hands of 13% of the population. Consequently, white South Africans wield real economic power while the overwhelming majority of black South Africans are still identified with unemployment and abject poverty' (CC, 1). It was then made clear that '[t]o address this gross economic inequality, legislative measures were taken to facilitate equitable access to opportunities in the mining industry' (CC, 1) and in particular to abolish 'the entitlement to sterilise mineral rights, otherwise known as the entitlement not to sell or exploit minerals ...,' which should be of 'no surprise in a country with a progressive Constitution, a high unemployment rate and a yawning gap between the rich and the poor which could be addressed partly through the optimal exploitation of its rich mineral and petroleum resources, to boost economic growth' (CC, 2). At the same time, this rationale underpinned the MPRDA, part of which included transitional arrangements, aiming at the protection of security of old-order rights-holders (CC, 27).

The final judgment analysed the right to sterilise minerals differently, adding thereto such a character that it is *undoubtedly property with economic value* (CC, 44). It was deemed as useful, for instance, to farmers attached to the land (CC, 45). Consequently, under past legislation it was not possible to compel the exploitation of privately-owned minerals, unless expropriation under compensation took place (CC, 45).

Considering the abovementioned circumstances, the holders of unused old-order rights were deprived of their property in the sense that their value resulted both from the possibility to sterilise minerals and, e.g., enhancing the value of the land, and from the potential to acquire the right to mine (CC, 50–51). The judgment tracked the definition of deprivation, which in its most basic form means limitation of use, enjoyment, and exploitation of property, like, e.g., zoning law.[41] Such deprivation was total and permanent, unless the application was filed (CC, 52). Though it was not arbitrary and was in line with MPRDA objectives as well as with transitional agreements, the judgment raised concerns as to whether deprivation amounted to expropriation (CC, 53).

Due to the evident interference with property rights at play, the issue of expropriation was more thoroughly analysed in the judgment. However, it was claimed that although Sebenza was no longer capable of holding its mineral rights, the state did not acquire them, and instead and had no right regarding prospecting or mining per se (CC, 68). Lacking state's acquisition, which would have to mean that the state would obtain a right to exploit affected mineral rights, the primary requirement of expropriation was said not to have been met.[42] Thus, Sebenza could have retained its rights based on the transitional agreements, and it was not the MPRDA, but the own situation of Sebenza, that made it impossible to do so (CC, 71); therefore, '[i]t was not the inadequacy of the MPRDA ... that caused it not to utilise those provisions' (concurring opinion to CC, 109).

[41]Marais, *supra* note 16, at 2983.

[42]*Id.* at 3021.

At the same time, the state was said to have been merely vested with the function of 'a facilitator or a conduit through which broader and equitable access to mineral and petroleum resources can be realised' (CC, 68). In particular, the concept of 'custodianship' is not supposed to mean that 'the state has acquired and thus has become owner of the mineral rights concerned' (CC, 71).

This view was not followed in the concurring opinion to this judgment, in which it was made clear that '[t]he MPRDA abolished private ownership of minerals, based either on land ownership or the holding of severed real rights to the minerals, which existed under the mining law dispensation enacted prior to the Constitution' (concurring opinion to CC, 80), which means that 'private owners of minerals had the power or competence to decide whether to exploit minerals they owned and to whom they could give their exploitation rights. It was an incidence of ownership. Now the state has that power or competence by virtue of its custodianship of mineral resources under the MPRDA' (concurring opinion to the CC, 81). It should be noted that this opinion adequately refers to the core of the state's right and their true content, and not the name attributed thereto.

Parallel to this, the judgment included extensive commentary on the purpose of the MPRDA. This is of significance for a range of questions concerning the extent and nature of the state's rights, as well as the analysis of the issue, whether such rights were acquired by means of expropriation. Article 25(3)(b) and (d) of the Constitution considers, for instance, the history of acquisition and the purpose of expropriation to calculate the amount of compensation. At the same time, it is within the state's legislative obligation to ensure equitable access to land to all citizens (Article 25(5) of the Constitution), while explicitly the public interest, which is a necessary condition for expropriation, 'includes the nation's commitment to land reform, and to reforms to bring about equitable access to all South Africa's natural resources' (Article 25(4)(a) of the Constitution).

Thus, it was held that the obligation imposed by Article 25 of the Constitution aimed at protecting private property means 'not to over-emphasise private property rights at the expense of the state's social responsibilities …'; rather, it 'must always be remembered that our history does not permit a near-absolute status to be given to individual property rights to the detriment of the equally important duty of the state to ensure that all South Africans partake of the benefits flowing from our mineral and petroleum resources' (CC, 62). To this extent the judgment makes possible the protection of property rights to a lesser extent than personal or political rights, as the state must undertake actions organising social life and realising the idea of the common good,[43] also at the expense of such private property rights.

This argument is, however, thoroughly developed, so that not only may property rights be curtailed by socially justified values, but they are even equalised with other values, often not regarded as human rights. Thus, eventually, '[e]qually important is a recognition of the need to protect individual property rights as well as the facilitation of sustainable development, eradication of all forms of discriminatory practices in

[43]With regard to protection of property according to Article 1 of the First Protocol to European Convention on Human Rights, see Wróbel [17, p. 476].

the mining industry and equitable access to the mineral and petroleum resources of this country, to all its people' (CC, 64). Then, in particular, because of the

> historical inextricable link between landownership and mineral rights ownership[,] [which] equally explains why the vast majority of black people do not have access to the mineral and natural resources of our land[,] [t]he determination of expropriation, in a matter like this, cannot therefore be merely surgical or mechanical. A fine balance must be struck between the interest of those deprived by the MPRDA, and the need to create jobs, grow the economy through the expanded development of the mining industry and open up opportunities for those sought to be made fellow partakers in the equitable access to mineral resources, brought into being by the MPRDA.
>
> (CC, 65).

The Constitutional Court of South Africa underlined also the function of transitional agreements as 'carefully designed to alleviate potential hardship and prevent expropriation' (CC, 74). At the same time, the concurring opinion to this judgment further emphasised the need for transitional agreements. Thus, in this opinion, the concept of state acquisition of ownership was agreed to, and this is why compensation must have been provided, like that which typically is required in case of expropriation. By means of compensation, the aim was 'making the transition fair and equitable to pre-existing rights holders, as well as to those who were previously deprived from the benefits of exploiting the country's mineral and petroleum resources' (concurring opinion to the CC, 87) Consequently, the transitional agreements were 'interpreted as "compensation in kind" measures that seek to give effect to the just and equitable compensation for property in terms of the provisions of section 25 of the Constitution' (concurring opinion to the CC, 90).

Also there is a special role for law in a period of social transformation. Notwithstanding the protection of private property under the European Convention of Human Rights, the European Court of Human Rights Grand Chamber judgment of June 30, 2005, in *Jahn v. Germany*, allowed for expropriation without compensation in exceptional circumstances, which could be understood as comparable to those present in *Agri*. In particular, the following similarities were drawn: 'property derived from a tainted past; the challenges of transformation; and the demands of justice' (concurring opinion to the CC, 99).

12.5 Conclusion

The MPRDA, regardless of concerns as to the necessarily extensive encroachment on the rights of old-order rights-holders, which should be (and, in fact, partly are) still afforded some property protection, is an interesting example of legislation adapting the notion of sustainable development to the particular field of mineral wealth exploitation. The analysis of the MPRDA, together with its rationale and relationship to the past law, as provided in the series of judgments regarding the effects of the act, helps one to understand the justification for, and manner by which, the necessary pursuit of economic development of the state and necessity to provide protection for investor rights have been balanced with non-economic values.

In particular, the new law observed the need to redress past racial discrimination in wealth distribution and to ensure environmental protection, as well as to care for local communities, inhabitants, and workers. It does so, whilst also ensuring the facilitation of mining, in order to allow the country to benefit from its latent wealth, as well as by granting old-order rights-holders privileges under new law. The scope for compromise between such contrasting values is evidently the source of much discussion, as also has been the case with the legal reasoning concerning certain legal constructions involved (such as the notion of 'custodianship' as theoretically different from the Royalty system of mineral ownership), and the admissibility of all legal means undertaken.

It is particularly worth noting, as the legislation under review in the present chapter deals with varied issues of mineral rights: From one perspective, such issues are highly prone to have implications for the natural environment, rights to participation, housing, and fair labour conditions. From another perspective, economic benefit of the state, market stability and investment protection, as well as private property rights are involved. Considering comparable challenges in a number of African countries—rich in minerals, but often unable to fully profit from them—the South African example could be one to follow.[44]

References

1. Cawood, F. T., & Minnitt, R. C. A. (1995). A historical perspective on the economics of the ownership of mineral rights ownership, 11/12. *Journal of Southern African Institute of Mining and Metallurgy*.
2. Munslow, B., & Fitzgerald, P. (1994). South Africa: The sustainable development challenge. *Third World Quarterly, 15*.
3. UNICEF. (2015). *Children's Rights and the Mining Sector*. http://www.unicef.org/csr/files/UNICEF_REPORT_ON_CHILD_RIGHTS_AND_THE_MINING_SECTOR_APRIL_27.pdf.
4. Human Rights Watch. (2014). *Whose Development? Human Rights Abuses in Sierra Leone's Mining Boom*. https://www.hrw.org/report/2014/02/19/whose-development/human-rights-abuses-sierra-leones-mining-boom.
5. Belinkie, S. F. (2015). South Africa's land restitution challenge: Mining alternatives from evolving mineral taxation policies. *Cornell International Law Journal, 48*.
6. United Nations Environment Programme. (2010). *Sierra Leone environment, conflict and peacebuilding assessment* 2, http://postconflict.unep.ch/publications/Sierra_Leone.pdf.
7. Brown, O. et al. (2012). Environmental assessment as a tool for peacebuilding and development: Initial lessons from capacity building in Sierra Leone. In D. Jensen & S. Lonergan (Eds.), *Assessing and restoring natural resources in post-conflict peacebuilding 9*. http://environmentalpeacebuilding.org/assets/Documents/LibraryItem_000_Doc_076.pdf.
8. Mostert, H. (2012). *Mineral law: Principles and policies*.
9. Dawis, K. E., & Michael, J. (2001). Trebilcock, legal reforms and development. *Third World Quarterly, 22* (2001).

[44]Belinkie, *supra* note 6, at 222.

10. de Gaay Fortman, B., & Mihyo, P. (1993). A false start—Law and development in the context of colonial legacy. *Law and Police in Africa, Asia and Latin America, 26.*
11. Merryman, J. H. (1977). Comparative law and social change: On the origins, style, decline and revival of the law and development movement. *American Journal of Comparative Law, 24.*
12. Gopal, M. G. (1996). Law and development. Towards a pluralist vision. *American Society of International Law Proceedings, 90.*
13. Marais, E. J. (2015). When does state interference with property (now) amount to expropriation? An analysis of the Agri SA court's state acquisition requirement: Part 1 (Vol. 18). *Potchefstroom Electronic Law Journal.*
14. Weiss, E. B. (1992). In fairness to future generations and sustainable development. *American University International Law Review, 8.*
15. Barral, V. (2012). Sustainable development in international law: Nature and operation of an evolutive legal norm. *European Journal of International Law, 23.*
16. Campbell, N. J., Jr. (1956). *Principles of mineral ownership in the civil law and common law systems*. In *Proceedings (American Bar Association. Section of International and Comparative Law).*
17. Wróbel, A. (2011). Ochrona własności. In L. Garlicki (Ed.), *2 Konwencja o ochronie praw człowieka i podstawowych wolności. Komentarz do artykułów 19–59 oraz do protokołów dodatkowych.*
18. Rakoczy, B. (2015). In B. Rakoczy (Ed.), *Prawo górnicze i geologiczne. Komentarz (LEX).*

Chapter 13
Sustainable Development as a New Trade Usage in International Sale of Goods Contracts

Daniel Zatorski

Abstract When one buys goods of a particular brand, one does not simply buy a physical object; one buys a lifestyle. When buying a car, one buys *jinba ittai*, (Mazda); when buying shoes, one wants to *just do it*, (Nike); when buying coffee, one wants it to be '100 percent ethically sourced', (Starbucks). What this means is that the goods contain for the buyer an emotional dimension. This is referred to as the *brand*. A brand can carry with it many emotional attributes, several of which may be associated with ethical values. It is not uncommon for such values often to relate to *sustainable development*. To some, however, it may seem counterintuitive for global brands—and the multinational corporations behind them—and ethical values to go hand-in-hand. After all, the lack of evident interrelation between business and ethics has been famously summed up by Milton Friedman's statement that 'the social responsibility of business is to increase its profits', (Friedman in New York Times (1970), [1]) or, as some paraphrase, that: 'the business of business is business' (Schwenzer and Leisinger in Commercial law challenges in the 21st century: Jan Hellner in Memoriam (2007), [2]). Conversely, global business pours enormous sums into creating and maintaining a brand, including associating it with such values including sustainable development (*e.g.*, Apple). This is because having a brand, albeit costly, wields great returns (Maley in 12 Int Trade Bus Law Rev (2009), [3]); Saidov in The law of damages in international sales: the CISG and other international instruments (2008), [4]). In other words, ethical standards may have value (Schwenzer and Leisinger in Commercial law challenges in the 21st century: Jan Hellner in Memoriam (2007), [2]). This becomes also important in the context of international trade in goods. It is naturally the case that for many international sales contracts, ethical values bear little meaning for the parties (Maley in 12 Int Trade Bus Law Rev (2009), [3]). However, how goods are produced has ramifications for their value (Schwenzer and Leisinger in Commercial law challenges in the 21st century: Jan Hellner in Memoriam (2007), [2]). This therefore gives rise to the question: is, indeed, the business of business, business? This chapter examines the parties' obligations under transactions governed by the 1980 United Nations Convention of

D. Zatorski (✉)
Faculty of Law and Administration, Jagiellonian University, ul. Gołębia 24, 31-007 Kraków, Poland
e-mail: daniel.zatorski@gmail.com

P. Szwedo et al. (eds.), *Law and Development*, Kobe University Monograph Series in Social Science Research, https://doi.org/10.1007/978-981-13-9423-2_13

Contracts for the International Sale of Goods. This contribution's main argument is that sustainable development may be deemed an internationally-recognised trade standard forming part of many global brands, which is witnessed at the international level in the plethora of signatories to the United Nations Global Compact. Thus, the standards underpinning sustainability may be used to supplement the content of international sales contracts. This may be achieved through supplementing the conformity requirements that the goods must meet as enshrined in CISG Article 35 in three ways: through an implied term, through the goods' particulars, or through their ordinary purpose. All of these conformity requirements are discussed.

Keywords Brands · Corporate social responsibility · Ethical consumption · International sale of goods · Sustainable development

13.1 The Brand and Its Incorporation of Sustainable Development

Goods are more than just the sum of their parts. For many buyers, the goods' physical qualities are just as important as their or their seller's reputation. And it seems more true than ever that consumers nowadays do not only buy a product—a good—but also feelings.[1] This is due to the fact that buyers nowadays do not only sell physical goods but with them the emotional connotations these goods contain. Indeed, Nike's chief executive officer, Phil Knight, implied that Nike does not sell shoes, Nike sells feelings.[2] These feelings associated with the goods can be brought under the umbrella-term of the *brand.*

The definition of a brand, adopted from a commercial perspective by legal writers, describes 'the impression of a product in the minds of potential users or consumers'.[3] Some brands are even referred to as *lifestyle brands*.[4] In other words, the image that the sold goods convey represents an entire lifestyle. The brand is thus a term that carries an emotional value, which may also impact the goods' economic value.[5] This was made abundantly clear by Howard Schultz—the chief executive officer of Starbucks—who wrote that 'if people believe they share values with a company, they will stay loyal to a brand'.[6] Moreover, goods associated with a strong brand have a competitive advantage compared to no-brand goods.[7] This is why, in addition to a strong brand, reputation and goodwill are important commercial assets for businesses.[8] What can thus be said for certain is that a brand can have enormous value.

[1] Dysted [5, 4].

[2] *See* Willigan [6, at 92].

[3] Maley [3, at 88].

[4] Dysted [5, at 3].

[5] *See* Maley[3, at 88].

[6] Schultz and Yang [7, 193].

[7] *See* Ramberg [8, 71, 72].

[8] *See* Saidov [4, at 60].

Brands that do not have emotional value attached to them are more susceptible to competition, and thus weaker on the market, as emotional qualities cannot be as easily replicated as physical qualities.[9]

To summarise, the brand may, among other things, represent a certain ethic, idea, or lifestyle. It is therefore unsurprising that the necessity arises to protect a brand in international sales transactions, which may include associating a brand with standards of sustainable development. The idea behind sustainable development is 'the idea that the current generation wants future generations to be able to benefit from … resources in much the same way that we have. The goal is to develop our natural resources, but to do so in a way that does not permanently destroy them'[10] or 'to meet the needs and aspirations of the present without compromising the ability to meet those of the future'.[11] This chapter refers to these standards as the *sustainability standards*. More than several private efforts have been made to associate various brands with sustainability standards. The private initiative deemed most successful is the United Nations Global Compact (the UN Global Compact).[12] In a nutshell, the UN Global Compact deals with corporate sustainability; in fact, these are the first two words of its preamble.[13] The underlying idea being that companies must apply a principles-based approach to business and operate 'in ways that, at a minimum, meet fundamental responsibilities in the areas of human rights, labour, environment and anti-corruption'.[14] The UN Global Compact imposes several broad, yet minimal, ethical standards, which boil down to ten principles dealing with: human rights, labour, the environment, and anti-corruption. By becoming a signatory to the UN Global Compact, a business declares that it will respect the ten principles. At the time of preparing this chapter, the number of signatories to the UN Global Compact exceeded 13,000 participants.[15] Since it is the most successful private initiative on an international scale, the UN Global Compact will serve as a beacon for establishing whether—firstly—sustainability standards have become interwoven into the brands of the signatories of the UN Global Compact; and secondly, whether, due to its great success, an international trade usage under the United Nations Convention of Contracts for the International Sale of Goods exists as to the obligation to respect sustainability standards embodied by the UN Global Compact's ten principles.

---

[9] *See* Ramberg [8, at 72].

[10] Ørebech and Bosselman [9, 12].

[11] World Commission on Environment and Development, *Report of the World Commission on Environment and Development: Our Common Future*, http://www.un-documents.net/our-common-future.pdf (last visited 20 Sept. 2018).

[12] *See* Schwenzer and Leisinger [2, at 257].

[13] United Nations Global Compact, *The Ten Principles of the UN Global Compact*, https://www.unglobalcompact.org/what-is-gc/mission/principles (last visited 20 Sept. 2018).

[14] *Id.*

[15] United Nations Global Compact, *See Who's Involved*, https://www.unglobalcompact.org/what-is-gc/participants (last visited 20 Sept. 2018).

13.2 Non-physical Qualities of Goods

The protection of a brand is a pertinent issue in international trade, including international trade in goods. The most prevalent legal document dealing with international sales in goods is the United Nations Convention of Contracts for the International Sale of Goods (CISG). No reference to brand equity, ethics, or sustainable development was made in the CISG itself or in its legislative history.[16] Nonetheless, the CISG imposes an obligation on the seller to, put briefly, deliver the right goods, to the right place, at the right time and at the agreed price.[17] The first of these obligations is defined in CISG Article 35. Namely, CISG Article 35(1) states:

> The seller must deliver goods which are of the quantity, quality and description required by the contract and which are contained or packaged in the manner required by the contract.

This provision encompasses the so-called principle of *conformity*, which is a term describing whether 'the goods concord with the parties' actual intent and presumed intent'.[18]

In relation to the term *goods*, these are, under the CISG, first and foremost tangibles.[19] Kristian Maley poetically wrote that '[t]he nucleus of an international sale is the provision of a good with certain defined physical characteristics'.[20] The obligation to deliver conforming goods refers undoubtedly to their physical attributes. At first glance the logical conclusion is that the violation of any non-physical standards—be it ethical, brand or sustainability standards—does not negatively impact on the goods.[21] However, the term *quality* used in CISG Article 35(1) is understood broadly as meaning not only their physical condition but also 'all the factual and legal circumstances concerning the relationship of the goods to their surroundings'.[22] Goods may thus also have an intangible dimension such as reputation, image, or intellectual property rights.[23] Such non-tangible qualities are what Maley deems to surround the nucleus of an international sales transaction.[24] Such qualities are considered *incorporated* into the goods as their subsidiary component, and becoming their non-physical characteristic.[25] However, it may be argued that allowing for non-physical qualities to be incorporated into the goods may engender problems under CISG Article 3:

(1) Contracts for the supply of goods to be manufactured or produced are to be considered sales unless the party who orders the goods undertakes to supply a substantial part of the materials necessary for such manufacture or production.

---

[16]Dysted [5, at 14].

[17]Henschel [10, 23].

[18]Maley [3, at 83].

[19]*See id.* at 85; *see also* Ramberg [8, at 77, 82].

[20]Maley [3, at 88].

[21]*See* Schwenzer and Leisinger [2, at 266].

[22]*Id.* at 267.

[23]*See* Dysted [5, at 12].

[24]*See* Maley [3, at 88].

[25]*Id.* at 85.

(2) This Convention does not apply to contracts in which the preponderant part of the obligations of the party who furnishes the goods consists in the supply of labour or other services.

A typical example may be that of a supply chain, whereby the buyer, who is the brand-holder, procures goods which will bear the buyer's brand. The brand itself may be of greater value than the goods. After all, the $31.4 billion Nike brand[26] is worth more than a shipment of hundreds of pairs of shoes. Christina Ramberg takes issue with this point, however, arguing that 'it is probable that courts and arbitrators will apply the CISG to international sales of goods irrespective of whether a substantial proportion of the price relates to emotions rather than the product's physical properties'.[27] Indeed, it seems that this may be the case, since the provision is not applicable to cases where the buyer provides industrial property rights, licences, plans or know-how.[28] Consequently, although such contributions may form a substantial part of the goods' value, they do not fall within the scope of CISG Article 3(1) per se.

Unlike CISG Article 3(1), Article 3(2) 'deals with mixed contracts, in which the obligation to deliver a good or goods is combined with the obligation to provide services'.[29] A contract partly for the sale of tangibles, and partly for the provision of non-tangible qualities may be deemed a mixed contract.[30] In this context it has been argued that '[t]o provide an emotional feeling is closely related to services'.[31] Consequently, it may be argued that non-physical qualities should not form the preponderant part of the seller's obligations, because—by operation of CISG Article 3(2)—such a contract would not be a contract for the international sale of goods, and thus the CISG would not apply.[32] Yet such an approach is predicated on the misunderstanding that CISG Article 3(2) applies when the services are employed in the manufacture of the goods, that is to say, they are merged with the obligation to deliver the goods.[33] This is not the case. The provision is applicable 'only if there are separate obligations to supply goods and to provide services in one entire contract, which could equally have been agreed upon in two or more contracts …'.[34] In other words, where sustainability standards form part of the goods' quality, there is no need to resort to CISG Article 3(2).

In sum, regardless of whether one shares this view, marketing is not inconsequential to the value of goods; the implications of marketing for the perceived value

[26] *See* Forbes, *The World's Most Valuable Brands*, https://www.forbes.com/powerful-brands/list/#tab:rank (last visited 20 Sept. 2018).

[27] Ramberg [8, at 77].

[28] *See* Schlechtriem and Schwenzer *Article 3*, in [11, 61, 66]; *see also* Schlechtriem and Butler [12, 24].

[29] Schlechtriem and Butler [12, at 26]; *see also* Schwenzer and Hachem, *Article 3* in [11, at 67].

[30] *See* Ramberg [8, at 77].

[31] *Id.*

[32] *See* Maley [3, at 88].

[33] *See* Schwenzer and Hachem, *Article 3* in [11, at 67].

[34] *Id.*

of goods demonstrates the increasing importance of non-physical characteristics, in particular brand equity, to the value of goods.[35] Ordinarily, brand equity is protected under intellectual property and notions such as *goodwill*.[36] Goodwill however is connected to the business, while brand equity can attach to the goods.[37] For this reason brand equity can be protected through various legal means, including through the enforcement of intellectual property rights or under tort law.[38] It can, lastly, as will be demonstrated, be protected through rules on conformity of goods.

13.3 Express or Implied Term?

Parties have great autonomy as regards their understanding of *conformity*. The parties' subjective intention is of the greatest importance under CISG Article 35(1), and thus it is first and foremost for the parties to decide what features the goods must contain.[39]

> The starting point is that there are no limits to the contractual requirements which the parties may agree with respect to the goods, for example, that the goods may not be made by child workers, that the goods should be produced in an environmentally-friendly way ... that the goods should satisfy the special safety and environmental requirements of the buyer's country, etc. Only the imaginations of the parties and mandatory public law rules can set limits to what can be validly agreed.[40]

It seems that the case is clear-cut if the parties are sufficiently diligent and explicitly provide in the contract—by means of an express term—the non-physical qualities the goods must possess.[41] Would this also be the case if a contract contained no reference to non-physical attributes? It is conceivable for a contract to contain, in addition to express terms, an implied term in regard to conformity.[42] This may however be subject to dispute, especially between parties from different jurisdictions.[43] The exact characteristics of the goods are namely subject to interpretation, which is the purview of CISG Article 8[44]:

(1) For the purposes of this Convention statements made by and other conduct of a party are to be interpreted according to his intent where the other party knew or could not have been unaware what that intent was.

[35] *See* Maley [3, at 88].

[36] *See id.* at 93.

[37] See *id.*

[38] *See id.* (N.B., with regard to providing examples of trademark dilution, the tort of passing off and breach of personality rights).

[39] *See* Schlechtriem and Butler [12, at 113]; *see also* Maley [3, at 122]; *see also* Kruisinga [13, 29].

[40] Henschel [10, at 162].

[41] *See* Dysted [5, at 14].

[42] *See* Schwenzer and Leisinger [2, at 267].

[43] Dysted [5, at 6].

[44] *See* Kruisinga [13, at 29].

(2) If the preceding paragraph is not applicable, statements made by and other conduct of a party are to be interpreted according to the understanding that a reasonable person of the same kind as the other party would have had in the same circumstances.
(3) In determining the intent of a party or the understanding a reasonable person would have had, due consideration is to be given to all relevant circumstances of the case including the negotiations, any practices which the parties have established between themselves, usages and any subsequent conduct of the parties.

The provision directs the interpreter's efforts towards—firstly—the parties' subjective intention; and secondly—when the first fails—towards the *reasonable person* standard. A breach of an express or implied term concerning the goods' conformity will constitute a *subjective defect*[45] and as a result a breach of contract under CISG Article 35(1).[46]

Lastly, under CISG Article 8(3), in both cases (subjective intention and the reasonable person standard) due consideration is to be given to all relevant circumstances of the case, including the negotiations, any practices which the parties have established between themselves, usages, and any subsequent conduct of the parties. The inclusion of the term *usages* draws attention to CISG Article 9,[47] which reads:

(1) The parties are bound by any usage to which they have agreed and by any practices which they have established between themselves.
(2) The parties are considered, unless otherwise agreed, to have impliedly made applicable to their contract or its formation a usage of which the parties knew or ought to have known and which in international trade is widely known to, and regularly observed by, parties to contracts of the type involved in the particular trade concerned.

CISG Article 9 supplements the terms of the contract[48] and Article 35(1) as to the implied terms on quality.[49] Moreover, CISG Article 9(2), unlike Article 9(1), supplements the contract independent of the parties' intent.[50] It namely supplements the contract similarly to the reasonable person standard of CISG Article 8(2)[51] by imposing the necessity to consider trade usages, which are 'rules of commerce which are regularly observed by those involved in a particular industry or marketplace'.[52]

[45] *See* Schlechtriem and Butler [12, at 114] (explaining that a subjective defect of the goods is in essence their non-adherence to the goods' description under the contract).

[46] *See* Schwenzer and Leisinger [2, at 267].

[47] *See generally* Dysted [5, at 16] (indicating that CISG Article 8 must be read together with CISG Article 9).

[48] Martin Schmidt-Kessel, *Article 9*, in [11, 182].

[49] *See* Schwenzer and Leisinger [2, at 266–267].

[50] Schmidt-Kessel, *Article 9*, in [11, at 183].

[51] *Id.* at 188.

[52] *Id.* at 187.

Through CISG Article 9(2), non-physical features may impliedly become part of the contractual description of the goods.[53] Ingeborg Schwenzer and Benjamin Leisinger made the argument that where CISG Article 9(1) is not applicable, ethical standards might still become part of the contract under CISG Article 9(2).[54] This will however depend on whether such standards constitute an international trade usage under said provision. In order for an international trade usage to apply it must—firstly—be 'acknowledged and widely observed by parties to contracts of the type involved in the particular trade concerned'.[55] Secondly, the parties knew or ought to have known of the international trade usage.[56] This gives rise to the question: can an international trade usage be established with regard to ethical standards, such as the standards underpinning sustainable development? It is arguable whether this is a futile exercise. Schwenzer and Leisinger argue that 'first and primary consideration should be given to usages and practices that have been established in certain trade branches'.[57] Codes of conduct common for particular trade branches are of particular relevance here, or general private initiatives.[58]

This brings one back to the UN Global Compact; the values underpinning the UN Global Compact may become, or may be perceived by consumers as, part of a company's brand, and may thus become part of the goods' description. This may be achieved in several ways: firstly, through express notice:

> when a buyer makes it known to a seller that the quality of the goods must be produced in compliance with Global Compact principles during the negotiation stages, under Article 35(1) the seller is under a contractual obligation to produce the goods in compliance with the quality demanded by the buyer.[59]

Expressly making known that a buyer's brand includes sustainable development standards can be achieved in more ways than one. The most obvious is explicitly stating such standards in a written contract. A less obvious avenue is making reference to or including as an annex to the contract a code of conduct, corporate social responsibility (CSR) policy, or standard terms.[60] Secondly, in case no express reference is made, sustainable development standards underpinning a brand may amount to an implied term under CISG Article 35(1) through contractual interpretation. Without explicit reference to sustainable development in a contract, or a CSR policy, the goods' description may still contain sustainable development standards. This may happen in a scenario when a buyer communicates its ethical standards to the world 'externally with the direct or indirect purpose of enhancing the surrounding society's

[53] *See* Schwenzer [14, 103, 107].

[54] Schwenzer and Leisinger [2, at 265].

[55] Schlechtriem and Butler [12, at 59] (referencing *BP Int'l Ltd. v. Empresa Estadal Petroleos de Ecuador*, 332 F.3d 333 (5th Cir. 2003)).

[56] *See* Schlechtriem and Butler [12, at 59].

[57] Schwenzer and Leisinger [2, at 265].

[58] *Id.*

[59] Williams [15, 299, 305].

[60] *See* Ramberg [8, at 78–79].

impression of the company'.[61] One such scenario may include, in the author's opinion, whether the buyer is a party to the UN Global Compact. The UN Global Compact expressly mentions in its contents sustainable development.[62] Is, however, merely being a party enough? On the one hand, Christina Ramberg (writing admittedly about a buyer's CSR policy) argues that 'I do not think that the purchaser's general CSR-policy could form a basis for a claim of non-conformity against a supplier even when the supplier is aware of the policy'.[63] Nonetheless, she goes on further to argue that there must exist certain additional factors for a CSR policy or non-physical attributes to apply to the goods' description, such as: 'the purchaser's interest in its CSR-policy [being] too obvious to need stating' or 'the very essence of the contract is to acquire a feeling more than a physical product'.[64] It seems reasonable that the requirements of conformity are dependent on context and the buyer's reasonable expectations.[65] Hence the crucial issue is whether the buyer may reasonably expect that the goods—be it through their production process or the materials they are made from—meet sustainability standards. For Schwenzer and Leisinger the answer seems straightforward; they go one step further to even advance an argument independent of any brand-protection issues. Namely, they argue that 'the observance of, at least, basic ethical standards can be regarded as an international trade usage and, thus, as an implied term in every international sales contract'.[66] In the author's opinion this seems to be a reasonable argument to make. Since Schwenzer and Leisinger's article was published, the number of signatories to the UN Global Compact has increased by approximately 5000 participants, suggesting increasing recognition of an international trade usage under CISG Article 9(2), or, at least, recognition that a party to the UN Global Compact may reasonably expect to associate its brand with minimum levels of global sustainability standards.

In sum, the principle of conformity in CISG Article 35(1) is wide enough in scope to encompass the goods' non-physical characteristics. These can be incorporated into the contract either through an express or implied term. In order to ascertain the existence of the latter, it is necessary to turn to CISG interpretive tools, among them the incorporation of any applicable international trade practice. An international trade practice to abide by sustainability standards may exist by means of the UN Global Compact. Nonetheless, if the principle of conformity is not sufficient, the subsequent part of CISG Article 35 provides additional ancillary objective rules and standards of conformity.

---

[61] *Id.* at 78.

[62] United Nations Global Compact, *The Ten Principles of the UN Global Compact*, https://www.unglobalcompact.org/what-is-gc/mission/principles (last visited 21 Sept. 2018).

[63] Ramberg [8, at 81].

[64] *Id.*

[65] *See id.* at 83.

[66] Schwenzer and Leisinger [2, at 267].

13.4 Particular or Ordinary Purpose?

Even if one does not recognise an international trade standard, and if efforts of contractual interpretation fail, meaning when 'the contract does not contain any, or contains only insufficient, details of the requirements to be satisfied by the goods for the purposes of Article 35(1)',[67] CISG Article 35(2) provides 'ancillary objective rules and standards'[68] or standards on a 'subsidiary determination of conformity'.[69] In other words, having received an unsatisfactory answer as to what the parties agreed to (in accordance with CISG Article 8), only then is CISG Article 35(2) applicable.[70] The provisions of CISG Article 35(2)—being based on an objective criterion as to the goods' intended purpose[71]—are deemed to be 'a continuum of the parties' presumed intention' based on a reasonableness standard.[72] CISG Article 35(2) seeks to settle any interpretative doubts by providing two implied obligations[73] based on the goods' fitness for their ordinary (CISG Article 35(2)(a)) or particular (CISG Article 35(2)(b)) purpose. Under such a framework, sustainability standards may have a role to play.

13.4.1 Particular Purpose Under CISG Article 35(2)(b)

On the one hand, sustainability standards may be viewed as the goods' *particular purpose* under CISG Article 35(2)(b). This provision should be analysed first, as it takes precedence over CISG Article 35(2)(a), viz, the ordinary purpose.[74] According to CISG Article 35(2)(b):

> Except where the parties have agreed otherwise, the goods do not conform with the contract unless they are fit for any particular purpose expressly or impliedly made known to the seller at the time of the conclusion of the contract, except where the circumstances show that the buyer did not rely, or that it was unreasonable for him to rely, on the seller's skill and judgement.

A particular purpose is understood as 'a purpose which lies outside what is considered the ordinary use of the goods'.[75] The application of the provision is broader than

[67] Ingeborg Schwenzer, *Article 35*, in [11, 103, 107].

[68] Schlechtriem and Butler [12, at 115].

[69] Schwenzer and Leisinger [2, at 267].

[70] *See* Schlechtriem and Butler [12, at 115] (stating that 'Article 35(2) CISG sets out what reasonable parties would have agreed upon had they put their mind to it. This is important since it means that the first inquiry has to be what the parties agreed upon and only if that inquiry is not satisfactory is Article 35(2) CISG applicable'.).

[71] *See* Schwenzer, *Article 35*, in [11, at 575].

[72] Schlechtriem and Butler [12, at 115].

[73] *See* Kruisinga [13, at 30].

[74] *See* Schwenzer, *Article 35*, in [11, at 575].

[75] Henschel [10, at 222].

merely specific technical requirements.[76] Namely, it may obligate a seller to abide by public law regulations of the buyer's state.[77] It may however be even broader than that, since it may also encompass other factors than public law regulations, including ideological, cultural or traditional.[78] For instance a buyer may buy goods in order to subsequently sell them in a specific market, where great emphasis is put on sustainability standards.[79] After all, fitness for resale in a particular market may be more limited than universal fitness for resale.[80]

The additional hurdle imposed by CISG Article 35(2)(b) is for the particular purpose to be expressly or impliedly made known to the seller at the time of the conclusion of the contract. The test whether this is indeed the case is objective: was the seller put in a position to be able to recognise the purpose?[81] Schwenzer and Leisinger propose that a seller is put on notice when 'the buyer's firm, i.e. the company's name, contains information in this regard or where its reputation in context with ethical values is widely known in the trade sector concerned'.[82] Here again the importance of context is highlighted. In the author's opinion a strong indication of a buyer's reputation—brand—in the context of ethical values—such as sustainable development—may be a buyer's participation in the UN Global Compact. The second hurdle is the buyer's reliance on the seller's skill and judgement. No obligation to provide goods meeting a particular purpose exists in circumstances that indicate that the buyer did not rely, or that it was unreasonable for him to rely, on the seller's skill and judgement. Generally, as a rule, it is presumed that the buyer did rely on the seller's skill and judgement.[83] It is questionable whether this principle applies to non-physical qualities of the goods, since—under the so-called *sphere of influence principle*—for such qualities the buyer, and not the seller, are a better judge of such characteristics.[84] Kristian Maley underlines here: 'where a product does not have existing brand recognition in the seller's country, it is unlikely that the buyer would reasonably rely on the seller to make judgements in respect of the product's brand'.[85] Nonetheless, he underlines that in the case of global brands, such as Coca-Cola, Kodak or Unilever, 'the brand recognition and reputation of the goods will typically be in the seller's sphere of influence'.[86] Here too, this author believes, participation on the part of the brand-holder in the UN Global Compact has ramifications, since it

[76] *See* Maley [3, at 93].

[77] Bundesgerichtshof [BGH] [Federal Court of Justice] Mar. 8, 1995, VIII ZR 159/94 (Ger.), http://cisgw3.law.pace.edu/cases/050302g1.html.

[78] *See* Maley [3, at 117].

[79] *See* Schwenzer and Leisinger [2, at 267].

[80] *See* Maley [3, at 117].

[81] Henschel [10, at 230].

[82] Schwenzer and Leisinger [2, at 267].

[83] *See* Maley [3, at 119].

[84] *See id.* at 119–120.

[85] *Id.* at 120.

[86] *Id.*

makes a brand's adherence to global sustainable development standards *global* and thus expands the seller's sphere of influence.

13.4.2 Ordinary Purpose Under CISG Article 35(2)(a)

Sustainability standards may, on the other hand, be viewed as the goods' *ordinary purpose*. Under CISG Article 35(2)(a): 'Except where the parties have agreed otherwise, the goods do not conform with the contract unless they are fit for the purposes for which goods of the same description would ordinarily be used'. Whether they indeed are fit for their ordinary purpose is objectively ascertained based on the view of a person in the specific trade.[87] One of the aspects of the goods' ordinary purpose is that they must be fit for commercial purposes, and among others, resaleable.[88] In order to objectively ascertain the goods' resaleability, they should be analysed through the scope of market expectations towards them, such as tradition, culture, economic circumstances, or legal requirements.[89] CISG case law indicates that reputation has implications for goods. Kristian Maley notes that case law under CISG chiefly concerns a party's entitlement to damages rather than whether a breach has occurred.[90] Nevertheless, the case law is informative. The ramifications that the negative reputation of the goods may have, have been apparent in cases concerning unfortunate advertising campaigns[91] or where the goods are unsafe.[92] However, with regard to the former, it is not always easy to prove a causal link between loss and reputational damage.[93] With regard to the latter, the so-called *Pocket ashtray* case[94] concerned an agreement between an Italian and a Scottish company whereby the latter was to deliver a number of pocket ashtrays. The first shipment contained defective and dangerous goods due to the excessive sharpness of the blades. The seller replaced the defective goods. Nonetheless, subsequent sales were prejudiced due to the reputational damage to the buyer, and hence the buyer instigated arbitral proceedings claiming damages for loss of earnings before the Chamber of Commerce, Industry and Handicraft of the Swiss Canton of Ticino. The arbitrator ruled that the first shipment was defective, since the ashtrays were unsuitable for ordinary use. The claim for damages was upheld, since the loss was caused due to the bad

---

[87] *See* Schlechtriem and Butler [12, at 115].

[88] *See* Henschel [10, at 211]; *see also* Schwenzer and Leisinger [2, at 267–268].

[89] Schlechtriem and Butler [12, at 116].

[90] *See* Maley [3, at 116].

[91] Oberlandesgericht Frankfurt [OLG] [Appellate Court Frankfurt] Mar. 15, 1996, 25 U 100/95 (Ger.), http://cisgw3.law.pace.edu/cases/960315g1.html.

[92] Bundesgerichtshof [BGer] [Federal Court of Justice] Oct. 10, 2005, 4P.146/2005/biz (Switz.), http://www.unilex.info/case.cfm?pid=1&do=case&id=1094&step=Abstract.

[93] *See* Maley [3, at 113].

[94] Bundesgerichtshof [BGer] [Federal Court of Justice] Oct. 10, 2005, 4P.146/2005/biz (Switz.), http://www.unilex.info/case.cfm?pid=1&do=case&id=1094&step=Abstract.

reputation of the goods as being hazardous. This judgment was subsequently upheld by the Swiss Supreme Court. The foregoing indicate in essence that goods may be deemed non-conforming due to their negative reputation, only if the non-conformity is due to a physical defect. Maley criticised this view:

> This reasoning … is problematic, because following the principle articulated, the buyer's right to return the goods owing to negative reputation would arise only if the seller had previously delivered defective goods. This seems to be a somewhat artificial distinction, as the direct cause of the poor sales was the negative reputation of the product rather than the non-conformance of the first shipment.[95]

Such criticism is valid, as negative reputation alone—without any physical defect—can be a source of financial loss. Indeed, this was made clear by the German Bundesgerichtshof in the so-called *Frozen pork case*.[96] The case concerned sold Belgian meat products which were suspected of being hazardous. Moreover, the risk of the goods' defectiveness had already passed in that case to the buyer. This, however, was irrelevant for the Bundesgerichtshof, which held that:

> Whether and to what extent the meat delivered to [Buyer] was actually contaminated with dioxin is irrelevant because the suspicion alone, which excluded the marketability, which became apparent later and which was not invalidated by the Seller, has a bearing on the resaleability and tradeability.[97]

In other words, conformity need not attach to the sheer physical qualities of the goods; it can be independent—just as sheer suspicion is.[98] For this reason, in the author's opinion, a breach of sustainability standards attached to a brand need not be connected to the physical qualities of the goods per se, since commercial reality suggests that a negative reputation can have vast repercussions, even when the physical state of the goods is entirely satisfactory.

13.4.3 Obviousness of Non-conformity

Lastly—regardless of the particular or ordinary purpose—it is important to note, however, that bad faith or lack of due diligence on the part of the buyer, fortunately, is unlikely to be rewarded within the CISG context. Namely, under CISG Article 35(3): 'The seller is not liable under subparagraphs (a) to (d) of the preceding paragraph for any lack of conformity of the goods if at the time of the conclusion of the contract the buyer knew or could not have been unaware of such lack of conformity'. Liability under said provision is excluded only for cases that are obvious.[99] This

---

[95] Maley [3, at 114].

[96] Bundesgerichtshof [BGH] [Federal Court of Justice] Mar. 2, 2005, VIII ZR 67/04 (Ger.), http://cisgw3.law.pace.edu/cases/050302g1.html.

[97] *Id.*

[98] It must however be underlined that the ruling was limited to cases where the suspicion led public authorities to enact measures precluding the goods' tradeability.

[99] *See* Schwenzer, *Article 35*, in [11, at 586].

means its application is limited to cases of gross negligence.[100] CISG Article 35(3) has relevant implications for the incorporation of sustainability standards into the description of the goods. In this context Schwenzer and Leisinger voice an important caveat, namely:

> It might be necessary to note here that, in cases where the buyer is only willing to pay a price that is so low that ethical production standards are impossible to be applied—and consequently cannot be expected—, the buyer cannot rely on an implied term of the contract.[101]

For this reason interpretative attempts under CISG Article 35(2),[102] or Article 35(1),[103] must be accompanied by attention to whether the price is too low to require adherence to sustainability standards. If the answer is that it obviously is, then one cannot rely on the goods' lack of conformity.

13.5 Conclusions

It may seem facile to attach emotional value to products of a particular brand. Yet it is this phenomenon that allows principles underpinning sustainability—environmental sustainability or humane labour conditions—to find their way into a contract for the sale of goods without express reference. This almost seems cynical, yet the broad scope of the conformity requirement of CISG Article 35 makes this possible. This may come practically into play when interpreting a contract for the sale of goods. Namely, in the course of contractual interpretation it seems prudent to ask a series of questions to ascertain whether sustainability standards form part of the contract. They do if:

(a) the interest in the goods being products in accordance with sustainability standards is too obvious to need stating;
(b) the contract would not be commercially viable without sustainability standards; or
(c) the very essence of the contract is to acquire a feeling of sustainability more than a physical product.

Regardless of these questions, one cannot neglect the caveat made clear by Schwenzer and Leisinger and must ask the additional question whether the price is so low that it is impossible to anticipate the use of ethical production methods. Indeed, in the final analysis, it is common sense that should dictate the contents of the contract—and common sense seems always to whisper that if the price is too good to be true, then

[100] *See* Schlechtriem and Butler [12, at 120].

[101] Schwenzer and Leisinger [2, at 265].

[102] N.B., CISG Article 35(3) does not apply to cases of Article 35(1); *see* Schlechtriem and Butler [12, at 120–121].

[103] Schwenzer and Leisinger's comment pertained to an *implied term*, suggesting that the comment's scope was beyond the scope of application of CISG Article 35(3).

it probably is not true; someone else, somewhere else in the process has had to pay for it in some way.

References

1. Friedman, M. (1970, September 13). The social responsibility of business is to increase its profits. *New York Times*.
2. Schwenzer, I., & Leisinger, B. (2007). Ethical values and international sales contracts. In R. Cranston (Ed.), *Commercial law challenges in the 21st century: Jan Hellner in Memoriam*. http://cisgw3.law.pace.edu/cisg/biblio/schwenzer-leisinger.html.
3. Maley, K. (2009). The limits to the conformity of goods in the United Nations convention on contracts for the international sale of goods. *12 International Trade & Business Law Review*. http://cisgw3.law.pace.edu/cisg/biblio/maley.html.
4. Saidov, D. (2008). *The law of damages in international sales: The CISG and other international instruments*.
5. Dysted, C. (2015). Ethical defects in contracts under United Nations convention on contracts for the international sale of goods. Unpublished master's thesis, University of Copenhagen Faculty of Law, on file with Albert H. Kritzer CISG Database. http://cisgw3.law.pace.edu/cisg/biblio/dysted.pdf.
6. Willigan, G. (1992). High-performance marketing: An interview with Nike's Phil Knight. *Harvard Business Review* (July–August). https://hbr.org/1992/07/high-performance-marketing-an-interview-with-nikes-phil-knight.
7. Schultz, H., & Yang, D. J. (1997). *Pour your heart into it: How Starbucks built a company one cup at a time*.
8. Ramberg, C. (2015). Emotional Non-conformity in the international sale of goods, particularly in relation to CSR-policies and codes of conduct. In I. H. Schwenzer & L. Spagnolo (Eds.), *Boundaries and Intersections: 5th Annual MAA Schlechtriem CISG Conference*, March 21, 2013. Vienna: Conference in Honour of Peter Schlechtriem.
9. Ørebech, P., & Bosselman, F. (2005). The linkage between sustainable development and customary law. In *The role of customary law in sustainable development*. Cambridge University Press.
10. Henschel, R. F. (2005). *Conformity of goods in international sales*.
11. Schlechtriem, P., & Schwenzer, I. (2010). *Commentary on the UN convention on the international sale of goods* (I. Schwenzer (Ed.), 3rd ed.).
12. Schlechtriem, P., & Butler, P. (2009). *UN law on international sales*.
13. Kruisinga, S. (2004). *(Non-)conformity in the 1980 UN convention on contracts for the international sale of goods: A uniform concept?*
14. Schwenzer, I. (2015). Conformity of the goods—Physical features on the Wane. In I. H. Schwenzer & L. Spagnolo (Eds.), *Boundaries and Intersections: 5th Annual MAA Schlechtriem CISG Conference*, March 21, 2013. Vienna: Conference in Honour of Peter Schlechtriem.
15. Williams, J. (2015). Analysis of CISG Article 35—Conformity of the goods in the changing power dynamics of corporate social responsibility. In *19 Hors Serie Trade Development through Harmonization of Commercial Law*. University of Victoria Wellington Faculty of Law. https://www.victoria.ac.nz/law/research/publications/about-nzacl/publications/special-issues/hors-serie-volume-xvi,-2013/Williams.pdf.

Correction to: Between Economic Development and Human Rights: Balancing E-Commerce and Adult Content Filtering

Adam Szafrański, Piotr Szwedo and Małgorzata Klein

Correction to:
Chapter 9 in: P. Szwedo et al. (eds.), *Law and Development*, Kobe University Monograph Series in Social Science Research, https://doi.org/10.1007/978-981-13-9423-2_9

In the original version of this book, the following change has been made: In the chapter 9, the affiliation "Faculty of Law and Administration, University of Warsaw" of the author "Małgorzata Klein" has been changed to "Faculty of Geography and Regional Studies, University of Warsaw." The erratum chapter has been updated with the changes.

The updated version of this chapter can be found at
https://doi.org/10.1007/978-981-13-9423-2_9

P. Szwedo et al. (eds.), *Law and Development*, Kobe University Monograph Series in Social Science Research, https://doi.org/10.1007/978-981-13-9423-2_14

If you have any concerns about our products,
you can contact us on
ProductSafety@springernature.com

In case Publisher is established outside the EU,
the EU authorized representative is:
Springer Nature Customer Service Center GmbH
Europaplatz 3, 69115 Heidelberg, Germany

Printed by Libri Plureos GmbH
in Hamburg, Germany